THE OXFORD HISTORY
OF ENGLAND

Edited by SIR GEORGE CLARK

THE OXFORD HISTORY OF ENGLAND

Edited by SIR GEORGE CLARK

The titles of some volumes are provisional
* These volumes have been published

THE
EARLY STUARTS
1603–1660

BY

GODFREY DAVIES

SECOND EDITION

OXFORD
AT THE CLARENDON PRESS
1959

Oxford University Press, Amen House, London E.C.4

GLASGOW NEW YORK TORONTO MELBOURNE WELLINGTON
BOMBAY CALCUTTA MADRAS KARACHI KUALA LUMPUR
CAPE TOWN IBADAN NAIROBI ACCRA

FIRST PUBLISHED 1937
REPRINTED 1938 AND 1945 (WITH CORRECTIONS)
1949, 1952
SECOND EDITION 1959

PRINTED IN GREAT BRITAIN

PREFACE TO SECOND EDITION

T HE changes in this new edition have had in view three main purposes: to correct errors; to incorporate the results of recent research, and to bring the bibliography up to date; and to assist the reader by identifying some of the minor characters and explaining some of the less familiar contemporary terms.

In the revision I have enjoyed the assistance of Clarence L. Ver Steeg of Northwestern University for colonial history and of F. P. Wilson of the University of Oxford for literature. Sir George Clark, the editor of the Oxford History of England, has once again placed me heavily in his debt by giving me many fruitful suggestions.

G. D.

1 September 1955

NOTE BY THE EDITOR

MR. GODFREY DAVIES, the author of this book, died on 28 May 1957. It therefore fell to my lot to see this second edition through the press. I have added references to some publications which appeared after the above Preface was written: several of them had been reviewed by Mr. Davies himself. I must also pay my tribute here to the devotion with which he carried on his historical studies in defiance of long-protracted illness, and to his generous friendship through many years.

G. N. C.

PREFACE TO FIRST EDITION

IN acknowledging with gratitude the assistance I have received, it is fitting that I should mention first those to whom my obligations are greatest—the trustees and director of the Huntington Library who have most generously allowed me to devote to this book whatever time I could spare from my official duties and other research projects. Without the liberty to carry on my researches while at the Library and to use its collections, I could not have completed this volume; with it, I could work as conveniently in San Marino as anywhere in the world. Moreover, I have had the advantage of being able to consult colleagues, both permanent and temporary, about different sections of my book. Mr. C. H. Collins Baker effected many improvements in my chapter on the arts; Dr. Max Farrand, the director of the Huntington Library, not only facilitated my studies in various ways, but also found time to improve the order and style of several of my chapters; Professor Edwin F. Gay read through 'Social and Economic History' and made some valuable additions; Dr. Hubert C. Heffner and Dr. Hoyt H. Hudson gave me much assistance with 'Literature', the former with the drama and the latter with poetry; Dr. Francis R. Johnson made a thorough revision of 'Science'; Dr. Fulmer Mood kindly read 'Foreign Trade and the Colonies'; Dr. Conyers Read went through many chapters and gave me much sound advice; Dr. Louis B. Wright allowed me to draw freely on his knowledge of literature, and Dr. Marjorie H. Nicolson has given advice on that subject and on science and education. In addition Dr. G. N. Clark exercised a very beneficial editorial supervision; the late Sir Charles Firth most generously lent me some unpublished lectures on the social history of the Protectorate, from which I have taken many references, facts, and comments; Dr. Edwin P. Hubble helped me by reading and discussing 'Science'; Dr. C. K. Judy commented on 'Literature'; and Professor Jacob Viner not only allowed me to make a very great use of his writings on mercantilism but also corrected 'Foreign Trade'. Finally I owe much to two members of the Huntington Library staff, Mr. M. H. Crissey and Mrs. Marion Tinling, for the care they have taken in the preparation of my manuscript.

G. D.

SAN MARINO

February 1936

TABLE OF CONTENTS

VII. POLITICAL AND CONSTITUTIONAL HISTORY, 1649–58

X. POLITICAL AND CONSTITUTIONAL HISTORY, 1658–60

XI. SOCIAL AND ECONOMIC HISTORY

LIST OF MAPS

At end

NOTE ON DATES

DURING this period two calendars were in use. The Julian, or Old Style, used in England, was ten days behind the Gregorian, or New Style, used in most continental countries. Moreover, on the Continent a year began on 1 January, but for most purposes in England a year began on 25 March. In this book dates are given according to the Old Style so far as the day and month are concerned, but the year is taken to begin on 1 January. Thus, an English contemporary would have dated the execution of Charles I, 30 January 1648; a foreigner, 9 February 1649. Here the date is given 30 January 1649.

LIST OF ABBREVIATIONS

TITLES	ABBREVIATIONS
Acts and Ordinances of the Interregnum, 1642–1660, ed. C. H. Firth and R. S. Rait (1911)	*Acts and Ordinances*
Bacon, The Works of Francis, ed. James Spedding, Robert Leslie Ellis, and Douglas Denon Heath (14 vols.; 1857–74)	Bacon, *Works*
Bibliotheca Lindesiana, ed. R. R. Steele (1910)	Steele
Carlyle, Thomas, *Life and Letters of Oliver Cromwell,* ed. S. C. Lomas (3 vols.; 1904)	Carlyle
Clarendon, Edward Hyde, Earl of, *The History of the Rebellion* (6 vols.; 1888)	Clarendon
Gardiner, S. R., *History of England* (10 vols.; 1884)	Gardiner
Laud, The Works of William (7 vols.; 1847–60)	Laud, *Works*
Milton, The Works of John (Columbia University Edition; 1931–40)	Milton, *Works*
Parliamentary History of England, The, ed. William Cobbett (36 vols.; 1806–20)	*Parliamentary History*
Parliamentary or Constitutional History of England (24 vols.; 1761–3)	*Old Parliamentary History*
Rushworth, John, *Historical Collections* (8 vols.; 1659–1701)	Rushworth
State Trials, A Complete Collection of, ed. T. B. and T. J. Howell (33 vols.; 1812–26)	*State Trials*
Thurloe, A Collection of the State Papers of John (7 vols.; 1742)	Thurloe

INTRODUCTION

THE keynote of the seventeenth century was revolt against authority. Modern times as distinct from the middle ages had begun under the Tudors and were now developing rapidly. The surviving elements of medievalism were being viewed with increasing scepticism.

The tide of discontent in England, which began to come in under James I (1603–25), swelled during the reign of Charles I (1625–49) and reached its high-water mark at the king's execution. For eleven uneasy years England was a republic, but as the commonwealth (1649–53) gave way to the protectorate (1653–9) the tide turned, became more conservative, and after a year's ebbing and flowing restored the monarchy. The return of the Stuarts did not entail setting back the clock to the *status quo* of 1603, or even 1642. The legislature might affect to ignore all that had been accomplished during 1642–60, but the minds of men had received an ineffaceable impression that can be traced in many directions.

In the realm of thought there was a definite break with the past. Scholasticism, after more than three centuries of dominance, was at length challenged by a new philosophy. The desire to learn the secrets of nature and to banish fear of the unknown was in conflict with the cosmic interpretation that had been accepted since the thirteenth century. The age of experiment was treading upon the heels of the age of dogma.

In political thought the sixteenth-century conception of the monarch as the saviour of society and the theory of the divine right of kings (which reached its highest exaltation under the early Stuarts) were violently assailed, and substitutes of almost infinite variety were offered by theorists. Many of the democratic, and not a few of the socialistic, doctrines that are commonly regarded as modern, or at least of the eighteenth century, were set forth in the seventeenth century. The greatest contribution then made to political theory, Hobbes's *Leviathan*, was written for all time, but even in a theocratic age its daring insistence upon a state of nature, a covenant as the basis of society, and the imperative need for a sovereign power in the state exercised a real if rather imperceptible influence.

In religion the Reformation had already rent in twain the

seamless coat of the catholicism of the middle ages and had substituted a national for a universal church. Under the Stuarts
the *via media* was troubled by many cross-currents. Arminianism
was a protest against the doctrinal tyranny of Calvinism, just
as independency was a protest against any closely organized
church. Quakerism arose from dissatisfaction with all existing
creeds. The concept of the inner light rendered prescribed doctrines or covenants unnecessary for those holding it. Socinian-
ism (later styled unitarianism) involved the rejection of one of
the cardinal tenets of Christianity. Numerous if ephemeral sects
also arose, whose votaries were inspired by the hope of finding
salvation in pastures new. The more enlightened and humane
members of most ecclesiastical organizations began to champion
toleration and thus challenged the right of the state to determine the religious worship of its citizens.

In politics occurred the most obvious instances of revolt
against authority. In some ways the 'great rebellion' is a better
label than the 'puritan revolution' for the movement that led to
the execution of Charles I and the establishment of the protectorate. It is true that most puritans sided against the king,
that the parliamentary commissions ran in the name of king and
parliament and thus afforded their holders a somewhat transparent screen against being called rebels, and that a war concerned mainly at the start with political sovereignty rather
changed its character and became a crusade for religious freedom. Nevertheless the struggle, though at no time a class war,
was to a large extent a revolt by the middle classes against
personal government. They had been steadily growing in power
under the Tudors, when they had been allowed to participate
in government at the will of the sovereign. Now they were no
longer content merely to register approval of royal edicts—
indeed, they had occasionally shown embarrassing independence, even under Henry VIII or Elizabeth. Their intention of
taking an active part in determining policy was due to many
associated causes: to consciousness of strength, to the desire for
a further reformation in the church, to an anti-sacerdotalism
which conflicted with the existing alliance between church and
state, to dislike of an economic policy which hindered though it
could not stop inclosures and aimed at restricting private gain
for the public good, and to impatience with a paternalistic
régime now that they felt they had outgrown leading-strings.

The parliamentary franchise and the distribution of seats assured them full representation in parliament, and they were bent upon fostering the strength of the legislature and of increasing its influence upon the executive. Then the cabinet did not link legislature and executive, so parliament tended to be in chronic opposition to the Crown. Such influence as the two houses could exert was usually indirect, through an imperfect control of taxation or the impeachment of ministers. Consequently, as parliament grew in importance, the machinery of government was thrown more and more out of gear—a condition in which it remained until the revolution of 1688, or perhaps until the accession of the house of Hanover.

The seventeenth century, therefore, began with the English constitution entering a transitional state, which lasted until the change from personal rule to parliamentary government was complete. A transformation was preordained, but whether it would be accomplished gradually and peacefully, or whether progress would be made by violent stages with intervening reactions, depended most of all upon the relations to be established between the middle classes and the new dynasty. Certainly Queen Elizabeth bequeathed no bed of roses to her successors. On the contrary they found awaiting them a steep and stony path whose end was invisible when the first of the Stuarts took the place of the last of the Tudors upon the throne of England.

I

POLITICAL AND CONSTITUTIONAL HISTORY, 1603-29

ELIZABETH I died early on 24 March 1603, but not before she had signified that James VI of Scotland should succeed her. The privy council at once issued a proclamation of the Scottish king's accession as James I of England, in a form to which he had previously assented. His peaceful accession was welcomed with practical unanimity, and, we are told, 'the like joy, both in London and all parts of England, was never known'.[1] The king spent a month on his progress from Edinburgh to London, and the first impressions his new subjects gained were favourable. His familiarity and courtesy were praised on every side,[2] and his zeal for hunting endeared him at once to many. The gentry who flocked to see him were rewarded with knighthoods, with a profusion far in excess of any previous grants.[3]

James VI, born in 1566 and crowned king of Scotland the next year, began to reign formally in 1578 and actually in 1583. Educated by George Buchanan, the Scottish humanist, he became one of the most learned of kings, especially in theology, his main interest. His knowledge did not broaden his mind but made him pedantic and pedagogic. Throughout his life he aspired to instruct his subjects and wrote treatises and delivered speeches to teach them the obedience they owed to God's vicegerent on earth. His precocious self-conceit increased with his success in suppressing the disorders in the Western Isles and along the Border and in attacking presbyterianism. He accepted the presbyterian doctrine but hated the discipline as incompatible with his theories of divine right. His confidence in his statecraft grew after his peaceful succession to the English

---

[1] *Hist. MSS. Com., Salisbury MSS.* (1930), xv. 26.
[2] Ibid., p. 28.
[3] In two months James created as many knights as Elizabeth in the last ten years of her reign. Bacon wrote to Cecil, 3 July 1603: 'For this almost prostituted title of knighthood I could now without charge by your means be content to have it; both because of this late disgrace, and because I have three new knights in my mess in Gray's Inn commons, and because I have found out an alderman's daughter, a handsome maiden, to my liking' (ibid., p. 167).

throne because he attributed it to his intrigues with English statesmen and continental rulers. It was really due to heredity and the absence of any suitable alternative. From an early age in Scotland until his death in England he felt a strange infatuation for favourites chosen for their youth, graceful and handsome figures, and willingness to flatter their master. His habit of fondling them, and especially Buckingham, in public gave rise to suspicions of baser intimacies in private, but these are not proved. Naturally indolent, he could concentrate on business only for short periods. He was at best in a small circle of intimates when his learning and pawky wit enlivened conversation: he was at his worst on state occasions because he wholly lacked kingly dignity.

James determined to make no radical changes among the ministers who had served Elizabeth. He had already assured Cecil that he regarded him as his principal upholder,[1] and continued him in office as chief adviser. The choice was the best possible, and until his death, in 1612, Cecil restrained the king from such graver follies as then followed. Unfortunately, however, Cecil, for all his integrity,[2] tireless industry, and administrative skill, could do little more than project into the future the worn-out ideals of the past. He was, like his royal master, totally unable to appreciate the aims or principles of those who differed from him, and could never understand either Bacon or Raleigh. In common with most sublime mediocrities, he distrusted original ideas of every kind, and never perceived that a changing world demanded policies far different from those in which he had been trained at the court of Elizabeth. At a time when the centre of political gravity was rapidly shifting, he left no mark at all upon constitutional history. An observation his cousin, Francis Bacon, is reputed to have made to James I exactly sums up his place in the national annals: 'I do think he was no fit counsellor to make your affairs better; but yet he was fit to have kept them from growing worse'.[3]

It is highly significant that one consequence of the king's retention of Cecil as his chief minister was the dismissal of Raleigh from his post as captain of the guard, though a generous pecuniary compensation was provided. Disappointed ambition

---

[1] *Hist. MSS. Com., Salisbury MSS.* (1930), xv. 10, 28.
[2] He wrote in 1603: 'Honesty having ever been the greatest study of my life' (ibid., p. 58).   [3] *Works*, xi. 278 n.

prompted Raleigh to listen to, though probably not to take an active part in, a wild project of Cobham's[1] to supplant James by his cousin, Arabella Stuart, an English-born descendant of Margaret, daughter of Henry VII, from whom the king's title was derived. For this Raleigh was tried, found guilty, and condemned to death, but reprieved and confined in the Tower. From a modern standard his trial was unfair, and posterity has reversed unanimously the contemporary verdict. Most of the blame must be laid to the procedure then followed in criminal trials, but Sir Edward Coke conducted the prosecution with a ferocity perhaps unequalled in English courts of law until the time of Jeffreys and the 'Bloody Assize'.

Another sign of the times was revealed at the beginning of 1604, when James issued a proclamation for the choice of members of parliament, because in it he directed that all election returns should be made into chancery, where any found contrary to the proclamation would be rejected as unlawful. This order was responsible for the first of many disagreements between king and parliament. When the houses met, the unusually large attendance testified to the importance men attached to the occasion.[2] From James's opening speech the future of the reign might have been foretold, for it disclosed at once the wide gulf fixed between the royal policy and public opinion. After eulogies on the peace with Spain[3] and the union of the crowns of England and Scotland, the king passed to religion. He praised the church of England, but regretted the existence of two bodies that refused to live within its folds. The puritans and 'novelists' he denounced for 'being ever discontented with the present government, and impatient to suffer any superiority; which maketh their sect unable to be suffered in any well-governed commonwealth'. Turning to the Roman catholics, he acknowledged theirs to be the mother church, although defiled by some infirmities and corruptions. The leniency he had already shown proved that he was against persecution, but he could not tolerate priests within his kingdom so long as they upheld the papal claim to dethrone princes and approved the assassination of heretical rulers.[4]

---

[1] Henry Brooke, eighth Baron Cobham (d. 1619), was the son of one of Queen Elizabeth's favourites and a rival of Essex's. He was involved in what was called the 'Main Plot' to be distinguished from the 'Bye Plot', a catholic conspiracy.

[2] *Commons' Journals*, i. 140–1.   [3] See below, p. 49.

[4] *Commons' Journals*, i. 142–4.

Before proceeding to other business, the commons took up two cases of privilege. The one finally secured freedom of members from arrest except for treason, felony, or breach of the peace. Shirley, a member, had been arrested for debt and held in the Fleet, and it was not until the warden of that prison had been committed to the Tower and acts of parliament asserting that members had always enjoyed this privilege had received the royal assent that Shirley was released to take his seat.[1] The other was of greater importance, for it produced the first clash between king and parliament. In the Buckinghamshire election Goodwin, an outlaw, had defeated Fortescue, but the court of chancery had declared the election void, and Fortescue was then chosen at a by-election. The house at once summoned Goodwin, and after hearing his statement ordered him to take his seat. James thereupon intervened and told the commons that, since all their privileges were derived from him, he did not expect them to be used against himself. Under the law, the house ought not to meddle with returns, which should be sent to chancery and there corrected if they needed it. The commons then realized that the question had suddenly assumed a new significance—that Goodwin versus Fortescue had become the case of the whole kingdom.[2] The commons therefore maintained a firm but conciliatory attitude, and at length James, after commanding them 'as an absolute king' to hold a conference with the judiciary, gave way and admitted that they were the proper judges of their own returns, while they in gratitude ordered the issue of a new writ for Buckinghamshire.[3] There can be no doubt that the commons had won their first skirmish with prerogative.

The commons then passed to the discussion of some practical grievances, such as purveyance and wardship. Both were relics of feudalism and both had long survived the reasons for their original existence. In a petition the commons summed up at length the case against purveyance, of which Bacon said to James: 'There is no grievance in your kingdom so general, so continual, so sensible, and so bitter unto the common subject.'[4] They mentioned that, in spite of thirty-six or more laws prohibiting the abuse of this privilege, there were still many grievances: that those responsible for requisitioning carts habitually

---

[1] *Eng. Hist. Rev.* viii. 733-40.   [2] *Commons' Journals*, i. 159.
[3] Ibid., p. 168.   [4] *Works*, x. 185.

demanded a number far beyond the requirement and exacted money before discharging those not wanted; that victuals and firing were taken at a price not greater than a fourth part of the true value, and that not in ready money; and that warrants were sent for excessive quantities of hay, straw, and oats of which the carriage alone often cost the subject twice as much as he received for his produce. In seeking the support of the lords, the commons struck a snag, for they found that there the opinion was held that compensation to the amount of £50,000 per annum should be granted.[1] This raised a most important question of principle, for the commons felt that, if purveyance was abused, there was no reason why compensation should be granted for the surrender by the Crown of these abuses; while the lords, voicing the opinion of the Crown, assumed that, as the royal revenue was already inadequate for the king's needs, no source should be abandoned unless an alternative were offered. There was much to be said for both sides, for unquestionably the Stuart monarchs, although extravagant, were never in possession of sufficient revenue to perform the functions pertinent to their office. On the other hand, instead of presenting the issue fairly to parliament, they preferred either to try to drive a hard bargain with the national representatives or to rely upon extra-legal devices to fill their coffers.

Wardship was in a position somewhat different from that of purveyance. The right of the king to the wardship of tenants-in-chief who were minors, to take the land of a minor into his own hand, to pocket the profits, and to arrange the marriage of an heiress under age, was unquestionable in point of law. But, here again, the legal right flourished long after the feudal duties that had once justified it had vanished. The court of wards had already become an obnoxious anachronism and a source of annoyance and expense to landowners. Fathers, in making their wills, had to face the difficulty of providing for the purchase from the king, or his officers, of the wardships of their children;[2] and a faithful servant of the Crown, like Strafford,

---

[1] *Commons' Journals*, i. 204. Sir Julius Caesar stated in 1610 that wardships were worth to the king £60,000, and purveyance £40,000 (*Parliamentary Debates in 1610*, ed. S. R. Gardiner [1862], p. 12).

[2] As an example, see *The Autobiography and Correspondence of Sir Simonds D'Ewes*, ed. J. O. Halliwell (1845), ii. 153. One of the concessions offered at an early stage of the discussion about the great contract was: 'The friends of every ward to have the wardship at certain reasonable rates' (*Parliamentary Debates in*

hoped that he might be rewarded with the wardship of his own son.[1] Moreover an odious traffic in the rights of wardship developed, often to the enrichment of greedy courtiers. In this case the commons, recognizing that the system was legal, offered to provide, in another way, a larger revenue than the king had ever obtained from the court of wards, but, instead of thanks, received one of the frequent scoldings that the king, 'as a father to his children', was wont to inflict upon them.[2]

The result was the Apology of the House of Commons, which is a statement, couched in firm, dutiful language, of parliamentary privileges and a defence of the proceedings in the lower house. It deserves the closest study, both because it reveals the position the commons took up and maintained for the next forty years—that their privileges were the general liberties of England—and because it was an authoritative pronouncement of the reforms or changes deemed necessary at the beginning of the new reign. After the statement that their privileges had been 'more universally and dangerously impugned than ever (as we suppose) since the beginnings of parliaments', the commons point out that freedom of election had been attacked and freedom of speech prejudiced by reproofs. Therefore they must protest, they say, because 'the prerogatives of princes may easily, and daily grow [while] the privileges of the subject are for the most part at an everlasting stand'. They declare that the liberties of the commons of England consist chiefly in free election, freedom from arrest during parliamentary sessions, and freedom of speech, and assert that these privileges are their right and due inheritance. As regards religion, they deny that the king could make any alterations or laws except by consent of parliament. They had not come, they say, in any puritan spirit to attempt the subversion of the ecclesiastical *status quo*, but, for the sake of peace and unity, ask that 'some few ceremonies of small importance' might be abandoned. After mentioning purveyance and wardship, they conclude by stating that 'the voice of the people, in the things of their knowledge, is said to be as the voice of God'.[3] Apparently the Apology was never presented

---

1610, p. 16). For a striking example of financial exaction, see *Salisbury MSS.*, xv. 276.

[1] *The Earl of Strafforde's Letters and Dispatches*, ed. William Knowler (1740), i. 370-1, 421.   [2] *Commons' Journals*, i. 230.

[3] *The Parliamentary History of England*, ed. William Cobbett (36 vols., 1806-20), i. 1030-42.

to the king, but it stands on record as an undelivered 'lecture to a foreign king on the constitutional customs of the realm which he had come to govern, but which he so imperfectly understood'.[1]

On the other hand there is little doubt that a copy of the petition reached the king's hands, for, in his speech at the prorogation, he scornfully observed that it was easy to make apologies when no man was present to answer them. His main complaint was that in the parliament there was 'nothing but curiosity, from morning to evening, to find fault with my propositions', and that he had not been accorded due respect. Here, like all the Stuarts, James was treating expressions of national grievances as if they were personal insults. He seems to have regarded parliamentary complaints as breaches of good manners, and persistence in the redress of grievances as disloyalty. His attitude towards the national representatives was both paternal and contemptuous. Like a father, he wished his people to believe that whatever he did was for their good; but the thesis that their representatives should decide what was good or bad for the country was rank sedition to him. Criticism seemed to emanate either from 'idle heads' or disloyal hearts. There was thus no sympathy between king and parliament because there was no understanding.

Disagreement on religion was greater than on any other question.[2] Probably the sentiments of the majority in parliament were voiced in the puritan appeal, presented to the king on his first entrance into England, which has become known as the Millenary Petition. At the resultant Hampton Court conference James's determination not to accede to the moderate demands for relaxation of ceremonial, and his declaration that he would make puritans conform, were fatal obstacles to a good understanding with parliament. In the Apology the commons had hoped that the relinquishment of a few ceremonies of slight importance would secure a perpetual uniformity, but James and Bancroft (who was nominated archbishop of Canterbury in October 1604) meant to achieve unity by the rigid enforcement of the law.[3]

Another difficulty in the way of a good understanding between king and parliament was presented by the catholic question.

---

[1] J. R. Tanner, *Constitutional Documents of the Reign of James I* (1930), p. 202.
[2] See below, pp. 69–71. [3] See below, p. 69.

James, hankering after a union with Rome, was averse to grati-
fying his protestant subjects by a uniform enforcement of the
penal code, and treated catholics according to dynastic or personal, rather than national or religious, considerations. By
alternately permitting and relaxing persecution he created distrust among protestants and failed to win the confidence of
catholics. The occasional martyrdom of priests[1] and the more
frequent exaction of recusancy fines[2] made some of the bolder
catholics despair of any lasting alleviation of their cruel lot.
The result was the Gunpowder Treason or Plot. A small band
headed by Robert Catesby hired a cellar under the houses of
parliament, had it well stored with barrels of gunpowder, and
arranged for Guy Fawkes to apply the torch. They hoped that
if king, lords, and commons were all blown up, they might
profit by the inevitable confusion among protestants to seize the
reins of government.[3] Their plot failed completely, but it inevitably deepened the national hatred against them, and increased
the severity of the penal code.

The next parliamentary session began under the shadow of
the Gunpowder Plot, and was adjourned immediately after a
speech from the throne, in which James tried to enlighten his
hearers by enlarging upon the true nature of monarchy, declaring that kings were God's 'vice-gerents on earth, and so
adorned and furnished with some sparkles of the Divinitie',[4] and
upon the function of parliament: 'Neither is this a place . . . for
every rash and harebrained fellow to propone new lawes of his
owne invention.'[5] Nevertheless, when parliament assembled
again, there was an unwonted harmony between king and
estates: a generous financial grant was made, and an act, passed
in the previous session, to appoint commissioners representing
England and Scotland to treat of a union between the two
kingdoms, was extended.[6]

The proposed union was the main topic of discussion in the
third session (1606-7). In his opening speech James strongly
urged the importance of the union, and stressed three essentials:

---

[1] See below, p. 208.   [2] See below, p. 206.

[3] For the view that the plot was mainly a fiction inspired by Cecil, see John
Gerard, *What Was the Gunpowder Plot?* (1897); for a refutation, S. R. Gardiner, *What
Gunpowder Plot Was* (1897).

[4] *The Political Works of James I*, ed. C. H. McIlwain (1918), p. 281.

[5] Ibid., p. 288.

[6] For the Articles the commissioners agreed to, see *Commons' Journals*, i. 320-3.

that all existing laws framed to provide for possible hostilities between the two kingdoms might be abrogated; that free trade should be established; and that those of his subjects born before his accession to the English Crown might be considered naturalized. When these preliminaries are completed the two nations 'shall ever acknowledge one church and one king; and be joined, in a perpetual marriage, for the peace and prosperity of both nations, and for the honour of their king'.[1] The ideal that James set before parliament was not destined to be realized for another century. The old hatred between England and Scotland had become less vehement but was still strong. Englishmen knew little of Scotland and cared less.[2] Many of the English despised the Scots as a nation of beggarly peasants or pedlars, or simply as men living by robbery or treachery. James's generosity to favourites whose sole merit was their nationality had made Scots more unpopular than ever, and it was easy to represent them as greedy adventurers who would devour the land like so many boars.[3]

The debates naturally turned on the question of free trade and naturalization. The London merchants protested that they would be ruined by the competition of Scots, who would be on hand whenever a bargain was to be made but would disappear across the border when taxes became due. Similarly the trading companies would soon be filled by Scots, and Englishmen deprived of a living. These and other arguments were utilized in the commons, where violent speeches abusing the Scots were listened to without disapproval until the king protested. In vain Bacon urged that England was not so overpopulated that the influx of a few Scots would make any real difference, that naturalization must precede any attempt to assimilate the laws of the two countries, and that to join them had been the lifelong effort of Edward I, one of the greatest English kings. He cited examples from classical as well as modern European history, to prove how beneficial unions similar to the one in question had proved, but his hearers remained unconvinced. They closed their ears to the opinion of the legal advisers of the Crown, that by the common law the Post-nati (the name given to those born

[1] Ibid., pp. 314–15.
[2] The striking remarks of Edward, earl of Clarendon (*The History of the Rebellion* [6 vols., 1888], ii. 18), refer to 1637 but apply equally well to 1607.
[3] C. H. Firth, 'Ballads Illustrating the Relations of England and Scotland during the Seventeenth Century', *Scottish Historical Review*, vi. 113–14.

in Scotland after James's accession) were *ipso facto* naturalized. They took up the position that they would have a 'perfect union' or nothing. By this they meant, as Sir Edwin Sandys stated, an incorporating union under which there would be one parliament and one law for both kingdoms.[1]

In view of the strength of the national prejudice, James had perforce to abandon his well-meant plan, and be content with the verdict at a collusive legal action, usually known as Calvin's case,[2] by which it was declared that the Post-nati were natural-born subjects of the king of England. Coke recognized that the action was 'the weightiest for the consequent, both for the present and for all posterity'; and in fact, as the historian of English law states, it made 'a uniform status for natural-born subjects, not only in England and Scotland, but also in the many lands which, in the succeeding centuries, were added to the king's dominions'.[3]

This use of the law-courts to declare as already existing law what parliament was unwilling to enact, was capable of dangerous extension. Both the first Stuarts were prone to appeal to the judges for confirmation of their own interpretations of legal points, and to regard them as natural upholders of the prerogative. This was the more serious inasmuch as there were many vital questions about which the law was not clear, for precedents might be cited on both sides. An example of extreme importance was now afforded of the prejudice a subject might suffer by the legal interpretation of a disputed right of taxation.

The case was that of John Bate, a merchant, who refused to pay a customs duty on currants. The previous history of this duty is somewhat complicated. Elizabeth had first granted a monopoly for the importation of currants from Venice, which then largely controlled the Levant trade. Later, when the Levant Company was formed, it had permitted non-members to import currants on payment of 5s. 6d. per hundredweight, but the company did not prosper, and, after various schemes

---

[1] *The Parliamentary Diary of Robert Bowyer, 1606-7*, ed. D. H. Willson (1931), pp. 258-9; Bacon, *Works*, x, chaps. vi, viii.

[2] Robert Colvill, or Calvin (afterwards the second Lord Colvill of Culross) was an infant born in Edinburgh, and an action was brought in his name relative to the ownership of land in England. The immediate point at issue was whether the child was or was not an alien, because if so he would be disabled from holding land in England.

[3] W. S. Holdsworth, *A History of English Law* (1922-31), ix. 80.

had been tried, its charter was surrendered, at the beginning of James's reign, and the trade thrown open, though an imposition was levied upon importation. Even so, the king had to remit arrears of duties amounting to £13,000 to the merchants. However, when Bate had a cartload of currants driven from the waterside before examination by the customs official and declared to the council that he had so acted because he believed the imposition to be illegal, the government decided to bring the whole question formally before the court of exchequer. The decision of Chief Baron Fleming is worthy of the closest analysis, inasmuch as it presents a theory of the royal prerogative widely held and long continuing. The impositions, he said, were duties newly levied by the king, without parliamentary authority, in order to augment his revenues. A king's power is both ordinary and absolute, and differs according to the ends it serves. The ordinary power concerns individuals, the execution of civil justice, and the determining of *meum*; is exercised in the ordinary courts of law according to common law; and is subject to parliament. The absolute power exists for the general benefit of the whole people, is governed by rules of policy, and varies according to what the wisdom of the king thinks is for the common good. Since all customs duties, be they old or new, are simply 'the effects and issues' of foreign trade, and since all foreign affairs, including commerce, are controlled by the absolute power of the king, impositions are rightly levied by this extraordinary prerogative. So far as foreign commodities are concerned, no act of parliament or petition was ever made against an impost upon alien goods, but the tax had been paid.[1]

On the whole, although Fleming's statement about the absolute or extraordinary prerogative of the Crown was capable of dangerous extension, he seems to have made it clear that this power was reserved for the regulation of foreign commerce, and his decision did not countenance its use solely for taxative purposes. The distinction he drew, by inference, between a duty to raise money and one to control trade, was probably sound according to precedent. Both Elizabeth and James had clearly been more concerned to foster trade with the Levant than to

---

[1] *A Complete Collection of State Trials*, ed. T. B. and T. J. Howell (33 vols., 1812–26), ii. 371–94. Salisbury probably correctly summed up the prevalent view in official circles, in the phrase that the king had the inherent right to levy impositions on foreign commodities 'with the due regard of the trade of merchandise' (*Parliamentary Debates in 1610*, p. 8).

raise a revenue from it. And the judgement in Bate's case apparently gave a legal justification for their policies. It was not the fault of the legal authorities concerned if James stretched the decision to cover additional impositions that were levied merely in order to increase the royal revenue.

To Salisbury, the treasurer, this decision seemed a godsend, and he proceeded to lay new impositions on merchandise,[1] though he was careful to make them as little onerous as possible and acted only after consulting the chief city merchants. Since the estimated yield of the new levies was £70,000, and the possibilities of raising further revenue from this source were not yet exhausted, the danger that the king might secure an adequate income independent of parliament was very real. Therefore it was natural that when parliament reassembled in 1610 impositions should be called in question. Salisbury explained in some detail the state of the national finances: that in spite of unparalleled exertions by which £700,000 of debt had been paid off, there was still owing £300,000, and that the revenue fell short of the requirements by £50,000, without allowing for extraordinary expenses. Members, however, were not impressed and they evinced more zeal for checking the prodigality of the court than for voting additional taxes. Wentworth's[2] speech is probably typical of the general sentiments: that it was useless to grant any more supplies unless the king would resume the pensions he had given to courtiers and reduce his own expenses. 'For his part . . . he would never give his consent to take money from a poore frize jerkyn to trappe a courtier's horse withall.' He was in favour of petitioning His Majesty to practise economy and to live of his own without further exactions from his poor subjects, especially in a time of peace. Otherwise, a precedent of Richard II's reign might be followed, when the king's excessive gifts and extravagance caused the appointment of a council to inquire into these excesses.

Other speakers were more eager to remove grievances, such as monopolies, purveyance, and wardship, than to suggest ways to make good the loss their abolition would entail. The unwillingness of the commons to grant an income that would have

---

[1] The higher duties appear in a book of rates issued in 1608.

[2] Thomas Wentworth, a lawyer, to be distinguished from his namesake, the future earl of Strafford, was the son of Peter Wentworth, imprisoned by Queen Elizabeth for his freedom of speech.

made the king largely independent of parliament was probably increased when attention was called to a law dictionary, *The Interpreter*, compiled by John Cowell. In this book the royal authority is enhanced to the highest point, and its writer leaves the impression that in his opinion the king is absolute and above the laws, and only admits the concurrence in legislation of the three estates through his benignity or by reason of his coronation oath.[1] Before there was time to prepare an address, the king prudently sent a message to the two houses in which he disavowed the theory of the prerogative, as set forth by Cowell, and acknowledged that he had no power either to make laws or levy subsidies without parliamentary assent. He therefore ordered the suppression of the obnoxious volume.[2]

After this interruption, attention once again centred on the state of the royal income. The commons were now willing that compensation should be given to the king in return for his surrender of all he received from feudal tenures except aids, but they offered only £100,000 when twice that amount was demanded by the court. They declined to proceed, and, instead, began to consider grievances (among them impositions). Forbidden to discuss them and told by James that he would not have his prerogative called in question, the commons engaged in an animated debate, in which claims were advanced that members might discuss any subject that concerned the welfare of the kingdom. Accordingly a petition was drawn up and, unlike the Apology, entered in full in the journal. The commons now asserted that parliament enjoyed the ancient and undoubted right to debate freely all matters affecting the subject, and sought permission to make a thorough examination of the new impositions. Thereupon James drew back, admitting that impositions were proper subjects for parliamentary inquiry. Accordingly a discussion of unusual length and gravity ensued, in the course of which the issue was fairly stated by a legal antiquary, William Hakewill: 'The question now in debate amongst us is, whether His Majesty may, by his prerogative royall, without assent of parliament, at his own will and pleasure, lay a new charge or imposition upon merchandises, to be brought into, or out of this kingdome of England, and enforce merchants to pay the same?'[3] The same speaker, in an exhaustive examination of

---

[1] Cowell, *The Interpreter* (1607), *sub* King, Prerogative, Parliament, and Subsidy.
[2] *Parliamentary Debates in 1610*, pp. 22–25.   [3] *State Trials*, ii. 407.

precedents, made out a good case against the right of the Crown to levy new customs for revenue purposes, and the general feeling of the house was clearly with him. Therefore Salisbury once more tried to arrange a compromise and eventually succeeded in inducing the commons to offer £200,000.[1] In a memorial the commons stated the concessions they expected from the king in return for the increased revenue he would receive. Purveyance, wardship, and other feudal relics were to be abolished (except aids, restricted in amount to £25,000), and possession of an estate for sixty years was to be a sufficient title against the king and his heirs. Four English counties now subject to the jurisdiction of the council of Wales were henceforth to be exempt therefrom.[2]

In his answer, delivered just before the prorogation, James took up other grievances as well as those mentioned above. He dealt at some length with various alleged ecclesiastical abuses, but, although his tone was conciliatory, he refused to promise more than that he would examine each point carefully and frame such remedies as his princely wisdom suggested. However adroitly he might contrive his answer to the commons' petitions, his feeling obviously was that ecclesiastical questions were no fit subjects for parliamentary interference, and that he meant jealously to safeguard his supremacy. Similarly, in touching upon the proposed restriction of the council of Wales, he would only promise to consider the matter.[3] In other words his attitude was that the commons after bringing grievances to his notice should thenceforth be content to leave their redress to him.

When parliament reassembled, the commons began to discuss the king's answer to their memorial, and it soon became evident that there was every intention to insist on a more definite and satisfactory response. On the other hand James now thought the proposed bargain unacceptable, and insisted that a grant should be made to pay his debts and also that his additional revenue should be augmented by another £100,000. The result of these fresh demands was to stiffen opposition, and there were plain speeches delivered against the Scottish favourites and the extravagance of the court. At last James lost patience and first adjourned and then dissolved parliament. Thereupon the 'great contract' vanished into oblivion.

[1] *Commons' Journals*, i. 451.   [2] *Lords' Journals*, ii. 660-2.
[3] Ibid., pp. 658-60.

The history of this first parliament of James I is most important as the prototype of many others. During its sessions the Tudor system of government had been on trial and its inadequacy was exposed. James had failed partly because he lacked the personality of his famous predecessor. Yet it is very doubtful whether even Queen Elizabeth could have succeeded, for both these sovereigns regarded parliament as an unwelcome and intrusive body that had to be cajoled by occasional concessions into granting much-needed subsidies. It was, they felt, a nuisance born of financial necessities. Consequently they directed all their efforts to excluding the estates from any share in administration and listened to criticisms only when they either became unusually vehement or when the fiscal situation was especially serious. There are other, less fundamental reasons why James failed to control parliament as successfully as Elizabeth. He allowed the dominant position which the privy councillors had occupied in the sixteenth century to be weakened by their paucity and slight influence. During this parliament there were only two or three councillors in the commons, and none of them ever acquired any real leadership in debate. The absence of such leadership as the Elizabethan councillors had supplied, naturally led back-benchers to accept guidance from private members. Although Sir Edwin Sandys cannot be regarded as the leader of the opposition, in any modern sense of that term, the feebleness of the court representatives gave him an opportunity which he skilfully utilized to concentrate the attention of the house upon such grievances as purveyance or impositions. In addition members found a way to free themselves from the control which privy councillors had exercised over committees, by enlarging them so that they became committees of the whole house. This change in procedure grew more and more important in the twenties and was admirably suited to training and developing leaders in the struggle against the court. Thus the tide was already advancing strongly in resistance to that system of monarchy which James loved so well.[1] His complete failure to appraise the new spirit that was animating members, and his entire lack of sympathy with popular opinion, were plainly revealed after the dissolution of his first parliament, in which

---

[1] Much of this paragraph is based upon Wallace Notestein, *The Winning of the Initiative by the House of Commons* (1925), and D. H. Willson, 'The Earl of Salisbury and the "Court" Party in Parliament', *American Historical Review*, xxxvi. 274–94.

criticism of his beloved Scots had been frequent. He now scattered £34,000 among his favourites, mostly fellow country-men, and created Robert Carr Viscount Rochester, thereby for the first time enabling a Scot to sit in the house of lords.[1]

Salisbury, who was mainly responsible for the royal policy, did not long survive the first parliament of the reign; and his death in 1612 removed a powerful restraint, for hitherto James had been kept from serious errors by the awe his minister inspired in him. Almost at once a change is noticeable, and a more frivolous tone perceptible. For the next nine years the domestic history of England largely consists of the annals of the court, where the most important events were the fall of one favourite and his supersession by another. The king seems to have felt that he had been unduly overshadowed by Salisbury, who had engrossed the two offices of lord treasurer and secretary of state. Accordingly the treasury was put into commission and the king was his own secretary of state for nearly two years, until the appointment of Sir Ralph Winwood. Both arrangements worked badly, for the treasury steadily increased its indebted-ness and the king was much too indolent to transact the business of an office that required daily attention. He came to rely more and more upon Rochester, whom he hoped to fashion into a useful instrument to carry out the royal policy, but was himself moulded to the wishes of the favourite, and thus became in-volved in an infamous tragedy. Rochester was enamoured of Frances (Howard), wife of the earl of Essex, and daughter of the earl of Suffolk and great-niece of the earl of Northampton, the leaders of the pro-Spanish faction in England. James was so infatuated with Rochester[2] that he must be held responsible for the success of the suit for nullity which the countess brought, inasmuch as he appointed new members, carefully chosen, to a commission that was evenly divided. To the great scandal of honest men, Lady Essex was thus enabled to marry her para-mour. One result of this unhallowed union between a daughter of the Howard family and the special friend of the king was the triumph of the Spanish faction at the court. Their influence over the king was much strengthened after the dissolution of the Addled Parliament.

[1] S. R. Gardiner, *History of England* (10 vols., 1884), ii. 111.
[2] Created earl of Somerset in 1613, but the earlier title is retained to avoid confusion.

The elections to this parliament (1614) created unusual excitement owing to the activities of some self-appointed 'undertakers' who hoped to secure the return of members likely to support the court. The extent of their interference was much exaggerated by rumour, and this in itself sufficed to secure their defeat. James made two speeches, early in the parliament, in which he acknowledged that there was a great increase of popery; this he attributed to the impunity the papists enjoyed in consequence of the failure of the proper officers to make presentments against them. He was careful to add that no religion or heresy had ever been extirpated by violence. He confessed his need of parliamentary grants and blamed his heavy family expenses—the burial of his son Henry and the marriage of his daughter Elizabeth whom he had sacrificed in the interest of religion and the commonwealth. He denounced as utterly false the reports that he had relied upon the undertakers, and denied that he had aided or hindered any man at the election. As for grievances, let each member present those of his own constituency, but let them not be heaped together in a scroll which would cast aspersions upon his government and evince discontent rather than desire for reformation.

Speedy disillusion awaited James's hope that the commons would revert to the earliest stages of parliament, when individual petitions were presented. Instead prompt consideration was given to a bill against impositions—a vexed question left over from the last parliament. In their desire for support the commons appealed to the lords, but their co-operation was denied in a close division in which the majority was largely composed of bishops, courtiers, and the two Scots who had been created English peers. To make matters worse, Neile, bishop of Lincoln and one of the worst of sycophants, who was possibly angered by a speech in the commons charging the clergy with leading scandalous lives,[1] delivered a strong attack upon the commons. Let not the lords enter into a conference, he said, on a bill that struck at the very root of the prerogative. They would be sure to hear undutiful and seditious speeches, tending to distract both houses and alienate the king and his subjects.[2] When the commons complained of this speech Neile apologized with tears, but the commons were still unsatisfied. Not content with debating the bishop's speech against them in

---

[1] *Commons' Journals*, i. 497.   [2] *Lords' Journals*, ii. 709.

the upper house, they strayed like lost sheep into all kinds of trifling accusations concerning his conduct in his diocese. When they were sharply pulled up by the king, angry complaints were made about the royal favourites and pensioners. The result was a dissolution. James gave his version of the trouble to the Spanish ambassador, Sarmiento:

> The house of commons is a body without a head. The members give their opinions in a disorderly manner. At their meetings nothing is heard but cries, shouts and confusion. I am surprised that my ancestors should ever have permitted such an institution to come into existence. I am a stranger, and found it here when I arrived, so that I am obliged to put up with what I cannot get rid of.[1]

The need for money, which had been responsible for calling a parliament, survived its dissolution. To raise funds James issued a general appeal for a benevolence. This began with genuinely free gifts, offered to the king by courtiers and others, and for a time retained its original character; but it soon became apparent that the example of generosity would not be generally followed. Thereupon the privy council attempted to use the sheriffs and justices of the peace as its local agents. These latter were instructed to inform people of means, within their respective counties, that free gifts to His Majesty would be regarded as proofs of good affections and held in grateful remembrance.[2] What happened in Devonshire is typical of the whole country. There the justices informed the privy council of their anxiety that posterity would suffer if they established such a precedent. 'Nothing but the fear of the just blame of after ages' impelled them to refuse what they would always be willing to give in accordance with the ancient and lawful customs of the kingdom. At this juncture they were summoned before the council, where it was proved that free gifts without coercion had often been made to the king's progenitors.[3] Nevertheless, in spite of these appeals, the amount raised from the whole country was only about £40,000, plus £20,000 from the City and courtiers.

Meanwhile Rochester's pre-eminence at court was being threatened by the appearance there of George Villiers, the son of a Leicestershire knight, first introduced to the king in 1614

---

[1] Gardiner, ii. 251.
[2] *Acts of the Privy Council, 1613–14* (1921), pp. 491–6.
[3] A. H. A. Hamilton, *Quarter Sessions from Queen Elizabeth to Queen Anne* (1878), pp. 42–52.

and appointed a gentleman of the bedchamber and knighted in April of the next year. The good looks and facile manners of the young man alarmed Rochester, and he upbraided the king bitterly. The royal apologia is one of the most curious documents in English history. The king confesses that the favourite had 'deserved more trust and confidence of me than ever man did,—in secrecy above all flesh, in feeling and impartial respect, as well to my honour in every degree as to my profit'. Yet these merits have recently been 'mixed with strange streams of unquietness, passion, fury, and insolent pride, and (which is worst of all) with a settled kind of induced obstinacy'. The favourite's sharp and bitter railing made Peacham's treatise[1] a gentle admonition in comparison, and seemed intended to persuade the writer that he was to be overawed rather than loved. This discourse proceeded from the infinite grief of a deeply wounded heart, which had suffered as much as it could endure. The king continues:

Neither can I bear it longer without admitting an unpardonable sin against God in consuming myself wilfully, and not only myself, but in perilling thereby not only the good estate of mine own people, but even the state of religion through all Christendom, which almost wholly, under God, rests now upon my shoulders. Be not the occasion of the hastening of his death through grief, who was not only your creator under God, but hath many a time prayed for you, which I never did for any subject alive but for you. . . . Hold me thus by the heart; you may build upon my favour as upon a rock that never shall fail you. [Reward me with your love and obedience for] it hath ever been my common answer to any, that would plead for favour to a puritan minister by reason of his rare gifts, that I had rather have a conformable man with but ordinary parts, than the rarest men in the world, that will not be obedient.[2]

Rochester's downfall, however, came about not from sullen rudeness to the king but from the discovery of a shocking crime. When Rochester first became involved in a liaison with Lady Essex, he had not infrequently profited by the superior intelligence of Sir Thomas Overbury, an early friend. But when the annulment permitted Rochester to regularize his relations with his paramour, Overbury did his utmost to dissuade him from marrying her. To get this inconvenient mentor out of the way,

---

[1] An unpublished treatise, justifying rebellion against oppression, sufficed to imprison its author, Peacham.

[2] *Letters of the Kings of England*, ed. J. O. Halliwell (1846), ii. 126–33.

James was induced to offer Overbury a diplomatic appointment, and, when that was refused, to confine the unfortunate knight in the Tower. This punishment failed to satisfy the bitter hatred of the countess, even when she had attained her ambition and become the wife of Rochester. After a number of failures Overbury was successfully poisoned. The crime was not unearthed for two years, but in spite of the lapse of time ample evidence was forthcoming to convict the countess. The earl was found guilty too, but it is by no means certain that he was an active participant in the crime. Both were pardoned, but the clemency encouraged a suspicion that the king had connived at the murder. This was grossly unjust, but James's infatuation for Rochester, and the active part he had taken in Lady Essex's case, justified the general disgust at the revelation of the character of one whom the king had delighted to honour. Probably no single event, prior to the attempt to arrest the five members in 1642, did more to lessen the general reverence with which royalty was regarded in England than this unsavoury episode.

Another event that gave public opinion a profound shock was the fall of Sir Edward Coke. For ten years he had been the champion of the common law against the prerogative. He had maintained that the prerogative was subject to definite legal limitations, and that the judges should see that it did not exceed them. In opposition to Coke's views, legalists like Bacon tended to magnify the prerogative until it seemed to be supreme in the state, and to regard upholding the royal power as the special duty of the judges. Just as parliament had attacked what they at least regarded as the unconstitutional proceedings of the Crown in the matter of taxation, so Coke and the common lawyers tried to restrain within due bounds the prerogative courts, such as the high commission. Ever since his appointment in 1606 as chief justice of the court of common pleas, Coke had been a thorn in the flesh of churchmen on account of the writs of prohibition he had issued against the court of high commission. Similarly, in the famous case of proclamations, he had laid it down once for all that the king could not by proclamation change the common law or create any new offences, although he admitted that if the king prohibited by proclamation what was already punishable by law future offenders would be guilty of an aggravated offence. To silence this troublesome critic,

James removed him from the court of common pleas and made him chief justice of the king's bench, but the promotion did not achieve its purpose. Coke continued to assert the independence of the judicature, and in Peacham's case expressed the opinion that judges should not be consulted individually and privately about a case already pending, although for the present he did not protest against their consultation in a body. The final quarrel between Coke and the king took place over the question whether the king could command the common-law courts to desist from hearing a case by issue of the writ *de non procedendo rege inconsulto*. The judges made it clear that in their view the king could not control cases pending, even if his interests might be involved. Summoned before the council, the other judges retreated, but Coke stood his ground and was dismissed from his office. The lord chancellor told Coke's successor that the dismissal was 'a lesson to be learned of all, and to be remembered and feared of all that sit in judicial places'.[1]

Although some further examples were necessary before all the judges were prepared to accept the subservient position assigned to them by Stuart theories of government, Coke's disgrace was a heavy blow to the independence of the judiciary. But his sacrifice of office rather than conform to royal dictation was not in vain. Henceforth men became less and less disposed to accept legal decisions as definitions of the constitution, until in time even thoughtful men like Hyde[2] felt that the decision in Hampden's case was against the plain and obvious meaning of the law. By the dismissal of independent judges and the appointment of subservient successors, the early Stuarts obtained servile instruments. But the very means they took to secure favourable decisions deprived those decisions of all moral weight.

During the years that intervened between the fall of Coke in 1616 and the meeting of parliament in 1621, domestic history contributes little worthy of remembrance, except the advance of Buckingham[3] in royal favour and the fall of the Howards. This

---

[1] Holdsworth, *History of English Law*, v. 423–56. James claimed that he appointed the best judges he knew and never influenced them to decisions not in accordance with right and equity. Speech to parliament 30 Jan. 1621.

[2] Clarendon, i. 150.

[3] George Villiers, the second son of a simple knight, was trained as a courtier. He was taught dancing and fencing in England and spent three years in France learning the language and acquiring the accomplishments of a French nobleman. These, plus a handsome figure, were his qualifications for becoming the virtual

family, which engrossed many of the offices of state, was headed by Nottingham, lord high admiral, and Suffolk, lord high treasurer. Buckingham, whose pride could not endure the presence at court of any who did not owe their advancement to his influence, soon secured the exclusion of both from the administration. Suffolk's conviction of accepting bribes came none too soon, for the financial position had steadily deteriorated under him. He was succeeded at first by a commission and then by its moving spirit, Cranfield, who had begun life as a London apprentice but who, after amassing a fortune in the City, had quickly won favour at court and secured the treasurership and the title of earl of Middlesex. Nottingham had to resign after a commission had presented a hostile report on the state of the navy. In this case, also, the change was all to the good, for corruption and incompetence had long reigned supreme in the navy. Although the annual cost of its upkeep was constantly rising, the number of serviceable ships was little more than half the total inherited from Elizabeth. James bragged that his choice fell not upon 'an old beaten soldier for my admiral' but upon a young man whose honesty he trusted (Buckingham), and there is no doubt that, thanks to the transformation of the commission into a permanent navy board, the condition of affairs vastly improved. Indeed it can be said that both at the treasury and at the admiralty greater efficiency at less cost was secured by Buckingham and his nominees than by their predecessors. Yet the price paid for these reforms was too high, for Buckingham exacted servility from all, and honest criticism and outspoken advice were no longer heard in James's court. Moreover the losses from the Howards' corruption would have been trifling compared with those sustained through Buckingham's overweening confidence in his capacity to rule England. And the time was at hand when his ignorance of foreign affairs made free discussion in the council essential.

The first stage of the Thirty Years War was now over, for the battle of the White Mountain (November 1620) ended Frederick's brief reign in Bohemia.[1] It soon became evident, however, that his enemies would not be content until they had

---

ruler of England for nearly a decade. He became earl, marquis, and duke of Buckingham in 1617, 1619, and 1623 respectively.

[1] See below, p. 55, for Frederick's acceptance of the Bohemian crown and the beginning of the Thirty Years War (1618).

also expelled him from the Upper and Lower Palatinate. James, who had no direct responsibility for the rash adventure in Bohemia, felt that he could not sit idly by while his son-in-law was despoiled of his hereditary lands. Therefore, having failed to induce his subjects to contribute liberally to a benevolence to help Frederick, he once again had recourse to a parliament. The time seemed opportune to profit by the warm sympathy Englishmen felt for Frederick, popularly regarded as a protestant champion threatened with destruction by a Roman catholic coalition. Probably never in previous English history had interest in public affairs, and particularly in foreign policy, been so intense. Sermons were often devoted to the danger to continental protestantism, and it is noteworthy that the earliest English newsbooks were printed in Holland (1620–1) and dealt with foreign intelligence.[1] James, however, regarded this popular absorption in foreign news with strong disapproval. It is wholly characteristic that, when Bacon drafted a proclamation to explain to the electorate the situation of foreign affairs, which necessitated a parliament, James's comment was that, as the people were incapable of understanding state affairs, it was not fit that the king should explain them.[2] He found it easy to punish ministers who talked politics in the pulpit, and to issue a proclamation against the excessive discussion of questions of state;[3] but the mass of Englishmen were too interested to be deterred. It is probable that, as Bacon suggested, the disappointing results of the elections were occasioned by recent events on the Continent and 'the general licentious speaking of state matters'.[4] A factor he overlooked was the depression lasting from about 1619 to 1624. Hard times are usually blamed on the government by electors and there is no reason to believe 1621 was an exception.[5]

James's contempt for the opinions of the man in the street and his determination to exclude members of parliament from all real influence upon the direction of foreign affairs were fatal to his relations with the legislature. He would need money to carry

---

[1] *First Newspapers of England*, reproduced and published by W. P. Van Stockum (1914). The presence of English soldiers in the Netherlands helps to explain the printing of these newsbooks.

[2] Bacon, *Works*, xiv. 123–9.   [3] Ibid., pp. 156–7.

[4] Ibid., p. 152. Elsewhere he speaks of these 'huffing elections and general licence of speech'.

[5] See below, pp. 291, 333.

on whatever foreign policy he judged best, but parliament would refuse grants unless it both knew and approved the policy that required the expenditure. At present James was in a curious position because parliament accepted one half of his foreign policy, his anxiety to prevent the catholic powers from over-running the Palatinate, but disliked the other half, the Spanish match.[1] It is just possible that, had the king given a strong lead in his opening speech to parliament (January 1621), domestic grievances would have been forgotten amid the excitement of a spirited attempt to preserve Frederick in his hereditary domains. Instead James disdained to take parliament into his confidence, and his remarks were singularly ill suited to enlist the sympathies of his hearers. 'But you of the Lower House,' he said, 'I would not have you to meddle with complaints against the King, the church or state matters, nor with princes' prerogatives.'[2] On the all-engrossing question of foreign policy, he merely said that he would never suffer the Spanish match to endanger religion and that he proposed to equip an army in the summer to preserve his children's patrimony, and for this reason supplies would be needed. No hint was afforded of the probable cost of the army or of the extent of his commitments with foreign powers. Accordingly parliament made the rather perfunctory grant of two subsidies, and then turned to redress of grievances.

For some time there had been indications of the storm about to break, because a writer of newsletters had noted that everybody was groaning under the burden of monopolies, whose number had been multiplied by a score since James's accession.[3] What made this burden the more unbearable was that Elizabeth's gracious surrender in 1601 had seemed to lighten it permanently, for she had agreed that the legality or otherwise of any or every patent might be tested in the law-courts. At the very beginning of the new reign the judges in the famous case, *Darcy* v. *Allen*, had delivered the unanimous decision that a monopoly was prima facie against both common and statute law, that it was burdensome to the kingdom because it raised the price of the commodity at the same time that it lowered the quality and threw artificers out of work, and that it was justi-

---

[1] For the negotiations to arrange a marriage between Prince Charles and the infanta see below, pp. 55, 59.

[2] *Commons Debates 1621*, by Wallace Notestein, Frances Helen Relf, and Hartley Simpson (1935), ii. 12.

[3] Gardiner, iv. 1.

fiable only when a new invention was made or introduced or when demanded in the interest of the state.[1] Nevertheless the law had been ignored, evaded, or broken. In 1606, 1610, and 1614 parliament had protested against the abuse of patents, but the evil was more rampant than ever during the early years of Buckingham's ascendancy. Then the relatives or dependants of the favourite enjoyed three monopolies—for the licensing of inns, and that of ale-houses, and for the manufacturing of gold and silver thread. No doubt these monopolies furnished pickings for their possessors, but the gain was small in comparison with the irritation caused. The country gentleman who was a magistrate was affronted at the implication that he was incapable of supervising the inns in his neighbourhood, the puritan protested that the new patentees licensed disorderly houses and multiplied drinking facilities far beyond the reasonable needs of the people, and the City mercers were annoyed at the privileged position given to a rival industry.

As soon as the commons began to discuss grievances, the proceedings of the monopolists came in for severe censure. In particular Sir Francis Mitchell and Sir Giles Mompesson were found to have been extortionate as licensers of inns, and the tale of their iniquities aroused the house to a fury. Mitchell was called to the bar and sentenced without a hearing.[2] Then, rather late in the day, the question was raised whether the commons had any right to punish offences which did not concern their privileges. A search for precedents having failed, it was resolved to repair to the lords.[3] The king, hearing of these proceedings, unexpectedly addressed the lords in a curiously vacillating speech intended to exempt himself and Buckingham (and his relatives) from all blame. He told the lords that the commons would be the accusers and they the judges, and that they must be careful to see that all charges against Mompesson were proved by witnesses. The speech ended characteristically with the pronouncement that 'I will give accoumpt to God and to my people declaratively, and he that will have all doon by parliament is an enemy to monarchie and a traitor to the king of

---

[1] Holdsworth, *History of English Law*, iv. 348–51; W. H. Price, *English Patents of Monopoly* (1913), pp. 21–24.

[2] Later Mitchell was formally judged before the house of lords (*Lords' Journals*, iii. 89, 95).

[3] Edward Nicholas, *Proceedings and Debates of the House of Commons in 1620 and 1621* (1766), i. 85, 109; *Commons' Journals*, i. 530–2, 540.

England'.[1] Undeterred, the lords heard witnesses and passed sentence. Now, having tasted blood, the commons flew at higher game. During their investigations of irregularities at the courts of law they unearthed evidence that Francis Bacon, Viscount St. Albans, lord high chancellor of England, had accepted presents from suitors, a few while their suits were actually pending but usually after judgement had been delivered. Bacon at once realized the uselessness of attempting a defence to the articles of impeachment exhibited against him, and acknowledged the substantial accuracy of the charges.[2] The king remitted most of the penalties imposed, but excluded him from all public business. He did not long survive his disgrace, dying in 1626. The only possible line of defence is that which he himself suggested in a letter written to the king at an early stage of the proceedings. 'I hope I shall not be found', he said, 'to have the troubled fountain of a corrupt heart in a depraved habit of taking rewards to pervert justice; howsoever I may be frail and partake of the abuse of the times.'[3] The most lenient view that can be taken, therefore, is that the highest legal dignitary in the kingdom accepted presents from suitors, when he must have known full well that these presents were either given in the hope of influencing decisions or in gratitude for favourable decisions. Whether the distinction between accepting presents under these circumstances and taking bribes is worth making, is a question that can be left to the casuist.

These judicial proceedings, and the time they consumed, seem to have alarmed and irritated the court. When the houses met, after an adjournment, members were told to avoid long speeches and malicious diversions from what should be the sole business before them, the grant of supplies to sustain the army in the Palatinate.[4] Once again the commons were left without any clear indication of the nature of the policy they were asked to finance. They naturally demanded that, first, they should know against what enemy the army to be raised was going to march. After voting a subsidy for the immediate support of the forces in the Palatinate, the commons drew up a petition in which they sketched the European situation as they saw it.

[1] *Notes of the Debates in the House of Lords*, ed. Frances Helen Relf (1929), p. 14; *Lords' Journals*, iii. 51, 72.
[2] *Lords' Journals*, iii. 84, 87, 98–101, 106.
[3] Letter to James I, 25 March 1621 (Bacon, *Works*, xiv. 226).
[4] Nicholas, *Proceedings and Debates*, ii. 185.

They represented what they conceived to be the causes of the unhappy state of affairs, and what the remedies. Briefly the causes were the Roman catholic league abroad, with the king of Spain at its head, and the connexion between the triumph of popery on the Continent and its increase at home. The remedies were to declare war against the head of the catholic league and to marry the prince of Wales to a protestant. Before this petition was formally presented, James, egged on by Gondomar, the Spanish ambassador, wrote to the Speaker. Hearing that 'some fiery and popular spirits' were debating questions far above their reach and tending to violate the royal prerogative, the king demanded that no one in the house should henceforth presume to meddle 'with anything concerning our government or matters of state', and particularly not with the Spanish match. Furthermore the king said that he felt himself 'very free and able to punish any man's misdemeanors in parliament, as well during their sitting as after. Which we mean not to spare hereafter upon any occasion of any man's insolent behaviour there.'

The commons then drew up an explanation of their petition, in which they acknowledged that to make peace and war and to marry the prince of Wales appertained solely to the royal prerogative. The reason for their petition, therefore, was merely to bring to the king's attention certain facts which might not otherwise come to his knowledge, and they now asked him to receive their answer and petition. This explanation was not unnaturally roughly handled by the king, who pointed out that it was idle to protest at one place that they did not intend to entrench upon the prerogative and yet in reality to usurp it by their advice. Thereupon the commons drafted the famous Protestation of 18 December 1621, in which they denied, by implication, the king's claim to the right to imprison members at his will, by asserting that their lives and privileges were 'the ancient and undoubted birthright and inheritance of the subjects of England'. They replied to the king's denial of their right to discuss foreign relations with the statement that what concerned the king, state, defence of the realm, and the church of England were proper subjects for counsel and debate in parliament and that they had every right to discuss and resolve them.[1]

This was too much for James's patience, and he first adjourned and then dissolved parliament. Coke and Sir Robert Phelips

[1] Tanner, *Constitutional Documents*, pp. 274-89.

were imprisoned, and Pym confined to his house, for their share in the proceedings. Further to mark his disapprobation, the king ordered the production of the journal of the commons, at a meeting of the privy council, and tore out the offending protestation. At the same time he made a speech condemning it because it was framed in ambiguous and general terms that might serve in the future as precedents for the invasion of most of the prerogatives of the Crown.[1] The criticism is just. The commons' right to give advice on all subjects was substantially new,[2] and if conceded would give them simultaneously an indirect control over the administration, for they would naturally refuse supplies whenever their advice was not accepted. James realized the logical consequences of their claims more clearly than they did themselves, but he entirely failed to gauge the strength of popular support the commons had at their backs and particularly failed to perceive that his pursuance of a pro-Spanish foreign policy was the surest way to alienate the sympathy of the middle classes, so strongly represented in parliament.

Bad as the mistake was in choosing friendship with Spain, and the Spanish match, as subjects for rebutting the pretensions of the commons, James gave his case away by the grossest inconsistency. After the failure of the long-drawn-out negotiations with Spain, he summoned parliament and virtually handed over the direction of foreign relations to the very body he had so recently rebuked. In his opening speech (February 1624) he said that full particulars of the negotiations would be given members. When they had heard about the negotiations, 'I shall then entreat your good and sound advice. . . . Never a king gave more trust to his subjects than to desire their advice in matters of this weight.' Later he said that no man dying of thirst longed for water more ardently than he desired a happy conclusion to his parliament.[3] On the whole his wish was gratified, and he parted on better terms with the houses, now, than on any previous occasion, for king and subjects were united against Spain—although the union was achieved only after the complete failure of a policy pursued consistently for a decade.

---

[1] *Acts of the Privy Council 1621–1623* (1932), pp. 108–10.

[2] Cf. a message from the commons to the lords in 1606, about naturalization of Scots: 'They hold it to be a matter of state, so as it is fitter to have beginning from the upper house, that is better acquainted with matters of state' (*Lords' Journals*, ii. 483).

[3] Ibid. iii. 210.

Moreover, judging by the course of events, the king's statecraft had been wrong and popular prejudice right. It was perhaps fortunate for his peace of mind that he died at the outbreak of hostilities, for his reign ended, as it had begun, with England at war with Spain.[1]

Miserably as James had failed in his most cherished plan, he furnished proof before he died that he was wiser than his son and his favourite. When they insisted on promoting the impeachment of the treasurer, Middlesex, the king warned Charles that he would live to have his fill of impeachments, and Buckingham, that he was merely pickling a rod for his own back. Perhaps the king realized that the proceedings against Middlesex were more significant constitutionally than those against Mompesson or Bacon. Then the commons had been content to turn over the evidence to the lords for investigation and punishment; now they presented definite charges as 'inquisitors general of the grievances of the kingdom'.[2]

Constitutionally the reign is the first of six that occupied the transitional period during which the Tudor monarchy was transformed into the Hanoverian. It is difficult, therefore, to gauge the advance made by parliament under James. That the two houses would no longer be content to occupy a subordinate position in the state was already clear. When not blinded by anger, the king was too shrewd not to see that a new power had arisen in the land, as was proved by his famous remark, on receiving a parliamentary deputation: 'Chairs for the ambassadors.' Yet the only privilege the house of commons asserted so decidedly that it was never called in question was the right to determine the validity of the election of its own members. Neither immunity from arrest for words spoken in parliament, nor the right to tender advice freely on all subjects, was acknowledged by the Crown, and both privileges were infringed by Charles I. During his last years James ceded the revived claim to call ministers to account by impeachment, but Charles utterly denied it in order to save Buckingham.

The future seemed to depend on two factors—how far the needs of the Crown could be supplied by its ordinary revenue, and whether the commons could count on the support of the

---

[1] There was no formal declaration of war either by James I or Charles I, at least, none has been traced. James may, therefore, have died technically at peace.

[2] *Lords' Journals*, iii. 307.

lords. James had been successful in establishing impositions as regular levies on merchandise, but his efforts to raise money by benevolences or forced loans had been foiled by the passive resistance of his subjects. At the end of his reign the Crown could rely upon funds nearly sufficient to meet ordinary expenses but would be forced to ask parliamentary grants for emergencies. In other words a peaceful policy would virtually obviate the necessity of calling parliament, but a war would compel recourse to one. The question of the co-operation of the two houses was still open, half-way through the reign. At its commencement the lords refused to join the commons in attempting to suppress the evils of purveyance, and in 1614 adopted the same attitude with regard to impositions. Yet during the last few years signs were not lacking that the two houses would present a united front. James's lavish creation of English peerages[1] and bestowal of Scottish and Irish peerages on Englishmen, the ascendancy of Buckingham in the royal counsels, and later the influence ecclesiastics exercised in politics, all combined to alienate the old nobility and to produce an opposition party—'the country lords', as its members were called in contradistinction to the court lords and the bishops. As generally happens, personal wrongs coincided with public grievances in estranging the lords from the court. No doubt the lords resented their exclusion from the royal confidence unless they deferred to Buckingham, but they were also disgusted at the national disasters for which he was responsible. Consequently they viewed with equanimity, or even encouraged, the growing pretensions of the commons.

The declension of the influence on public affairs of those who prided themselves on being the natural-born counsellors of the king was not due solely to the early Stuarts and their idiosyncrasies. The time had come when the enlargement of the sphere of governmental activity required more elaborate administrative machinery than had previously sufficed. During Elizabeth's reign, even the tireless energy and business acumen of Burghley and Walsingham, with the assistance of a small group of councillors, could scarcely keep pace with the daily routine of the government. After the death of Salisbury in 1612 his successors had neither the ability nor, for the most part, the devotion to duty that had inspired the Elizabethan ministers of state. It is

---

[1] See below, p. 266.

not surprising, therefore, that the group of privy councillors that served Elizabeth was only half as large as that under James. The privy council now contained the chief officers of state and of the household, and such personages, English and Scottish, as the king thought fit to honour. By the end of his reign there were about thirty-five privy councillors, a number which was increased to about forty by 1630 but restored by 1640. The increase in size did not make for greater efficiency, and the non-official members rarely gave constant attendance. Consequently recourse was had to committees, some temporary, some permanent. The standing committees of James's reign were numerous and gave preliminary consideration to matters concerning Ireland, the navy, &c. Most important of them was that for foreign affairs, for this was the direct ancestor of the cabinet. Apparently it began with the appointment of a committee in or about 1615 to treat of the Spanish marriage. By the end of James's reign it was already discussing questions of state in no way directly concerned with foreign affairs and had achieved sufficient importance to be referred to as the junta, or cabinet council. Charles I continued the practice of his father, and it was in the cabinet council that Strafford spoke the words that brought him to the block.[1] However, although by 1640 the cabinet council had become established in fact and was legally what it has always remained, a committee of the privy council, it bore little resemblance to the modern cabinet. Above all, its members were not selected from among the leaders in parliament, and it contributed nothing to bridge the gulf that was rapidly widening between king and parliament. Indeed in the absence of well-defined political parties in parliament it would have been difficult to make the seventeenth-century cabinet a means to create harmony between legislature and executive.

Looking both backwards and forwards, there is no doubt that the relations of the early Stuarts with their parliaments were vitiated throughout by their firm belief in the theory of the divine right of kings. Englishmen had ample opportunity of learning what James thought about monarchy. In 1598 he published his *Trew Law of Free Monarchies*. In 1616 *The Workes*

---

[1] For the view that the Scottish committee became identical with the committee for foreign affairs, see E. R. Turner, *The Cabinet Council of England* (1930), i. 307. Cf. below, pp. 91, 95–96, 100.

of the Most High and Mighty Prince, James were collected and published. In addition the king rarely lost an opportunity of setting forth his theories in speeches. In so doing he was not actuated solely by a vain desire to display his learning but had the deliberate intention, as he said, to set *cor regis in oculis populi* and to act as the 'great schoolmaster of the whole land'. From his utterances and writings, therefore, it is possible to deduce his conception of the royal office with greater definition than for any other English king. By a free monarch he meant one free from all control. Even though 'a free and absolute monarch' owed duties to his subjects and was ordained for their advantage, no degree of tyranny on his part justified them in resisting.[1] He could make laws without the co-operation of parliament or suspend laws passed by parliament, and, notwithstanding that 'a good king will frame all his actions according to the law, yet he is not bound thereto but of his own good will'. The state of monarchy was the supremest thing on earth, because kings are not only God's lieutenants here below and sit upon God's thrones, but even by God himself are called gods. Therefore, as it is blasphemy to dispute what God can do, and as good Christians content themselves with his will revealed in his word, so it is presumption and high contempt in a subject to dispute what a king can do, and a good subject cheerfully abides by the king's pleasure revealed in his law.

James was far from successful in persuading the masses of his subjects to accept these views. The school of divines which contemporaries came to style 'Arminian', but which modern writers often call 'Laudian', wholeheartedly adopted them and preached them fervently. Among laymen, however, there were few imitators of these clerics. In particular parliament, which formed the audience for many of the king's utterances, remained wholly unconvinced. A well-informed observer, writing, in 1610, after one of the more hyperbolical of the king's speeches, noted of it: 'I hear it bred generally much discomfort, to see our monarchicall power and regal prerogative strained so high, and made so transcendent every way, that yf the practise should follow the positions, we are not likely to leave to our successors that freedome we received from our forefathers.'[2] Thus the persistence

---

[1] It is reported that James said he would govern according to the good of the common weal, but not according to the common will (*Original Letters*, ed. Henry Ellis, 2nd ser. iii [1827], 240).

[2] *Memorials of Sir Ralph Winwood* (1725), iii. 175.

with which James thrust down his subjects' throats his theory of the constitution almost compelled them in their turn to formulate their views of the limitations of monarchy and the rights of parliament, which might otherwise have remained undefined for a generation longer. James had called into existence, therefore, an opposition that in less than twenty years advanced from the modest position of the Apology of 1604 to the bold stand of the Protestation of 1621. These contradictory theories of the respective powers of king and parliament contained material for a bitter conflict, but James was by temperament adverse to pushing matters to extremes and too indolent to pursue any path persistently. Hence the day of the constitutional battle was postponed to the next reign.

Charles I never attempted elaborately to define his conception of kingship. He did not share his father's fondness for abstract speculation or his considerable literary and oratorical gifts. His views have to be gleaned, therefore, from occasional utterances, not from full-length discourses. Nevertheless he stated, time after time, one postulate of the theory of the divine right of kings. 'I must avow', he said in June 1628, 'that I owe the account of my actions to God alone.' While on trial for his life he was equally definite. 'A king', he told Bradshaw, the president of the court, 'cannot be tried by any superior jurisdiction on earth.'[1] But for Bradshaw's interruption, he would have continued that the Scripture[2] saith, 'Where the word of a king is, there is power, and who may say unto him "What doest thou?"'[3] He cited the legal maxim that a king can do no wrong as proof that he could not be impeached. He was equally convinced that there was a divine law commanding subjects to obey their king, under penalty of God's judgement. At the time of the negotiations at Uxbridge, in February 1645, he suggested to Sir Edward Nicholas, then secretary of state, that if, during his arguments with the parliamentary commissioners, 'in your privat discourses, . . . you would put them in mynde that they were arrant rebelles & that their end must be damnation, ruine,

---

[1] J. G. Muddiman, *Trial of King Charles the First* (c. 1928), p. 90.
[2] Eccles. viii. 4. In a proclamation explaining why he had dissolved his first two parliaments, Charles says of the two dissolutions: 'of which, as of his other regal actions, he is not bound to give an account to any but to God only, whose immediate lieutenant and vicegerent he is in these his realms and dominions by the divine providence committed to his charge and providence' (Rushworth, i. 410).
[3] Muddiman, p. 231.

and infamy, except they repented, . . . it might doe good'.[1] He remained consistent to the last hour of his life. From the scaffold he declared that the people had no claim to any voice in the government. Their freedom consisted in the enjoyment of laws by which their life and liberty would be secure. It was not in having a share in the government: that did not pertain to them —'a subject and a soveraign are clean different things'.[2]

Both James and his son were thus devoted adherents of the theory of the divine right of kings, though they stressed different postulates. The father, however, was usually content to be logical and consistent on paper, whereas the son was consistent in trying to translate his theories into action. Charles had been a very sickly child, not expected to survive. He was very slow in beginning to walk and to talk, but whereas he became a good horseman and walker, he suffered from an impediment in his speech all his life. This defect may account for the gravity and reserve which caused his elder brother, Henry (d. 1612), to tease him by calling him the archbishop of York.[3] Unlike his father's, his disposition was inflexible. His intellect was rigid, yet he was capable of quibbling and giving evasive answers that might mislead. He himself said that he could never be a lawyer: 'I cannot defend the bad nor yield in a good cause.'[4]

Charles's character augured ill for the future, inasmuch as both the general trend of events—the spirit of the age—and the particular circumstances in which the new reign opened called for conciliation in order to win support for the expensive policy now being pursued abroad.

When Charles succeeded James in 1625, he found that the financial needs of the Crown compelled the prompt summoning of parliament. When it met the king and those who spoke in his name did little more than assert that, as the previous parliament had advised the present policy, the present one would no doubt provide the necessary funds. There was from the start, however, a disinclination among members to recognize in the extravagant schemes now on foot the true offspring of their predecessors. They voted two subsidies, or about one-seventh of the amount the king needed, and then began to discuss the state of affairs,

---

[1] *The Diary and Correspondence of John Evelyn*, ed. William Bray (n.d.), p. 796.
[2] Muddiman, p. 262.
[3] *Memoirs of Robert Cary Earl of Monmouth*, ed. G. H. Powell (1905), pp. 83-85.
[4] *State Papers, Venetian, 1603-1607* (1900), p. 513; Laud, *Works*, iii. 146-7.

particularly the way in which the previous grants had been spent. Different speakers stressed different points: that no one seemed to be any the better for the expenditure; that the king would do well to follow Queen Elizabeth's example and rely upon a grave and wise council rather than upon one or two favourites; that the journey to Madrid was the real cause of the war with Spain, not any parliamentary action; that it was well known that then articles that benefited Roman catholics had been sanctioned, and it might be that the recent marriage treaty with France included similar provisions; and that, after all, the best way to secure national safety was to suppress Roman catholicism at home.[1] In vain Buckingham took upon himself the defence of the royal policy and urged prompt grant of supplies. The commons by this time had made up their mind that redress of grievances must have precedence. Voices were even heard hinting that the favourite was the greatest grievance of all. Charles thereupon hurriedly dissolved his first parliament, and thus terminated the opening scene in the long tragedy that ended twenty-four years later upon the scaffold.

His position continued to grow worse, for the expedition to Cadiz[2] returned in disgrace and the tension between the English and French courts was increasing so rapidly as to threaten war. The attempt to raise money by the issue of privy seals asking individuals to lend specific sums of money failed so completely that it was plainly necessary to summon another parliament. Charles did his best to smooth his path by ordering strict enforcement of the penal laws against papists, by appointing as sheriffs the leaders of the opposition in the late parliament, and by appointing Laud to preach to the two houses when they assembled. His sermon is a remarkable exposition of the views, on the unity of church and state, that prevailed at court. It was declared that a royal command must be God's glory, and obedience to it the subject's honour. It was asserted that the king would never depart from God's service, from the care of his people, or from the wise managing of his treasure. Laud's biographer remarks that this was sound doctrine but was not acceptable to the auditors.[3] Soon they were listening to an

---

[1] *Debates in the House of Commons in 1625*, ed. S. R. Gardiner (1873), pp. 77–91.
[2] Below, pp. 62–63.
[3] Laud, *Works*, i. 63–90 (text from Ps. cxxii. 3–5); Peter Heylyn, *Cyprianus Anglicus* (1668), p. 146.

orator of very different type—Eliot—on the late disasters. He roundly declared: 'Our honour is ruined, our ships are sunk, our men perished; not by the sword, not by the enemy, not by chance, but, as the strongest predictions had discerned and made it appear beforehand, by those we trust.'[1] His speech really determined the history of this parliament, for it convinced members that a strict accountability for the past must precede any provision for the future. The commons soon found that in their endeavour to establish the responsibility for Mansfeld's disastrous expedition[2] they were hampered by the refusal of the council of war to testify as to the opinions of individual members. Charles upheld them in their refusal: 'It is not you that they aim at, but it is me upon whom they make inquisition, and for subsidies, they will not hinder it. Gold may be bought too dear.'[3] Undaunted, the commons now attacked Buckingham as the author of all the national ills, and, once fairly started after their prey, they could not be called off. On one occasion Charles warned them not to question the man whom he delighted to honour and whom he cherished so dearly. A second time he threatened them in unmistakable terms: 'Remember that parliaments are altogether in my power for their calling, sitting, and dissolution; therefore, as I find the fruits good or evil, they are to continue, or not to be.'[4]

Perhaps the commons were emboldened by the knowledge that they could count on the support of the peers, for the upper house had revealed an independent spirit from the start of the session. They began by resolving that no peer should hold more than two proxies, thus striking a shrewd blow at Buckingham, who had thirteen. They presented three successive petitions to the king for the release of Arundel, nominally confined for an offence personal to Charles but in reality for opposition to Buckingham. The king did not give way until there was a probability that they would refuse to transact any business in Arundel's absence.[5] When Charles attempted, by having Bristol

---

[1] Gardiner, vi. 62. Sir John Eliot (1592–1632) had been the companion of George Villiers, later duke of Buckingham, in foreign travel and appointed through his influence vice-admiral of Devon. His alienation from the favourite was due to his conviction that Buckingham was wholly incapable of conducting the foreign policy of England and the war against first Spain and then France.

[2] See below, p. 59. [3] Gardiner, vi. 75.

[4] *Parliamentary History*, ii. 60; Rushworth, i. 229.

[5] Rushworth, i. 367–75. Thomas Howard, 2nd earl of Arundel, a great collector of works of art.

accused of high treason, to prevent his revealing what had actually happened at Madrid during the visit there of the prince and Buckingham, the house simultaneously accepted Bristol's charge of high treason against Buckingham.[1] They foiled all the king's efforts to deprive Bristol of a fair trial and allowed the earl to put in an answer full of damaging revelations. It was therefore clear, when the commons in their turn drew up an impeachment of Buckingham, that nothing could save him but the dissolution of parliament. When the lords prayed the king that they might sit a little longer, his reply, 'not a minute',[2] showed that he realized the peril in which his favourite stood.

The need for money remained as pressing after the dissolution of parliament as before. A demand for a free gift, equal in amount to the subsidies proposed but not voted by parliament, was dispatched to the justices of the peace, whose panels were purged of the names of all those obnoxious to the court. The response, however, was extremely meagre, for men refused to give except in a parliamentary way. A very rickety fleet was collected from the maritime towns and counties, and those who objected were sharply told that in times of danger ordinary precedents no longer applied.[3] There was still no money, however, to feed or pay mariners, although the probability of a war with France made the equipment of the fleet more imperative than ever. Therefore the king had recourse to a forced loan, to be raised by commissioners who were to exact from all men rated in the subsidy-books sums equivalent to what they would have paid if parliament had voted five subsidies. To make the scheme more palatable, Charles called upon the clergy for help from their pulpits. In a letter to the archbishop—doubtless intended to serve as a text for many a sermon—the king urged that, having been led into war by the advice of parliament, he could not now be abandoned but with the sin and shame of all men.[4] The section of the clergy that good protestants were beginning to label 'Arminian' willingly responded to the call. Sibthorpe[5] and Roger Manwaring preached sermons magnifying

---

[1] Ibid., pp. 253–67, 273–306. John Digby, 1st earl of Bristol (1580–1653), ambassador to Madrid, 1611–24.

[2] *The Court and Times of Charles the First* (1848), i. 112; Rushworth, i. 402.

[3] Rushworth, i. 419–20.

[4] Gardiner, vi. 143.

[5] Robert Sibthorpe was a Northamptonshire vicar. Roger Manwaring (1590–

the prerogative above law and parliament. Charles was so pleased with the former's effusion that he directed the archbishop to license it. The archbishop refused. Thereupon he was ordered to confine himself to his house and was supplanted in the church courts by a commission headed by Laud. Other methods than persuasion were adopted in dealing with those who refused to contribute. By way of warning, the lord chief justice, Sir Randolph Crew, was dismissed for refusing to acknowledge the legality of the loan. Some of the recalcitrants were sent to prison, or into confinement, or to serve on board ship, and an attempt was even made to compel fifty men from Essex to accept press-money for service with the king of Denmark. Among those who refused to contribute were Eliot, destined to be a martyr for parliamentary liberties, Hampden, the future hero of the struggle against ship-money, and Wentworth, who, after changing sides, became the great exponent of personal government.

During the year 1627 the situation went from bad to worse. The king of Denmark was expelled from Germany, and the protestant cause lay at the feet of the victorious Roman catholics; the French Huguenots were encouraged to rebel, but Buckingham suffered a decisive defeat on the Isle of Ré when he tried to relieve La Rochelle.[1] These disasters increased the need of money at the same time that they made borrowing more difficult. As one of Buckingham's parasites acknowledged, 'No man that is moneyed will lend upon any security, if they think it to go the way of the court, which now is made diverse from the state.'[2] The failure off La Rochelle was regarded as the greatest and most shameful defeat England had suffered since the loss of Normandy. Indeed, according to Denzil Holles, who was one of the five members whom Charles tried to arrest in 1642, England had never received so dishonourable a blow.[3] Exasperation at the manifest misgovernment naturally strengthened resistance to the forced loans, and before the end of the year an attempt was made to test the legality of confinements for refusing to contribute. In a famous case[4] five prisoners applied for a

---

1653) was a royal chaplain when he preached the obnoxious sermon which was printed. In 1635 he was named bishop of St. Davids'.

[1] See below, pp. 65–66.   [2] Gardiner, vi. 193.

[3] *Strafforde's Letters*, i. 42. Cf. Rushworth, i. 470.

[4] Sometimes called Darnel's case, in spite of Darnel's withdrawal at an early stage in the proceedings; and sometimes called the case of the five knights, although after Darnel's withdrawal there were only four.

writ of habeas corpus in order to bring their case before the king's bench. The writ was not one of right but of grace, yet it was granted because of the great public interest in the issue at stake. Probably the five knights hoped that the question would be raised whether a refusal to contribute to the loan was a legal cause for commitment. The return to the writ, however, merely stated that they were committed by the special command of the king, and assigned no other reason whatsoever. Thereupon one of the prisoners, Darnel, refused to proceed, but the other four contended that they should be released on bail, since they had been committed without cause shown. The attorney-general argued that they should be kept in prison until the king was ready to bring them to trial. The precedents, as well as the statutes, were by no means clear, and accordingly the decision of the judges was: 'We cannot deliver you but you must be remanded.' The judges apparently intended to postpone further consideration of the case because, as one stated later, there was no record that, upon such a writ as the present one, a man had ever been bailed without the king being first consulted, and the prisoners might have sued out another habeas corpus the next day. Actually both they and the general public assumed that a final verdict had been given and that the judges had lent their authority to the view that the loan and the imprisonments for refusing to contribute to it were legal, and that the king had the right to commit for indefinite periods without his victims' having any redress at law.[1]

The prison doors were opened at the beginning of 1628, but this clemency did not evoke any gratitude in the country at large. When Charles caused elections to be held for a third parliament, the main issues were the forced loan and arbitrary punishment. Popular interest ran high and considerable pressure was brought to bear in favour of court candidates, but the royal influence was powerless against appeals on behalf of those who had suffered imprisonment rather than contribute to the exchequer in an unparliamentary way.[2] An observer summed up the results of the election as follows: 'It is feared . . . because such patriots are chosen every where, the parliament will not last above eight days.'[3] When the houses met, the debates

---

[1] Frances Helen Relf, *The Petition of Right* (1917), chap. i.
[2] Mary Coate, *Cornwall in the Great Civil War* (1933), p. 21; *State Papers, Venetian, 1628–1629* (1916), pp. 10, 21.   [3] *Court and Times of Charles the First*, i. 327.

turned almost exclusively upon the question how to prevent extra-parliamentary taxation and imprisonment without cause shown. The commons began by passing resolutions against un-parliamentary taxation, against the retention of any man in prison by command of the king or council unless the cause were expressed, against the denial of the writ of habeas corpus, and against the refusal to release or bail a prisoner confined without cause shown. These resolutions occasioned a great debate in the house of lords, where it was thought by a contemporary that the majority stood 'for the king's prerogative against the subject's liberties'.[1] Generally speaking, the old nobility opposed the court, but the new creations and most of the bishops favoured it. The parties were so evenly divided that in the end a compromise was reached which attempted to prevent the king from interfering with due process of law in normal times but would permit him to override it in an emergency.

The commons, however, were unwilling to acknowledge explicitly that the king possessed these extraordinary powers, especially as no satisfactory form of words could be devised to define them.[2] Abandoning their own resolutions, they now de-termined to proceed by a bill which should both reaffirm the validity of old statutes safeguarding the liberty of the subject and interpret them in the sense the commons thought right. Thereupon the king declared that, as he was willing to promise to observe the old statutes, so his subjects should be content to contain themselves within the laws of their forefathers, without enlarging them by new explanations or additions. The flat refusal of the king to suffer his prerogative to be curtailed by law prompted Sir Edward Coke to hit upon the happy idea that the two houses should join in a Petition of Right[3] to the king for the redress of their particular grievances. Such petitions had been used by individuals in the past, when they felt that the sovereign or his servants had exercised his prerogative to over-ride the law, and merely sought permission for the petitioners to enjoy the benefit of the law. The Petition of Right emanating from parliament, however, was intended to go farther and to declare what the law was, as well as to secure for individuals the

---

[1] C. H. Firth, *The House of Lords during the Civil War* (1910), pp. 48-51.
[2] Rushworth, i. 552-3.
[3] The two best modern studies are Relf, op. cit., and E. R. Adair, 'The Petition of Right', *History*, v. 99-103.

benefit of it. The king was deterred from a speedy dissolution only by his financial needs and by the knowledge that the majority of the house of lords sided with his opponents. In vain he attempted ambiguous and evasive answers to the Petition, for both houses requested a clear and satisfactory answer, and in the end the king assented in the style, *Soit droit fait come est desiré*.[1] The Petition, 'concerning divers rights and liberties of the subjects', begins with a recital of the statutes alleged to have been broken and of the grievances for which redress was now provided. It then proceeds to ask: (1) that no man hereafter should be compelled to make any gift, loan, benevolence, tax, or such like charge, without common consent by act of parliament; (2) that no free man should be imprisoned or detained without cause shown; (3) that soldiers and mariners should not be billeted upon private individuals against their will; and (4) that commissions for proceeding by martial law should not be issued in the future.[2]

Previous to the royal assent to the Petition, the commons had been careful to consult the lords at every stage, and together the two houses had prevailed. Thenceforth the commons rashly attempted to stand alone, and made no effort to secure the co-operation of the upper house. After the failure, under Wentworth's leadership, to embody in a bill such a compromise as would both satisfy the king and safeguard the liberty of the subject, Eliot had recovered the ascendancy he had exercised over the house in 1626. The greatest orator of his generation, he was fiery and impulsive by nature, prone to idealize the commons at the expense of king and lords, and scornful of the daily compromises so essential in political life. Through his impatience he had hazarded the fruits of the session by proposing remonstrances and attacking Buckingham, for only by the action of the lords was the king dissuaded from a dissolution, and only by their intervention was he induced to accept the Petition. The necessity of conciliating the upper house proved irksome to Eliot's democratic ardour. On one occasion he had said, 'I am confident that, should the lords desert us, we should yet continue flourishing and green';[3] and the commons proceeded, under his guidance, to test the truth of this assertion. In particular

---

[1] *Lords' Journals*, iii. 843–4.
[2] S. R. Gardiner, *Constitutional Documents* (1906), pp. 66–70.
[3] Gardiner, vi. 284.

they passed a remonstrance—a prototype of the more famous measure of 1641—detailing grievances in both church and state and naming their authors, Laud and Neile of the first and Buckingham of the second. The lower house followed this up by a second remonstrance, denouncing the collection of tonnage and poundage as a breach of the fundamental liberties of the kingdom, because these duties had never been granted to Charles I by parliament. The king interrupted this hot pace by a prorogation. The speech that preceded it contained a statement of his view of the Petition of Right: 'The profession of both houses, in time of hammering this Petition, was no ways to intrench upon my prerogative, saying, they had neither intention nor power to hurt it. Therefore it must needs be conceived that I have granted no new, but only confirmed the ancient liberties of my subjects.'[1] This view prevailed at law during the years prior to the meeting of the long parliament. When those members who were imprisoned after the dissolution in 1629 tried to take advantage of the Petition, they were met by the attorney-general with the following argument:

A petition in parliament is not a law, yet it is for the honour and dignity of the king, to observe and keep it faithfully; but it is the duty of the people not to stretch it, beyond the words and intention of the king. And no other construction can be made of the Petition, than to take it as a confirmation of the antient liberties and rights of the subject. So that now the case remains in the same quality and degree, as it was before the Petition.[2]

Thus its immediate effects were slight, and proof would be difficult to find that the king's government during the years 1629 to 1640 was hampered by the Petition, except possibly with regard to forced loans, which were no longer exacted. Nevertheless the very reluctance of the king, first to accept the Petition at all, and then to accept it in an unequivocal manner, suggests at least that he was conscious that something more was at stake than the mere confirmation of ancient liberties. In fact he had sustained a severe defeat at the hands of both houses of parliament, although the foolish tactics of Eliot, by ruining all hope of the continuance of that union between the two houses which had already accomplished so much, enabled the king to

---

[1] Gardiner, *Constitutional Documents*, p. 74.
[2] Rushworth, i, App., p. 40.

represent the proceedings of the lower house as the work of a seditious minority.

In the interval between the two sessions of parliament the assassination of Buckingham revealed the wide gulf that had opened between king and people. A naval lieutenant, John Felton, brooding upon his own wrongs (especially the refusal of Buckingham to promote him or to see that he received the pay due to him), read the remonstrances passed by the commons and believed that it was his duty to sacrifice his life to rid England of the hated favourite. His deed was welcomed by the populace, who compared him to David slaying Goliath. Verses and ballads celebrated England's delivery, and the duke's body was conducted to Westminster Abbey with few mourners but with an escort of the train-bands lest the citizens of London should defile the corpse. 'And this', says a newsletter, 'was the obscure catastrophe of that great man.'[1]

The death of Buckingham had removed one obstacle to a good understanding between king and parliament, and there were other hopeful signs that the ruinous foreign policy which had alienated the two houses was about to be changed. The restoration to favour of Abbot and Bristol, and the admission to the king's counsels of such men as Richard Weston, named lord high treasurer in 1629 and created earl of Portland in 1633, and Wentworth, were sure guarantees against further adventures like the expeditions to the Isle of Ré. Nevertheless the disagreements about impositions and religion still remained. Charles ordered that the customs duties be collected as if they had been granted by parliament. When merchants tried to land their goods without paying the duties, the goods were seized, and all attempts to recover them by legal action failed. One merchant, Richard Chambers, being summoned before the council, bitterly complained that 'the merchants are in no part of the world so skrewed and wrung as in England; that in Turky they have more incouragement'.[2] After committal to prison he was released on bail, whereupon he was cited before the Star Chamber, whose proceedings had been in no way interfered with by the Petition of Right. Another merchant, John Rolle, whose goods were confiscated, was a member of parliament. As regards religion, whereas the commons, in their

---

[1] *Original Letters*, 2nd ser. iii. 265. Cf. *State Papers, Venetian, 1628–1629*, p. 337.
[2] Rushworth, i. 682.

remonstrances, had demanded the suppression of the Arminians, there were obvious signs, such as the promotions of Montague[1] and Manwaring, that this party was in full favour at court.

When parliament reassembled it was soon evident that a stiff contest was in prospect. It must be confessed that the popular leaders in the commons chose their ground badly. Instead of presenting a united front with the lords, as they had done with very satisfactory results in the earlier part of the previous session, they now elected to stand alone. They failed to assume the general position that all unparliamentary taxation was illegal, and chose rather to assail the alleged breach of privilege involved in the seizure of Rolle's goods. They then launched forth into a general attack on the religious policy pursued, displaying a strong bias that was at once Erastian and puritan. Thus Pym boldly asserted that parliament was the only power in the land competent to deal with the new disease of Arminianism, and Eliot that the bishops could not be trusted with the interpretation of the Thirty-nine Articles. In fact, the latter orator continued, the presence on the episcopal bench of men like Montague threatened the total overthrow of sound religion, which was already undermined by the innovations introduced by the sect to which he belonged. Most speakers contrived to represent the Arminians as akin to the Jesuits and to suggest that the inevitable result of the teaching of the first would be the ultimate triumph of the second.

Once the religious issue had been definitely raised, there was no longer any possibility of a compromise. The commons were claiming the right to determine the religion of England. They insisted that the leaders of the branch of the Anglican church that was most popular at court should be silenced. Such demands could never be admitted by Charles. His sympathies were wholly with those new churchmen who headed the revolt against the Calvinistic theology that found favour in the sight of the commons. Montague, at the close of his *Appello Caesarem*, had written: 'Popery is for tyranny, puritanisme for anarchy: poperie is originall of superstition; puritanisme, the high-way unto prophanenesse; both alike enemies unto piety. . . . Domine Imperator, defende me gladio, et ego te defendam calamo.'[2]

---

[1] Richard Montague, a controversial divine who attacked Selden's history of tithes, both wrote and preached in favour of the royal prerogative. In 1628 he was named bishop of Chichester.

[2] Richard Montague, *Appello Caesarem* (1625), pp. 321-2.

Eliot's impetuosity had brought matters to a crisis, and the king felt he had no option but to defend the church. In his eyes, as in Montague's, the puritans intended to disrupt both church and state, and Charles firmly shared his father's belief, 'No bishop, no king'. He therefore determined to set a term to the commons' interference in ecclesiastical affairs and order the speaker to adjourn the house. When the speaker signified this command, he was met with a loud cry of 'Noe noe'. On his attempt to leave the chair, he was restrained until three resolutions had been passed: that whoever should introduce any innovation in religion to bring in either popery or Arminianism should be accounted a capital enemy of the king and kingdom; that whoever should advise the levying of tonnage and poundage without parliamentary sanction should incur like denunciation; and that whoever should pay tonnage and poundage, under those conditions, should be held a betrayer of the liberty of the subject and a capital enemy of the king and kingdom.[1] A week later Charles formally dissolved the parliament, with a speech in which he contrasted 'the undutiful and seditious carriage in the lower house' with the 'dutiful demeanors' of the lords.[2] In a sense the contrast is fair, and at least some of the blame for the eleven years' prerogative government that followed must be laid at the door of Eliot, whose headlong course had provoked the inevitable; and, moreover, the fact that one house of parliament was now neutral, or perhaps even favourable to the king, helps to explain the acquiescence of the country at large in the intermittence of parliament. On the other hand it is characteristic of Charles—and the explanation of his ultimate downfall— that he failed to see in the action of the commons anything more significant than that 'some few vipers' had cast 'this mist of undutifulness' over the eyes of the majority. He could never conceive that to many of his subjects puritanism was a living faith for which they were as ready to suffer as had been the martyrs during the Marian persecution. Similarly he never realized that probably a majority of the people were deeply attached to parliamentary government and were anxious to see its extension rather than its curtailment.

He could see Eliot, who embodied the new aspirations of the

---

[1] *Commons Debates for 1929*, ed. Wallace Notestein and Frances Helen Relf (1921), p. 267.
[2] *Lords' Journals*, iv. 43.

house of commons, only as a rebel, and converted him into a martyr for parliamentary privileges by confining him in the Tower until his death in 1632. The successive dissolutions of 1625, 1626, and 1629 had been terrible disappointments to Englishmen in general, and especially to the classes represented in parliament, which were rapidly growing in power and wealth.[1] The comments of the puritan diarist, D'Ewes, on these dissolutions are worth noting. In the first instance he refers 'to the great grief of all good subjects that loved true religion, their king, and the commonwealth'. In the second he says, 'Infinite almost was the sadness of each man's heart, and the dejection of his countenance that truly loved the church or commonwealth.' Finally he laments that the day which witnessed the breach between king and parliament in 1629 'was the most gloomy, sad, and dismal day for England that happened in five hundred years last past'.[2]

---

[1] 'The house of commons was both yesterday and to-day as full as one could sit by another. And they say it is the most noble, magnanimous assembly that ever those walls contained; and I heard a lord estimate they were able to buy the upper house (his majesty only excepted) thrice over, notwithstanding there be of lords temporal to the number of 118. And what lord in England would be followed by so many freeholders as some of those are?' (21 March 1627/8 [*Court and Times*, i. 331]).

[2] *Autobiography*, i. 279, 301, 402. It is noteworthy that D'Ewes says that 'divers fiery spirits in the house of commons were very faulty, and cannot be excused'. Clarendon wrote in 1646 that 'no man can shew me a source from whence these waters of bitterness we now taste have more probably flowed, than from this unseasonable, unskilful, and precipitate dissolution of parliaments' (*Rebellion*, i. 6).

II

FOREIGN RELATIONS, 1603–30

THE relations between England and foreign countries during the seventeenth century are peculiar in that their importance does not consist so much in their influence upon Europe as in their repercussions at home. Except for a brief but dramatic period under Cromwell, English diplomacy and English arms were singularly futile, and it would be difficult to name any event of the first rank in European history, during the reigns of James I and Charles I, which was determined by English intervention. Nevertheless the reaction upon domestic policies of the foreign policy pursued by the early Stuarts was so outstanding that it justifies separate treatment, even though a certain amount of repetition of the subject-matter of other chapters is inevitable from time to time.

Until the seventeenth century control of foreign policy in England had rested exclusively in the hands of the sovereign[1] and had been little influenced directly by either parliament or people. Elizabeth had been able to abstain from active intervention in the Netherlands for a decade after the more venturesome of her subjects had demanded war with Spain, and her successful defence of the realm against the Armada had set the seal of popular approval upon her policy. Although in some other respects there were signs that the country was getting tired of an attitude of passive acquiescence in whatever its ruler did, there is no indication that parliament or any considerable body of public opinion wished to dictate foreign policy in the sixteenth century. James I therefore had some basis in history for his view that the direction of English foreign relations was the especial prerogative of the Crown. He regarded any criticism as the highest presumption in a subject, and was quick to rebuke the commons in 1621 when they made their first serious attempt to influence foreign policy. Apart from the changed attitude, in general, of parliament towards the king, there were three main reasons why it was improbable that there would be

---

[1] See the long list of precedents to support this thesis, quoted in a speech of the earl of Salisbury in 1607 (Bacon, *Works*, x. 355–8).

abstinence from comment much longer: that the principal feature of James's policy—friendship with Spain—ran contrary to the prejudices of most Englishmen; that his statecraft produced no triumphs to justify it; and that the rapidly increasing importance of trade was likely to compel a new orientation in foreign relations.

James's policy was based chiefly on personal and dynastic considerations. Of his personal sentiments none was stronger than his love of peace. Contemporaries suggest that this was due to cowardice and that he was afraid his own life would not be safe if war broke out.[1] Be this as it may, James was swayed by worthier sentiments than fear. As a great and Christian king, he said, he simply desired that each ruler should enjoy his own possessions and not try to rob his neighbour;[2] and he may have felt sincerely that military glory was mere vanity.[3] He was certainly easily flattered by adroit references to the reputation for power and prudence he enjoyed abroad, and he loved to be called the King of Peace, or the Peacemaker. Unfortunately he did not fully understand the extremely critical position in Europe; but at least he can be given credit for realizing that an outbreak anywhere on any question might end in a universal war of religion.[4] He saw more clearly than his subjects that a war based merely on religious animosity or national prejudices was not likely to prosper. Indeed a purely religious war, if such a catastrophe had been possible, would have found the protestants heavily outweighed. No doubt there was much to be said for an attitude of complete aloofness from the troubles which were shortly to plunge Europe into the horrors of the Thirty Years War. Similarly a case can be made out for the view that England should maintain her Elizabethan role of the protestant champion, and that, after a few more years of warfare, the chief catholic champion, Spain, must inevitably collapse from sheer exhaustion.[5] Unhappily, however, James followed neither policy consistently. His statecraft prevented his joining wholeheartedly

---

[1] *State Papers, Venetian, 1621–1623* (1911), p. 460. Cf. ibid., p. 449, for Gondomar's opinion that 'fear alone guides the king'. The Tuscan resident reported: 'He was pacific by nature, which many called timidity, as well as lenient, and averse to the shedding of blood' (*Hist. MSS. Com., Skrine MSS.* [1887], p. 4).

[2] *State Papers, Venetian, 1619–1621* (1910), p. 18.

[3] Ibid., p. 415.

[4] Ibid., p. 264. Cf. ibid., p. 91, for the king's anxiety lest, if the war became one of religion, France would side with the catholic powers.

[5] This was the main argument of Raleigh and the war party in general.

in the Thirty Years War on the protestant side, and he may have served England well by his abstinence. Nevertheless he abandoned his own policy when his son-in-law was expelled from his hereditary lands, the Palatinate. Then James was moved to action, but justified his intervention on the ground that he could not suffer ill treatment of his children, and consequently went to war to effect reparation for the injuries inflicted on them.[1] There is no evidence at all that he ever considered whether the true interests of England or of protestantism demanded that a war be waged to recover the Palatinate. It is also typical of the dynastic control of foreign policy that the Spanish match should ultimately have broken down over the question of the restitution of the Palatinate.

At his accession the immediate question James had to answer was whether he would continue the war with Spain, which had been going on for nearly twenty years. By the treaty of 1598 England was allied with the United Provinces against Spain, but was not pledged to furnish any specific armed assistance to the Dutch in their struggle for independence. They acknowledged the debt to England of £800,000, left the 'cautionary' towns Flushing and Brill, and fort Rammekens in English hands as security, and took into their pay the regiments hitherto maintained by the queen under the treaty of 1585. Henceforth these soldiers were to take the oath of allegiance to the United Provinces and thus enter upon a new phase of their long and honourable service in the Dutch armies.[2] There was no longer any compelling reason why England should make further sacrifices for the Dutch, who were able to hold their own, and prudence suggested that she might now withdraw. Other factors, however, had equal weight in the decision to abandon the war.

James, like all the Stuarts, disliked and despised the Dutch. In his eyes they were rebels,[3] and this was the unforgivable sin to a monarch who believed implicitly in the theory of the divine right of kings. Moreover, now that the Spanish invasion of Ireland had been decisively repulsed, the disputed right to trade with the Indies was the only issue between England and

---

[1] State Papers, Venetian, 1619–1621, p. 428; Acts of the Privy Council, 1619–1621 (1930), pp. 332–3.

[2] Thomas Rymer, Foedera, xvi (1727), 340–3.

[3] State Papers, Venetian, 1603–1607, pp. 34, 520–1. The Venetian ambassador notes that James called the Dutch 'rebels' and declared that their bad example should not be encouraged (ibid., pp. 40–41. Cf. Original Letters, 2nd ser. iii. 216).

Spain. But it is symbolic of James's whole outlook upon foreign affairs that he was less influenced by these considerations than by a more personal one: that, as Scotland had taken no part in the conflict, he did not regard himself as at war with Spain. Consequently he at once ordered the cessation of hostilities at sea.[1] Negotiations for peace consumed the summer of 1604. There were three or four points in dispute. The English representatives refused to brand the Dutch as rebels and to renounce intercourse with them, because their trade was so important that England could not spare it; because they owed her a great debt; and because if forsaken by her they might seek other protection, which might be dangerous both to her and to Spain. On the other hand Cecil's demand for full liberty of trade to Englishmen in all the dominions of the king of Spain and the archdukes, and freedom from molestation by the Inquisition, was granted only so far as Spanish possessions in Europe were concerned. In vain Cecil urged the extension of this liberty to the Indies. Commerce, he argued, was of great concern to Englishmen, who could not suffer 'those wooden walls . . . which are the ramparts of Brittany to rot for want of use'. If not engaged in lawful commerce, they would perforce be driven to acts of hostility. Moreover, by the law of nature and of nations, the sea ought to be common to all men. To such argument the inexorable reply always was that the king of Spain could not grant to foreigners the liberty he had prohibited to even his own subjects. When in their turn the Spaniards demanded that James should recall English troops in Dutch service, the only concession they received was permission to make levies in England on their own account.[2]

There can be little doubt that the peace was the best that could be made. Nevertheless it was, and remained, unpopular in the country and was often denounced from pulpits.[3] There was a feeling that the kingdom flourished in time of war, whereas in reality, although a number of individuals had profited by the war against Spain in the late reign, the Crown had been severely impoverished. Moreover resumption of trade rather embittered than modified the national animosity towards Spain.

---

[1] *Tudor and Stuart Proclamations*, ed. Robert Steele (1910), no. 952.
[2] Robert Watson, *History of the Reign of Philip the Third* (2nd ed., 1786), ii, App.
[3] *State Papers, Venetian, 1607–1610* (1904), p. 6; ibid. *1610–1613* (1905), pp. 231, 335, 419; *Memorials of Sir Ralph Winwood*, ii. 217.

English vessels were frequently seized on the suspicion that they were carrying Dutch goods, or were pirates, or were trading with Jews or Turks, the enemies of the Christian religion. According to a complaint of London merchants to the house of commons in 1607, not only did they suffer confiscation of ships and goods upon trivial or false grounds but most of the seamen lost their lives, by torture, imprisonment, or other cruel usage. Even if a favourable verdict were obtained in a Spanish court, the release of the captured ship was delayed intolerably.[1] The commons suggested the issue of letters of marque, but Salisbury replied with a long series of precedents to show that to make war or peace was a prerogative of the Crown, with which parliament should not meddle.[2] In spite of every effort by the government, complaints of these grievances continued until the arrival in England of Gondomar, when the negotiations for the Spanish match diverted attention to larger issues.

The relations of England and the United Provinces steadily deteriorated during the reign of James I. So long as the war continued between Spain and her revolted subjects, Englishmen were not fully aware of the strength of the new trade rival they had helped to establish at their very door. Thus many were sorry to see the twelve years' truce arranged between Spain and the Netherlands in 1609. For the rest of the reign the English and Dutch were competitors in several spheres. From 1613 onwards there was a constant dispute about the whale-fishery off Greenland (i.e. Spitzbergen)—an island of which both countries claimed the sovereignty by right of prior discovery.[3] More serious was the dispute about herring-fishing in the North Sea. Hitherto foreign competition had been negligible, but now, according to Salisbury, two or three thousand sailing ships at a time might be seen engaged in fishing for herring and cod.[4] James therefore issued a proclamation (6 May 1609) that every alien must obtain a licence before engaging in the fishing-trade off the English coast.[5] The Dutch promptly dispatched an embassy to England to claim freedom of fishing, on the two

---

[1] *Commons' Journals*, i. 341–2. Cornwallis, English ambassador to Spain, writes thence: 'Here some end their lives and all their means, before they can bring any thing that toucheth upon justice or restitution to conclusion' (*Winwood Memorials*, ii. 151–2).   [2] Bacon, *Works*, x. 347–59.

[3] *Acts of the Privy Council, 1613–1614* (1921), pp. 322–4.

[4] *Winwood Memorials*, iii. 20.

[5] *Tudor and Stuart Proclamations*, no. 1077.

grounds that privileges granted by treaties were still in force and that the sea is like the air and hence is free for all to use—an argument which had been set forth earlier in the year by Grotius in his *Mare Liberum*, a work primarily against Spain but capable of use against any other maritime power. Interest dwindled during the Cleves-Jülich dispute, when an English contingent served with Maurice of Nassau and assisted in enforcing a satisfactory compromise. On another political question harmony also prevailed, for in 1616 the cautionary towns were handed back to the Dutch in return for £215,000, a sum in ready money which James was willing to accept as full payment for the debt incurred in Elizabeth's reign. No similar agreement could be reached in the effort to settle economic rivalries. Furthermore public opinion was hardening, for pamphleteers were beginning to emphasize the growth of Dutch commerce and its danger to English trade. An able tract[1] pointed out that the British seas were the 'chiefest, principall, and only rich treasury' of the Dutch, and, under provocation,[2] they themselves contributed to the reopening of the question in 1616 by a proclamation[3] forbidding the importation of dyed cloth into their territories, which was answered by an attempt to enforce tolls on the Dutch fishing-fleet. Simultaneously Anglo-Dutch relations in the East Indies became hostile.

The first Dutch voyage to the Malay Archipelago, in 1595, yielded such a promising return that what was known as the United Company was formed in 1602 and was soon sending out an annual fleet a dozen strong. Meanwhile the prospect of sharing in the lucrative trade in pepper and spices had led to the formation of the East India Company[4] in England in 1600. It is noteworthy that the earliest voyages financed by the new company were to the islands in the Far East and not to India. However, whereas the English settlements were on the mainland, notably at Surat, the Dutch tended to concentrate first

---

[1] Tobias Gentleman, *Englands Way to Win Wealth* (1614), p. 5 (reprinted in *Harleian Miscellany* [1809], iii). John Keymer says much the same, in his *Observations Touching Trade and Commerce with the Hollander* (1664)—formerly attributed to Raleigh. On its authorship see T. W. Fulton, *The Sovereignty of the Sea* (1911), pp. 127-8.

[2] For the attempt to compel the Dutch and other foreigners to buy English cloth already dressed and dyed instead of unfinished, as heretofore, see the description of Alderman Cokayne's project, below, p. 333.

[3] *State Papers, Venetian, 1615-1617* (1908), p. 343.

[4] See J. B. Black, *The Reign of Queen Elizabeth*, p. 211.

on the Moluccas and then on Java. It was natural that the Dutch, at war with Spain in Europe, should attempt the conquest of Portuguese possessions in the Pacific. They secured as allies some of the native chiefs, promising them protection against the Portuguese in return for the exclusive enjoyment of the trade in spices. This monopoly naturally led to disputes with the English, which continued in spite of the attempts of the home governments to find a satisfactory adjustment. In 1613 and 1615 Anglo-Dutch conferences were held but failed to reach an agreement. The fundamental difference was that the Dutch felt that trading within the area adjudged by the papal bull of Alexander VI to be Portuguese or Spanish—Portugal was annexed to Spain 1580–1640—was or might be regarded as an act of war, and that if the English wished to participate they must be prepared to maintain a squadron in Indonesian waters to carry on a defensive war against Spain. The English contended that peaceful trading was possible in territories not actually occupied by Spain. In 1619 an elaborate agreement was drawn up, which provided for a joint council of defence at Batavia and a division of trade. However, this treaty was speedily cast aside by Coen, the real founder of the Dutch eastern empire. He solved the problem of how to meet English intervention in the Spice Islands by having ten English settlers put to death after torture. This massacre of Amboyna exercised an influence upon Anglo-Dutch relations out of all proportion to the number of victims. It weakened permanently England's position in the nearer East Indies and forced her to concentrate upon the mainland;[1] and it became a running sore which public opinion in England never overlooked. Fortunately the news of this outrage did not reach England for a year, but even then an account of it in a pamphlet aroused much bitterness against the Dutch.[2] However, as in 1610, the exigencies of European politics temporarily proved more powerful than mercantile or colonial jealousies. Whereas prolonged negotiations in 1618, and then in 1622, failed to settle satisfactorily any of the points in dispute

[1] Until Borneo and New Guinea were occupied in comparatively recent times.
[2] *A True Relation of the Unjust, Cruell and Barbarous Proceedings against the English at Amboyna* (1624). It is noteworthy that the pamphlet was reprinted in 1651 and 1672. The work of Sir George Clark and Jonkheer W. J. M. van Eysinga, *The Colonial Conferences between England and the Netherlands in 1613 to 1615*, 2 vols. 1940–51, is exhaustive and also contains much of great value for Anglo-Dutch relations in James's reign.

between the merchants of the two nations, a treaty of alliance was easily arranged as soon as James began war against Spain.

In other respects English foreign relations during the first decade of the reign were mainly favourable to protestantism. James in 1612 joined the Protestant Union, formed in the empire in 1608, and the next year sanctioned the marriage of his only daughter Elizabeth to Frederick, the Elector Palatine and champion of militant Calvinism in Germany. When the States General adhered to the Union at James's request, he was in a fair way to becoming the leader of a protestant alliance against the Habsburgs. This policy was abandoned shortly after the arrival in England of a new Spanish ambassador, Diego Sarmiento de Acuña, later count of Gondomar. Hitherto Spain had relied upon presents (which even Salisbury had accepted) for the maintenance of her interests, but her new representative was able to establish an almost complete personal ascendancy at the English court.

Gondomar soon took the measure of the king and realized that his vanity, timidity, love of peace, and dislike of persecution might all be utilized for Spanish ends. On the other hand he never understood the English national character. In particular he failed to perceive that protestantism and hatred of popery, and of Spain as the champion of popery, were ruling passions with the majority of Englishmen.[1] He seems to have believed that most Englishmen were either catholics who disguised their real religion through fear of persecution, or protestants whose religion had been assumed to please the head of the state and who would revert to catholicism if the penal laws were repealed. However, he was not so much concerned about the position of catholics under the law in England as upon the effect the withdrawal of England from the protestant group of states in Europe might have on the balance of power. If the weight of England could be thrown into the scale against European protestantism, its downfall was certain. Even if England could be kept neutral during the conflict which was approaching, the victory of the catholic countries seemed inevitable.

The character and circumstances of James helped Gondomar

---

[1] Most Englishmen would have agreed with the sentiments expressed in Ben Jonson's *The Alchemist* (Act IV, sc. ii):

Dame Pliant. Truly I shall never brook a Spaniard.
Subtle. No!
Dame Pliant. Never since eighty-eight could I abide them.

materially. The king was as thoroughly anxious to avoid participation in war—especially a war of religion—as the Spaniards could have wished. Apparently he thought that an alliance between the chief protestant and the chief catholic powers would be the surest way to avoid such a disaster. At the same time his financial needs made him particularly eager to obtain the dowry which might be expected with a Spanish princess. He seems to have viewed the question much as one of wardship. The emptiness of his purse was a strong inducement to try to get a good marriage portion with his son's bride. As the dowry of the infanta was expected to amount to £600,000[1] his anxiety becomes intelligible. The immediate difficulty in the way of the Spanish match arose from the exorbitant demands emanating from Madrid. Not only were any children of the marriage to be baptized and educated by their mother as catholics and to be free to remain such without forfeiting their right of succession to the throne, but also the execution of the penal laws was to be suspended.[2]

There were, however, other parties to the question—the pope and Spanish theologians, and the English people. The theologians insisted that the marriage treaty must be sanctioned by the English parliament, and that three years should then elapse before the marriage in order to ensure that freedom of worship for English catholics was really granted. James dared not make any public announcement of freedom of worship for catholics, but attempted to satisfy the Spaniards by suffering Raleigh to be executed in 1618,[3] under the sentence passed upon him for treason in 1603 (although it was perfectly obvious that he was in reality the victim of Spanish influence at court), and by releasing a hundred priests, who were allowed to leave the country in 1618.

At this stage the Bohemian revolution began the Thirty Years War. In August 1619 Frederick of the Palatinate accepted the crown of Bohemia without waiting for the approval of his father-in-law.[4] A year later Frederick's forces were defeated at the battle of the White Mountain, and a Spanish army invaded the Palatinate. Public opinion in England whole-heartedly

---

[1] Gardiner, iii. 104.   [2] Ibid. ii. 323–4.
[3] For Raleigh's release from the Tower and his expedition to Guiana see below, p. 326.
[4] Anton Gindely, *History of the Thirty Years' War* (1898), i. 153–5.

adopted Frederick's side,[1] but the king stood aloof from this enthusiasm. His attitude was an odd mixture of delight that his daughter's husband should have become a crowned king, fear lest Spain should hold him responsible for his son-in-law's rashness, and anger at the affront to regality.[2] His remarks to Dohna, Frederick's envoy, are typical of his whole position on foreign policy: 'Can you show me a good ground for the Palatine's invasion of the property of another? ... So you are of the opinion that subjects can dispossess their kings? You are come in good time to England, to spread these principles among the people, that my subjects may drive me away, and place another in my room?'[3] Whereas James was concerned solely with the dynastic question and with the rights of crowned heads, the people of England were concerned with the interests of protestantism. Some called for a war to recover the Palatinate, and James went so far as to permit the enrolment of volunteers and the subscription of money to aid his unfortunate son-in-law. Others, however, wished for a naval conflict with Spain so that the cost of a war for protestantism might be maintained from the wealth gained from prizes at sea. A ballad entitled 'Gallants to Bohemia' well illustrates the twofold attraction of a war with Spain. 'One verse speaks of fighting "for true religion's right" and "for God and his gospel", others talked of "gold prizes" and of Indian silver and pearls, and bade pilots take card and compass in hand,

> "And hye again to Neptune's seas
> Where we'll have riches when we please".'[4]

A war with Spain was the last thing James wanted, and on the return of Gondomar to England in March 1620 the king made frantic efforts to enlist Spanish support for his son-in-law. To secure such an end James became the prey of the wildest

---

[1] *Tom Tell-Troath* (in *Somers Tracts*, ii [1809], 472) says that, in taverns, for one health to the king ten were drunk to the Palatine and his wife.

[2] *State Papers, Venetian, 1619–1621*, pp. 53, 92 (where he is said to have declared that he could not countenance the practice of deposing kings). In his speech at the opening of parliament in 1621, he explained why he had been loath to meddle with the question. Among the reasons is: 'I would not make religion the cause of deposing kings' (*Old Parliamentary History*, v. 317–18).

[3] Mary Anne Everett Green, *Elizabeth, Electress Palatine and Queen of Bohemia* (1909), p. 150, n. 1.

[4] C. H. Firth, 'Ballad History of the Reign of James I', in *Transactions of the Royal Historical Society*, 3rd ser. v (1911).

projects. He even proposed to Gondomar a partition of the Netherlands, of which his share was to be Holland and Zeeland. It is noteworthy that the Spaniard, not the king, refused to believe that the English troops in the service of the States General would betray the land they were paid to defend; and without the certainty of their co-operation the plan could not be attempted. At first James had been confident that the Spaniards would not attack the Palatinate; after they had successfully invaded it he thought they would surrender their conquests to arrange the Spanish match. He became even more anxious to secure the Spanish alliance after his quarrel with parliament in 1621. There the feeling in the beginning was unanimous in favour of helping to recover the Palatinate, and a motion pledging members, and those they represented, to assist the king in war, with their lives and fortunes, if pacific means failed to restore his 'children abroad, and the general afflicted estate of the true professors of the same Christian religion, professed by the church of England, and other foreign parts', was received with unexampled enthusiasm;[1] but later popular leaders became more concerned that a stout blow should be struck at Spain than that a great effort should be made to intervene in Germany. They felt that Spain was the head and paymaster of the confederation that had ejected Frederick from his hereditary dominions, but that, if the Indies could be captured, Spain would lose her purse, and her armies would be broken by mutiny within two years.[2] A war after the Elizabethan style would enable them 'to enrich ourselves as well as to defend our right and ourselves'. Moreover papists in England looked to Spain to protect them;[3] and their numbers had increased rapidly as a result of the pro-Spanish policy lately pursued. Thus a war with Spain was the best and cheapest way to aid the cause of protestantism in general and that of the Palatinate in particular. The commons therefore drew up a petition in which, after dilating upon the causes and effects of the growth of popery, they

---

[1] Nicholas, *Proceedings and Debates . . . in 1620 and 1621*, ii. 170, 172; *Commons' Journals*, i. 639.

[2] Nicholas, ii. 211–17.

[3] This point is emphasized in *Vox Populi* (1620; in *Somers Tracts*, ii. 512). Cf. Nicholas, ii. 210–17. The Venetian ambassador wrote, 9/19 March 1620: Gondomar 'has been awaited by all the catholics of this country with the utmost expectation, as it is announced that he brings the marriage upon which they found extensive hopes of seeing the true religion restored and established in these parts' (*State Papers, Venetian, 1619–1621*, p. 204).

proposed as remedies that the king should prepare for war and stand side by side with protestants abroad, and especially direct his sword against that prince mainly responsible for the loss of the Palatinate.[1] James angrily complained that members were trenching upon his prerogative, and ordered the house not to meddle with mysteries of state. When the commons replied with the Protestation, he dismissed the parliament.[2]

This breach between king and parliament, said Gondomar, was the best thing that had happened for Spain and the catholic religion since Luther began to preach heresy. James would no longer be able to help his son-in-law or to hinder the catholic advance. According to the same authority, James was deeply distressed, but said that if he acted otherwise his discontented puritan subjects would cause him to die miserably.[3] The king's decision to throw himself unreservedly into the arms of Spain came at a time when Frederick's cause was desperate, for he was put under the ban of the empire, and his electorate was conferred on Maximilian of Bavaria. James's urgent representations that Philip should intervene at Vienna to stay the course of events received only procrastinating replies. By the end of 1622 Frederick had lost every foot of his native land.

Meanwhile the marriage negotiations were proceeding so slowly that Prince Charles set out with Buckingham for Madrid in order to conduct his wooing in person. That romantic errand was as remarkable for the extraordinary complacency of the prince as for the *naïveté* that inspired it. Charles, in addition to agreeing that his wife should have the sole charge of their children till they were twelve, that her chapel should be open to all Englishmen, and that a bishop and twenty priests should be attached to her household and be exempt from the law of the land, also gave assurance of the immediate suspension of the penal laws and their repeal by parliament within three years.[4] Nevertheless pledges that could certainly never be redeemed did not suffice to bring the match to a happy conclusion, for the Spaniards refused to allow the infanta to leave for England until a period of probation should have revealed whether the catholics had enjoyed the promised freedom of private worship. This was too much. Charles's patience, already strained by his

---

[1] Spain was not named, but there could be no doubt which power was meant (*Parliamentary History*, i. 1323-6).   [2] Cf. above, p. 27.
[3] Gardiner, iii. 266.   [4] Ibid. v. 48, 68, 90.

complete failure to induce the Spaniards to move a finger on behalf of his brother-in-law Frederick, wore so thin that after wearisome delays some plain speaking took place. The prince asked Philip's chief minister, Olivares, 'if the emperor proves refractory will the king, your master, assist us with arms to reduce him to reasonable terms?' 'No', replied Olivares, 'we have a maxim of state that the king of Spain must never fight against the emperor.' 'Look to it, sir', said Charles, 'for if you hold yourself to that, there is an end of all; for without this you may not rely upon either marriage or friendship.'[1] Thus the rock on which the Spanish alliance split was the Palatinate. Charles was willing to yield virtually everything that was asked in the interest of English catholics, and thereby to sacrifice the penal laws, but he was unwilling that his marriage should entail the irretrievable ruin of his sister. In this he was at one with his father, who said, 'I like not to marry my son with a portion of my daughter's tears.'[2]

The return of the prince and duke without the infanta, said Laud, was greeted with 'the greatest expression of joy by all sorts of people, that ever I saw'.[3] The reason for this rejoicing was that Englishmen felt delivered from the fears, that had beset them for the last six or seven years, that a Spanish match would mean the ruin of protestantism in England and on the Continent.[4] The country in general was quite willing to support Charles and Buckingham in a war against Spain. When parliament met anti-Spanish sentiment ran high. Eliot probably expressed the feelings of the majority when he said: 'Are we poor? Spain is rich. There are our Indies. Break with them; we shall break our necessities together.'[5] On the other hand the suggestion that simultaneously war should be waged on land for the recovery of the Palatinate was now coldly received. Such a plan, one member stated, is 'not fit for the consideration of the house in regard to the infinite charge'. These views were reflected in the address accompanying the grant of £300,000, which was to be expended by the direction of commissioners appointed in parliament and was voted in order to achieve four objects: the defence of the realm, the securing of Ireland, assistance of the United

[1] *Lords' Journals*, iii. 226; Gardiner, v. 105–6.

[2] Ibid., pp. 131, 137.

[3] Laud, *Works*, iii. 143, 149–50; John Nichols, *Progresses of King James* (1828), iv. 927–30; Rushworth, i. 104.

[4] *D'Ewes Autobiography*, i. 182–3.   [5] Gardiner, v. 199.

Provinces (again at war with Spain), and equipment of the navy.[1]

Charles and Buckingham, whose influence over James was now so strong that they virtually ruled the kingdom, favoured war on a large scale. Their desire to be avenged for the failure of the Spanish match made them willing enough to listen to parliamentary voices calling for a naval war, but they were also anxious for a war on land to recover the Palatinate. Therefore English ambassadors were soon journeying in all directions, seeking alliances. It proved easy to arrange a treaty with the Dutch (5/15 June 1624) by which England agreed to pay 6,000 soldiers to aid them in their struggle for independence. Negotiations for a French marriage treaty made speedy progress, and the announcement of its conclusion was generally welcome.[2] A force under Mansfeld, a soldier of fortune, was assembled at Dover, but money was wanting to equip as well as to pay it. Neither the Dutch nor the French wished to receive it, and when it eventually landed at Flushing the rate of mortality was so high that soon the 12,000 men that started were reduced to 3,000. The attempt to enlist the services of Gustavus Adolphus for the recovery of the Palatinate failed because that sovereign made demands too onerous for the English treasury to assume. Christian IV of Denmark, however, was more venturesome, and his offer to lead a force into Germany if England would provide payment for seven thousand men was accepted. Hence when James I died he bequeathed to his son a Spanish war, Dutch and Danish alliances, and the support of Mansfeld's ill-fated army.

Charles I then proceeded with the French alliance, and his marriage to Henrietta Maria took place within three months of his accession. At Paris, as at Madrid, the demands were conceded that the members of the queen's household should be of her own religion, and that the penal laws should be suspended.[3] On the other hand Buckingham, who went to Paris in person to conduct the final negotiations, found that Richelieu was unwilling openly to take part in a war for the recovery of the Palatinate. Thus the French marriage had lost much of its

---

[1] *Lords' Journals*, iii. 275.   [2] *D'Ewes Autobiography*, i. 257.

[3] Yet in 1624 James had assured parliament: 'It is against the rule of wisdom that a king should suffer any of his subjects to be beholding and depend upon any other prince than himself; and what hath any king to do with the laws and subjects of another kingdom . . . I will be careful that no such condition be hereafter foisted in upon any other treaty whatsoever' (*Lords' Journals*, iii. 318).

charm even before it was consummated, for Charles found he
would have to bear the brunt of the struggle to restore his
brother-in-law. In all, his foreign commitments were likely to
cost him a million pounds a year—if he fulfilled them.

When parliament met, however, Charles briefly appealed for
subsidies to carry out a war that he asserted parliament had
advised, and allowed Sir Richard Weston to relate how the
king had learnt in Spain that nothing brought his father into
so much contempt as the coldness between him and his people;[1]
but he made no effort at any time to acquaint members with the
details of the alliances he had formed. Without knowledge and
leadership, parliament voted only an interim grant of two subsidies—about one-seventh of the royal needs—before its further
proceedings were cut short by dissolution.

The spring and summer of 1625 were consumed in preparations for the great expedition against Spain. The alliance with
the States General provided for a Dutch fleet to blockade the
Flemish coast and an English one the coast of Spain. The Dutch
also agreed to supply one ship for every four English ships that
sailed on a joint enterprise.[2] The English navy furnished several
men-of-war that rendered a good account of themselves, but
the merchantmen and colliers that were forced to accompany
them proved to be manned by base cowards. Some 10,000
soldiers and half as many seamen were pressed to take part in
the expedition. Most of the former, at least, seem to have been
rogues and vagabonds and caused a worthy diarist to denounce
soldiers as one of the greatest plagues of the country. In their
half-starved and half-naked condition, their presence made the
inhabitants of any locality they passed through offer gratuities
to their officers to march them farther, in order to avoid demands for 'hose, shoes, shirts and conduct money'.[3] Half a
crown a week was the nominal sum allowed for the upkeep of
each, but lack of funds delayed its payment. When one of the
generals, accustomed to the well-disciplined and well-equipped
army that fought in the Dutch wars, saw these levies, he recognized at once that they could not be made serviceable without
the prompt provision of supplies of every kind. Moreover he
noticed that a great many of the men were lame or decrepit and

---

[1] *Debates in the House of Commons in 1625*, p. 83.
[2] Treaty of Southampton, 8 Sept. 1625 (Gardiner, vi. 6).
[3] *Diary of Walter Yonge*, ed. George Roberts (1848), p. 82 n.

wholly unfit. Since arms were lacking to drill the men, they wasted the summer in such riotous living as their scanty pay or frequent outrages on the countryside could furnish.

At length the expedition started, in October, but it speedily became evident that neither the soldiers nor the sailors had any heart in their work. When the fleet arrived off Cadiz a chance to surprise a Spanish fleet in the bay was ruined because the merchant-captains and their crews were too sluggish or too timid to advance. Similarly the bombardment of Fort Puntal was a failure because the colliers neglected to go into action during the night, and after their pusillanimity became evident in the daylight they took refuge behind the ships of the royal navy and tried to fire over them at the fort, but actually shot so wildly that after a cannon-ball had been sent through the stern of a warship they were allowed to obey their cowardly instincts and withdraw. Eventually the fort surrendered to a landing-party, and the army marched on Cadiz. After the men had toiled for miles under a semi-tropical sun, it was discovered that their knapsacks were empty. The neighbourhood yielded no food, but wine in abundance was found. Thereupon, wrote an eye-witness, what with their emptiness and heat, the soldiers became so drunk that their officers were in danger of having their own throats cut for trying to stop the debauch. Five hundred men could have defeated the whole army, for such dissolute wretches the earth had never brought forth, but the Spaniards failed to take advantage of their opportunity. After this it was idle to think of attacking Cadiz, now warned and garrisoned, so the army was embarked and sail was set in the hope of surprising the treasure-fleet from Mexico.

It soon became obvious that the fleet could not stay long at sea. The victuals and drink were so bad, said an officer, that no stray dog in London would have touched them. The ropes were rotten, and some of the sails dated back to the time of the Armada. Therefore there was nothing to be done but to return home—disgraced, shattered by a storm, and having daily cast overboard scores of soldiers and sailors who had died from malnutrition. The plight of those who survived to reach England was pitiful to the last degree. Sir John Eliot, the vice-admiral of Devon, saw seven die, and many more fall exhausted in the streets of Plymouth on a single day. 'In this unfortunate journey', wrote one of the officers to Buckingham, 'God's judgments have followed us by sickness, mortality and otherwise.' Some who took part in the expedition had different views, however, about the cause of their misfortunes: among these men was Lieutenant John Felton, Buckingham's future assassin.[1]

The war with Spain dragged on for another four years, but actual hostilities were practically confined to private enterprises. Parliament refused to grant money so long as Buckingham managed everything, and the Londoners followed suit. At a public meeting in Westminster Hall citizens were exhorted to give freely because the kingdom was in danger of invasion and they themselves threatened with the total loss of their 'goods, honour, wives, children and life itself'. The people listened attentively, but their only response was, 'Parliament, parliament'.[2] Private adventurers proved totally unequal to emulating the feats of their Elizabethan predecessors. The earl of Warwick received a commission to attack any Spanish dominions in Europe, Africa, or America, but achieved little, and Sir Kenelm Digby's semi-piratical expedition to the Mediterranean was equally futile. On the other hand the privateers from Dunkirk levied heavy toll on English commerce. In fact people grumbled that they did not enjoy the advantages of peace or of trade, but suffered the losses and dishonour of war.[3]

Disastrous as this naval warfare was to English commerce, it was even more serious as the main cause of the outbreak of hostilities with France in 1627. Three years before, high hopes had been entertained of an Anglo-French alliance against Spain, and now England was at war with both France and Spain. The two countries on opposite sides of the Channel had begun to drift apart soon after Richelieu had applied to the English and Dutch governments for aid against the Huguenots because their leader, Soubise, had seized and carried to La Rochelle six vessels belonging to the royal navy. James was influenced partly by the thought that the Huguenots were rebels, and partly by the hope of securing active French co-operation in Germany if Richelieu's request was granted. Moreover this request came at the very time when the French marriage was on the point of completion. Therefore contracts were signed by which a ship of the royal navy, and seven merchant vessels hired for the

---

[1] The best account of the expedition is in Charles Dalton, *Life and Times of Sir Edward Cecil, Viscount Wimbledon* (1885), ii. 83–241.

[2] *State Papers, Venetian, 1625–1626* (1913), p. 495.   [3] Ibid. *1628–1629*, p. 128.

purpose, were lent to Louis with the stipulation that they might be used against any enemy except the king of Great Britain.[1] Almost immediately afterwards Buckingham went to Paris and found to his indignation that Louis XIII was neither willing to pledge himself to a joint attack on Spain nor to wage open war for the recovery of the Palatinate. In revenge, Buckingham indulged in a love-scene with Louis's wife, Anne of Austria, which naturally did not promote harmony between the two Crowns. The failure of parliament to make adequate grants rendered the king more anxious than ever to secure the French alliance, but the means he had originally chosen now proved a fertile source of friction. The small English fleet Louis had hired was inflexible in its determination not to take part in an attack on La Rochelle. When at Dieppe, its commander, Pennington, refused to receive French troops on board and soon brought the ships back to England, where the captains lodged a violent remonstrance against being forced to shed the innocent blood of protestants on behalf of a popish king. Charles and Buckingham by this time realized how unpopular the employment of these ships against La Rochelle would be in England, and, while ostensibly doing their utmost to effect the transfer, secretly put every obstacle in the way of their delivery to the French. After weeks of quibbling, the news that terms of peace had been agreed upon between Louis and the Huguenots induced the seamen to hand over their ships, although all of the men but one (who, as good protestants noticed, was almost immediately killed by accident) refused to enter French service. This hesitation of the English government in surrendering the ships was due not only to an increasing distrust of France but also to the desire to gain popularity in England by posing as a protestant champion in Europe. By now the court had two divergent and incompatible objectives: the formation of a protestant league in Germany for the recovery of the Palatinate, and the conclusion of an alliance with France against Spain. In accordance with the first, Buckingham negotiated a treaty at The Hague between England, the United Provinces, and Denmark, but his success was fatal to his chances of securing French co-operation, for Louis felt that he should have been consulted beforehand and that the real object of the treaty was the destruction of catholicism. Other causes of friction with France were the enforcement of the

[1] Gardiner, v. 328.

penal laws of England, in complete contradiction to the promises made at the time of the French marriage, and the attempt of Charles to mediate between Louis and the Huguenots.

These causes of irritation might have been removed peacefully but for a grave conflict of principle as to belligerent rights at sea. The English fleet had seized in the Channel a number of ships owned by Calais merchants and suspected of carrying merchandise whose ultimate destination was the Spanish Netherlands. Charles weakened his case at the outset by permitting part of the cargoes to be sold as contraband before their condemnation by the court of admiralty. He seems to have regarded these prizes as hostages for the return of the English ships Louis was using against La Rochelle. The conclusion of peace between the Huguenots and their sovereign did not solve the problem, but rather made it more intricate, because the treaty could not be consummated without the intervention of the English ambassadors in France, who persuaded the Rochellese not to insist on certain demands. They agreed, but made it clear that having yielded to English mediation they would expect Charles I to preserve their liberties in the future. Hence the momentary cessation of the Huguenot war did not improve Anglo-French relations. Charles was dissatisfied because in the treaty he had desired open acknowledgement of his position as mediator and because he expected Louis to share equally with him the burden of the war in Germany. On the contrary France made peace with Spain in April 1626, and all hope of an Anglo-French alliance against the Habsburgs had to be abandoned. This happened just at a time when the protestant cause in Germany reached its nadir and Mansfeld's defeat at the Bridge of Dessau and Christian IV's at Lutter left no organized army to continue the struggle against the forces of the counter-reformation. While these grave issues were at stake Anglo-French relations were further disturbed by Charles's expulsion of the French attendants of Henrietta Maria, by new seizures of French ships, and by an embargo on English ships in French ports. Thus the two countries drifted into war.

The year 1627 saw the preparation of a large armament at Portsmouth. To the miserable survivors of the Cadiz expedition were now added more pressed men, and eventually about 6,000 foot were assembled. Buckingham's instructions defined the objects of his expedition as the defence of English commerce and the destruction or capture of the ships of France or Spain; the convoy to La Rochelle of regiments to garrison that city if the citizens thought the danger of possible attack from Louis sufficient to justify their reception; the assertion of English supremacy at sea along the French coast; and the interruption of Spanish trade between Flanders and the West Indies.[1] The expedition duly arrived at the Isle of Ré, just off La Rochelle, but found the Rochellese very unwilling to cast in their lot with their would-be deliverers, so that only a few score joined Buckingham's force. The fortress on the island, St. Martin, was ably defended, and before starvation compelled surrender Richelieu had collected an army on the mainland and transported much of it to the island. Fearing to be crushed between the besieged and their relievers Buckingham set out for his ships but lost heavily before regaining them. A contemporary truly remarked that the expedition returned to England 'with no little dishonour to our nation, excessive charge to our treasury, and great slaughter of our men'.[2] Charles was now more than ever bent upon protecting the Huguenots. Louis XIII, he said, 'is determined to destroy La Rochelle, and I am no less resolved to support it'; and Buckingham added, 'as long as this punctilio exists, it is useless to think or speak of peace'.[3] A new expedition was made ready and sailed under the command of Denbigh, but found that Richelieu had erected such formidable moles across the narrow channel that led to La Rochelle that to attack was to invite disaster. The obstinacy of Charles and his favourite was proof even against this discouragement, and Buckingham was at Portsmouth getting ready still another expedition when he was assassinated.

But the favourite's death did not produce harmony between king and legislature. When Charles dissolved parliament in 1629, with the intention of ruling without it for the future, peace became essential, because to wage war without parliamentary grants was impossible. To arrange the treaty of Susa with France was comparatively easy, since the fall of La Rochelle had removed the ostensible cause of the war, and the difficulties about belligerent rights at sea were ignored. To come to terms with Spain proved more difficult, because at first Charles was unwilling to treat except in concert with the States General, and

---

[1] Gardiner, vi. 170.   [2] *Original Letters*, 2nd ser. iii. 251.
[3] *State Papers, Venetian, 1626-1628* (1914), pp. 542-3.

he was still anxious to insist upon Spanish aid to recover the Palatinate. Eventually the treaty of Madrid was signed on 5 November 1630, and was very similar in terms to the treaty of 1604; but its conclusion entailed the abandonment by Charles of both his sister Elizabeth and his allies. These two treaties mark the end of the only attempt of the early Stuarts to pursue an active foreign policy. Their efforts had been totally devoid of any success on the Continent, and were largely responsible for the loss of the Palatinate, the defeat of Christian IV, and the downfall of La Rochelle. The results in England, however, were no less important. Clarendon[1] in his old age painted in vivid colours the cumulative effects of the successive disasters that had befallen English expeditions. Both services were mutinous not only for want of pay but also for detestation of Buckingham's authority. The counties were incensed at having to provide billets for raw and undisciplined soldiers whose frequent lack of pay almost excused the outrages they committed. The exaction of forced loans to equip these men, the imprisonment of those who refused to lend, and the imposition of martial law were directly responsible for the Petition of Right, the one great achievement of the opponents of the early-Stuart methods of government. First of all, distrust of the foreign policy of the Crown had ruined all hope of harmony between king and parliament in 1621. Later the attempt to call to account the favourite held responsible for the disasters that attended the expeditions of 1625 and 1627 was the main cause of the quarrel between Charles I and the commons during 1625–8. Moreover the consequences of these national humiliations were not confined to the present, for they tended to alienate the nation permanently from the Crown. They had made it apparent to all that the old constitution no longer sufficed, nay more, was definitely defective. In fact this exhibition of incompetence strengthened the determination of the commons to share in, and subsequently even to change, the government of England.

[1] *History*, i. 87–88.

III

RELIGIOUS HISTORY, 1603-40

IN many ways the church of England was in a more satisfactory condition at the end of the sixteenth century than at any previous time.[1] The immediate dangers, from without that a foreign invasion might restore Roman catholicism, and from within that puritanism might wreck the Elizabethan settlement through substituting a presbyterian for an episcopal form of government, had been met and defeated. Roman catholicism had so declined that its acknowledged adherents no longer numbered more than a small percentage of the population, although there were probably many more who attended Anglican services so as to avoid persecution; but most Englishmen continued to believe that the restoration of popery was an ever present threat. Puritanism, which in the third quarter of the sixteenth century had seemed likely to prevail, had received a very definite set-back during the nineties. The reasons for its failure were varied. In the first place a new school of theologians had arisen (of which Hooker and Andrewes were the brightest ornaments), who no longer thought of the writings of Luther or Calvin as the last court of appeal but relied on the co-ordinated authority of Scripture and patristic literature. They supplied a learned and reasoned basis for the theological position of the church of England, and commended the *via media*, not as a convenient half-way house between Rome and Geneva, but as the true, if reformed, descendant of the primitive church. In the second place puritanism, with its strict and inquisitorial morality, was opposed to the spirit of the age that produced William Shakespeare. Thirdly the official view then prevalent, that church and state were one society in a twofold aspect and that to assail the former inevitably involved the latter, was not yet repugnant to the class with political power. At that time the theory of the divine right of kings was accepted, and the most damaging accusation brought against the oppo-

[1] Much of this chapter is based on an article by the present writer, 'Arminian versus Puritan in England, *ca.* 1620-1640', in *Huntington Library Bulletin*, No. 5 (1934), where full references are given. In order to secure continuity, Roman catholicism and independency are not treated here but in chap. viii.

nents of Anglicanism was that they were attempting to introduce a popular or democratic form of government both in church and state. Nevertheless, although the puritan attack had been repulsed, there resulted merely a sullen truce rather than a lasting peace. However, this breathing-space gave the church leaders time to take stock of the position and to try to set their house in order. There was undoubtedly much room for improvement.

The poverty of many of the clergy was disgraceful in an age steadily growing richer, and the ignorance, slackness, and occasional misconduct of a fair number, together with the widespread pluralism, provided critics with solid ground for complaint. Churchmen had long been conscious of these evils but had been unable to remedy them. Whitgift had declared in 1585 that out of 9,000 benefices more than half had incomes of not more than £10 and most of these not more than £8,[1] that the majority of clerics had no university degree, and that a thousand were pluralists. Less than 4,000 of the clergy were licensed to preach, and the remainder were the 'dumb mouths' decried by puritans. Reform was almost impossible without increasing the income of the church, for the miserable pittance that awaited the parish priest would hardly warrant the previous expense of a university education, and pluralism was the only way to attract and retain learned scholars without private means. Something was done by a statute passed early in James's reign to prevent the alienation of episcopal lands, thus stopping the systematic pillage Elizabeth had allowed Raleigh and other favourites to enjoy. Decisions in ecclesiastical courts in some cases improved the incomes of benefices by restoring payment of tithe in kind whenever unfair commutations could be legally voided. The close inspection of impropriations restored to the church a fraction of the revenues that had been alienated to laymen during the disorders of the reformation. Such efforts, however, were mere palliatives, and left the majority of the clergy still scandalously underpaid.

Simultaneously with these attempts to increase clerical emoluments, Bancroft tried to improve ecclesiastical discipline. Hitherto many puritan ministers had dispensed with such ritual and parts of the Prayer Book as were objectionable to them. The nature of their scruples is revealed in a petition usually called

[1] R. G. Usher, *Reconstruction of the English Church* (1910), i. 219 ff.

the Millenary Petition (1603) because its authors claimed that it expressed the views of more than a thousand ministers. In studiously moderate language it urged that some practices should be abolished, as the sign of the cross in baptism, or the ring in marriage, and that others should be left optional, as the cap and surplice. These demands were debated in the Hampton Court conference (1604), when James presided over a disputation between the heads of the church and four puritans. The arguments of the latter completely failed to convince the king, who roughly told them that he would make them conform to existing usage or harry them out of the land. He would have, he said, 'one doctrine and one discipline, one religion in substance and in ceremony'. At the same time his reiterated phrase, 'No bishop, no king', emphasized his belief in the interdependence of episcopacy and monarchy.[1] The conference had one good result, however, for a new translation of the Bible was undertaken. The task was entrusted to some fifty scholars, divided into six groups, each with its allotted part of the Scriptures. They did not finish their labours until 1611, when there appeared the King James version, generally styled 'authorized'. Even though it received no formal authorization beyond the words on its title-page, 'appointed to be read in churches', it soon superseded its former rivals, the Geneva Bible and the Great Bishops' Bible, and its apt phraseology, rhythmic beauty, and generally faithful, if not always literally accurate, rendering of the original have given it for more than three centuries a unique position in literature.[2]

Having decided to deny puritan demands for a revision of the Prayer Book, the church adopted the other alternative and enforced conformity. The constitution to which all ministers must now subscribe was defined in the canons of 1604, which codified existing practice and combined whatever was deemed valuable in previous canons and injunctions with additions designed to meet the present needs. The new clauses were largely concerned with discipline, and among other requirements demanded that the minister should acknowledge that each of the Thirty-nine Articles was agreeable to the Word of God, should wear a cope and surplice during divine service, and should see that his congregation received the communion kneeling. The general

---

[1] Edward Cardwell, *A History of Conferences* (1840), pp. 198-9, 203.
[2] For a further discussion of the Authorized Version, see below, p. 407.

enforcement of the new subscription caused the deprivation of some puritan ministers, whose number is disputed.[1] The sympathy that naturally goes out to those who suffer because of conscientious scruples should not be allowed to obscure the correctness of Bancroft's decision that ministers of the church must loyally accept its constitution or lose their benefices.

The church might have enjoyed comparative peace had it not become inextricably involved in grave political issues. James I, proud of his ecclesiastical supremacy in England in contrast with the lowly position assigned to him in presbyterian Scotland, on all occasions championed the bishops against their puritan critics in parliament, while the bishops in their turn adopted enthusiastically the theory of the divine right of kings and preached passive obedience. Thus James's aphorism, 'No bishop, no king', was literally true. The Stuart system of government would have collapsed ignominiously early in the century but for the support of the hierarchy, and Jacobean and Caroline bishops would, but for the royal favour, have been called to account before the Long Parliament met. Hence a position was created in which the puritan found that any opposition to the church was regarded as sedition at court and any criticism of the monarchy was denounced as blasphemy in the pulpit. Courtly divines frequently argued that those who were eager to cast mitres and copes under foot were equally anxious to throw down crowns and sceptres.[2] As Bacon said, religion was the chief bond of human society, and Laud was emphatic that divisions would at once appear in the state if unity did not prevail in the church. So the voice of criticism was to be hushed in the pulpit as in the market-place.

This unqualified acceptance of the will of his ruler was all the harder for the puritan inasmuch as protestantism seemed in imminent danger, not only from the advance of the counter-reformation in Europe, but also from the spread of Arminianism[3] in England. To the Calvinist the reliance of Arminians on the practice of the primitive church, and their insistence on the con-

---

[1] For various estimates and comments on them see W. H. Frere, *The English Church* (1904), pp. 320–1; cf. Usher, *Reconstruction of the English Church*, chap. 6.

[2] e.g. John Pocklington, *Sunday No Sabbath* (1636).

[3] The term was derived from a Dutch theologian, the latinized form of whose name was Arminius. In England the Arminians were those who rebelled against the intellectual tyranny of Calvinism, especially against predestination, and corresponded, in some respects, to the Anglo-catholics of to-day.

tinuity of the Anglican church with the pre-Reformation church, seemed to presage a drift Romeward. These suspicions were apparently justified by the pro-Spanish foreign policy of James I and the favour shown to papists by Charles's wife Henrietta Maria. Moreover the complete failure of the early Stuarts to strike even one stout blow for continental protestantism appeared to indicate lukewarmness if not something worse. Therefore there were many vital issues at stake during the struggle between Arminianism and puritanism, although the points around which the actual disputes raged were often not of the first importance.

The fundamental issue between Arminian and puritan arose over the question of episcopacy. Many puritans, like Bastwick, were indifferent about prelacy, so long as it was merely 'an order established by the king and state';[1] but their keenest antagonism was aroused when the theory of episcopacy *jure divino* was emphasized. This theory, although advanced in Elizabeth's reign, was first brought prominently before the public by Alexander Leighton's denunciatory pamphlet,[2] published in 1628, and thenceforth was the main subject of contention between puritans and episcopalians. As Archbishop Laud said, 'Our main crime is . . . that we are bishops. . . . And a great trouble 'tis to them [puritans], that we maintain that our calling of bishops is *jure divino*.'[3]

The answer to attacks on the Laudian position was that a system of church government which had continued from the time of the Apostles to the present day and which had been established both by law and by custom in England ever since the introduction of Christianity was more likely to suit Englishmen than a system such as presbyterianism, which was newly created, not recognized by the laws, and incompatible with monarchy.[4]

Perhaps the bishops' claim to an apostolic succession for their order was rendered more odious to puritans by the increasing dignity and pomp of the episcopate. Malicious eyes noted that Laud went abroad with forty or fifty mounted attendants and ushers crying, 'Roome, roome for my Lords Grace. Gentlemen

---

[1] *The Second Part of the Letany* (1637), p. 6.
[2] *An Appeal to the Parliament; or Sions Plea against the Prelacie.*
[3] *Works*, vi. 42-3; cf. pp. 573-4.
[4] This is a paraphrase of Laud's argument, in *Works*, iii. 387.

be uncovered my Lords Grace is coming.' To make way for the archbishop, his attendants are said to have exhibited great contempt for the common folk, 'tumbling downe and thrusting aside the little children a playing there: flinging and tossing the poore costermongers and soucewives fruit and puddings, baskets and all into the Thames'.[1]

Nevertheless the general unpopularity of the bishops in the early 1640's was due to many reasons besides the puritan hatred of prelacy as unlawful and unchristian. Their enjoyment of high public offices and engrossment of the royal confidence, as Clarendon says, 'exposed them to the universal envy of the whole nobility'.[2] Puritans were not slow to point out the inconsistency in the claim of the clergy to the exclusive control of matters of religion, when they were themselves simultaneously taking a leading part in directing the national policy.[3] When that policy caused such opposition in Scotland that the bishops' wars ensued, its general unpopularity was revealed for the first time. Until then the puritan propagandists, finding that the sympathy of the ordinary citizen could not be enlisted by theological arguments, utilized to the full the widespread hatred of popery. They were careful to point out that popery and tyranny went hand in hand,[4] and thus to link together constitutionalism and fanaticism. In their attempts to frighten the plain man into the belief that there was a real danger of the restoration of Roman catholicism, they were much aided by the more rigid insistence of Arminian bishops upon a ceremonial church service which seemed to many to foreshadow a return to pre-Reformation usages.

The attempt to introduce uniformity and decency of external worship aroused opposition, and ministers who were formalists found themselves denounced as corrupt time-servers. As Laud complained in 1637, "tis superstition now-a-days for any man to come with more reverence into a church, than a tinker and his bitch come into an ale-house'.[5] Furthermore, in the controversy about ceremonial the puritans had the great advantage

---

[1] John Bastwick, *Letany* (1637), p. 6.   [2] *History of the Rebellion*, i. 184.
[3] Henry Burton, *An Apology of an Appeale* (1636), pp. 29–30.
[4] See Peter Heylyn's remarks in the preface to his *A Briefe and Moderate Answer* (1637).
[5] *Works*, vi. 57. Cf. Thomas Cheshire, *A True Copy of That Sermon* (1641), p. 12: 'Another will maintaine, that there is no more holinesse in the church then in his kitchen, nor in the Lords table then in a dresser-board.'

that they could denounce ritual as pre-Reformation and therefore popish and abominable. Moreover they regarded all practices not prescribed in the Scriptures as heathenish, for they had constituted the Bible their sole authority[1] and held it up as a uniform manual of docrine and an absolute law of truth.

In their propaganda against the church, however, the puritans were at a great handicap, for they were officially denied the use of both the main organs of public opinion—the pulpit and the press. The early Stuarts imitated Elizabeth, who 'used to tune the pulpits, as her saying was'.[2] Since the sermon was both the mainstay of the puritan service and often the sole channel by which news filtered down to the masses, the government tried to exercise a rigid control. Thus in 1622 instructions were issued that preachers should adhere strictly to their texts, that their afternoon sermons should be confined to some part of the catechism or to a text from the Creed, the Ten Commandments, or the Lord's Prayer.[3]

This royal order caused the greatest consternation among puritans, who deplored the loss of half the preaching in England, by the restrictions placed on the afternoon sermons.[4] What made these restrictions still more onerous was the freedom, both to preach and to publish, enjoyed by the Arminian faction.[5] Montague might taunt the puritans with having annexed to their pens and pulpits the infallibility of the papal chair and with remaining in the church in order to betray it by installing popes (i.e. presbyters) in every parish and a democratic anarchy in the state;[6] but the puritan ran the risk of severe punishment if he replied in an unlicensed pamphlet—his controversial writings were unlikely to be licensed. Whereas the puritan was forbidden to preach against the prerogative, the Arminian was

---

[1] John Selden made the very acute observation that the puritan 'would be judged by the word of God. If he would speak clearly, he means himself, but he is ashamed to say so; and he would have me believe him before a whole church, that has read the word of God as well as he' (*Table Talk* [1927], p. 104).

[2] Heylyn, *Cyprianus Anglicus*, p. 161.

[3] Further restrictions were imposed in 1629, after which, as Burton complains, nothing was allowed on Sunday afternoons except catechism by question and answer out of the Book of Common Prayer (*Apology of an Appeale*, sig. A 2ᵛ).

[4] Thomas Fuller, *Church History* (1868), p. 110.

[5] John Rushworth (i. 417) comments as follows on the proclamation of 1626 against writing or preaching about controversial matters in religion: 'The effects of this proclamation how equally soever intended, became the stopping of the puritans mouths, and an uncontrouled liberty to the tongues and pens of the Arminian party.'   [6] *Appello Caesarem*, pp. 6–7, 44.

permitted to support it with vehemence. In the first speech he made in the Long Parliament, Pym included in his enumeration of the principal grievances of the kingdom, 'preaching for absolute monarchy that the king may doe what hee list'.[1]

The puritans were similarly at a disadvantage with regard to the press, for a proclamation was issued in 1624 forbidding the printing or importation of any book dealing with religion, church government, or matters of state, until it had been approved. To reinforce this edict, a new star chamber decree was issued, in July 1637, to the effect that no book or pamphlet should be printed or reprinted unless licensed, that no foreign books should be sold until sanctioned by representatives nominated by the church, and that, if any unauthorized printer should establish a press, he was to be set in the pillory and whipped.

The campaign against puritan critics of the Laudian system was waged bitterly, and, with the exception of the burning of two heretics in 1612, the severest punishment inflicted for ecclesiastical offences was for pamphlets against the religious policy of the Crown. Even so, the extreme sentences passed upon Puritan writers like Leighton, William Prynne, and John Lilburne were unlikely to deter those who were convinced that they were called upon to testify publicly for a great cause. The punishment by mutilation of Prynne, John Bastwick, and Henry Burton, in 1637, only brought forth fervid appeals from the sufferers to the onlookers to stand firm for their religion and liberty, lest they should sink into perpetual slavery. All the sympathies of the crowds that watched were with the victims, and every care was taken to ensure the widest publicity. Prynne addressed himself particularly to the intelligencers[2] standing around, and pious hands described in detail the heroic bearing of the champions of puritanism and recorded the comforting words that passed between them and the spectators. Burton might well boast: 'This day will never be forgotten . . . through these holes (poynting to the pillary) God can bring light to his church.' A woman answered: 'There are many hundreds which by Gods

---

[1] *The Journal of Sir Simonds D'Ewes*, ed. Wallace Notestein (1923), pp. 8–9. It is noteworthy that, during the negotiations at Newcastle after the first civil war, Charles showed more anxiety to control sermons than the militia. 'If the pulpits teach not obedience', he wrote, 'the king will have but small comfort of the militia' (*Charles I in 1646*, ed. John Bruce [1856], p. 79).

[2] The equivalent of the modern newspaper reporters.

assistance would willingly suffer for the cause you suffer for this day.'[1]

Another subject of bitter dispute between Anglican and puritan was the observance of the Lord's day. During the last decade of the sixteenth century there was a marked growth of sabbatarianism. The puritans eagerly supported the attempt to apply the provisions of the Mosaic law to the English Sunday and to suppress the May games, morris dances, and other sports indulged in after service in the countryside.[2] Such an attempt by the Lancashire magistrates, in 1617, caused James to issue a declaration that those who had already attended divine service might engage in certain lawful recreations afterwards. The next year the application of this order was extended from Lancashire to the whole country, and every minister was directed to read from the pulpit the declaration in favour of certain lawful sports, often called the Book of Sports. Nevertheless a renewed puritan attempt to suppress Sunday games—this time in Somersetshire—was responsible for the reissue of the Book of Sports in 1633, which was also to be read in every parish church. The bishop of Bath and Wells provides a clue to the eagerness with which episcopalians welcomed Sunday sports, when he suggests that if people were denied their recreations they would go either into inns and talk, over their ale, of matters of church or state, or else into conventicles.[3] The puritans continued to be extremely indignant at what they regarded as a profanation of the Sabbath. Notwithstanding the Book of Sports, some, in a furious kind of ardour, used to run into the streets, and even dash into private houses, in search of those engaged in their lawful pastimes, scatter the company, and break the instruments, and even the heads, of any musicians they found. Some would not suffer either baked or roast meat to be prepared on the Sabbath, or provender to be carried to a horse, or a pint of wine to be sold. Such scruples were not the monopoly of the middle classes, for we are told that maidservants refused to wash their dishes or clean their kitchens on the Sabbath.[4] Not infrequently

---

[1] *A Briefe Relation* (1638). On Sunday, says Nicholas Bownd, 'We are bound straitly to rest from all the ordinarie workes of our calling' (*Sabbathum Veteris et Novi Testamenti* [1606], Dedication).

[2] *Eng. Hist. Rev.* xxxii. 561-8.

[3] Letter of 5 Nov. 1633, in William Prynne, *Canterburies Doome* (1646), pp. 141-3 (misprinted 151).

[4] Heylyn, *The History of the Sabbath* (1636), ii. 255-7.

a group of zealots assembled and threw down the Maypole.[1] The extreme opponents of the puritans sneered at their adoring the Sabbath 'as an image dropt downe from Jupiter', and often mocked at the alleged perplexity of those who could not tell whether the sin were the greater to bowl or dance on the Sabbath or to commit murder.[2] Nevertheless it is evident that the Book of Sports was a direct defiance of a growing mass of public opinion, and its compulsory reading in church was an unnecessary affront to the puritan conscience.

It is clear, therefore, that king and bishops had their hands full when they tried to enforce the religious unity so dear to them. The means of coercion they used were provided by custom, by legislation, and by the ecclesiastical supremacy of the Crown. According to the Elizabethan Act of Uniformity all persons were bound to attend divine service every Sunday, under penalty of forfeiting twelvepence for each absence; and this regulation was re-enacted early in the reign of James I.[3] In addition there was a church regulation that all parishioners should receive the sacrament three times a year.

If the few presentments, at quarter sessions, of absentees from church services be accepted as adequate evidence, the people of England, during the first half of the seventeenth century, were certainly regular churchgoers. The apparent regularity of attendance, however, may not be proof of anything more than that the bare requirements of the law were satisfied. The fact that around Eastertime there was usually a rush to take the sacrament three times and that the Communion was often neglected during the rest of the year would seem to indicate that compulsory attendance did not produce devout enthusiasm for the church.

Judging by sermons, attendance was slack, and, moreover, the behaviour of the congregation left much to be desired. One preacher complains, for example, that even in times of famine few come to church, and these so carelessly and sleepily that they can scarcely be called present at all.[4] Another churchman deplores that bad weather or the least indisposition, which would never prevent men from attending to their own pleasures, were

---

[1] *Hertfordshire County Records*, v (1928), 249.

[2] Pocklington, *Sunday No Sabbath*, p. 20.

[3] *Statutes of the Realm*, iv (1819), pt. 2, p. 1075.

[4] George Abbot [later archbishop of Canterbury], *An Exposition upon the Prophet Jonah* (1600), p. 420.

thought sufficient reasons for staying away from church. The market, he said, was always better attended than God's church.[1] Even those who did attend were said to have spent their time in gazing about to see what others did and who had the newest fashion.[2] No doubt these are rather conventional complaints, but they suggest, at least, that Anglican services engendered no great zeal.

The discipline of the church was maintained by both spiritual and temporal means. The former consisted of penance or excommunication. By an Elizabethan statute,[3] excommunication might be pronounced against those guilty of heresy, of refusal to have a child baptized, to receive communion, or to attend church, or of incontinency, usury, simony, perjury in ecclesiastical courts, and idolatry. The complaint was made in the Millenary Petition that excommunications were issued for trivial offences. These sentences were the more serious inasmuch as the accused, if he failed to make his submission within forty days after being excommunicated, was liable to imprisonment.[4]

The courts for ecclesiastical causes were archidiaconal, diocesan, and provincial, with a court of delegates to which appeals might be made. The court of high commission was easily the most important of all the ecclesiastical tribunals and bore much the same relation to the church as the court of star chamber did to the state. As the result of the attempts of Coke and other common-law lawyers to limit the jurisdiction of this prerogative court by issuing prohibitions, new letters patent were issued in 1611, whereby the high commission was to inquire concerning all matters of heresy and schism, recusancy, writings or speeches against the Book of Common Prayer or any official of the established church, any crime done on holy ground, or interruption of divine service, and all sexual offences and all misdemeanours whatsoever committed by any cleric.

These vast powers, which could be exercised in an inquisitorial fashion, gave the greatest umbrage to the legal profession at the time, and have been condemned by posterity. Recent investigations, however, have shown that only 5 per cent. of the cases seem to have been initiated by the commissioners them-

---

[1] Percy H. Osmond, *A Life of John Cosin* (1913), pp. 21-22.
[2] Robert Shelford, *Five Discourses* (1635), p. 52.
[3] 5 Eliz., c. 23.
[4] Felix Makower, *Constitutional History of the Church of England* (1895), p. 452.

selves, and the rest by individuals who, presumably, had confidence in the fairness and legality of the court. The majority of cases that came before it were, in numerical order, suits for alimony and divorce, then adultery and other moral offences, and thirdly simony, drunkenness, and other sins of the clergy.[1]

However there is no doubt that the court of high commission was intensely disliked. Since the number of ministers deprived for puritanism is so small as to be almost negligible,[2] the court's unpopularity must be explained on other grounds. Certainly its abolition, together with that of the coercive powers of ecclesiastical courts in general, was voted in 1641 without any opposition, after many speeches had been previously made condemning it.[3] Presumably animosity arose from the feeling that the existence and procedure of the court were alike contrary to the principles of English law. It may be, too, that many shared the sentiments Burton expressed in 1636, that it was manifestly unfair that bishops and other ecclesiastics, when charged with innovations, should sit as judges upon their accusers. In other words, the court first aroused keen resentment when the judges were also parties to suits.[4]

It is clear that by 1640 the puritans were wholly estranged from the church. Whereas in 1603 they had asked only for the modification of, or permission to omit, certain ceremonies acknowledged by the heads of the church to be 'things indifferent', forty years later they clamoured for the abolition of episcopacy. The propaganda they directed against the Laudian bishops was often unfair, inasmuch as it either treated Arminianism and popery as synonymous terms or implied that the one inevitably led to the other. Much of its success was due to the national prejudice against Roman catholicism, and to fervid appeals to the people to stand firm in the religion for which the Marian martyrs had died. Nevertheless it is probable that the Anglican leaders were mainly to blame for their own downfall, partly because of the disastrous effects of trying to impose a liturgy on Scotland and partly because they sought to buttress the church by an alliance with the Crown, instead of depending on the inherent strength of Anglicanism. They deliberately

---

[1] R. G. Usher, *Rise and Fall of the High Commission* (1913), pp. 256–7, 323–4.

[2] See Gardiner, x, App. ii.

[3] It is remarkable that ecclesiastical courts supply the first head of Pym's first speech to the Long Parliament (*D'Ewes Journal*, p. 8).

[4] *Apology of an Appeale*, p. 6.

accepted, on behalf of the church, a theory of monarchy that rapidly grew out of date, and inculcated passive obedience upon a generation eager for constitutional reforms of far-reaching character. They therefore incurred all the unpopularity attendant upon Stuart methods of government, and paid the penalty when they became involved on the losing side in the civil war.

IV

POLITICAL AND CONSTITUTIONAL
HISTORY, 1629-40

WHEN Charles I dismissed his parliament in 1629 he hoped never to have to summon another. Observers noticed that, on his return from Westminster after the dissolution, he was in high spirits, as if he had freed himself from the yoke.[1] He was now at liberty to practise that form of government which commended itself to him. In his own eyes he was the guardian of the church and constitution against iconoclasts and anarchists. He declared that he was going to maintain the established doctrine of the church of England, as well as the just rights and liberties of his subjects;[2] and he meant what he said. The difficulty was that he was to be the sole judge of true doctrine and just rights. If the very elasticity of the Reformation settlement permitted the adoption of Arminianism as the true doctrine, then the suppression of puritanism was inevitable. Charles held strongly, if unconsciously, the theory that was embodied in such legislation as the Corporation Act after the Restoration—that only a devoted adherent to the national church could be a loyal citizen. At court nonconformity and sedition were synonymous terms, and puritans were time-servers who stayed in the church only to betray it or revolutionaries who made zeal for religion the cloak for their nefarious designs. Absolute unity of church and state was the ideal that Charles and Laud, his favourite ecclesiastic, set before them. They regarded all their opponents as both morally and politically dangerous—guilty of blasphemy and disaffection alike. They intended that disputes about doctrine or ritual should be settled by the clergy in convocation—subject to the royal leave— and the layman was to accept their decisions without question.

Just as the ordinary citizen had no voice in determining the discipline of the church, so the intermission of parliament deprived him of any share in shaping the law of the land. His only concern with the law was to obey it. True, Charles had promised to observe it, but events were to prove that he meant

[1] *State Papers, Venetian, 1628–1629*, p. 589.
[2] Gardiner, *Constitutional Documents*, pp. 97–98.

no more than that he would regard as legal whatever the judges so declared; and he was wont to make up his mind what the law was and then dismiss judges who disagreed with him and appoint others more subservient. As the great lawyer John Selden remarked: 'Now the judges they interprett the law, & what judges cann be made to doe wee all knowe.'[1] Consequently legal decisions soon came to have little weight in the country at large, and the judges, like the bishops, were popularly regarded as the willing instruments of despotism. This was the more serious because the whole basis of the royal revenue rested, or came to rest, on the law courts and not on parliament.

During most of the years 1629 to 1640 the success or failure of the attempt to dispense with parliament seemed to depend on the treasury. Provided that the king was content to cut his coat according to his cloth, he might be able to avoid the odious necessity of summoning the estates. He realized this himself, and abandoned the costly foreign policy which had yielded little except debts and humiliations. By making peace with France and Spain he stopped the main drains on the exchequer. Even so the situation did not look very promising in 1629, for the royal debts were over £1,000,000, and there was general resistance to the payment of tonnage and poundage. Nevertheless it was not financial stringency but the Scottish wars that ultimately brought to an end eleven years of unparliamentary government.

Perhaps the task before the lord high treasurer, Richard Weston (created earl of Portland in 1633), would have been hopeless if repayment of the debt had been essential. Actually much of it was quietly ignored and little of it discharged in cash. A grant of crown lands, a pension, the proceeds of fines, the reversion of an office, a share in a monopoly—these and other sops gave debtors some compensation if not complete satisfaction.[2] However, it is nearly certain that Weston could not have succeeded in making both ends meet had he not pared down the cost of the royal household and other charges on the revenue. But the greatest economy occurred after his disgrace in 1635, when ship money practically saved the exchequer the entire cost of the navy.

---

[1] *Table Talk*, p. 66. Cf. Holdsworth, *History of English Law*, v. 351-2.
[2] According to a document printed by Gardiner (x. 223), the king's debts on 30 July 1635 were £1,173,000.

At the outset Weston had to overcome opposition to the payment of tonnage and poundage. By abstaining from trade some merchants offered a passive resistance to these taxes, but this course could hardly be prolonged indefinitely, when the conclusion of peace with Spain opened lucrative markets. One trader after another yielded and paid his duties. Apart from the pertinacious Chambers, henceforth the king met with no further resistance in this direction, even when some additions were made to the Book of Rates. Moreover the large increase of trade during this decade meant an expanding revenue from customs, although the system in vogue of farming them prevented the Crown from enjoying the full benefit.

The royal revenue averaged about £600,000 for the five years ending 1635, leaving an annual deficit of not more than £20,000. Thus, if the debt could be ignored, the national budget was already nearly balanced, and Charles was likely to be free from all anxiety on the side of finance, provided that he could avoid any extraordinary expenditures. The additional sources discovered to augment the royal revenue usually took the form of the revival of old exactions rather than the invention of brand-new ones. Among the earliest and most profitable was the fine imposed upon all owning land worth forty pounds a year, who had neglected to be knighted. Here there was no question of legality, for that was indisputable, but the energetic enforcement of high rates for composition gave great umbrage to the landed classes. Much more questionable was the attempt to restore the forest laws. By threats and intimidation juries were induced to inflict large fines for obsolete offences and to pronounce that the forest law held good over large tracts where it had long been in desuetude. Thus the earl of Salisbury was fined £20,000, and Rockingham Forest was enlarged from six to sixty miles. The antiquary D'Ewes notes that the county of Essex, with the exception of a single hundred, was found to be forest, although the inhabitants had lived quietly for four hundred years free from forest laws.[1] Another financial expedient that hurt the larger landowners was the enforcement of the statutes against inclosures. One of Strafford's correspondents notes that in 1635 money to compound for depopulations was coming in apace, the guilty being fined various sums rang-

[1] *D'Ewes Autobiography*, ii. 136–7; *Victoria County History: Essex*, ii (1907), 227–8.

ing up to £4,000, with the additional penalty of restoring many farms that had been demolished.[1]

The exactions of the court of wards became more vexatious than ever, with the result, says Clarendon,[2] that all the rich families of England were exceedingly incensed against the Crown, because they felt that what the law had intended for their protection and preservation was now applied to their destruction.

The most productive of all these financial expedients was ship money. This was no new levy, so far as the coast-towns were concerned, for their obligation to provide ships for the navy was acknowledged. The first writ of ship money, in 1634, was strictly in accordance with precedent. Thus the one addressed to the City of London demanded the delivery at Portsmouth of a number of ships of specified tonnage and equipment, on the ground that pirates were endangering commerce.[3] It is noteworthy that the Londoners were alone in petitioning against this impost. The next year writs were again issued, but this time they were directed to the inland counties as well as to the ports. In the following year a third series of writs called on all to contribute. By then it was clear that ship money was likely to be transformed into a permanent source of revenue, and signs that it would be resisted were discernible. Charles therefore asked the judges whether he might command his subjects to furnish such a number of ships as he should think fit for the defence of the kingdom in time of danger, and they gave an affirmative answer.[4] Their opinion was published, in the hope of deterring men from appealing to the law-courts against the legality of ship money. Nevertheless the persistence of John Hampden resulted in a test case. Its importance was universally recognized. As one of the judges said, 'This is one of the greatest cases that ever came in judgment before the judges of the law.'[5] By the narrowest possible margin the decision went against Hampden, but the grounds on which the majority of the judges based their verdict were more alarming to constitutionalists than the decision itself. In particular the judgement of Sir Robert Berkeley was significant for its support of the prerogative. The law, he said, is an old and trusted servant of the king's and the instrument or means which he uses to govern his people

---

[1] *Strafforde's Letters*, i. 335, 491.   [2] *Rebellion*, ii. 102.
[3] *State Trials*, iii. 830-2; Gardiner, *Constitutional Documents*, pp. 105-8.
[4] *State Trials*, iii. 1264-5.   [5] Ibid., p. 1078.

by. 'I never read nor heard, that lex was rex; but it is common and most true, that rex is lex, for he is "lex loquens", a living, a speaking, an acting law.'[1] For the rest, it was decided that in times of danger the king had a right to charge his subjects with the defence of the kingdom and that he was the sole judge of the existence and gravity of danger.[2]

Contemporaries bewailed and condemned this decision, in no uncertain terms, as contrary to law; and henceforth the collection of ship money became increasingly difficult.[3] Among the main objections were: that the judges, by upholding ship money, had in reality given the king the legal right to exact as much and as often as he pleased;[4] that the tax was unfairly assessed, so that farmers paid more than large landowners, and the poor met the demands on them only by selling their bedding;[5] and that the fleet thus maintained was employed to convoy Spanish goods to Flanders while English shipping was left exposed to pirates.[6]

The legality or illegality of ship money is incapable of proof, but its political inexpediency is unquestionable. Charles might claim with every justification that all the money thus collected was spent on the fleet,[7] and he probably hoped that the assertion of the sovereignty of the Narrow Seas against the Dutch would reconcile men to this impost.[8] He may have expected that, as taxes were certainly light in proportion to the wealth of the country, their dubious origin would excite little opposition; and royalist writers in after days looked back upon this decade as a golden age, when peace and plenty abounded.[9] These fond hopes were doomed to disappointment, for puritan England did not live by bread alone, and no material prosperity could reconcile her to a pro-Spanish foreign policy, to an Arminian system of church government, and to personal rule in which parliament had no share. Open opposition was rare, but

[1] Ibid., p. 1098. [2] Ibid., pp. 1105, 1243.

[3] Of the amounts demanded by the writs of 1634, 1635, 1636, 1637, 1638, and 1639, the following approximate percentages could not be collected: 1, 2½, 3½, 9, 20, 80. See Miss M. D. Gordon, in *Trans. Royal Hist. Soc.*, 1910, pp. 143–4, 154.

[4] Clarendon (i. 148) is in agreement with Prynne (*An Humble Remonstrance against the Tax of Ship-Money* [1643], p. 5). Cf. *D'Ewes Autobiography*, ii. 129–32.

[5] Prynne, p. 15. Cf. Gordon, p. 148.

[6] Prynne, p. 17.

[7] The value of the argument is small, however, because in normal times the fleet was a regular charge upon the exchequer.

[8] See below, p. 216.

[9] Clarendon, i. 163; Sir Philip Warwick, *Memoirs of the Reign of King Charles I* (1813), p. 63.

disaffection was rife; and the ensuing troubles with Scotland were to prove that, although Englishmen in general were not prepared to start a rebellion, most of them would not stir a finger against their ancient enemies so long as they appeared as champions of protestantism and opponents of Thorough.

Although at first sight it might appear that the movement in Scotland which culminated in the bishops' wars was of the nature of a sudden explosion, in reality the causes of the revolt were deep-seated and of long standing. On the surface it might have seemed as if Charles I would encounter none of the difficulties that beset his father's path in Scotland. James, both before and after his accession to the English throne, had been bent upon shackling presbyterianism, and succeeded in establishing bishops and enforcing the 'Five Articles of Perth'.[1] On the whole he had prevailed, because he had skilfully, if unscrupulously, divided the nation and left the ministers without their former allies of the Reformation struggles, the nobles. His son, however, totally failed to perceive that only by playing upon the antagonism of the nobility to the ministers' persistent intrusion into private affairs had it been possible to curb presbyterianism. He at once incensed the nobility by the famous Act of Revocation (1625), which re-annexed all the church and crown lands that had been alienated since 1542. Between that year and 1625 there had been so many confiscations of church lands, and forfeitures and alienations of baronial estates, that few Scottish families of substance were unaffected by this new act. With the question of land was bound up that of tithes. During the confusion of the Reformation they had been seized with the same rapacity as other forms of church property. The new owners extorted their dues with a business-like relentlessness that was in drastic contrast with the former leniency of the church. Charles redressed the grievances of the tithe-payers and arranged a compromise with the owners of alienated lands.

Ultimately this thorough-going land-revolution produced real benefits, inasmuch as it made possible adequate remuneration for the ministers of the national church. Probably, too, the farmer profited by the various restrictions placed upon the exaction of tithes. The immediate result, however, was that the alliance between Crown and nobility that had enabled James I

---

[1] Passed by the general assembly in 1618. The most obnoxious to a presbyterian prescribed kneeling to receive the communion.

to get the better of general assemblies was shattered at a stroke. The official account[1] of the first bishops' war fully acknowledges the importance of the land question in making the nobility bitterly hostile to the Crown.

The discontent remained concealed for the moment, but Charles's visit in 1633 to the land of his birth did nothing to relieve it. The coronation ceremony at the royal palace of Holyrood, and the ritual used by Laud and other English divines at church services elsewhere, did much to revive those twin sentiments which had produced the Scottish Reformation—hatred of foreigners and hatred of popery.

The one thing lacking to convert stealthy discontent into open opposition was soon forthcoming. Shortly after Charles returned to England, he decided that the great need of Scotland was a Book of Common Prayer, together with canons enjoining uniformity of service. This was no new project, for a prayer book had been prepared as early as 1619, but James I, observing the unpopularity of the Articles of Perth, wisely avoided the risk of arousing opposition through imposing additional religious innovation. Charles was less prudent, and insisted that a prayer book be forced upon Scotland, but the attempt in 1637 to read services from the prayer book in St. Giles's, Edinburgh, caused a riot. The 'she-zealot' who called out, 'The mass is entered amongst us!' expressed the opinion of nine-tenths of the Scots. To the suspicion of popery was added the sure knowledge that the hated book largely emanated from England. Patriotism and protestantism therefore combined in resistance.

Soon royal authority ceased to exist in Scotland. Baillie, a moderate presbyterian, was startled at the popular fury:

What shall be the event, God knows: there was in our land ever such ane appearance of a sturr; the whole people thinks poperie at the doores; the scandalous pamphlets which comes daily new from England, adde oyl to this flame; no man may speak any thing in publick for the king's part, except he would have himself marked for a sacrifice to be killed one day. I think our people possessed with a bloody devill, farr above any thing that ever I could have imagined, though the masse in Latine had been presented. The ministers who has the command of their mind, does disavow their unchristian humour, but are noways so zealous against the devill of their furie, as they are against the seduceing spirit of the bishops.[2]

[1] *A Large Declaration* [mainly written by Walter Balcanquhall] (1639).
[2] *Letters and Journals of Robert Baillie*, ed. David Laing (1841), i. 23.

It is reported that when Charles heard of these happenings his first remark was, 'I mean to be obeyed'.[1] His refusal to conciliate the Scots induced them to appoint a permanent body of commissioners, far more truly representative of Scotland than ever her parliament had been; and henceforth this body, together with a select committee—often called 'The Tables'—was the real ruler of Scotland.

Then came the covenant—one of the most important measures of the seventeenth century and a landmark in English as well as Scottish history. It prevented any lasting compromise between Charles and Scotland and became a bone of contention between the Scots and the English and even between England's parliament and army. For fifty years it was the source of the bitterest sectarian strife and the touchstone of political adherence.

The subscribers to the covenant swore to resist to the death the recent innovations, which were declared to be unwarranted by the word of God, contrary to the Reformation and to acts of parliament, and tending to the re-establishment of popery and tyranny. They disclaimed the intention of attempting anything that might turn to the dishonour of God or to the diminution of the king's greatness. On the contrary they promised to uphold their sovereign, his person and authority, in defence of the true religion and the liberties and laws of the kingdom. Time was to prove how stoutly they sought to redeem this pledge. Unfortunately it was also to prove the impossibility of sustaining, at the same time, both the king's authority and the presbyterian form of government. Loyalty to church and loyalty to king proved incompatible, and most often the former prevailed over the latter.

Popular subscription to the covenant was almost unanimous. The significance of this new unity of all classes in Scotland was not lost upon the king's advisers there, and they at once urged that the service book should be abandoned. Charles, however, refused to listen, and bitterly complained that so long as the covenant existed he had no more power than the doge of Venice.[2]

Nevertheless he gave way for the moment, and a general assembly was summoned to meet in November and a parliament in the following May. The mode of election to the former, however, at once raised a fundamental issue, for it involved, not

---

[1] Gardiner, viii. 321.   [2] G. Burnet, *Lives of the Hamiltons* (1852), p. 59.

only the representation of each presbytery by a lay leader as well as by three ministers, but also the membership of laymen in the constituent body electing representative ministers. This participation by non-clerical elements was anathema to Charles and Laud.

It was fitting that the responsibility of the bishops to answer to this assembly for their misdeeds should have been the cause of the breach between Charles and his Scottish subjects. 'If the bishops', said a Scottish peer, 'decline the judgment of the national assembly, I know not a competent judgment seat for them but the King of Heaven.' 'I stand to the king's prerogatives', replied the marquis of Hamilton, the royal commissioner, 'as supreme judge over all causes civil and ecclesiastical.' Thereupon he declared the assembly dissolved; but it continued to sit. It abolished the service book, the canons, and the Articles of Perth, together with episcopacy itself. It re-established the presbyterian form of government and declared that ministers who were not sound presbyterians had forfeited their livings. War was inevitable. To Charles and his advisers in London the doctrine summed up in the trite phrase, 'No bishop, no king', was fundamental. The bishops had become the great prop of the Stuart monarchy: kingship by divine right could not exist without them. From this point of view Charles was perfectly right in accusing the Scots of a direct attack on his regal authority. On their side they were equally convinced that the general assembly was the ordinary remedy prescribed by divine authority for the redress of their grievances. Unlike Charles their leaders could count on the whole-hearted support of most of the people. The official apologist for Charles's policy in Scotland notes that the common people were always cursing popery and bishops;[1] it was clear that they had come to believe that these two were one and the same thing.

Both parties now began to prepare for military operations. On 9 May 1639 Alexander Leslie, later earl of Leven, a veteran of the Thirty Years War, was appointed by the parliament general of all the Scotch forces. He succeeded in enlisting under his banner a considerable number of officers and men who had served with him in the Swedish armies.[2] With the nucleus of a

---

[1] *Large Declaration*, pp. 86, 105, 117.
[2] The commission is printed in C. S. Terry, *The Life and Campaigns of Alexander Leslie*, pp. 54–56.

military force thus ready at hand, it is not surprising to read, 'We are busy preaching, praying, and drilling.'

Matters did not go so smoothly for Charles. Without the money to pay a regular force, he had of necessity to call upon the nobility to serve at their own expense, and to summon the train-bands (i.e. militia). Probably the presence of the nobles did more harm than good, for most of them were disaffected—some, like Lords Brooke and Saye and Sele, because they were puritans; others for personal reasons or on account of resentment at the preferences Charles had shown for Laud and his kind over natural-born counsellors. The train-bands, coming mainly from the northern counties, where animosity to Scotland was a tradition, probably would have been willing enough to fight if they had been well armed, drilled, and led. But discipline is impossible in a force irregularly paid, and there was a lack of competent officers to whip the raw militia into shape. Before the summer was over it was evident that the king could not afford to risk a battle, and consequently the first bishops' war ended without the striking of a blow. It was not difficult to come to terms. By the treaty of Berwick (18 June) the Scots were to disband their army, and Charles, on his side, gave assurance that all ecclesiastical matters should be determined by the general assembly and civil matters by the parliament.[1]

Events now moved rapidly in Scotland. The assembly, as a matter of course, swept away episcopacy and the service book, and enacted that every Scottish subject should subscribe to the covenant. Parliament proved that it, too, was determined to cut loose from its servile past by reconstructing the lords of the articles—a committee of almost absolute authority. Hitherto the mode of election of this committee had given the Crown complete control over procedure, but now each estate could choose its own lords of the articles. This in itself marked a revolution as important in politics as the covenant was in religion, for the emancipation of the Scots estates from royal control ultimately was a direct cause of the Union.

A more immediate result was the formation of the parties that struggled for ascendancy in Scotland during the first civil war. Whereas Argyll[2] realized that the growing power of the middle class must be recognized by their representation in the

---

[1] Rushworth, iii. 943-4.
[2] Archibald Campbell, eighth earl and first marquis of Argyll.

lords of the articles and that henceforth they would have the same weight in politics as in religion, Montrose,[1] hitherto known only as the covenanter who had suppressed the incipient royalism of the Gordons, hated to see the authority of the nobles undermined by this new class and was anxious to effect a reconciliation between the nobles and the king. He would have been content with such a situation as existed under James VI before the establishment of episcopacy or the Articles of Perth, when the alliance of king and nobles kept presbyterianism within due bounds.

Charles viewed the proceedings of the Scottish parliament with the utmost dislike. Before the year was out he made up his mind that it was impossible for him permanently to acquiesce in the overthrow of his authority in Scotland, and he began to cast round for the means of waging war again. For some time he had largely entrusted the management of Scottish affairs to a body of privy councillors, known either as the Scottish Committee or the Committee of Eight (the number of its members). Its debates furnish some of the most important illustrations of the system of government that commended itself at this time to the royal advisers. On this occasion it was Strafford, supported by Laud and Hamilton, who successfully argued for calling a parliament. The secretary of state, Windebank, sums up the motives that influenced the councillors:

But the lords being desirous that the king and his people should meet if it were possible, in the ancient and ordinary way of parliament, rather than any other, were of opinion his Majesty should make trial of that once more, that so he might leave his people without excuse, and have wherewithal to justify himself to God and the world, that in his own inclination he desired the old way; but that if his people should not cheerfully according to their duties meet him in that, especially in this exigent, when his kingdoms and person are in apparent danger, the world might see he is forced contrary to his own inclination to use extraordinary means, rather than by the peevishness of some few factious spirits to suffer his state and government to be lost.[2]

To raise money by parliamentary authority would take time. Meanwhile the councillors agreed to make a loan to the king, which eventually amounted to about £230,000, a sum large

---

[1] James Graham, fifth earl and first marquis of Montrose.
[2] *Clarendon State Papers*, ii (1773), 81.

enough to permit the first steps towards raising an army. This time the train-bands south of the Humber were to be called upon for service, inasmuch as those north of the river had borne the burden of the previous war. But the formation of this military force was irretrievably damaged by the failure of the Short Parliament to vote any supplies at all.

It is unfortunate that details of the elections to this parliament are almost completely lacking. Apparently, although Clarendon[1] stated that the parliament was 'most welcome to the whole kingdom', its election does not seem to have caused any great excitement, perhaps because people were too surprised at so great a novelty to have room for other emotions.[2] Most of the old leaders from 1628-9 were re-elected, but less than one-fourth of the members in 1640 had sat in the earlier body.[3]

On the opening day Finch, the new lord keeper, explained the king's wishes. He asked members to lay aside all other debates and to pass a bill granting as many subsidies as they thought fit. When this had been done, the king would give time for the discussion of petitions for the good of the commonwealth. There was but one reference made to the grievances that must have been in the minds of his hearers—namely, tonnage and poundage were declared only to have been taken *de facto*. Against this procedure a vigorous protest was made by Pym, who now became the undisputed leader of the group opposed to Charles I. In a famous utterance, he catalogued with studious moderation the grievances of the land. He began by enumerating the attacks on the members and privileges of parliament, followed this up with the religious innovations, and concluded with what he called 'grievances against the propriety of our goods'. On such an occasion Pym was at his best. Probably no parliamentarian could have marshalled the unpopular acts of the last fifteen years so calmly yet so comprehensively. As a negative programme, Pym's statement leaves nothing to be desired. Generally speaking, he anticipated the work of the first nine months of the Long Parliament. On the other hand there is little in the speech to show that Pym realized that he was virtually proposing a revolution. It is true, as Gardiner points out, that Pym

---

[1] *Rebellion*, ii. 62.

[2] Thomas May, *History of the Long Parliament* (1854), p. 54.

[3] 'Much the greatest part having never before sat in parliament' (Clarendon, ii. 68).

said that 'the parliament is that to the commonwealth which the soul is to the body'.[1] But he did not explain how this political ideal was to be attained. Nevertheless, whatever the limitations of the speech, quite clearly it was admirably suited to the occasion. Within the house it was greeted with loud cries of 'A good oration!',[2] and abbreviated copies of it were eagerly read throughout the kingdom.[3]

As parliament devoted the next few days to discussing breaches of privilege and to the examination, by a committee for grievances, of ship money, the king demanded an immediate grant of supplies, promising that once funds were voted he would be willing to listen to whatever they should propound in order to secure their liberties.[4] The commons remained determined that their grievances should have priority over the king's needs, for, as a member said, 'till the liberties of the house and the kingdom were cleared they knew not whether they had anything to give or no'.[5] Charles induced the lords to intervene on his side, but even then, with the shadow of dissolution looming over them, the commons disdained the suggestion that twelve subsidies should be granted on condition that ship money should be no longer collected. Moreover 7 May had been fixed for a debate on the Scottish question, and it is likely that a petition against the war would have been presented. The king, having hastily summoned his council and heard from Vane that there was no hope that the commons would give one penny, dissolved parliament on 5 May. The dissolution was a serious political blunder, and was immediately so recognized by the opponents of the court. They rejoiced at the king's hasty act, for they were convinced 'that this parliament would never have done what was necessary to be done'. Certainly a conciliatory policy would have been far more likely to succeed now than six months later. In May 1640 timely concessions would probably soon have produced a reaction in the royal favour. To begin with, the king would have found a substantial minority in the parliament.[6] Moreover, during the Long Parliament the king's concessions

---

[1] Cf. Rushworth, iii. 1132, and Gardiner, ix. 102.
[2] Ibid. x. 101.   [3] May, p. 60.
[4] Rushworth, iii. 1137. Cf. Gardiner, ix. 107–8.   [5] Ibid. ix. 108.
[6] In the division whether the commons would consent to a second conference with the lords, 148 voted for the affirmative and 257 for the negative. If Rushworth is correct in his remark that this division 'fully discovered the temper' of the house, it is clear that the king had already many supporters.

were so obviously extorted by the indirect pressure of the Scottish army and were so clearly against his inclination that they did him little good, whereas probably a tenth of the concessions made later would have sufficed in the spring of 1640.

Convocation had met at the same time as the Short Parliament, but to the surprise of all men, including Laud, the king ordered it to continue sitting after the dissolution of the latter body. A grant of £20,000 a year for six years was made under the name of a benevolence or free contribution. The most important work, however, was the promulgation of seventeen new canons. There can be little doubt that these canons were intended to contribute to the support of the monarchy and to define what should be the attitude of all loyal subjects. They are in their way as much a manifestation of Thorough as the 'Grand Remonstrance' was to be of the opposition to that policy. On this account they deserve the closest analysis.

The first, concerning the regal power, is easily the most important. Every clergyman was to read aloud at morning prayer, once every quarter, the following definition:

The most high and sacred order of kings is of divine right, being the ordinance of God himself, founded in the prime laws of nature, and clearly established by express texts both of the Old and New Testaments. A supreme power is given to this most excellent order by God himself in the Scriptures, which is, that kings should rule and command in their several dominions all persons of what rank or estate soever, . . . For subjects to bear arms against their kings, offensive or defensive, upon any pretence whatsoever, is at least to resist the powers which are ordained of God; and . . . they shall receive to themselves damnation.

Furthermore all clerics were to teach their congregations to obey, honour, and serve the king. For any minister to maintain an argument contrary to these explanations of regal power was to incur excommunication and suspension or, in case of obstinacy, deprivation of all spiritual promotions.

Another article (XV) established an oath for the prevention of all innovations in doctrine and government—commonly known as the 'etcetera oath'. The name arose from the oath to be imposed on all bachelors and doctors of divinity, law, or medicine, and all schoolmasters, as well as all dignitaries of the church, not to alter its government by 'archbishops, bishops, deans, and archdeacons, etc.', as it stands 'now established'.

The seventh article declared that, although the position of the communion table at the east end of the chancel was 'in its own nature indifferent', yet it was now directed that for the sake of decency and order it should be at the east and railed off. Moreover members of the congregation were commanded to observe reverence and obeisance on entering and leaving all churches.[1]

Taken as a whole, these canons represent the zenith of Laudian Arminianism. Virtually every clause was offensive to puritans, and not a few to ordinary protestants. The insistence upon the railed-in altar at the east end and bowing towards the east on entering and leaving the church seemed, to many, outward and visible signs of a drift Romeward. The restriction on preaching, and the prescription of certain subjects for sermons, were alike offensive to puritans and were the more important inasmuch as the pulpit was the great organ of public opinion at this time. Finally the royal 'explications' gave form and definition to a theory of monarchy which the growth of new political forces was rendering obsolete and which was recognized by many as already obsolete. Just at a time when episcopacy had provoked an unsuccessful war with the Scots, these canons were concerned to show the inseparable interdependence of monarchy and episcopacy. Accordingly, henceforth an attack on Laudism could hardly fail to be also an attack on the divine right of kings.

After the dissolution of the Short Parliament there recurred the old problem of finding money elsewhere. The Scottish Committee met on 5 May 1640, and the record of its debate will repay careful inspection. Strafford began by laying it down as a maxim that the Scots must be reduced by force. To provide the necessary funds, the City of London was to be called upon immediately to lend a hundred thousand pounds, and ship money was to be collected with vigour. He was whole-heartedly in favour of an offensive war, which would end the Scotch resistance in a few months. When Northumberland[2] queried what was to be done if money were not after all forthcoming, Strafford replied:

Goe on with a vigorous warr, as you first designed; loose and

[1] Edward Cardwell, *Synodalia* (1842), i. 380–415.

[2] Algernon Percy, tenth earl. He wrote the same day to Conway: 'We are going upon a conquest with such a power that nothing in that kingdom will be able to resist us' (*Notes of the Treaty of Ripon* [1869], p. viii).

obsolved (*sic*) from all rules of government, beinge reduced to ex-
treame necessitie, everythinge is to bee done that power might admitt,
and that you are to doe. They refuseinge, you are acquitted towards
God and man, you have an army in Ireland, you may imploy here to
reduce this kingdome. Confident as anythinge under heaven Scotland shall not hold out five monthes. One sumer well imployed will
doe it. Venter all I had, I would carry it or loose it.

This line of argument won the vigorous approval of Laud:

Tried all waies, and refused alwayes; by the lawe of God you
should have subsistance, and ought to have it, and lawfull to take it.[1]

In practice, however, it did not prove so easy to raise money
by any method. The attempt to exact 'coat and conduct' money
for the train-bands met with much resistance, and the produce
of ship money was also small. The City refused to lend and
treated threats of distraint of their property with derision.
Charles thought of device after device to fill his empty coffers.
The debasement of the coinage was ordered, but countermanded
in view of the threat of merchants to increase the price of their
goods to correspond. Loans were successively begged in vain
from the kings of Spain and France and the pope.

Under these conditions it is not surprising that Charles failed
ignominiously to raise an army equal to looking the Scots in
the face. Desertion was frequent, and not even the execution of
martial law sufficed to keep men to their colours. Mutinous out-
breaks of the train-bands assumed the form of demonstrations
against the church policy associated with Laud's name. Com-
munion-rails, in particular, incurred the hostility of the militia
of the southern counties and furnished material for several
bonfires. The result was that the Scottish army crossed the
Tweed at Coldstream unopposed. The cannonade at Newburn
(on the Tyne) was sufficient to make many under the king's
standard throw down their arms and run. Strafford paints the
situation vividly:

The army altogether necessitous and unprovided of all necessaries.
That part which I bring now with me from Durham, the worst I
ever saw. Our horse all cowardly; the country from Berwick to York
in the power of the Scots; an universal affright in all; a general disaffection to the king's service, none sensible of his dishonour.[2]

There seemed only one remedy—a parliament—but Charles

---

[1] *Hist. MSS. Com., Third Report* (1872), p. 3.   [2] Gardiner, ix. 195.

was extremely averse. Not so his subjects. During August the leaders of the opposition—Essex, Warwick, Bedford, Saye and Sele, and Brooke among the peers, and Pym and Hampden among the commons—were in close conference. The result was the 'petition of the peers' (28 August), in which the subscribers enumerated various evils, under seven headings, from which they believed the realm to be suffering, and named one remedy —a parliament—to cure them all.[1]

Charles, not yet convinced, adopted instead the suggestion that a great council of peers should be summoned. This council performed notable service in negotiating a treaty with the Scots at Ripon, even though the terms were very like a royal surrender. The Scots were to remain in possession of Northumberland and Durham and to receive £850 a day until matters in dispute were finally settled, and it was plainly implied that parliamentary assent was necessary for final settlement. At length the king gave way. The Scots had beaten him, but their triumph evoked little resentment in England. The news of the royal defeat at Newburn had been celebrated in London as if it had been a national triumph. The Scots themselves had carried on propaganda to prove that their grievances were also England's and that the preservation or ruin of religion and liberty in the one kingdom would immediately affect the other. 'We must now stand or fall together. . . . We are Brethren.'[2] They had conciliated the citizens of London by promising them that the sea-borne coal trade should not be interfered with by their occupation of Newcastle. Robert Baillie, when he first came to London, in November 1640, found that all men professed that, under God, they owed their religion, liberties, and parliament to the Scottish army.[3]

The elections to the Long Parliament created far more excitement than those to the Short Parliament, and are more fully described. Generally speaking, the electors voted for the men who had represented them in the earlier body. Apparently about 60 per cent. of those elected had sat in the previous spring. There was an obvious intention not to accept courtiers. Of twelve lawyers named by the king as fit to be provided with seats only three were actually chosen. Sir Edward Osborne was rejected by the city of York because he had Strafford's

---

[1] *State Papers, Domestic, 1640*, pp. 639-40.
[2] *Notes of the Treaty of Ripon*, App. i.   [3] *Baillie Letters and Journals*, i. 275.

recommendation, but peers used their influence successfully in a number of instances. Contests were many and keenly fought. Frequently four, and sometimes five, candidates competed for two seats, and in some cases at least presents of beer and tobacco were used to influence voters. There seems to have been some electioneering, in the modern sense: Anthony Wood says that Pym 'rode about the country to promote the elections of the puritanical brethren to serve in parliament'. The results were almost uniformly unfavourable to the court, except in Wales, Somerset, and some northern counties.

The richest and most populous part of the country (with the exception of Somerset) thus declared against the king. . . . It was the heart of England, in wealth, population, and progressive quality, that appealed, through its chosen representatives, against past oppressions and apprehensions for the future.[1]

[1] R. N. Kershaw, in *Eng. Hist. Rev.* xxxviii. 508.

V

POLITICAL AND CONSTITUTIONAL HISTORY, 1640-1

PARLIAMENT met on 3 November, and it soon became evident that, now as six months ago, grievances were to have precedence over all other questions. Once again Pym gave a masterly analysis of the misrule that had prevailed. His advice was to seek out and punish the authors of a design to alter both the religion and the government of the kingdom, which was the highest treason, and to land an Irish army 'to bring us to a better order'.[1] The need to move very quickly soon became evident, for Pym learnt that Strafford had formed the daring design of anticipating his own plan of impeaching the king's ministers by accusing the parliamentary leaders of treasonable relations with the Scots, a charge of which the evidence has never come to light.

When the house met, wildly excited by this and other rumours, the speeches betrayed the fear the members felt lest some *coup d'état* was intended. Immediately, the resolution to impeach Strafford was taken, mainly on account of his alleged intention to bring the Irish army over to subdue England.

News that the commons had requested the lords to sequester him reached Strafford at the court. Hastily he went to the house of lords, and was proceeding to his seat, when many voices bidding him withdraw forced him in confusion to stand at the door until he was called in. Then he was commanded to kneel and was delivered to James Maxwell, Black Rod, to be kept a prisoner until the commons were ready to proceed with his trial. He offered to speak, but was ordered to be gone without a word. Deprived of his sword by Maxwell, Strafford made his way through the throng of people to his coach. All eyes were fixed on him, but no one 'capped to him before whom that morning the greatest of England would have stood uncovered'. To the general question, 'What's the matter?' he answered, 'A small matter, I warrant you'; and the spectators replied, 'Yes, indeed, high treason is a small matter.'[2] Then he was taken to the Tower amid the scorn of the insulting multitude.[3]

[1] *D'Ewes Journal*, pp. 7-11.   [2] *Baillie Letters and Journals*, i. 272-3.
[3] *Hist. MSS. Com., Cowper MSS.* (1888), ii. 262.

The rest of the year was mainly devoted to attacks on, and impeachments of, other ministers. The first of these to be accused was the secretary of state, Windebank, who was identified in the popular mind with the lenient policy towards Roman catholics.[1] The commons, however, never discovered that Windebank had negotiated with the papal agent, Rossetti, for aid in men and money from Rome to crush opposition in England. Nevertheless enough had been revealed to make Windebank fear a complete disclosure. Accordingly he fled to France, the first of a long procession of the followers of Charles I to eat the bitter bread of exile. Next to follow him was Lord Finch, against whom articles of impeachment had been exhibited, and whose share in the ship-money trial was denounced on all sides.[2]

The proceedings against Strafford were, as Rushworth says, 'the concern of every man in England'; and Scotland and Ireland were equally interested in his fate. The trial itself lasted for three weeks, without a verdict being returned. Instead of waiting for a judgement by the house of lords, the commons substituted a bill of attainder, to which the king assented on 10 May. It is clear from the proceedings that what was on trial was really the policy of Thorough of which Strafford was the foremost exponent. It is true that Pym's hatred of the great apostate of 1628 led him to bring charges of cruelty and avarice, but they were never substantiated. Indeed it was the impossibility of demonstrating that Strafford had been guilty of any crime against the known laws of the land that caused the commons to abandon the impeachment. The necessity of punishing Strafford for the crimes he was alleged to have committed filled the speeches of his accusers; but it is doubtful whether they were not actuated more by fear of the future than anger at the past.

As time went on, it became increasingly evident that the attempt to prove Strafford guilty of treason was likely to fail. Undoubtedly the strongest weapon which Pym possessed was the copy of Vane's notes of the deliberations in the Committee of Eight on 5 May.[3] Yet no one actually present supported Vane. Hamilton and Northumberland, Juxon and Cottington, who had all been present, declared that they could not remember that Strafford had ever proposed to bring the Irish army to England; and, of the others, Laud and Windebank would almost

---

[1] *D'Ewes Journal*, pp. 31–32, 89–90.   [2] Ibid., pp. 123–4.   [3] See above, p. 95.

certainly have supported Strafford's own denial. In a court of law this would have been decisive, and even in the house of lords it was clear that the tide was running in favour of the accused. Unluckily for him, just at this moment the leaders of the popular party learnt of the first army plot.[1] Possibly 'plot' is too strong a word to apply to the series of discussions which had taken place between some of the discontented leaders of the English army and courtiers like Henry Jermyn the queen's favourite or Sir John Suckling the poet. Pym did not reveal this plot forthwith to the house; but there can be little doubt that it was in the minds of many and doubtless gained credence from the king's refusal to disband the Irish army.[2]

Unfortunately the origin of the bill of attainder is shrouded in darkness; but it seems to have had its rise in a group around Sir Arthur Hesilrige, whose subsequent career proved the intensity and rigidity of his political convictions. These members, impatient of the delays in Strafford's trial, took control away from Pym and Hampden and passed the bill for the third time, on 21 April, by 204 to 59. The fate of Strafford now rested with the lords and the king. Whatever chance there might otherwise have been of evading the death-penalty was ruined by the prevalence of every kind of random report about the army plot. Moreover doubts of the use the king hoped to make of the Irish army, the attempt to introduce new troops into the Tower (which the lieutenant would not permit), and Suckling's enlistment of men for some purpose or other, contributed to an atmosphere of panic. The nerves of the commons seem to have been completely on edge, for on a certain occasion, when the house was in full debate, a board cracked beneath the weight of some of the members, whereupon one cried out that he smelt gunpowder, and so caused the rest to rush out helter-skelter.

At such a time fair play gave place to rancorous bitterness. The argument of St. John that it was idle to discuss the legality of the bill of attainder because it was never accounted either cruel or foul play to knock foxes and wolves on the head as beasts of prey wherever they were found, was symptomatic of the prevailing sentiments in the commons. The house of lords did not remain uninfluenced by the rumours abroad, and accepted the bill. All now depended on Charles. He had recently reassured Strafford that he should not suffer in life, honour, or

---

[1] Gardiner, ix. 317. [2] Ibid., pp. 334-5.

fortune. He had been absolved from this promise by Strafford himself, who urged him to sign the bill rather than allow a subject's life to be the obstacle in the way of a good understanding between sovereign and people.[1] Meanwhile a mob, sometimes composed of well-dressed citizens and sometimes of the rabble, surrounded Whitehall, shrieking for justice. Panic was as acute there as at Westminster. The danger of an attack on the palace seemed grave, and popular animosity was likely to be directed against the queen. At length Charles yielded. 'If my own person only were in danger', he said, 'I would gladly venture it to save Lord Strafford's life; but seeing my wife, children, and all my kingdom are concerned in it, I am forced to give way unto it.' A few years later, when his own turn came to mount the scaffold, Charles stated that nothing lay so heavy on his conscience as having consented to Strafford's death, for which his own death by an unjust sentence would be a punishment.[2]

Strafford's execution attracted perhaps the biggest multitude that had ever assembled in England. It is said that there were 200,000 people on Tower Hill or in the vicinity. They had come to witness the beheading of one whom they regarded as the great apostate from the cause of parliamentary government and as the great incendiary of all the troubles with Scotland. If they expected any sign of repentance, they were most grievously disappointed. Strafford died as he had lived, in the full consciousness of duty performed to the best of his ability. If his life was an acceptable sacrifice to the king, he gladly made it. 'I am not afraid of death', he said, '. . . but doe as chearfully put off my doublet at this time, as ever I did when I went to bed.'[3] He was satisfied that there was no further place for him in the new political world that was arising. He owed his fate, Clarendon states, to the two things he most despised, Sir Henry Vane and the people.[4] It was well for him that he was removed before he was forced to witness the people's further triumph over the monarchy he revered.

The punishment of evil ministers was followed by the destruction of their instruments. The Triennial Act[5] provided machinery for summoning parliament in case the king omitted

---

[1] Gardiner, ix. 362. [2] Muddiman, *Trial of King Charles the First*, pp. 152-3.
[3] S. R., *A Briefe and Perfect Relation* (1647).
[4] *Rebellion*, iii. 205. [5] 16 Car. I, c. 1, *Statutes of the Realm*, v (1819), 54-58.

to do so when three years had elapsed from the dissolution of the previous parliament. The next important measure was designed 'to prevent inconveniences that may happen by the untimely adjourning, proroguing, or dissolving of this present parliament'[1] except by its own consent. To this revolutionary measure Charles assented on the same day that he agreed to the bill of attainder against Strafford. Probably his anxiety about the one prevented his giving adequate consideration to the other. Only on this hypothesis is it credible that he would have passed the measure without a protest. Some at least of his subjects realized the importance of this 'Act for the perpetual parliament', as it came to be called,[2] for one of the most astute of them asked him, 'Whether it would be possible for his truest lieges to do him service any more?'[3]

The next few months witnessed much remedial legislation. A grant of tonnage and poundage[4] was accompanied by the declaration that the previous exaction of these duties, together with the impositions, had been against the laws of the land and that henceforth they could not be levied without the consent of parliament. Moreover, by this and similar acts, they were granted for only short periods. A comprehensive measure for regulating the privy council abolished the star chamber, the council of the Marches of Wales, and the council of the north.[5] Also, the court of high commission was swept away and provision made that no new court of like nature should ever be erected.[6] Writs of ship money, together with the judgement against John Hampden, were denounced as contrary to law.[7] The boundaries of forests were asserted to be the limits and bounds that obtained in the twentieth year of the reign of James I.[8] To compel any one to take upon himself the order of knighthood was declared illegal.[9] Clarendon, in discussing most of these acts, says that they will be

hereafter acknowledged by an incorrupted posterity to be everlasting monuments of a princely and fatherly affection to his people, and such an obligation of repose and trust from the king in the hearts of his subjects that no expressions of piety, duty, and confidence,

---

[1] Ibid., c. 7, pp. 103–4.
[2] Clarendon, iii. 206.
[3] John Hacket, *Memorial of Williams* (1693), pt. ii, p. 162.
[4] 16 Car. I, c. 8, *Statutes of the Realm*, v. 145.
[5] Ibid., c. 10, pp. 110–12.
[6] Ibid., c. 12, pp. 112–13.
[7] Ibid., c. 14, pp. 116–17.
[8] Ibid., c. 16, pp. 119–20.
[9] Ibid., c. 20, p. 131.

from them, could have been more than a sufficient return on their parts.[1]

The enactments that Clarendon thus commends constituted most of the permanent work of the Long Parliament, and formed the legacy accepted as the law of the land at the Restoration. They were not accorded in 1641 the gratitude that Clarendon felt was their due, because men realized that Charles's assent had not been freely given. Indeed he had on occasion declared that he would never pass such legislation, although it is true he did so in the end. Moreover many felt that he did not intend to accept the permanent curtailment of his prerogative which this legislation implied. Since Henrietta Maria informed the papal agent, Rossetti, that according to the law of England whatever was granted by the king under compulsion was null and void,[2] it can hardly be said that those who distrusted Charles's good intentions were unreasonable.

With the punishment of the agents of the king's unparliamentary rule and the passage of legislation designed to prevent its recurrence, the unanimity that hitherto had generally marked parliamentary proceedings vanished. During the summer the division of the commons into two groups grew more noticeable, and at the same time disagreements between the two houses of parliament became more frequent. The causes of division or dispute were church affairs. Much time was spent on a bill designed to exclude the clergy in general from all participation in temporal affairs, and bishops in particular from the house of lords. The latter body not unnaturally regarded this as an unwarranted attempt to alter the constitution of their house and rejected the bill.[3]

Meanwhile the commons had been discussing the 'root and branch' bill, had voted that the present government of the church had long been a hindrance to the full reformation of religion, and had proposed to appoint nine lay commissioners to exercise all ecclesiastical jurisdiction in England.[4] The debates were remarkable for the contrast between the vehemence of the opponents of episcopacy and the lukewarmness of its supporters. Lord Falkland 'was wont to say that they who hated bishops hated them worse than the devil, and that they who loved them did not love them so well as their dinner'.[5]

[1] *Rebellion*, iii. 271.   [2] Gardiner, ix. 404.   [3] 8 June (ibid., pp. 378–83).
[4] Ibid., pp. 388–9, 407.   [5] Clarendon, iii. 241.

Another subject that came to the front was the protestation to maintain protestantism. The two houses had accepted this at the beginning of May,[1] but when the commons proposed that it should be made obligatory upon every one the lords threw out the bill introduced for that purpose.[2] The commons thereupon voted that all who refused the protestation were unfit to hold office in church or state, and ordered this vote to be printed and sent down to the constituencies. When the lords objected, the commons avowed their desire that their votes should be 'a shibboleth to discover the true Israelite'.[3]

The commons now determined to act alone. On 8 September they drew up a declaration that the communion table should be removed from the east end of the church and the rails destroyed, that bowing during service should cease, that dancing or other recreation on the Lord's day should be forborne, and that the authorities concerned should certify the performance of this order or report non-compliance to the commons. The next day, upon the lords' refusal to concur, the commons voted to print their declaration, together with a brief order of the upper house of 16 January,[4] that divine service should be performed in accordance with the law of the land.[5] What Clarendon calls 'so transcendant a presumption and breach of privilege'[6] was perhaps the clearest indication hitherto afforded that the commons were grasping at something beyond a restoration of the old constitution, for in the two disputed questions they had aimed, first at imposing a test on the whole nation by their sole authority, and second at a radical change in church affairs. They were not only invading the royal prerogative, but even entrenching upon the just rights of the house of lords.

It is noticeable, however, that the most remarkable innovation was the joint work of the two houses. In order to give formal authority to the parliamentary commissioners who were deputed to watch Charles's proceedings in Scotland (which he visited in the summer of 1641) the lord keeper was asked to set the great seal to their commission. On his refusal an ordinance passed both houses giving authority to the commissioners to attend his Majesty in Scotland. Apparently to issue an ordinance

---

[1] *Lords' Journals*, iv. 234.   [2] Gardiner, ix. 413.
[3] *Lords' Journals*, iv. 337–8.
[4] Firth, *The House of Lords during the Civil War*, pp. 95–96.
[5] John Nalson, *Impartial Collection*, ii (1683), 481–5.   [6] *Rebellion*, iv. 8.

of parliament without the concurrence of the king was unprecedented. Soon this method of procedure was applied to much more important questions.

In spite of the bitter opposition of parliament, Charles insisted on visiting the northern kingdom because he had made up his mind to try to win over the Scottish leaders by personal persuasion. He spared no pains to ingratiate himself with the covenanters, and listened to Henderson's preaching and sang the Psalms in the manner of the Scottish kirk.[1] He ratified all the acts of the Scottish parliament establishing presbyterianism, but could not conceal his chagrin at the insistence of the estates that they should control the nomination of the royal officers.[2] Moreover, whatever chances he may have had of enlisting the aid of presbyterian noblemen were ruined by the 'incident'— an obscure plot to kidnap Argyll. After its discovery Charles realized that no help could be obtained from the Scottish army.

England meanwhile had had an opportunity to take stock of the situation. The result seems to have been a conservative reaction. The Venetian ambassador notes that during September and October parliament was slowly yielding ground. The fear of an army plot seemed idle after the disbandment of the army. The expenditure which the payment of the rival forces in the north had entailed[3] meant that England had been taxed more heavily than ever before. Parliament, the ambassador wrote, 'is losing the great credit which it enjoyed henceforth [i.e. hitherto], since it appears that instead of relief it has brought expense and discomfort to the people'.[4]

Undoubtedly one cause of the reaction in public opinion was the extravagance of the sectaries. Churchmen observed with wonder that now cobblers and weavers, feltmongers and tailors, and even butchers, presumed to interpret God's word.[5] Apart from the antics of such sects as the Adamites or the novelties of women preachers, there was much in the actions and writings of the more sober puritans to cause serious concern among

[1] Sir Henry Vane to Nicholas, 7 Sept. 1641 (*Nicholas Papers*, ed. G. F. Warner [1886], i. 41).

[2] Gardiner, x. 20–21.

[3] According to 'A Declaration concerning the Generall Accompts of the Kingdome . . . unto the 1st of June, 1642' (*Somers Tracts*, iv), the amount paid to the Scots to date was £286,000, and to the royal army £396,000.

[4] 10/20 September (*State Papers, Venetian, 1640–1642* [1924], p. 215; cf. pp. 213, 226, 251).   [5] Cheshire, *True Copy of That Sermon*, p. 11.

churchmen. John Milton stood far above the other puritan pamphleteers, but even in his works there is a rancorous bitterness against the church, which must have convinced many of the hopelessness of any compromise. His tract, *Of Reformation Touching Church-Discipline in England*, appeared in June 1641, and may be taken as a fair sample of the attacks upon Anglicanism that were then prevalent. The clergy, said Milton, through the

fraud of deceivable traditions, . . . backslide one way into the Jewish beggary, of old cast rudiments, and stumble forward another way into the new-vomited paganisme, of sensuall idolatry attributing purity, or impurity, to things indifferent, that they might bring the inward acts of the spirit to the outward, and customary ey-service of the body, as if they could make God earthly, and fleshly, because they could not make themselves heavenly, and spirituall.[1]

He then denounced the altar, 'pageanted about, like a dreadful idol', which since it had been railed in had become a 'table of separation' between priest and congregation. But it was for the bishops that Milton reserved most of his vituperation. They had driven free-born Englishmen and good Christians across the ocean, where the savage deserts of America could shelter them. They had by the Book of Sports urged men forward to 'gaming, jigging, wassailing, and mixed dancing', and they had tried to force upon Scotland what England was weary of—'the skeleton of a Mass-book'. Probably to the reader the implied comparison with the Book of Common Prayer was most offensive. So long as the attack was concentrated on the Laudian bishops there was little dissension. But to assail the form of service was to arouse enmity. Here the churchman definitely parted company with the man who demanded extempore prayers and the abolition of all ritual. Moreover every form of reverence seems to have become obnoxious to some of these fanatics. In the streets of London the clergy were bawled after, as 'There goes a Jesuit, a Baals priest, an Abbey-lubber, one of Canterburies whelps. . . . Divers ministers have had the surplisse torne from their backes and well they scap'd with their skins.'[2]

It was inevitable that the parliamentary cause should suffer from the extravagancies of its more extreme supporters. Sir

---

[1] p. 2.   [2] Cheshire, p. 14.

Edward Nicholas, the secretary of state, noted that parliament appeared to be losing the reverence hitherto paid it. The great obstacle, he thought, to the king's regaining the affections of his people was the universal fear of popery.[1] It was most unfortunate for the king that, coincident with a distinct revival of monarchical sentiment, the gravest suspicions of popery seemed to receive fresh justification from the Irish massacre.

The causes of the rebellion of 1641 were of long standing. The difficulties of the English government in Ireland during most of the Tudor period sprang from the sporadic disorder inherent in the clan system rather than from any acute racial or religious differences. The risings were usually not very formidable, for the lord deputy could rely upon the loyalty of the Anglo-Irish in the Pale against the native or 'mere' Irish. A new factor entered with the Jesuit missions, which were so successful that the question of religion, which had been negligible during most of the century, became of great importance at its close. For the first time the Anglo-Irish gentry shared a common interest with the native Irish, and their mutual hostility to the administration tended to draw them still closer together as puritanism grew in strength in England. Elizabeth had been wise enough to avoid inciting religious antagonism by persecution, and she had even winked at the non-enforcement of the Acts of Supremacy and Uniformity. Moreover mass had been held during the last years of her reign in private in many parts of Ireland, and openly in Munster under James I. 'Masses and processions were celebrated as frequently and upon as grand a scale as in Rome herself', said a Jesuit report.[2]

At present land rather than religion was the disturbing factor. In Ulster the earls of Tyrone and Tyrconnel headed the clans of O'Neill and O'Donnell, and the extreme pretensions of both were a constant source of trouble to the smaller chieftains as well as to the English government. Eventually the English lord deputy determined that Tyrone and his principal adversary should come to England, where the king would settle their differences. Thereupon Tyrone and Tyrconnel boarded ship, landed in France, and never again visited their native land. The reasons for 'the flight of the earls' appear inadequate, except

---

[1] Letters of September 1641 from Sir Edward Nicholas to Charles I, in *Diary of John Evelyn*, ed. William Bray [n.d.].

[2] R. Bagwell, *Ireland under the Stuarts* (1909), i. 7.

in the aggregate. The fundamental cause of this voluntary exile seems to have been that the earls felt that their claims were incompatible with English authority, and rather than submit they preferred to leave the country. Their departure was followed by an insignificant rising led by O'Dogherty. When this had been subdued, there remained the question of the disposal of the land which the English government considered had escheated to itself. The result was the plantation of Ulster.

The plan for the division and plantation of the forfeited lands in the six counties of Ulster (Tyrone, Coleraine, Donegal, Fermanagh, Armagh, and Cavan) provided that a careful survey should be made of every county and the land first divided into four parts, which in turn were to be subdivided: two into parcels of 1,000 acres apiece, a third into parcels of 1,500 acres, and a fourth into parcels of 2,000 acres—all to form parishes, in each of which a church should be erected and endowed with glebe land. These parishes were to be occupied by undertakers, who were to be: English or Scottish, who should plant their land with English or Scottish tenants; servitors[1] in Ireland, who might take English or Irish tenants at their choice; and native Irish, who should be freeholders. Various conditions were laid down, by which the undertakers were to build stout houses and courtyards, capable of standing a siege. All were to pay rent.[2]

Chichester, then lord deputy, criticized the scheme on account of its uniformity and especially for the assignment of too little land to the native freeholders. Actually the project was never carried out in its entirety. It proved difficult to secure enough undertakers, and a number of them were speculators, like Lord Audley—who received 7,000 acres for himself and his two sons, but upon whose land it was reported in 1619 there was 'no building at all, either of bawn [courtyard] or castle, neither free-holders'.[3] Moreover the stipulation that undertakers should plant only English or Scottish tenants was often ignored, and the Irish were allowed to remain as tenants on land they had once owned. A muster taken twenty years after the beginning of the settlement gives 13,000 as the number of British males in Ulster, and of these only about 7,000 were settled on land escheated in 1607. There were then less than 2,000 fire-arms in the province, so that the hope of forming permanent English

---

[1] Those who had served the Crown as civilians or soldiers.
[2] George Hill, *The Plantation of Ulster* (1877), pp. 78–88.   [3] Bagwell, i. 76.

garrisons to keep the native Irish in check was doomed to disappointment.

Such success as the plantation achieved was largely due to those Scottish presbyterians who sought in Ulster the religious freedom denied them in their native land, and to the Londoners who were granted Coleraine and who changed the name to Londonderry. The Londoners set to work so briskly that Sir John Davies, the attorney-general for Ireland, was reminded of Virgil's description of the building of Carthage. But there were not enough settlers to people the whole county. The towns of Londonderry and Coleraine were largely built of stone, but as in 1689 their surrounding ramparts were of earth, liable to crumble easily. On the whole there was little justification for Ben Jonson's praise of James as one destined to relieve Ireland and free

> Her fame from barbarisme, her state from want,
> And in her all the fruits of blessing plant.[1]

This policy of plantation was continued in other parts of the island. Wexford, Longford, Leitrim, and King's County were all planted to some extent. Generally enough was done to fill the Irish with a burning sense of injustice, but not enough to clear them out and to bring in sufficient new settlers. The result is well summed up by David Rothe, Roman catholic bishop of Ossory, whose words could be applied to any of the plantations:

Since these Leinster men, and others like them, see themselves excluded from all hopes of restitution or compensation, and are so constituted that they would rather starve upon husks at home than fare sumptuously elsewhere, they will fight for their altars and hearths, and rather seek a bloody death near the sepulchres of their fathers than be buried as exiles in unknown earth or inhospitable sand.[2]

Apart from these confiscations of land, there is little to record in Irish history from the retirement of Chichester in 1615 to the advent of Wentworth in 1632.

Hardly had Wentworth arrived at Dublin before he had made up his mind how Ireland was to be governed. In reply to a letter from Laud, in which the newly created archbishop complained that the church was so bound up in the forms of the common law that he could not do all the good he would, Wentworth wrote:

No such narrow considerations shall fall into my counsels as my

---

[1] 'The Irish Masque', in *The Workes of Beniamin Jonson* (1616), p. 1003.
[2] Bagwell, i. 161.

own preservation, till I see my master's power and greatness set out of wardship and above the exposition of Sir Edward Coke and his year-books, and I am assured the same resolution governs in your lordship. Let us then in the name of God go cheerfully and boldly; if others do not their parts I am confident the honour shall be ours and the shame theirs, and thus you have my Thorough and Thorough.

On another occasion he asserted that the king was able to carry any just and honourable action

thorough all imaginary opposition, for real there can be none; that to start aside for such panick fears, phantastick apparitions, as a Prynn or an Elliot shall set up, were the meanest folly in the whole world.[1]

The new lord deputy as speedily made up his mind that autocracy was the only possible form of government. His council he described as a company of men the most intent upon their own selfish interests of any he had ever met with, and he plainly told them that there was no necessity for him to consult them and that if need be he could get along without their help.[2] His only confidants were his cousins, Christopher Wandesford and George Radcliffe, who alone knew, so he said, what he wrote or intended.[3]

Wentworth certainly found Ireland in a parlous condition. To begin with, the seas were infested with pirates. In 1630 they had landed at Baltimore and carried off over a hundred inhabitants, and had prevented the new lord deputy from crossing the Irish Sea for six months, and even then managed to capture five hundred pounds' worth of his linen.[4] Wentworth, however, infused some of his own energy into the few royal ships allowed him, and, aided by Rainsborough's successful expedition against the pirates at Sallee, claimed to have cleared the seas by 1637.

Then the army, on which the maintenance of English authority ultimately rested, was a sorry force, consisting of not more than 400 horse and 2,000 foot. Even so, it was paid very irregularly. Consequently discipline was almost non-existent. In addition horses, arms, and equipment were defective, drills were infrequent, and the officers were often absentees. Here again Wentworth, by careful examination of every troop or company, was able to point out to each officer what was wrong and to

---

[1] *Strafforde's Letters*, i. 111, 173; Bagwell, i. 192.
[2] *Strafforde's Letters*, pp. 201–2.   [3] Ibid., p. 193.   [4] Ibid., p. 198.

cashier him if no improvement took place. He himself, 'clad in a black armour, with a black horse, and a black plume of feathers', trained a troop near Dublin. He was also able, later, to secure better arms for the soldiers.

The church of Ireland, moreover, was so contemptible that it is no wonder if there were complaints that Jesuits and other priests were swarming everywhere. The church buildings were often ruinous or devoted to secular purposes. Thus in Dublin one was a stable, a second a residence, a third a tennis-court, and a fourth permitted its vaults to be hired to Roman catholic publicans. Simony and pluralism were the order of the day. A certain bishop was reported to have held twenty-three benefices, but the curates in charge to have received only a few pounds a year.

Money was needed to deal with these and other abuses, and Wentworth determined to call a parliament in 1634. It was with great difficulty that he could secure the necessary permission from Charles. 'As for that hydra', wrote the king, 'take good heed, for you know that here I have found it as well cunning as malicious.'[1] Every care was exercised to prevent the Irish house of commons from bearing the least resemblance to the English. Pressure was shamelessly exerted in all the boroughs, and patrons were allowed little freedom of choice, as is evidenced by Lord Cork's observation, in his diary, that he received six letters from the lord deputy ordering him to arrange for the return of the individuals who were named.

Wentworth's speech to both houses illustrates precisely his view of the functions of parliament. The debt of the Crown must be paid and an annual deficit provided for. The houses were simply to devote their time to these two needs. That was the business of the first, or king's, session. Then there would be a session of their own, when the king would grant whatever favours he thought suitable, and these they were to receive with the proper gratitude. Let them avoid private meetings or consultations. 'I am commanded to carry a very wakeful eye over these private and secret conventicles, to punish the transgression with a heavy and severe hand, therefore it behooves you to look to it.'[2]

The result of this exhortation was that six subsidies were granted—two to be levied in the first and second years, and one

---

[1] *Strafforde's Letters*, p. 233.   [2] Ibid., pp. 286, 290.

each in the third and fourth. So far so good. Even the Irish parliament, however, was reluctant to miss the second opportunity that had been afforded it since 1603 of raising grievances in a parliamentary way. The house of lords was told that the proper method of procedure was to offer humble prayers to the lord deputy. This the commons did, to the effect that a law might be enacted making sixty years' possession a good title, even against the Crown—a concession that had been promised, but not fulfilled, earlier in the reign.[1] Since titles to land in Ireland were generally defective, the question was of the first importance. The commons also requested that the 'free and easy exportation and vent . . . of natural commodities' be permitted, and vagabonds and beggars employed, which would help Irish manufactures. By this time, however, Charles was out of patience with the very name of parliament and rejected Wentworth's plan that the Irish houses might be retained by prorogations. His experience in England had taught him, he said, that parliaments 'are of the nature of cats, they ever grow curst with age'.[2] Therefore a dissolution was prescribed.

Simultaneously with parliament, the convocation of the Irish church met in 1634, and established the Thirty-nine Articles, together with canons to enforce their subscription. This fresh weapon against the Scottish presbyterians in Ulster was vigorously wielded by Bramhall, bishop of Derry and a close friend of Laud. By compelling all ministers to subscribe to the new canons or to vacate he forced many to return to their native land, where a number played a prominent part in defeating the Laudian policy of 1637–8.

During the bishops' wars Wentworth did everything he could to render the Ulstermen powerless to aid their fellow countrymen across the sea. He invented what is usually known as the 'black oath', by which the subscriber had to swear not to bear arms against the king or resist any of his commands, and not to enter into any covenant, but to renounce all such bonds.[3] The general imposition of this oath in Ulster gave the greatest offence, especially since only Roman catholics were exempted. The utmost severity was used against all recalcitrants. Thus a man and his wife, their two daughters, and a servant were fined

---

[1] Bagwell, i. 182, 221. The petition of the commons is printed in *Strafforde's Letters*, i. 310–28.

[2] *Strafforde's Letters*, i. 365.   [3] Ibid. ii. 345.

£13,000 and condemned to imprisonment for life, for refusing to abjure the Scottish covenant—in spite of the fact that the 'black oath' had no legal authority whatsoever.

Not satisfied with the success of this oppressive measure, Wentworth actually proposed to banish from Ulster, by proclamation, all the Scots who were not considerable landowners. It is not surprising that the Scots regarded him as their bitterest enemy. There can be little doubt of the interdependence of events in Ulster and in Scotland. Because the Scots at home thought that Wentworth was 'bringing a verie Spanish inquisition on our whole Scottish nation' in Ulster, they resisted the more stoutly the introduction of Thorough across the Tweed.[1]

In addition to alienating the Ulster planters, Wentworth antagonized the landowners of Connaught. A strong believer in the plantation system, he was anxious to extend it in all directions. He began with Roscommon, where the jury was induced to find that the king had a valid title to the land there—an achievement rendered easy by the generally defective titles to land in Ireland. Wentworth justified his proceedings on the ground that the king, in restoring three-quarters of the land, would take from the landlords nothing that was theirs and would even give them something that was his. Another way of stating the result of these legal proceedings would be to say that the king took from the landowners one-quarter of the land whose possession they had enjoyed unchallenged for some time.

In Galway the jury was less complacent, whereupon the sheriff was fined heavily and the jury bound over to appear before the castle chamber, a sort of Irish star chamber. This severity was effective, and a later jury declared in favour of the king, who thought it was just and reasonable that the resistance should be punished by confiscating half the land instead of a quarter.

A somewhat analogous method of raising money was applied in the north. Proceedings in the star chamber against the Corporation of London for failure to carry out the conditions under which Coleraine had been granted resulted in a fine of £70,000 and forfeiture of the charter. It is curious to find Wentworth suggesting that Londonderry would make a suitable appanage for the duke of York, for in 1689 that city sustained the famous siege by the same duke, then James II.

---

[1] *Baillie Letters and Journals*, i. 199.

The arbitrary treatment thus applied to whole counties or corporations was equally meted out to individuals. For some rash words spoken after dinner Mountnorris, half a year later, was summoned at twelve hours' notice to a court martial and there condemned to death. His sentence was not carried out, but he was imprisoned from time to time and deprived of his offices. For the alleged failure to pay a marriage settlement promised fifteen years before, the octogenarian Chancellor Loftus was suddenly charged and committed, and not released until he had made over his property to trustees who were friends of Wentworth's. A third victim was the earl of Cork, who wrote that he thought no man living had suffered so much injustice from Wentworth as himself and that the lord deputy had taken from him by his prerogative alone, without any suit at law, £40,000 of his personal estate and £1,200 a year of his income, together with '£4,200 within this five years for subsidies which might have ransomed me if I had been prisoner with the Turks'.[1] At Strafford's trial, the earl of Cork had his revenge, for he testified that the lord deputy had said: 'Call in your writs, or if you will not, I will clap you in the Castle; for I tell you, I will not have my orders disputed by law nor lawyers.'[2]

When Wentworth left Ireland for the last time, in 1640, he thought the Irish were 'as fully satisfied and as well affected to his Majesty's person and service, as can possibly be wished for'.[3] Superficially this boast seemed justified. Ireland certainly appeared more prosperous and more peaceful than it had been, probably, at any other time in its history. Unfortunately for his reputation as a statesman, his system of Thorough depended upon the strong right arm of the lord deputy and signally failed to secure the support of protestant or catholic, English interest or Ulstermen, or 'mere' Irish. Beneath the surface all detested Wentworth, though their divisions prevented their making a united stand against his tyranny. The result was that Thorough collapsed in Ireland as easily and as completely as Laudian episcopalianism in Scotland.

The year and a half that followed his departure are noteworthy for the reviving independence of the Irish parliament. During

---

[1] Bagwell, i. 269; Dorothea Townshend, *The Life and Letters of the Great Earl of Cork* (1904), p. 287.

[2] John Rushworth, *The Tryal of Thomas Earl of Strafford* (1680), p. 175.

[3] *Strafforde's Letters*, ii. 403.

the early months of 1641 the Roman catholics had a majority, which they employed to submit twenty-two queries to the judges on the legality of many of Strafford's acts. Taken together, these queries form an impressive indictment of Thorough. When the judges had submitted their replies, the commons answered their own queries. Their most noteworthy declaration was the first: that Irishmen were a free people, to be governed only according to the common law of England and the statute laws and lawful customs of Ireland.[1]

Another important feature was the formation of an army in Ireland to intervene in Britain. During 1640, 1,000 horse and 8,000 foot were raised. They could not be brought over to fight the Scots, for lack of money. Even after the treaty of Ripon with the Scots the king obstinately refused many petitions from parliament to disband these forces, and did not give way until a few days before Strafford's execution. His intention then was that a number of officers should transport the 8,000 foot for foreign service, mainly Spanish. Parliament vigorously protested and the design was abandoned. In May the army was paid off at the rate of about 45 per cent. of what was due. The effect was that these disbanded soldiers—discontented Roman catholics—in many cases took an active part, often a leading part, in the Irish rebellion that occurred five months later.

This rebellion, or massacre (as contemporaries called it), had its roots in the past. Strangely enough, in the remonstrance that the Irish leaders drew up and presented to the government on 17 March 1642-3 the question of land is not specifically mentioned. They were necessitated to take up arms, they say, for the preservation of their religion, maintenance of the king's rights and prerogatives, and the natural and just defence of their lives and estates and the liberties of their country.[2] Probably it is safest to leave it at that. The immediate occasion was the weakness of the Irish executive. Very likely the council was blind and supine, but whether abler men could have done much more,

---

[1] Nalson, *Impartial Collection*, ii. 572–90.
[2] *The False and Scandalous Remonstrance of the . . . Rebells of Ireland* (1644), p. 3. Cf. Lord Macguire's 'Relation', in Nalson, *Impartial Collection*, ii. 543–4: Rory O'More, the originator of the rebellion, 'began to particularize the suffering of them that were the more antient natives, as were the Irish; how that on several plantations they were all put out of their ancestors estates. All which sufferings he said, did beget a general discontent over all the whole kingdom in both the natives; to wit, the old and new Irish.'

with king and parliament at loggerheads in England and with
no clear policy for the council in Dublin to carry out, is not at
all certain.

The controversy about the extent of the massacre is of long
standing, but there is no gainsaying Hume's remark that the
Irish catholic who denies the massacre of 1641 must be considered beyond the reach of argument or reason. The exact
number of victims matters little. It is sufficient to know that
certainly several thousands were killed in cold blood and probably two or three times as many perished from exposure and
privation. What is more important is that contemporaries in
England and Scotland believed, however unjustifiably, that
there had been a plot formed by the Irish for the universal ex-
tirpation of all British settlers, and that many thousands of men,
women, and children had been barbarously murdered without
any provocation.[1]

Moreover the priests were generally regarded as the ring-
leaders. It was said they impressed upon their flocks that it was
a mortal sin to give relief or protection to any of the English and
that killing them was a meritorious act that would save them
from purgatory.[2] Pamphlets of the time enlarged upon the
cruelty of the Irish; for example, *The Rebels' Turkish Tyranny*[3]
accuses them of ravishing women and of toasting children on
spits before their parents' eyes, burning them to ashes, or muti-
lating them.

The news of the Irish massacre raised public excitement in
England to fever heat. The partial revelations of the two army
plots and rumours about the queen's intrigues with Roman
catholic powers on the Continent had already inflamed public
opinion. Soon reports circulated that the rebels claimed to be
acting in the king's name, and even that one of their leaders
had exhibited a commission, under the broad seal of England,
authorizing him to restore Roman catholicism in Ireland. Beyond any doubt this was a forgery, but there is at least a possibility that some of the catholic leaders had been encouraged
by the king to seize strongholds in Ireland and to maintain them
against the English parliament.[4] Unquestionably the rebellion,
as Clarendon says, 'proved of infinite disadvantage to the king's

---

[1] Sir John Temple, *The Irish Rebellion* (1646), pp. 1–2.
[2] Ibid., pp. 40, 86.   [3] Printed for W. R., 1641.
[4] Gardiner, x. 92–94.

affairs which were then recovering new life'.[1] The inevitable result was that those who believed or suspected the complicity of Charles became more and more determined to impose still further shackles upon him.

The news from Ireland reached London just at the time when the Grand Remonstrance was under discussion. The knowledge that an army must be created to suppress the Irish rebellion introduced a fresh factor into the situation. Pym held that it would have been madness to entrust the command of this force to royal nominees. He therefore succeeded in carrying through the commons instructions to be sent to the committee attending the king in Scotland. These instructions stated that there was just cause to believe that the Irish rebellion was the effect of evil counsellors, and that so long as they continued in office any financial grants for the suppression of the Irish rebels would be applied to fomenting that rebellion or encouraging similar attempts by papists in England. If, therefore, the king refused to employ such ministers as enjoyed the confidence of parliament,

we shall be forced in discharge of the trust which we owe to the state and to those whom we represent to resolve upon some such way of defending Ireland from the rebels as may concur with securing of ourselves from such mischievous counsels and designs as have lately been and still are in practice and agitation against us . . . and to commend those aids and contributions which this great necessity shall require to the custody and disposing of such persons of honour and fidelity as we have cause to confide in.[2]

This, says Dr. Gardiner, 'was the signal for the final conversion of the episcopalian party into a royalist party'.[3] The Irish rebellion had, therefore, brought civil war in England much nearer. Moreover, since Pym's position in parliament was now precarious, he felt it necessary to issue an appeal to the people. Accordingly the remonstrance which had been talked of since the early days of the Long Parliament was at last produced on the very day that the instructions to the Scottish committee were carried.[4]

Probably the remonstrance did not begin to take definite form until after 3 August, when a committee of eight, of whom the most important were Pym and Henry Vane, was appointed. Quite likely, however, different parts of it were the work of

---

[1] *Rebellion*, iv. 26.
[2] *Lords' Journals*, iv. 430-1.
[3] *History*, x. 59.
[4] *Commons' Journals*, ii. 25, 221, 234.

different hands, for it is disjointed and contains repetitions. It opens with an enumeration of grievances, in 119 clauses, which suggests that it had been designed originally as a statement of misgovernment. Some of these clauses, at least, may be the work of the original committee of twenty-four appointed on 10 November 1640 and ordered on 23 July following to complete promptly a remonstrance on the state of the kingdom when parliament met and on the proceedings of the houses since then.[1] Then comes a list of the remedies already carried. This section seems to have been hurriedly compiled, because, while the star chamber and the high commission are allotted clauses to themselves,[2] nothing whatever is said about them, although the very next clause specifically says the council of the north has been abolished.

Apparently, therefore, clauses 120 to 180 represent in part the work of the committee at the end of July and the beginning of August, and in part what was done hastily to comply with the order of the house, on 25 October, to complete the declaration within the week.[3] It is here that unmistakable evidence is to be found that the remonstrance was designed to win popular support. Some of the clauses were drafted with the definite purpose of counteracting the conservative reaction that had set in during the summer of 1641, for they denounce as a scandal the impression that parliament had obtained from the king many things very prejudicial to the Crown, in respect of both prerogative and revenue. Moreover it is acknowledged that the king had passed more bills to the advantage of the subject than had been enacted in many ages.[4] Furthermore there are clauses bearing directly on the recent disagreements between lords and commons. Thus it is stated that a party of bishops and popish lords in the upper house prevented the passage of bills reforming corruptions both in church and state.[5]

Clauses 181 to 204 deal chiefly with religion and seem from internal evidence to have been drafted by a different hand. Although a number of amendments and additions were made to the remonstrance between 8 November, when it was introduced, and 22 November, when it was passed,[6] the main debates concerned religion and the form of church government which the

---

[1] Ibid., pp. 25, 221. [2] Clauses 127–8.
[3] *Commons' Journals*, ii. 294. [4] Clauses 145–6, 154, 156, &c.
[5] Clauses 170, 181. [6] *Commons' Journals*, ii. 309, 311, 317, 320, 322.

majority of the commons proposed to substitute for episcopalianism. After acknowledging the intention to limit the exorbitant power of the bishops, the remonstrance proceeds:

... it is far from our purpose or desire to let loose the golden reins of discipline and government in the church, to leave private persons or particular congregations to take up what form of divine service they please, for we hold it requisite that there should be throughout the whole realm a conformity to that order which the laws enjoin according to the word of God. And we desire to unburden the consciences of men of needless and superstitious ceremonies, suppress innovations, and take away the monuments of idolatry.

And the better to effect the intended reformation, we desire there may be a general synod of the most grave, pious, learned and judicious divines of this island; assisted with some from foreign parts, professing the same religion with us, who may consider of all things necessary for the peace and good government of the church, and represent the results of their consultations unto the parliament, to be there allowed of and confirmed, and receive the stamp of authority, thereby to find passage and obedience throughout the kingdom.[1]

At the very end occurs the oft reiterated demand that the king should employ only such counsellors and ambassadors as parliament had cause to confide in, 'without which we cannot give his Majesty such supplies for support of his own estate, nor such assistance to the protestant party beyond the sea [in Ireland], as is desired'.[2]

The Grand Remonstrance is rightly regarded as one of the most important documents in English constitutional history. That contemporaries fully recognized this is shown by the unprecedented length and heat of the debate that preceded the final division. To royalists it seemed, then and always, as foul a libel as could be framed against the king.[3] To a sympathizer with him, like the Venetian ambassador, it appeared that Pym and his associates, fearful lest the support of the people was failing them, were trying all methods of discrediting the monarch's past and present actions. To such men the remonstrance was plain sedition.[4] On the other hand the opponents of the court felt its passage to be a matter of life and death. The extreme importance they attached to it is shown by Cromwell's famous remark 'that if the remonstrance had been rejected he would

---

[1] Clauses 184-5. [2] Clause 197.
[3] Warwick, *Memoirs*, p. 221; Clarendon, iv. 49.
[4] *State Papers, Venetian, 1640-1642*, p. 254.

have sold all he had the next morning and never have seen England more; and he knew there were many other honest men of the same resolution'.[1]

As soon as the remonstrance was passed, a motion was made that it should be printed forthwith, whereupon an even sharper debate ensued than on the main question. Edward Hyde and Sir John Culpepper contended that to publish it would sow divisions among the people and hence be dangerous, and another speaker on the same side urged that to remonstrate to the people was without precedent.[2] By this time the excitement had reached boiling-point, and when a member rose to demand that a protest should be entered 'in the name of himself and all the rest', there were wild shouts of 'All! All!' Many drew their swords, and one present stated, 'I thought we had all sat in the valley of the shadow of death'; but Hampden's calmness averted a fight on the floor of the house and further discussion was adjourned.[3]

The remonstrance, together with a petition, was presented to the king on 1 December. By chance he was afforded an indirect opportunity, the next day, of answering the remonstrance at Westminster, and declared that he meant not only to maintain the laws already passed but to 'grant what else can be justly desired for satisfaction in point of liberties, or in maintenance of the true religion that is here established'.[4] Charles was on firm ground and, had he been content to stand still, it is likely that he could have defeated the parliamentary leaders. Already a position of stalemate had been reached, for the house of lords was now definitely on the king's side. Charles need only have watched, without interfering, the increasing differences between the two houses. How acute these differences were, may be seen from the commons' assertion

that this house being the representative body of the whole kingdom, and their lordships being but as particular persons, and coming to parliament in a particular capacity, that if they should not be pleased to consent to the passing of those acts, and others, necessary to the preservation and safety of the kingdom, that then this house, together with such of the lords that are more sensible of the safety of the kingdom, may join together, and represent the same unto his Majesty.[5]

---

[1] Clarendon, iv. 52.
[2] Willson H. Coates, 'Some Observations on "The Grand Remonstrance",
Journal of Modern History, March 1932, p. 7, n. 19.
[3] Gardiner, x. 77; Warwick, pp. 221–2.   [4] *Lords' Journals*, iv. 459–60.
[5] *Commons' Journals*, ii. 330.

Charles, however, was unwilling to wait. Probably the provocations from the house of commons had become unbearable. Among them were the resolution to print the Grand Remonstrance[1] and the introduction of a bill to nominate a lord general with powers to raise men, to levy money to pay them, and to execute martial law.[2] Moreover the elections to the common council in London resulted in the return of puritans. Thereupon the king determined to act. He dismissed the puritan Sir William Balfour from the lieutenancy of the Tower and appointed the notorious swashbuckler Thomas Lunsford to that post. He answered the Grand Remonstrance directly by declaring his ignorance of the existence of any malignant party in the country and of the need of any reform in the church. With his very life, he said, he was ready to maintain the church of England against popery on the one hand and separatists on the other.[3] When fear of the mob kept the bishops from attending the house of lords and when Pym refused to take any action against the rioters, on the ground that the house of commons could not dishearten the people from obtaining 'their just desires in such a way',[4] Charles encouraged the bishops to protest that all that had been done in their absence was *ipso facto* null and void. This was a stupendous blunder and at once alienated the house of lords. Worse was to follow. Apparently enraged at the suspected decision of the commons to impeach the queen for conspiring against public liberty and instigating the rebellion in Ireland,[5] the king determined to impeach five members. Pym, Hampden, Holles, Hesilrige, and Strode, together with Lord Mandeville, were charged with treason for attempting to subvert the fundamental laws, to deprive the monarch of his rightful power, and to alienate the affections of his people, and for inviting and encouraging a foreign (Scottish) army to invade England. When these articles were presented before the house of lords, the peers not only refused to order the arrest of the accused but instead appointed a committee to inquire whether the impeachment was according to precedent. Charles then sent the serjeant-at-arms to the commons to arrest the five members; the commons replied that this concerned their privileges and that they would consider the matter. The next day

---

[1] On 15 December (*Commons' Journals*, ii. 344).
[2] Gardiner, x. 95.
[3] Rushworth, iv. 452.
[4] Gardiner, x. 118.
[5] *State Papers, Venetian, 1640-1642*, p. 276.

the king yielded to his wife's entreaties. 'Go, you coward,' she is reported to have said, 'and pull these rogues out by the ears, or never see my face more.'[1] Thereupon Charles, followed by three or four hundred armed swordsmen, went down to Westminster, entered the house of commons (which none of his predecessors had ever done), and told the members present that no person had any privileges when charged with treason. Therefore he was come to know if any of the accused were there. Looking round he saw that 'all the birds are flown'. The five members had taken refuge in the City and the king withdrew, baffled. He soon realized that he was powerless to compel the citizens to surrender them. Instead, the City appointed Philip Skippon major-general, to take command of the train-bands, and the seamen of the ports volunteered to help in the defence of parliament. A week later the five returned to Westminster, escorted by cheering multitudes.

The only possible excuse for a *coup d'état* is success, and Charles failed dismally. Although his final hesitations were overcome by the queen's reproaches, he did not yield to a sudden impulse but rather put into effect what had been contemplated for some time. At the very opening of the Long Parliament Strafford had planned an impeachment of the parliamentary leaders, but the project had not been taken up again until the following autumn. Then it became common knowledge that some such scheme was under discussion. Indeed the verses with which 'J. H.' (? John Hall) greeted King Charles, when he was entertained in the City on his return from Scotland, broadly hinted that members of parliament who were inclined to practise mischief should have 'regall judgement and a legall grave'.[2] The attempted arrest was frustrated by betrayal, but, even if it had taken place, the outcome would probably have been still more disastrous, for the consequence of the mere attempt was the immediate closing of the ranks in parliament. Differences between lords and commons disappeared and unanimity once more prevailed in the lower house.

---

[1] Gardiner, x. 136.
[2] *King Charles His Entertainment and London's Loyaltie* (1641).

VI

POLITICAL AND CONSTITUTIONAL
HISTORY, 1642-9

CHARLES left Whitehall the day before Pym's triumphal
return to Westminster. For the time being he was again,
as he had been in November 1640, without substantial
support anywhere. And yet ten months later he was able to
meet the parliamentary army on equal terms at Edgehill. The
explanation is partly that henceforth the policy that Hyde persuaded the king to adopt won him a party in the nation. Under
Hyde's guidance he took up an almost purely negative position
in the war of declarations that preceded the actual fighting.
Hyde chose as his text a remark Pym had made during Strafford's
trial: the law is that which distinguishes right from wrong. The
king, in this insistence upon the legality of his position and the
illegality of the parliamentary demands, was much helped by
the general unwillingness at Westminster to admit that the existing constitution would no longer suffice. As late as 2 August
parliament, wholly without realization that the old order was
passing away, resolved that a parliamentary majority would
never agree to set up an arbitrary government and that it was
'most improbable that the nobility and chief gentry of this kingdom should conspire to take away the law, by which they enjoy
their estates, are protected from any act of violence and power,
and differenced from the meaner sort of people, with whom
otherwise they would be but fellow servants'.[1] Since the parliamentary leaders were imposing constitutional and ecclesiastical
changes upon a country which by now they probably represented very imperfectly, they might fairly be accused of setting
up an arbitrary government, especially as they had expelled
all their opponents by imposing tests impossible for any supporter of the king to endure.

Granted, however, that Charles had the best of this paper
warfare, it seems certain that he would never have been strong
enough to take the field but for the increasing danger to the
church. He himself assented to a bill removing bishops from

[1] *Lords' Journals*, v. 258.

all temporal positions and depriving them of all courts of jurisdiction. With this stumbling-block out of the way, the majority
of churchmen would have been willing that matters should
remain as they were. This was impossible, because one section
of puritans wished to substitute presbyterianism for Anglicanism and another wished for toleration, which was disliked by
Anglicans and hated by presbyterians. By this time puritanism
had become a term having political as well as religious connota-
tions. The puritan publicist, John Vicars, defines as puritans
'all that were zealous for the laws and liberties of the kingdom
and for the maintenance of religion'.[1] If this had been the whole
story, civil war would not have come. But sober puritanism was
being replaced by enthusiastic Brownism. Milton complained
that 'the word puritan seemes to be quasht, and all that heretofore were counted such, are now Brownists'.[2] The Brownists,
or sectaries, were becoming the driving force of puritanism.
Their zeal and extravagances incurred the general condemnation of churchmen. The fear that the church was in danger
from seditious sermons by laymen who dared to arrogate to
themselves the functions of the ministry, and from 'heresy,
schism, prophaneness, libertinism, anabaptism, atheism',[3] rallied
half the nation under the king's banner.

So far as parliament had a definite political programme it is
to be found in the Nineteen Propositions, which were ordered
to be delivered to the king on 1 June.[4] Their importance is
attested by Ludlow's statement that they were in effect 'the
principal foundation of the ensuing war'.[5] They can be summarized as follows: that privy councillors, the great officers of
state, and the governors of fortifications should be appointed
only with the approval of parliament; that the king's children
should be educated by, and married to, those in whom parliament had confidence; that the laws against Roman catholics
should be strictly executed and popish peers excluded from the
house of lords; that the king should accept such a reformation
of the church as parliament advised; that he should sign the
militia ordinance; that he should abandon delinquents to the

[1] *Jehovah-Jireh. God in the Mount* (1644), p. 12.
[2] *The Reason of Church-Government Urg'd against Prelaty* (1641), in *Works*, iii, pt. i,
p. 214.
[3] See the Kentish Petition, drawn up 25 March (*Lords' Journals*, iv. 677; cf.
Gardiner, x. 179–80).					[4] *Lords' Journals*, v. 100.
[5] *Memoirs of Edmund Ludlow*, ed. C. H. Firth (1894), i. 29.

justice of parliament; and that peers created thereafter should not be admitted to the house of lords without the consent of both houses of parliament.[1]

In his reply Charles said that these propositions would appear 'a mockery and a scorn' and that they would, if accepted, annihilate the royal power and leave nothing but the empty forms of majesty. His answer would be, he said, *nolumus leges Angliae mutari*. As regards the church, he declared that nowhere on earth could be found a church that professed the true religion with more purity of doctrine than the church of England, or where the government and discipline were jointly more beautified and free from superstition than were here established by law; and he would maintain it not only against papists but also against separatists.[2]

Defence of the church was undoubtedly the most powerful motive in enlisting men under the royal standard. Next to loyalty to the church Charles owed most to the traditional loyalty to the throne: the 'anointed king' was still the deputy of the Lord.[3] Many who disapproved of Charles's policy and dreaded the results of the queen's popish zeal nevertheless felt they had no option but to take sides with the king. The words of Sir Edmund Verney probably apply to numerous royalists:

I do not like the quarrel, and do heartily wish that the king would yield and consent to what they [parliament] desire; so that my conscience is only concerned in honour and in gratitude to follow my master. I have eaten his bread and served him near thirty years, and will not do so base a thing as to forsake him; and choose rather to lose my life (which I am sure to do) to preserve and defend those things which are against my conscience to preserve and defend: for I will deal freely with you, I have no reverence for the bishops, for whom this quarrel [subsists].[4]

Social reasons, too, determined for some the choice of a party. Royalist landlords noted with alarm, about September 1642, that vulgar men were saying that the gentry 'have been our masters a long time and now we may chance to master them,

---

[1] Gardiner, *Constitutional Documents*, pp. 249-54.

[2] Rushworth, pt. iii, vol. i, pp. 725-35.

[3] Cf. Edmund Verney to his brother, Sir Ralph: 'I beseech you consider that majesty is sacred; God sayth "Touch not myne anointed"' (*Memoirs of the Verney Family*, ed. Frances Parthenope Verney [1892], ii. 136).

[4] *The Life of Edward, Earl of Clarendon . . . Written by Himself* (1857), i. 135. According to a family friend, Sir Edmund was sad and thoughtful, saying little except that if he received the king's commands he must go (*Verney Memoirs*, ii. 87).

and now they [the lower classes] know their strength it shall
goe hard but they will use it'.[1] Such fears were expressed by a
popular rhymester, who put into the mouths of roundheads
the following:

> Since then the anti-christian crew
>   Be prest and over-throwne,
> Wee'l teach the nobles how to crouch,
>   And keepe the gentry downe;
> Good manners hath an ill report,
>   And turnes to pride we see;
> Wee'l therefore cry all manners downe,
>   And hey then up go we.[2]

It is not surprising that a majority of the peers and greater landlords became cavaliers. They felt instinctively that the royal
prerogatives and their own privileges went hand in hand.[3]

Zeal for church and king was reinforced by class prejudice
against the upstart merchants and shopkeepers, among whom
puritanism was rampant. Ludlow directly accuses the royalists
of taking up arms so that they could continue to trample on the
lower classes. Probably considerations such as these had more
weight than is generally allowed. Many, too, seem honestly to
have believed, with a captain of the Leicestershire train-bands,
that the parliamentarians, under pretence of settling the ancient
laws of the kingdom, were really only intent upon fulfilling 'their
aspiring humours'.[4]

The parliamentary side was supported by all who held, with
Rushworth, that the royalists and parliamentarians were 'the
respective advocates for prerogative and liberty'.[5] It may well
be that the point of view of the puritan gentleman was the same
as Cromwell's: 'Religion was not the thing at first contested for,
but God brought it to that issue at last; and gave it unto us by
way of redundancy; and at last it proved that which was most
dear to us.'[6]

---

[1] *Verney Memoirs*, ii. 69.

[2] 'The Round-heads Race', appended to *The Distractions of Our Times* (1642). Cf.
Rump (repr. from 1662 ed.), p. 16; and Humphrey Willis, *Times Whirligig* (1647).

[3] Clarendon (viii. 82) says of Newcastle: 'He loved monarchy, as it was the foundation and support of his own greatness.' Cf. Ludlow, i. 96: 'Many of the nobility
and gentry were contented to serve his [Charles's] arbitrary designs, if they might
have leave to insult over such as were of a lower order.'

[4] *Lords' Journals*, v. 132. Cf. Ludlow (i. 96), who says of his own party in 1644:
'every one striving to enlarge his own power in a factious and ambitious way.'

[5] Preface to vol. i.   [6] Speech IV, in Carlyle, ii. 417.

The presbyterian and the sectary united in 1642 in an attack on a form of kingship that was based upon the exclusive privileges of the church. The spirit in which they set forth on their crusade is revealed in such pamphlets as *A Spirituall Snapsacke for the Parliament Souldiers*,[1] in which men are urged to

> Consider the parties against whom you fight are a most idolatrous, superstitious, delinquent, prophane, ignorant, or hypocriticall generation, take them where you will, from one degree to another, and you may fitly ranke them under some of those unworthy denominations; for either they are papists and so idolatrous; praelaticall, and so superstitious; offenders of several kinds and so delinquents; men of cursing, deboist, lips and lives, and so prophane.

But religious enthusiasts, though powerful in influence, were probably a relatively small proportion of the total population. Doubtless the majority of Englishmen were neither liberals nor puritans and were not generally interested in politics, except that they shared the almost universal hatred of popery. This prejudice the parliamentarians exploited to the full. They were continually declaring or insinuating, as Nicholas told the king,

> that popery (which is generally exceeding distastefull to yor subjects of this kingdome) is too much favoured by yor clergy here, & in yor owne court, & that this opinion (how unjustly soever laid by Brownists on yor Majesties government) hath & doth (more than any thing) prejudice yor Majesty in ye esteeme & affecc'on of yor people.[2]

On a later occasion he said that the alarm of popish plots frightened people more than anything else, that, therefore, it was a drum beaten upon all occasions, and that the suspicion of an intention to introduce popery was the primary cause of the unpopularity, in church and state, of Charles's government.[3] This fear was much augmented by the unwise intrigues of the queen (some of whose appeals to Roman catholic powers abroad were known to the parliamentarians), but especially by the Irish rebellion, when the exaggerated accounts of atrocities seemed to justify the worst fears of protestants.

Finally men with any kind of grievance—political, social, or economic—tended to find their way into the parliamentary ranks. The merchants and capitalists had been vexed by the

---

[1] By J. P. [? John Price] (1643).
[2] Nicholas to Charles I, 19 Sept. 1641.
[3] Nicholas to Charles I, 27 Oct. 1641.

financial devices of the Crown, and many a small shopkeeper had suffered from the disruption of trade caused by monopolies of common articles. In addition the debates in the general council of the army, in 1647, proved that among the common soldiers, as represented by their agitators or agents, were many striving after radical reforms, and pamphlets of levellers and diggers demanded important, or even revolutionary, changes in the social order. It is impossible to know the extent in 1642 of this discontent with the existing structure of society, for it was certainly not then articulate. Nevertheless there was a vague hope that better times would await the rank and file at the end of the war; that, as the paternal government of the nation would give way to popular government, so privilege and monopoly in the economic field would vanish; and 'the poor and middle sort of people' would enjoy a 'due and proper freedom'.[1] Perhaps it is not altogether fanciful to believe that the words the old Cromwellian soldier, Rumbold, uttered in 1685 have some application to 1642: 'I am sure there was no man born marked of God above another; for none comes into the world with a saddle on his back, neither any booted and spurred to ride him.'[2]

The uncompromising attitude parliament maintained during the summer of 1642 was largely due to confidence that the king could not raise an army, and for a long time this belief seemed justified. When Charles left London in January his position was desperate, for only some thirty or forty attendants went with him. He arrived at York in March, and a month later appeared before Hull but was refused entrance. His appeal to the Yorkshire gentry was accorded a mixed reception. Some 2,500 of the Yorkshire train-bands accompanied him when he again summoned Sir John Hotham, the governor, to surrender Hull, but meeting with refusal he was forced to dismiss the militiamen. His persistence before Hull is explained by his desire to secure the arms stored there when the forces raised to fight the Scots were disbanded. He then turned south and in August set up his standard at Nottingham. Even then, however, he had no more than 800 horse and 300 foot at his command, apart from the train-bands, whose loyalty was doubtful and military value slight. Many trusted advisers, therefore, gave up all hope of his being able to raise an army and urged him to hasten to London

[1] John Lilburne, *Englands New Chains Discovered* (1649), pp. A2–A2ᵛ.
[2] *State Trials*, xi. 881.

and, by a sudden appearance at Westminster, startle the houses into granting favourable terms.[1]

The king was saved from an unconditional surrender by a gross error on the part of his enemies. On 6 September the parliamentarians issued a declaration that they would not discharge their forces until Charles should abandon to the justice of parliament all persons voted to be delinquents, that the cost of raising their forces should be borne by delinquents and other malignant and disaffected persons, and that those who had lent money to parliament should be repaid out of the estates of the malignant party.[2] In this vague but comprehensive category were included—or might have been—all who had not actively assisted parliament. Consequently many who would probably have been content to remain neutral were now almost forced to take up arms in their own defence. Clarendon notes that the pride and perversity of the parliamentarians gave the king an advantage not to be imagined, and that henceforth his levies proceeded apace.[3] The parliamentary diarist, D'Ewes, agrees with the royalist historian. This declaration, he said, 'made not only particular persons of the nobility and others but some whole counties quite desperate . . . by which means without the special providence of God they were likely to help the king in his distressed condition with those considerable forces which he was never else likely to obtain'.[4]

Prominent royalists, who now had everything to lose by a parliamentary triumph, were zealous in raising a regiment of foot or a troop of horse out of their attendants and neighbours, and their efforts were so successful that by the end of September Charles had about 2,000 horse and 6,000 foot.[5] Weapons, however, proved as difficult to secure as men had been. The navy's adherence to the parliamentary cause prevented Henrietta Maria from transporting from Holland more than one small shipload of arms.[6] Accordingly the king called together the militiamen of the different counties and disarmed and then dismissed them. The result was that, while the royalists were not completely armed, nearly all had some kind of weapon, though a few carried only cudgels.[7] The artillery train was very small. What Clarendon calls 'the incurable disease of want of money' ultimately proved fatal to

---

[1] Clarendon, vi. 1, 15.   [2] *Lords' Journals*, v. 341.   [3] *Rebellion*, vi. 22.
[4] S. R. Gardiner, *History of the Great Civil War*, i (1914), 18, n. 3.
[5] Clarendon, vi. 62 n., 66 n., 71.   [6] Ibid. v. 374, 430; vi. 73.   [7] Ibid. vi. 73.

the royalist cause. Since Charles never obtained an adequate and regular supply of money, he never commanded a well-disciplined army. He had to rely upon private contributions and voluntary or forced requisitions, and the result was that, on the death or retirement of prominent supporters, the regiments they had raised melted away. Only at the beginning of the struggle was the royal treasury fairly full, thanks to the plate of the universities of Oxford and Cambridge and the generosity of wealthy individuals such as Worcester[1] and Newcastle.[2]

The parliamentarians had no difficulty in raising an army which, on paper, was adequate. It is true that the train-bands, for the most part, proved as useless to parliament as to the king. A parliamentarian complains that they were 'effeminate in courage and uncapable of discipline';[3] and two years after the war had started Waller branded the militia of the puritan counties of Essex and Hertfordshire as 'only fit for the gallows here and a hell hereafter'.[4] The London militia was an exception to the general worthlessness of the train-bands. Their presence on Turnham Green prevented Charles from attacking London in November 1642; their aid made possible the relief of Gloucester in 1643; and their stand at Newbury saved the day for Essex. In spite of this excellent record, however, they were not dependable for permanent service in the field. As Waller says, they soon came 'to their old song of "Home! Home!"'[5]

Parliament, therefore, followed the same procedure as the king and issued commissions to its prominent supporters to raise troops of horse or companies of foot. There is the difference to be noted, however, that, whereas Charles merely issued a commission and its recipient raised the men at his own cost, parliament gave grants of money for equipment as well. The result was that in a very short time Essex, the commander-in-chief, nominally commanded 5,000 horse and 25,000 foot. Actually he had only about half that number at Edgehill, the first battle in the civil war, in consequence partly of faulty dispositions and

---

[1] Henry Somerset, fifth earl and first marquis of Worcester. He is said to have spent £700,000 or £800,000 in the royal cause (Eliot Warburton, *Memoirs of Prince Rupert*, iii [1849], 517).

[2] William Cavendish, successively created earl (1628), marquis (1643), and duke (1665) of Newcastle. His losses due to the civil war are said to have been £930,000 (see his wife's *Life of William Cavendish*, ed. C. H. Firth [n.d.], p. 79).

[3] *Bibliotheca Gloucestrensis* (1823), p. 10.

[4] C. H. Firth, *Cromwell's Army* (1921), p. 17.

[5] Gardiner, *Civil War*, ii (1911), 5.

partly of the reluctance of some of the regiments to serve except as garrisons. This would give him a few thousand more men than the king had at that battle; yet his advantage in numbers was more than neutralized by his opponents' superiority in cavalry.

At Edgehill the royalist horse easily routed the two wings of Essex's army, but, rushing blindly forward in pursuit, missed the finest opportunity they ever had of annihilating their enemies. Meanwhile the parliamentary foot, aided by several troops that the royalist cavalry had missed, defeated Charles's foot, and might have overwhelmed them but for the return of the cavalier horse at nightfall. The actual fighting had resulted in a drawn battle, but Essex, by permitting the king to take Banbury unmolested, yielded the fruits of victory to the royalists. He retreated to London, while Charles took Oxford on his way before proceeding towards the capital. Reinforced by the London train-bands, Essex had double the king's numbers, so that, when the two armies came face to face at Turnham Green, Charles had to withdraw to Oxford, which became his headquarters for the rest of the war.

The advantage in battle had lain with the king; but his failure to conquer in a single campaign proved fatal. So slender were his resources, compared with those at the disposal of parliament, that time was against him. Not to have won a decisive victory in the autumn of 1642 really spelt final defeat.

At first it seems to have been the general impression that the civil war could be limited to the main armies of king and parliament and that they would soon reach a decision one way or the other. Accordingly, until the end of the year, there was little fighting outside the areas in which Charles I and Essex operated. After that the struggle was waged, in various degrees of intensity, throughout the country.

In the north, interest centres in Yorkshire. There the parliamentarians had two elements of strength: the possession of Hull, valuable alike as a base of operations and as a port for landing supplies of men, money, and arms; and the firm adherence of the manufacturing districts of the West Riding. 'Leeds, Halifax, and Bradford', said Clarendon,[1] 'three very populous and rich towns, (which depending wholly upon clothiers naturally maligned the gentry,) were wholly at their disposition.' Most of the gentry

---

[1] *Rebellion,* vi. 261.

were for the king, but were unable to face the parliamentarians under the two Fairfaxes, father and son, until the advent of the earl of Newcastle, who arrived just in time to rescue York from the besieging roundheads.

The first attempt of the royalists against the towns in the West Riding ended with their expulsion from Leeds in January 1643; the second was foiled by the resistance of Leeds and by Sir Thomas Fairfax's capture of Wakefield—which, to his admiring father, seemed rather a miracle than a victory;[1] the third was successful, for at Adwalton Moor (30 June 1643) Newcastle completely routed the Fairfaxes, who had but half his numbers. After this the clothing towns had no choice but to surrender, and for a year the royalists were supreme in Yorkshire (except for Hull).

In the west of England serious fighting began later than in the north. Sir Ralph Hopton, the royalist leader, after defeating the parliamentarians at Stratton, proceeded rapidly into Devonshire, which soon passed into his control, except for such puritan strongholds as Barnstaple, Exeter, and Plymouth. Sir William Waller, following a fruitful campaign around Gloucester, advanced to check his old friend Hopton. At Lansdowne, outside Bath, Waller's position was stormed by the Cornishmen. Their losses were so severe that they had to take refuge in Devizes. Reinforcements sent from Oxford, under Prince Maurice, completely defeated Waller at Roundway Down.[2] They marched farther north to join Rupert before Bristol. An attempt to storm the city was made and although only partially effective induced its surrender.

The royalist cause was now at its zenith. Charles, an excellent strategist but a hesitant tactician, planned a threefold attack on London. This provided that he should advance down the Thames with his main army, that Hopton with the western army should make his way along the right bank into Kent, and that the northern army, under Newcastle, should come down through the eastern counties, crush the nascent forces of the Eastern Association,[3] and assault London from the north. Provincialism proved too strong for the king. The western army,

---

[1] Rushworth, v. 268–71.   [2] 13 July.

[3] On 20 Dec. 1642 Norfolk, Suffolk, Essex, Cambridgeshire, and Hertfordshire were associated for their common defence. On 26 May 1643 Huntingdonshire was added and on 20 Sept. 1643 Lincolnshire.

which had lost severely in storming Bristol, now insisted on returning to guard their homes against raids from the garrison at Plymouth, and frittered away the summer in besieging that port. The northern army entered Lincolnshire, and, in spite of Oliver Cromwell's brilliant success in the skirmish near Gainsborough, captured that town and Lincoln. Then Newcastle, too, determined to retrace his steps in order to invest Hull, whence Sir Thomas Fairfax headed a number of raids in the North and East Ridings; but the operations before the town were badly conducted, and after a dashing sortie on 11 October Newcastle desisted.

When Charles saw that his strategic plan could not be carried out he decided to besiege Gloucester. The reasons for his choice are clearly stated by Clarendon: this was the only garrison the parliamentarians had between Bristol and Lancashire in the west, and its capture would give the king full command of the Severn, which would enable him to supply his troops at Worcester and Shrewsbury from Bristol; the trade of Gloucester might yield a substantial revenue; and if it were conquered the posts in Wales might be joined to the main army. Perhaps the decisive argument, however, was the expectation that the governor, Massey, would betray the city, as he had apparently promised to do. If this had been his intention, the militant puritanism within the walls caused him to change his mind, and Charles was successfully defied from 10 August to 5 September, when Essex's approach forced him to withdraw.

On his return Essex found that the cavaliers had reached Newbury before him and thus obstructed the road to London. Dearth of provisions made it essential that he should at once get into touch with the base of supplies, so he determined to cut his way through. The first battle of Newbury (20 September) was bitterly contested all day without a definite outcome. By nightfall Essex had made slight progress, but the undefeated royalist army still lay between him and the capital. However, Charles withdrew—according to one report, because his forces had exhausted their ammunition, or, according to another, because they had suffered severely during the unexpectedly fierce fighting.

The second year of the civil war was coming to an end without decisive results. Accordingly both sides began to look for outside assistance. The king turned to Ireland, the parliamentarians to Scotland. The situation in Ireland had gone from bad to worse. The Anglo-Irish of the Pale had cast in their lot with the native Irish, and the rebellion had spread from Leinster and Ulster to Munster and Connaught. Moreover the Irish were slowly organizing themselves. In May 1642 the heads of the Roman catholic church met at Kilkenny and drew up an oath of association to bind the Irish together into a confederation whose main object was declared to be the re-establishment of Roman catholicism. A supreme council, consisting of two members from each province, together with a president, was appointed. In October 1642 was convened a general assembly, which again pledged the confederation to maintain the Roman catholic faith and to observe the allegiance due to King Charles. Steps were taken to appoint a general over the armed forces of each province, the most important being Owen Roe O'Neill for Ulster. The lands of protestants and neutrals, and all church temporalities, were confiscated. It was with this confederation that the king ordered his representative in Ireland, the marquess of Ormonde, to treat. The 'cessation' was concluded 15 September 1643, and provided that hostilities should be suspended for a year, during which time negotiations might be conducted with a view to a definite settlement. For the present the confederates declined to send an army to England to fight for the king, but they granted him £30,000.[1]

Actually all that Charles gained was the use of the English forces released from service against the Irish; but it was generally believed in England and Scotland that the regiments from Ireland were composed of natives, 'idolatrous butchers' brought to England to exterminate protestantism.[2] In point of fact these troops had no great enthusiasm for the royal cause, and, when the largest body was defeated at Nantwich, about half of them willingly changed sides. The king, therefore, received very slight military advantage from the 'cessation', while his loss of reputation was enormous. Just as the Irish massacre had appeared to confirm the extreme fears of protestants in 1641, so the constantly reiterated charge that Charles's evil counsellors meant to introduce popery seemed to be substantiated by the 'cessation'. Certainly it was of the greatest assistance to the English in their negotiations for a military alliance with the Scottish presby-

---

[1] Bagwell, ii. 50–51.
[2] *Baillie Letters and Journals*, ii. 103.

terians. As Baillie says, 'most of all the Irish cessation made the mindes of our people embrace that meanes of safetie'.[1]

The difficulties in the way of a union with the Scots were caused by the opposing aims of the two parties. Whereas the English desired a political alliance for military purposes, the Scots wanted a religious covenant. Whereas the former were anxious not to shut the door upon independency, the latter were adamant against any toleration of sectarianism. At length a formula was devised to suit both parties, though the sequel shows that there was the widest divergence in its interpretation.[2] By the Solemn League and Covenant, the signatories were pledged to 'the reformation of religion in the kingdoms of England and Ireland, in doctrine, worship, discipline and government, according to the Word of God, and the example of the best reformed churches, and that popery and prelacy should be extirpated'.[3] In accordance with this treaty, the earl of Leven conducted an army across the border in January 1644.

His advent soon effected a remarkable transformation. Whereas previously Newcastle had outnumbered his enemies, he had now to face a new army superior to his own. To prevent the conjunction of Leven and Fairfax, he hastily marched north and confronted the Scots, first at Newcastle and then, when the Scots made a detour, at Durham. A disaster in his rear shattered his plans. Lord Bellasis, who now commanded the Yorkshire royalists, took up his position at Selby to prevent the Fairfaxes from advancing from Hull and attacking Newcastle in the rear. He was completely overwhelmed on 11 April—a disaster that had greater results than most of the battles in the civil war. This one well-planted blow ruined the royalist cause in the north. Newcastle retreated from Durham, with Leven at his heels, and took up his position at York, where he was promptly blockaded by Leven and the Fairfaxes and six weeks later by the army of the Eastern Association under Manchester and Cromwell.

Rupert, who had marched north, outmanœuvred the parliamentarians and relieved Newcastle. Believing that he had positive orders from the king to compel the enemy to fight at all costs, he insisted on following the parliamentarians to Marston

---

[1] *Letters and Journals*, ii. 103.
[2] Ibid., p. 90; Gardiner, *Civil War*, i. 229-36.
[3] Idem, *Constitutional Documents*, pp. 267-71.

Moor. There, on 2 July 1644, the two armies faced one another —the parliamentarians to the number of 26,000 or 27,000 on the top of a rolling slope, and the royalists, with 10,000 or 11,000 fewer men, farther down—with only a long ditch between them. Rupert meant to attack the next morning, but instead was set upon that very evening, when many of his men had left their ranks—like himself, to cook their suppers, or, like Newcastle, to enjoy a pipe of tobacco.

After a hard fight the royalists were badly defeated, losing some 3,000 through casualties and about half as many more as prisoners, together with guns and muskets that could ill be spared. The number of victims was not unduly large for the number engaged, but nevertheless the battle was decisive. Rupert and his horse had been worsted by a cavalry superior in discipline and leadership. Whereas his men had shown the faults first exhibited at Edgehill, Cromwell had trained a body of men capable of withstanding the chivalry of England.

The battle settled the hitherto fiercely contested question of the mastery of the north, for, although a few fortresses held out stubbornly, Newcastle and a considerable number of officers abandoned the struggle and embarked for the Continent. Rupert was made of sterner material and managed to rally 6,000 men, but he had to leave York practically undefended, and the city surrendered a fortnight later.

It is typical of the way in which the civil war was fought that the three armies which had conquered at Marston Moor now separated in order to pursue local objectives, with little reference to general strategy. Leven and the Scots marched north to besiege Newcastle; Sir Thomas Fairfax remained in Yorkshire, where royalist centres like Pontefract and Scarborough held out until July 1645; Manchester withdrew to the eastern counties and, disgusted at the rapid spread of independency in his army, did as little as possible until he reappeared as an unwilling participant in the second battle of Newbury.

In the south Charles revived in a modified form his plan of 1643 for an attack on London. He meant to remain on the defensive in the valley of the Thames and to push forward his right wing so as to join the royalists in Sussex and Kent and thus be able to threaten the capital from the south or at all events straiten it for supplies. Forth and Hopton, with an army of about 10,000 men, outgeneralled Waller, who had 1,000 or so more, and seized Alresford in Hampshire. Bad discipline and contempt for the enemy led the royalist cavalry, stationed on a slope, to descend into the valley, where they fought under great disadvantage and sustained a serious defeat.[1] This battle put an end for ever to the royalist plans for the invasion of Sussex and Kent.

Meanwhile Essex's army was slow to attempt a move, because it was still much under strength. Accordingly Waller was ordered to co-operate. Together the two armies drew near Oxford. But the mutual jealousies of the two leaders prevented them from acting in concert for very long. Charles managed to slip away from Oxford to Worcester, whereupon Essex, tired of acting jointly with Waller, decided to leave him alone to follow the king and to march himself into the west to succour Lyme Regis. Charles inflicted a severe check on Waller at Cropredy Bridge (6 June), and no longer had anything to fear from that general, whose army mutinied for want of pay and determined to return home to London, where most of them had been recruited. The king therefore turned and followed Essex into the west. The parliamentarians soon found themselves in a hostile land, penned in at Lostwithiel with no hope of relief. The parliamentary horse escaped to Plymouth, and Essex sailed away, leaving his infantry to make the best terms they could. The treaty stipulated that all arms and munitions were to be surrendered, but that the men were to be released, on condition they would not fight again until they reached Southampton or Portsmouth. As they were ruthlessly plundered by the royalists in spite of the articles of capitulation the hope of revenge kept them together. When re-equipped they served again under Essex at the second battle of Newbury (27 October). There the three armies, of Essex, Waller, and Manchester, numbering only some 19,000 men, attacked about half as many royalists. Thanks to ill-concerted strategy and the reluctance of Manchester to engage an army in which the king was present in person, the royalists succeeded in their aim of revictualling Donnington Castle.

The immediate military results of the second battle of Newbury were nil, but it had important reverberations in other spheres. The latent antagonism between Manchester and his lieutenant-general, Oliver Cromwell, now produced open recriminations.

[1] 29 March.

They were fighting for ideals fundamentally divergent. Manchester hoped that war would end with some compromise establishing presbyterianism in England but leaving Charles still king. 'If we beat the king ninety and nine times', said Manchester, 'yet he is king still and so will his posterity be after him; but if the king beat us once we shall all be hanged, and our posterity made slaves'—to which Cromwell replied: 'If this be so, why did we take up arms at first? This is against fighting ever hereafter. If so, let us make peace, be it never so base.'[1] He perceived the folly of trying to maintain the transparent pretext that the parliamentarians were fighting for the king against the evil advisers alleged to surround him: the parliamentary commissions ran in the name of king and parliament, as if political kingship could be supported by waging war against the person of the sovereign. Cromwell hated the idea of imposing presbyterianism on England with the aid of a Scottish army, and saw, as Waller had seen before him, that the contest would never be ended so long as reliance was placed upon local forces, brave enough in battle but prone to desert or mutiny before the end of a campaign. In a great speech on 9 December he urged that now was the time to speak out, or for ever to keep silence; unless effectual measures were taken for a vigorous prosecution of the struggle, it would be protracted until the kingdom would be tired of parliament and would hate its very name. Even those who were friends in the beginning were saying that the members of both houses

have got great places and commands, and the sword into their hands; and, what by interest in the parliament, what by power in the army, will perpetually continue themselves in grandeur, and not permit the war speedily to end, lest their own power should determine with it.[2]

This and similar arguments prevailed, and the New Model army was formed. It consisted of eleven regiments of horse with 600 men each, twelve regiments of foot with 1,200 men each, and 1,000 dragoons—in all, 22,000 men. The original intention had been to combine the three armies of Essex, Waller, and Manchester into one, but the campaign of 1644 had so reduced these forces that together they could supply only about 7,000 infantrymen. To provide the deficiency 8,500 were to be pressed from London, the Eastern Association, and the south-

---

[1] *The Quarrel between the Earl of Manchester and Oliver Cromwell* (1875), p. 99; Gardiner, *Civil War*, ii. 59.   [2] Carlyle, i. 186–7.

eastern counties. Each county had to contribute a fixed quota, and there was the greatest difficulty in filling it. The only particulars that have survived come from the Rape of Pevensey in Sussex. These show that three presses, in April, July, and September 1645, yielded 44, 49, and 56 men, and that they were escorted to the headquarters of the New Model army by 29, 49, and 56 guards respectively.[1] The ranks of the cavalry of the old army had never been depleted to the same extent as the infantry, and the high rates of pay made the former service much more popular. Accordingly it was usually unnecessary to obtain cavalrymen by impressment. Sir Thomas Fairfax, the commander-in-chief, was given authority to nominate his senior officers, subject to the approval of parliament.[2] A little later the Self-denying Ordinance was passed, discharging members of both houses from every office or command, civil or military, granted since 20 November 1640.[3]

The New Model had many advantages over its predecessors. Its cavalry, derived in the main from the old army of the Eastern Association, was composed for the most part of veterans led by officers in whom the troopers had every confidence. The foot were mainly raw recruits, stiffened with survivors of the first three campaigns of the civil war. The technical services were well supplied, and for a time at least pay was fairly regular. But the great advantage the New Model enjoyed was in its commanders. Fairfax and Cromwell—the latter retained as leader of the horse after he had quieted a mutiny in his old regiment, the Ironsides—made a very fine combination. With certain exceptions, the soldiers of fortune who had originally served beyond the seas, together with the pluralists and the military equivalent of placemen, disappeared. In their stead were stern enthusiasts, men who knew what they were fighting for and loved what they knew. Although the parliamentary ordinance prescribed that every member of the army, officers and privates alike, should take the covenant,[4] the former tended to be independents and the men indifferent to forms of church discipline. Inasmuch as the army was paid by parliament, and not by any association of counties or any single region, its movements were dictated by military exigencies, not by local fears or jealousies. At length

---

[1] *Journal of Modern History*, iii. 70–71.
[2] *Acts and Ordinances*, i. 614–26, 650–1, 653.
[3] Ibid., pp. 664–5.   [4] Ibid., p. 625.

parliament had an army able and willing to serve wherever the enemy was to be found.

The first two engagements of the New Model were the relief of Taunton and a cavalry raid by Cromwell around Oxford. On his way to the west Fairfax made it clear that the disorders so prevalent in the earlier armies would no longer be tolerated. Two offenders were hanged upon a tree by the road along which the army passed, as a sign that indiscriminate plundering would be severely punished. Before Fairfax reached Taunton he was recalled by the committee of both kingdoms to besiege Oxford. A brigade of four infantry regiments sent by him to the assistance of Robert Blake, the future admiral, at Taunton entered the town, but was itself then beleaguered.

Fairfax had made no progress before Oxford, when the news that Leicester had been stormed and sacked by the king caused him to start in pursuit of the main body of the royalists, whom he found near Naseby (14 June). The strategic withdrawal of the army to a position behind the skyline of the Naseby plateau was mistaken by Rupert for a general retreat. Accordingly the royalists pressed forward in pursuit, although they were outnumbered by nearly two to one and were attacking uphill. Nevertheless the parliamentary left wing was routed by Rupert and the infantry in the centre were hard pressed and in danger of defeat. But Cromwell, on the right, dispersed the opposing cavalry and then fell upon the royalist infantry. One brigade resisted, although set upon front, rear, and flank, until eventually broken by a combined assault of Fairfax's foot, his life-guard, and Cromwell's Ironsides. During the rout that followed the pursuit lasted ten or twelve miles and practically wiped out the king's army.

The remainder of the civil war was almost entirely given over to sieges. Fairfax first advanced into the west and defeated Goring at Langport—perhaps the most glorious achievement of the New Model, inasmuch as 700 horse, with a little assistance from the artillery and musketeers, won a victory over ten times as many royalists. Turning back, Fairfax stormed Bristol, but ever humane in the hour of triumph offered honourable conditions, which Rupert accepted. The popular hatred which the prince's exactions had excited is shown by the fierce cries of the countrymen as he marched out: 'Give him no quarter, give him no quarter!'[1]

[1] Joshua Sprigg, *Anglia Rediviva* (1854), p. 122.

Probably many royalist fortresses were induced to surrender without prolonged resistance by the fate of Basing House. After its successful storm Cromwell wrote: 'We have had little loss; most of the enemy our men put to the sword, and some officers of quality; most of the rest we have prisoners.'[1] Fairfax now returned to the west, where he was welcomed as a deliverer in the very parts where royalism had been strongest, for the tyranny of the hated leader Grenville had completely alienated the countryside. Even the chivalrous Hopton, who replaced him, could make no defence, and in March 1646 formally disbanded his forces. In the same month Charles's sole remaining army was beaten. Its commander, Sir Jacob Astley, acknowledging that the end had come, told his captors, 'You have now done your work and may go play, unless you will fall out amongst yourselves.'[2] The king gave himself up to the Scots early in May, Oxford surrendered in June, and to all intents and purposes the first civil war was over.

Charles, like Astley, anticipated that his opponents would quarrel among themselves. Indeed he had nothing further to hope for, for it soon became obvious that he could not obtain effective aid from either catholic Ireland or presbyterian Scotland. During the later stages of the civil war he had been planning Irish intervention on a large scale. He had employed both Ormonde, the lord lieutenant, and Glamorgan (Edward Somerset, later marquis of Worcester, commonly known as the earl of Glamorgan) to negotiate with the confederate Irish. The former filled an honourable role throughout, but the latter, a Roman catholic, signed three different treaties of progressive liberality, in all of which he exceeded his instructions. By the first (25 August 1645), the Irish were promised the free and public exercise of their religion and the sole possession of all churches not actually in use by protestants. It is typical of the ill luck that dogged the king's intrigues to secure outside assistance in the civil war that a copy of this treaty should have been captured in battle and published by the English parliament. The second and third treaties Charles repudiated. It is idle to spill learned ink in trying to determine how to allot censure for these ill-conceived and abortive treaties, because there can be no doubt that the king was playing fast and loose with the Irish.

---

[1] Joshua Sprigg, *Anglia Rediviva*, p. 149.
[2] Gardiner, *Civil War*, iii (1911), 80.

He wrote to his wife that he proposed 'the business of Ireland, but only in case there be no other way to save the Crown of England (for which at all times it must be sacrificed)'.[1] The confederate Irish may have been deceived, but Rinuccini, the papal nuncio, who landed in Ireland in October 1645, correctly gauged Charles's attitude. He wrote:

> I am alarmed by the general opinion of his Majesty's inconstancy and bad faith, which creates a doubt that whatever concessions he may make, he will never ratify them unless it pleases him, or, not having appointed a catholic viceroy, whether he might not be induced by his protestant ministers to avenge himself on the noble heads in Ireland, and renew more fearfully than ever the terrors of heresy.[2]

Nevertheless, at the king's absolute order, Ormonde succeeded in making a treaty with the confederate Irish. It promised to relieve Roman catholics of the oath of supremacy and of penal statutes, to open all offices to them, and to pardon all offences, civil and criminal, committed since 23 October 1641, with some trivial exceptions. This treaty, like the others, was absolutely in vain, inasmuch as, by the time it was concluded, Charles no longer possessed a port in England where an Irish army could land, even if one had been forthcoming. On the other hand his loss of popularity and prestige in England and Scotland, as these intrigues to employ the native Irish on English soil became known, can hardly be overestimated.

The king's negotiations with the Scots all hinged upon the covenant, whose acceptance they made an absolute *sine qua non* of military aid. To agree to establish presbyterianism in England Charles thought a sin of the highest nature. He had yielded against his conscience in the past, he told his wife, and his acquiescence in Strafford's execution had been deservedly punished. To give way again would only draw upon him God's further justice, both in this world and in the next. Besides, presbyterians taught as their main doctrine that the king must submit to Christ's kingdom, of which they were the sole governors on earth, and that the church should be absolutely independent of the Crown. Presbyterianism, wherever it existed, had originated as the creed of rebels, and, after all, if the pulpits failed to enjoin obedience, to dispute about the control of the militia was

---

[1] *Charles I in 1646*, p. 5.
[2] *The Embassy in Ireland of Monsignor G. B. Rinuccini*, tr. Annie Hutton (1873), pp. 145–6. Cf. Gardiner, op. cit., p. 55.

idle.[1] Instead of submission, presbyterians taught that supreme power is in the people, to whom kings ought to render an account. He explained his willingness to consent to the establishment of presbyterianism, for three years, as 'but a temporary permission to continue that unlawful possession (which, for the present, I cannot help), so as to lay a ground for a perfect recovery of that, which, to abandon, were directly against my conscience, and, I am confident, destructive to monarchy'.[2] Holding these opinions it is not surprising that Charles found it hard to come to terms with the Scots.

The king was no more fortunate in his negotiations with the English than with the Scots. When a prisoner in the north, he received from the parliament in London the Propositions of Newcastle. In nineteen clauses, they enunciated the parliamentary conditions under which Charles might be permitted to resume the throne of his ancestors. They required that he should swear to the covenant and suffer it to be imposed on all his subjects; that episcopacy should be abolished; that religion should be reformed according to the covenant, in such manner as parliament should agree after consultation with the Assembly of Divines sitting at Westminster; that he should grant to parliament complete control over the armed forces of the nation, for a space of twenty years; and that he should consent to the punishment, with varying degrees of severity, of all of his leading supporters.[3] When Hyde read the parliamentary demands, he expressed the opinion that if the king accepted them there would be no longer 'any seeds left for monarchy to spring out of'.[4] Charles, too, realized immediately that the propositions were wholly unacceptable, but characteristically thought that a positive rejection should be deferred as long as possible, and 'how to make an handsome denying answer is all the difficulty'.[5] He delayed so long that, instead of quarrelling, parliament came to terms with the Scots, who left England in January and February 1647, on the receipt of half the sum due to them for their services in England. Charles therefore passed into the

---

[1] On another occasion he wrote that his opponents wanted 'to take away the dependancy of the church from the Crowne; which, lett me tell you, I hould to be of equall consequence to that of the militia; for people ar governed by pulpits more then the sword, in tymes of peace' (*Clarendon State Papers*, ii. 243).

[2] *Charles I in 1646*, p. 83.

[3] Gardiner, *Constitutional Documents*, pp. 290–306.

[4] Idem, *Civil War*, iii. 129.   [5] *Charles I in 1646*, p. 51.

control of the English parliament and was brought to Holmby House in Northamptonshire.

For the moment interest shifts from the king to the army. Some reduction of its strength seemed necessary now that the civil war was over, and some part of it was likely to be sent to Ireland to subdue the confederate Irish. Parliament had at length issued its schemes for cutting down the number of soldiers in its pay and for organizing a force to reconquer Ireland. By the first the establishment for England was fixed at 6,600 horse and dragoons, and such infantry as were necessary for the garrisons. The Irish army was to consist of 4,200 horse and dragoons and 8,400 foot, all to be drawn out of the New Model.[1] At the same time the commons passed a vote that no member of parliament, and no one refusing to subscribe to the covenant, should continue to hold any commission.[2] Apparently parliament had accepted literally Cromwell's statement that the army would disband immediately upon order of the two houses.[3] They were soon to be undeceived. When they sent a deputation to the army headquarters at Saffron Walden, to enlist volunteers for service in Ireland, they were confronted with a unanimous demand for information about the payment of those who should serve in Ireland and concerning the satisfaction to be given for back pay, and indemnity for actions in the late war.[4] It is noteworthy that the quarrel between the army and parliament started over pay and indemnity. The arrears of the foot soldier now amounted to eighteen weeks, those of the horse to forty-three—parliament offered only six weeks' pay in cash on disbandment. The need for indemnity for any damage to life or property during the war had recently been emphasized in a legal action. At this stage the soldiers themselves, as distinct from their officers, began to petition, and, in addition to the demands already mentioned, to require that old volunteers might be exempted from impressment in the future, that the widows and orphans of soldiers killed in the war might receive pensions, and that soldiers might be compensated for any losses suffered. Parliament rejoined by denouncing all petitioners and threatening to proceed against them as enemies of the state.[5] A new parliamentary commission met with little success, and induced

---

[1] Gardiner, *Civil War*, iii. 217–19.

[2] Ibid., p. 220.

[3] Clement Walker, *History of Independency* (1648), p. 31.

[4] Gardiner, op. cit., p. 223.

[5] Ibid., p. 229.

only some 2,300 men, out of about 21,500, to volunteer for Ireland.[1] Consternation grew when first eight cavalry regiments, and then all the regiments, chose representatives, who came to be called either agitators or agents. The result was that the army soon had a council qualified to speak in its name.

Parliament for a time maintained an unyielding attitude. At first it seems to have contemplated meeting force with force: independents were weeded carefully from the London militia and only staunch presbyterians left. A stronger support might be found in the Scottish army, for which parliament was angling. The basis of agreement with Scotland was laid when Charles accepted the Newcastle propositions in a drastically altered form. He consented to the establishment of presbyterianism for three years and to a parliamentary control of the militia for ten. This agreement made possible an alliance between the Scots and presbyterians and cavaliers, which gave rise to the second civil war and ultimately to the Restoration.[2]

Meanwhile parliament made one more attempt at disbanding the army, and ordered each infantry regiment to a separate rendezvous, where the soldier was to take his choice between service in Ireland and immediate discharge. The result was that all the regiments, horse and foot alike, made for Newmarket, and there the Solemn Engagement of the army was read to, and unanimously approved by, the men. In it they declared that they would not disband until they received such treatment as should be thought satisfactory by a council consisting of the general officers of the army and two commissioned officers and two soldiers to be chosen for each regiment.[3] Simultaneously Cornet Joyce was sent by Cromwell with 500 horse to secure the king and to stop his removal to Scotland or elsewhere, and thus prevent his becoming the centre of resistance to the army. Joyce seized the king and brought him to Newmarket.[4]

The army was now in a stronger position: it had the king in its hands, and it became more unified after the rank and file had expelled unpopular officers.[5] It now embodied its political programme, for the first time, in the Declaration of the Army. Its signatories asserted that they were not 'a meer mercinary

---

[1] Gardiner, op. cit., p. 242.
[2] Ibid., pp. 252-3.
[3] Rushworth, pt. iv, vol. i, pp. 510-12.
[4] Ibid., pp. 513-16.
[5] Gardiner, op. cit., p. 284.

army, hired to serve any arbitrary power of a state, but called
forth and conjured by the several declarations of parliament, to
the defense of our own and the peoples just rights and liberties'.
Since they had enlisted in order to vindicate fundamental rights
and liberties, they would continue to assert them. Accordingly,
to secure their own and the kingdom's 'common right, freedom,
peace, and safety', they demanded: that parliament be purged
of delinquent, corrupt, or unfairly elected members; that it
should name a day for its dissolution, in view of the people's
right to choose their representatives at frequent intervals; and
that, after public justice had been satisfied by some few examples,
an act of oblivion should be speedily passed.[1] This declaration
was quickly followed by the impeachment, in the name of the
army, of eleven members of parliament—the leaders of the
presbyterian majority.[2] Their withdrawal was forced by a threat
of an advance on London.

By this time relations between the majority of parliament
and the army were so inflamed that it seemed more feasible to
the army leaders to reach an agreement with the king than
with the legislature. Cromwell and Ireton, who were mainly
concerned, soon found that they had undertaken no easy task.
They suspected that Charles was more anxious to make a total
breach between the army and parliament than to come to terms.
Ireton told him plainly, 'Sir, you have the intention to be an
arbitrator between the parliament and us, and we mean to be
it between your Majesty and the parliament.'[3] In conversation
with Berkeley, Cromwell declared that, 'whatever the world
might judge of them, they would be found no seekers of themselves, farther than to have leave to live as subjects ought to
do, and to preserve their consciences; and that they thought no
men could enjoy their lives and estates quietly, without the
king had his rights'. On the other hand the king 'discovered
not only to me, but to every one he was pleased to converse
with, a total diffidence of all the army . . . and grounded it
chiefly upon the officers backwardness, to treat of receiving any
favour, or advantage from his Majesty'.[4]

During July the council of the army had been slowly elaborat-
ing the conditions to be offered to Charles I. The Heads of the

---

[1] Rushworth, pt. iv, vol. i, pp. 564–70.   [2] Ibid., pp. 570–1.
[3] 'Memoirs of Sir John Berkeley', in Francis Maseres, *Select Tracts* (1826), i. 360.
[4] Ibid., p. 361.

Proposals suggested that parliament should set a date for its own termination; henceforth there should be biennial parliaments lasting for not less than one hundred and twenty days and enjoying control over the army and navy for ten years; no royalist should be permitted to hold any office in the state for five years or to be elected as a member until the second biennial parliament was over; there should be a council of state, composed of persons, to be agreed on now and serving for seven years, who should conduct all foreign negotiations but should require the consent of parliament to make war or peace; parliament should nominate great officers of state, directly for ten years and indirectly after that; all coercive power should be taken away from bishops and other ecclesiastical officers; all acts should be repealed enjoining the use of the Book of Common Prayer; no one should be compelled to take the covenant; and royalists should be allowed to compound on easy terms for their delinquency.[1] The Proposals seem to have angered the king. He spoke to Ireton and others with much bitterness and said, 'You cannot be without me; you will fall to ruin if I do not sustain you.' At length the loyal Berkeley whispered to him, 'Sir, your Majesty speaks as if you had some secret strength and power that I do not know of; and since your Majesty hath concealed it from me, I wish you had concealed it from these men too.' Charles soon recollected himself, but it was now too late, for many of the army leaders were already convinced of his duplicity.[2]

Meanwhile decisive events had been happening in the capital. Angered at the conciliatory attitude of parliament towards the army, a London mob pressed into each house in turn, and compelled the members present to rescind their votes. Thereupon the speakers of both commons and lords, together with about sixty members, who were independents, fled to the army. In their absence the eleven members returned, and preparations were made to put the City into a state of defence. At this stage the patience of the army gave way; the long deferred march on London took place, and a bloodless occupation ensued. The independent members were restored to their places in parliament and they forthwith appointed Fairfax constable of the Tower. While there he was shown Magna Carta. 'This is that',

---

[1] Gardiner, *Constitutional Documents*, pp. 316–26.
[2] Maseres, pp. 368–9.

he exclaimed, 'which we have fought for, and by God's help we must maintain.'[1]

Contrary to expectations events at Westminster still went against the army's wishes. Cromwell by this time was thoroughly out of patience with the presbyterian majority. 'These men', he told Ludlow, 'will never leave till the army pull them out by the ears.'[2] Unable to gain Fairfax's consent to use the army to expel obnoxious members, Cromwell, taking the initiative into his own hands, achieved his ends by a display of force. He had no sooner secured an independent predominance in parliament than he was faced with the possibility of losing his influence in the army. By October the inferior officers and rank and file were exasperated at the long-drawn-out negotiations with the king and at the failure of parliament to attend to the grievances they had enunciated in the Solemn Engagement.[3] Five regiments dismissed the agitators they had originally chosen and elected others, and their example was generally followed. These new agitators drew up the Case of the Armie Truly Stated, in which they asserted that, while they claimed arrears and indemnity as soldiers, as free commons they demanded rights and liberties. There was to be a law paramount that parliament should meet every two years and that it should be elected by all the free-born of England, of the age of twenty-one or upwards. Since 'all power is originally and essentially in the whole body of the people' and 'their free choice or consent by representors is the only originall or foundation of all just government', the authority to make or repeal laws should reside in the house of commons. Finally this document is remarkable for its insistence upon the removal of general social grievances. In order to relieve the poor from the oppressive excise upon beer, cloth, stuffs, and all manufactures and English commodities, the demand was made for a substitute duty on foreign products.

This was speedily followed by the Agreement of the People,

---

[1] Sir William Sanderson, *King Charles* (1658), p. 1002. Cf. John Lilburne's *Just Mans Justification* (1647): 'Magna Charta itself being but a beggarly thing, containing many marks of intolerable bondage.'

[2] *Ludlow Memoirs*, i. 148.

[3] In *A Cal to All the Souldiers of the Armie* (1647), Cromwell and others are accused of making the king an idol, of kneeling before him and fawning upon him, 'a man of blood; over head and eares in the blood of your dearest friends and fellow commoners'. If Cromwell should repent, let the soldiers follow him; if not, 'ye have men amongst you as fit to governe, as others to be removed and with a word yee can create new officers'.

in which the levellers, as the extremists were beginning to be called, embodied their constitutional theories. This proposed that constituencies should conform to population, that the present parliament should be dissolved on the last day of September 1648, that henceforth biennial parliaments should be chosen, and that representatives of the nation should have sovereign power, except that those represented reserved to their own decision the following subjects: (1) matters of religion, (2) impressment for military service, (3) punishment for participation in the late differences, and (4) equality before the laws, which 'must be good, and not evidently destructive to the safety and well-being of the people'. These were declared to be native rights, to be upheld against all opposition whatsoever.[1]

Both papers were discussed for a fortnight in the council of the army, in the presence of the field officers and of two officers and two agitators chosen by each regiment. The debates are of the utmost importance, not only because they gave all sorts and conditions of men opportunities to explain the principles for which they had fought, but also because they reveal the existence of fundamental differences in outlook. The higher officers, like Cromwell and Ireton, tended to be conservative, particularly in social questions, while the inferior officers often professed a rather doctrinaire radicalism or even levelling principles. These differences were overcome, now and later, by the masterly personality and general popularity of Oliver Cromwell, but they persisted and ultimately endangered the protectorate.

On the first day Sexby, one of the agitators, explained why they had drawn up the Agreement. It was essential to act quickly, for so far they had 'dissatisfied all men. Wee have labour'd to please a kinge, and I thinke, except wee goe about to cutt all our throats, we shall nott please him; and wee have gone to support an house which will prove rotten studds,[2] I meane the parliament which consists of a company of rotten members.'[3] Thereupon Cromwell shrewdly remarked that the Agreement was framed on the notion that it was possible to make a complete break with the past and to fashion a brand-new constitution. To the objection that the difficulties were great the

---

[1] Gardiner, *Constitutional Documents*, p. 333.
[2] 'Studds', i.e. the uprights in a lath-and-plaster wall.
[3] *The Clarke Papers*, ed. C. H. Firth (1891–1901), i. 227–8.

reply might be that faith could overcome them. Yet it should
be remembered that 'wee are very apt all of us to call that faith,
that perhaps may bee butt carnall imagination, and carnall
reasonings'.[1] Moreover they must be true to the engagements
already made in the declarations issued in the name of the army;
and he moved that a committee be appointed to consider the
nature of these obligations. Goffe, a religious enthusiast akin to
the fifth-monarchy[2] men, now and later spoke like one inspired.
To understand his speeches is to understand the spirit that
animated the New Model army. Let them not be ashamed to
declare to all the world, he urged, that their councils and their
ways were not altogether such as the world hath walked in. For
they had a dependency upon God. He seemed to be throwing
down the glory of all flesh and had thrown down the glory of the
king and his party and the presbyterians in the City of London.
Let them therefore beware lest they in their turn be thrown
down as a punishment for their timidity and worldliness.[3]

He proposed that the next day should be set apart to seek the
Lord in a prayer meeting. Wildman, the leveller, tried to show
that engagements need not be kept if they worked unexpected
hardships. Then Ireton, a great champion of the existing social
order, laid down the sole basis of right, 'that wee should keepe
covenant one with another'. He poured scorn on the law of
nature and argued that security of property rested upon the
observance of contracts.[4] In the end both Cromwell's and
Goffe's suggestions were adopted. A committee was appointed
and the prayer meeting arranged. At the latter Goffe was the
spokesman for those who believed that the army had a divine
mission to perform. Antichrist, he said, had been at work a
long time, and had entwined himself with the church. It was
said in the Book of Revelation that the kings of the earth should
give up their power unto the beast and in fact they had surrendered it to the pope. In England kings had been instruments
to cast off the papal supremacy and yet they had assumed the
same place. Now was the time when this mystery of iniquity
should be destroyed and in this work there should be a company
of saints, many of whom had been employed those last five or

---

[1] Ibid., p. 238.
[2] The last of the five universal monarchies foretold by Daniel (chap. 2) was to
be the reign of Christ.   [3] *The Clarke Papers*, i. 254.
[4] Ibid., pp. 263-4.

six years. Let them beware lest they endeavour to set up again that power whose ruin had been decreed on high.[1] He concluded with a strong plea for unity and patience.

Later the Agreement itself was discussed—particularly manhood suffrage. Rainborow, who represented the section of the army that had fought to make England a democracy, said, 'I thinke that the poorest hee that is in England hath a life to live as the greatest hee',[2] and ought therefore to be allowed to vote. Ireton, on the contrary, laid down the principle that no one had a right to the vote unless he had a permanent fixed interest in the kingdom, or, in other words, that the voters should be confined to 'persons in whom all land lies, and those incorporations in whom all trading lies'. In fact Ireton was arguing, very much like the nineteenth-century conservative, that the franchise should be restricted to those who had a stake in the country.[3] Rainborow rejoined that the foundation of all law is in the people and that every man born in England could not by law of God or by law of nature be deprived of his vote. Ireton replied that, if one man had an equal right with another in the choosing of him that should govern him, 'by the same right of nature, hee hath an equal right in any goods hee sees'.[4]

Cromwell thought that manhood suffrage tended to anarchy. Probably his fears were increased when one speaker hoped to live to see the day when king and lords and property would all be thrown down.[5] Later the same speaker thought that the power of kings and lords was a branch of tyranny.[6] In the end the discussion left the more general question of kingship and turned to Charles I. He was reviled as a man of blood, and any agreement with him was denounced as the maintenance of those principles of tyranny which God had declared against, as the many successes he had granted the army proved.[7] By this time Cromwell was getting impatient. He was also alarmed at the decline of discipline. He carried a resolution that representative officers and agitators should be sent back to their regiments.[8] Although there were meetings of the general council of the army as late as January 1648, for all practical purposes the experiment of governing an army by a system of representation was over. The representative general council of the army was re-

---

[1] *The Clarke Papers*, i. 282-3.
[2] Ibid., p. 301.   [3] Ibid., pp. 301-2.   [4] Ibid., p. 307.
[5] Ibid., p. 312.   [6] Ibid., p. 352.   [7] Ibid., p. 383.   [8] Ibid., p. 412.

placed by a general council of its officers. The re-establishment of the general council of the army and the acceptance of the Agreement of the People figured prominently among the demands of the mutineers for the next eighteen months. The most important and last mutiny in the army was crushed at Burford in May 1649. Henceforth the levellers ceased to be an organized group, though Lilburne continued to trouble the government almost until his death in 1657. Nevertheless, their democratic programme influenced the lower officers who remained republicans or commonwealthsmen until the Restoration.

Meanwhile royalists had observed the army's increasing hostility to the king. Charles noted the appeals made in the general council of the army to bring him, the chief delinquent, to justice, and being anxious to secure liberty of action he escaped and fled to Carisbrooke in the Isle of Wight. He had expected to find a welcome there, but after some hesitation the governor treated him as a prisoner. The flight, together with the discovery of the king's intrigues with the Scots, exasperated his opponents. They did not learn the actual terms of the Engagement, signed on 26 December 1647 by Charles and the Scottish commissioners, by which presbyterianism was to be established for three years and independency in all its branches rigidly suppressed, but they soon perceived that an agreement had been reached. Parliament therefore passed a Vote of No Addresses to the king, dissolved the Committee of Both Kingdoms, and substituted its English representatives, generally known from their place of meeting as the Derby House Committee.

The first sign that Charles had succeeded in allying presbyterian with royalist, to start a second civil war, came from Wales. Oliver Cromwell was ordered thither to suppress an insurrection, but, before the army was divided to meet the dangers threatened from all sides, the most famous of its prayer meetings was held at Windsor. There Goffe spoke on the text, 'Turn you at my reproof: behold, I will pour out my spirit unto you, I will make known my words unto you.' His denunciations of the recent 'carnal conferences' with the king, as a result of worldly wisdom and lack of faith, cut his hearers to the heart, and thereupon, we are told,

The Lord led us not only to see our sin, but also our duty; and this so unanimously set with weight upon each heart, that none was able hardly to speak a word to each other for bitter weaping, partly in the sense and shame of our iniquities of unbelief, base fear of men, and carnal consultations (as the fruit thereof) with our own wisdoms, and not with the Word of the Lord, which only is a way of wisdom, strength, and safety, and all besides it ways of snares; and yet were also helped with fear and trembling to rejoice in the Lord, whose faithfulness and loving-kindness we were made to see, yet failed us not; but remembered us still, even in our low estate, because his mercy endures for ever. Who no sooner brought us to his feet, acknowledging him in that way of his, viz. searching for, being ashamed of, and willing to turn from our iniquities, but he did direct our steps, and presently we were led and helped to a clear agreement amongst ourselves, not any dissenting, that it was the duty of our day, with the forces we had, to go out and fight against those potent enemies, which that year in all places appeared against us, with an humble confidence in the name of the Lord only, that we should destroy them; also enabling us then, after serious seeking his face, to come to a very clear and joint resolution, on many grounds at large then debated amongst us, that it was our duty, if ever the Lord brought us back again in peace, to call Charles Stuart, that man of blood, to an account for that blood he had shed, and mischief he had done to his utmost, against the Lord's cause and people in these poor nations.[1]

At first sight it seemed that the position of the army was well-nigh desperate. There were revolts actually begun in Kent, in Essex, and in south Wales; there was mutiny in the navy, as a result of which nearly half the ships in commission joined Batten in adherence to the Stuart cause; and an invasion from Scotland might be expected at any moment. In addition to this open hostility, the army was generally unpopular, especially in presbyterian centres like London or in districts in which it had been compelled to live at free quarter through lack of pay. Nevertheless it triumphed, thanks to its discipline and valour and to the skill of its commanders. Even these might have failed if there had been unity of purpose among the king's supporters. Unfortunately for his chances of success, the Anglican royalist and the ex-parliamentarian presbyterian were uneasy allies, agreed upon nothing except detestation of the army of sectaries. Englishmen in the mass remained neutral. Just as the presbyterian majority at Westminster could not make up their minds whether the Scots were to be treated as enemies or friends, so the majority of Englishmen did not feel sufficient concern in the outcome

---

[1] *Somers Tracts*, vi (1811), 501.

of the second civil war to take any part in it. Ten years more of puritan intolerance, as embodied in social legislation, were required before ordinary Englishmen were vitally interested in the suppression of the army, and even then they achieved their ends by splitting the army into factions, not by defeating it in the field.

Scotland, too, was hopelessly divided. The Engagers (who derived their name from the Engagement) were in the main the Scottish nobility, and those dependent upon them, and were bitterly denounced by the ministers for taking up arms on behalf of an uncovenanted king. Consequently the well-trained army under Leven was not available to Hamilton, who had perforce to lead raw recruits against the veterans of the New Model, when he crossed the border in July 1648. Under such circumstances it is not surprising that the royalist efforts were ill-concerted and their risings subdued piecemeal.

Fairfax crushed the royalists south of the Thames at Maidstone and besieged the Essex forces in Colchester, which stubbornly resisted until the end of August. By that time Cromwell, having subdued south Wales, had made a forced march northwards. The enthusiasm of his soldiers may be judged from the privations they manfully endured. One of them wrote of the hurried journey north: 'Our marches long, and want of shoes and stockings gives discouragement to our soldiers, having received no pay these many months to buy them, nor can we procure any, unless we plunder, which was never heard of by any under the lieutenant-general's conduct nor will be, though they march barefoot, which many have done, since our advance from Wales.'[1] On his junction with the northern levies Cromwell had to make a critical decision, for he could either bar the way of the Scots in their march south or pass round and place himself between them and Scotland. His choice of the second alternative received ample justification, for he found the Scotch army divided into sections near Preston and crushed them so completely (August 1648) that the second civil war was at an end.

The renewal of the struggle embittered the army, and made them resolve to exact an eye for an eye. After Colchester Fairfax had ordered the execution of two royalists who had already compounded for their participation in the first civil war. This bitterness seems to have sprung from the army's conviction that

[1] Gardiner, *Civil War*, iv (1911), 178.

their enemies in the second civil war had deliberately sinned against the light, when so many proofs of the divine favour had been manifested in the victories that had previously attended the New Model. Moreover, as Cromwell complained, whereas the former quarrel had concerned Englishmen alone, the present had involved an attempt 'to vassalize us to a foreign nation, and their fault that ordered in the summers business is certainly double to theirs who were in the first [civil war]'.

Meanwhile parliament, which had repealed the Vote of No Addresses, had entered upon a personal treaty with Charles I at Newport. Agreement was still impossible, but that mattered little now, for the army was determined to enforce its will. Its commanders believed that they had clear proof of the king's insincerity, and they were convinced that their recent victories were providences not to be resisted. They had lost confidence in the integrity of parliament, which, said Cromwell, 'would have put into his [the king's] hands all that we had engaged for, and all our security should have only been in a little paper'.[1] Charles himself was seized and brought to Hurst Castle on the Solent and later to Windsor, and London was occupied once again. Colonel Pride and his musketeers guarded the house of commons and arrested or kept out about 140 members, leaving a remnant rarely numbering more than 50 or 60. The original design had been a forcible expulsion of parliament, but the independent minority had persuaded the officers to purge rather than to dissolve it. The remnant passed an ordinance creating a court of 135 commissioners to try the king, and ignored the refusal of the house of lords to pass the ordinance.

Of the commissioners only about half could be induced to act, and Bradshaw was chosen as president of the court, with John Cook acting as prosecutor. When the king was brought before the court Bradshaw told him that the commons of England assembled in parliament, being sensible of the evils and calamities brought upon the nation and of the innocent blood which had been shed, had resolved to make inquisition for this blood and to bring him to trial and judgement. The charge itself was that Charles Stuart, having been trusted with a limited power to govern according to the laws of the land, had violated that trust and chosen to erect an unlimited and tyrannical power.

[1] Speech 1, in Carlyle, ii. 275-6.

For his part the king refused to acknowledge the authority of the court. Throughout he demanded to know by what authority he was brought to judgement. He argued that the liberties of his people were bound up with his own, and to acknowledge a usurped authority would be to betray these liberties. 'The king', he said, 'cannot be tried by any superior jurisdiction on earth. But it is not my cause alone, it is the freedom and liberty of the people of England.' He maintained this position unchanged for three days—whereupon, evidence having been offered of his participation in the civil war, Bradshaw pronounced sentence in a long, rambling discourse full of legal tags, scraps of history, and reference to Scripture. At the end the clerk of the court read the sentence, that Charles Stuart, for levying war against the present parliament and people therein represented, should be put to death by beheading, as a tyrant, traitor, murderer, and public enemy of the good people of this land. The king attempted to address the court in rebuttal of Bradshaw's charges, but was refused a hearing. His last words were: 'I am not suffered for to speak. Expect what justice other people will have.' He was led forth amid cries from the soldiery of 'Justice! Justice! Execution! Execution!'—at which he remarked, 'Poor soldiers! For a piece of money, they would do so for their commanders.'[1]

Even at the eleventh hour there was great difficulty in getting the members of the court to sign the death-warrant. The services of Hugh Peter were solicited to stiffen the backs of the hesitant, and he chose as his text, 'To bind their kings in chains, and their nobles with fetters of iron; to execute upon them the judgments written: this honour have all the saints.'[2] Threats are said to have been freely used, particularly by Cromwell, to force the commissioners to sign the death-warrant. According to one of the regicides, he at first refused, but Cromwell said, 'I will have their hands now'; and thanks to his vehement importunity fifty-nine signatures were ultimately obtained.

On 30 January the king was led forth to a scaffold erected outside the banqueting-house at Whitehall. The scaffold was surrounded by ranks of soldiers too deep to enable his voice to

---

[1] Muddiman, *Trial of King Charles*, pp. 130–1.
[2] Ps. clxix. On the same day Bishop Juxon preached before the king on the text 'In the day when God shall judge the secrets of men by Jesus Christ' (Rom. ii. 15).

carry to the crowd beyond. He therefore was content to address a few words to those in his immediate neighbourhood:

That he dyed a good Christian he affirms, for he had forgiven all the world, yea, those who chiefly caused his death (naming none). He wished their repentance and that they may take the right way to the peace of the kingdom, which was not by way of conquest, the way he apprehended hitherto designed. He did not believe the happiness of people lay in sharing government, subject and sovereign being clean different. And if he would have given way to an arbitrary government, and to have all laws changed according to the sword, he needed not to have suffered, and so said he was a martyr for the people.[1]

An eyewitness records that when the executioner struck the fatal blow, 'There was such a grone by the thousands then present, as I never heard before and desire I may never hear again.'[2] Troops of horse quickly dispersed the crowds but the memorable scene was never effaced from the minds of Englishmen. After the execution the king's body was embalmed and then buried in St. George's Chapel at Windsor. There is a tradition to the effect that, on the night before the body was removed from Whitehall, the watchers saw a man enter with his face quite hidden in his cloak. He approached the body, and then said, 'Cruel necessity.' It was thought that the speaker was Oliver Cromwell. If so, the words certainly represent only a passing mood, for the regicides did not order the king's execution as a measure of safety, but as a righteous judgement, a just retribution upon the author of the civil wars.[3] Like Ludlow,[4] they were 'convinced by the express words of God's law: "That blood defileth the land, and the land cannot be cleansed of the blood thus shed therein, but by the blood of him that shed it." '[5] Therefore, as Harrison stated at his own trial eleven years later, the king's arraignment and execution were not things done in a corner but upon the stage, in the light of the sun. They had acted, he said, 'in the fear of the Lord'. His remarks were silenced by the indignant question, 'Will you make God the

---

[1] *Moderate Intelligencer*, 8 Feb. 1648/9.

[2] Cromwell's view is well expressed in Letter CXLVIII (Carlyle, ii. 126), where he says that the king's execution will be mentioned with honour by Christians and with fear by tyrants.

[3] *Diaries and Letters of Philip Henry*, ed. Matthew Henry Lee (London, 1882), p. 12.

[4] *Memoirs*, i. 207.   [5] Num. xxxv. 33.

author of your treasons and murders?'[1] This was virtually what
Harrison wished to do, for he, and those who acted with him
in January 1649, believed in all sincerity that they were the
instruments God had fashioned to fulfil his will. Holding such
a view, it was natural that the regicides could never understand
the intense bitterness aroused throughout Europe by the execution of the king. General sympathy for him was much enhanced
by the appearance of Εἰκὼν Βασιλική, *The Pourtraicture of His
Sacred Majestie in His Solitudes and Sufferings*. As a contemporary
says, reading the book aggravated grief at the loss of so excellent
a prince, who had reached human perfection through adversity.
The contemplation of his virtues would render more odious the
wickedness of his persecutors.[2] Edition after edition appeared
in spite of all endeavours to suppress them, and translations
into European languages were rapidly made.[3] The enormous
influence of the book both at home and abroad forced the
council of state to take steps to counteract it, and recourse was
naturally had to Milton. During Charles's trial he had been
engaged upon *The Tenure of Kings and Magistrates: Proving That
It Is Lawfull, and Hath Been Held So through All Ages, for Any, Who
Have the Power, to Call to Account a Tyrant or Wicked King, and after
Due Conviction to Depose and Put Him to Death*. Seeing now that the
people were apt to set *Eikon Basilike* next the Bible and were
ready to fall down and give adoration to the image and memory
of the king, Milton prepared his *Eikonoklastes* to destroy the idol
erected by the 'mad multitude' in their 'besotted and degenerate
baseness of spirit'.[4] That two editions in English and one in
French sufficed for the *Eikonoklastes*, whereas some fifty in a year
were all too few for the *Eikon Basilike*, proves the complete
failure of the counterblast.

---

[1] *State Trials*, v. 1024–5.
[2] Walker, *History of Independency, The Second Part* (1649), pp. 138–9.
[3] See Francis F. Madan, *A New Bibliography of the Eikon Basilike* (1950), which
lists many issues in addition to the fifty editions published in 1649.
[4] *Eikonoklastes*, in Milton, *Works*, v. 64, 69.

VII

POLITICAL AND CONSTITUTIONAL HISTORY, 1649–58

THE establishment of the commonwealth really began on
4 January 1649, when the house of commons voted
that the people are, under God, the original of all just power: ...
that the commons of England, in parliament assembled, being
chosen by, and representing, the people, have the supreme power in
this nation: ... that whatsoever is enacted, or declared for law, by
the commons, in parliament assembled, hath the force of law; and all
the people of this nation are concluded thereby, although the consent and concurrence of king, or house of peers be not had thereunto.[1]

On the day of Charles's execution an act was passed against
the proclamation of any successor to him, and the above vote
was read again and ordered to be printed. A week later it was
resolved 'that the house of peers in parliament is useless and
dangerous, and ought to be abolished: and that an act be
brought in, to that purpose'.[2] On the morrow it was further
resolved 'that it hath been found by experience, and this house
doth declare, that the office of a king in this nation, and to have
the power thereof in any single person, is unnecessary, burdensome, and dangerous to the liberty, safety, and publick interest
of the people of this nation; and therefore ought to be abolished:
and that an act be brought in, to that purpose'.[3] Finally the
two acts, for abolishing the kingly office and the house of lords
respectively, were passed on 17 and 19 March of this year.[4]

The supreme legislative and executive authority therefore
resided in the one remaining estate. The Speaker of the house
of commons was first in dignity in the land, and the house itself
was unhampered by any check except whatever prudential
restraint might be imposed by the knowledge that its authority
rested solely upon the army. It was, of course, merely a fragment of the parliament elected in 1640. Membership was
practically confined to those who approved of the proceedings
against the king, and they numbered only about a tenth of

---

[1] *Commons' Journals*, vi. 111.   [2] Ibid., p. 132.
[3] Ibid., p. 133.   [4] *Acts and Ordinances*, ii. 18–20, 24.

the former body. They represented a very small section of the people of England, and were not wholly acceptable to the army, whose leaders had intended a dissolution of parliament—a step which the republican members managed to postpone, on one pretence or another, until they were ejected in April 1653.

The administration was conducted through the council of state, chosen for one year. There were 41 members of the first council, of whom 31 sat in parliament and 16 were regicides. The membership remained almost unchanged when the council was reappointed for a second year, but the composition of the third, fourth, and fifth councils was radically altered by the re-election, in each case, of only 21 members of the previous council and the appointment of 20 new members. The council of state transacted its business by standing committees, of which the most important were for the army, the navy, Ireland, and foreign affairs. Generally speaking, the members were extremely diligent, incorrupt, and efficient, and their conduct of public affairs compares favourably with the work of either their predecessors or their successors.

One of the most urgent tasks before the new republic was the reconquest of Ireland. That unhappy island had been left, for the most part, to her own troubles during 1641–9. Ormonde, the head of the English interest against the rebellious Irish,[1] had been ordered by Charles to arrange a truce to enable negotiations to take place between the confederate Irish and the king. The 'cessation' (15 September 1643), however, had not been recognized by the English parliament or by the Ulster Scots, and did not lead to any permanent treaty. Later Glamorgan had been sent to Ireland by the king, with a special commission of large but vague powers. As we have seen, he exceeded his authority in agreeing to all the demands of the confederates. When a copy of the Glamorgan treaty had been captured in battle its publication by the English parliament had caused a great sensation. Charles had been obliged to disavow his rash agent, with the result that suspicion of his sincerity had deepened both in England and in Ireland.

At that juncture Rinuccini, the papal legate, had arrived in Ireland and had at once formed a clerical party in opposition to the confederates. He had cared only for the interests of the catholic church and had been entirely indifferent to those of

[1] See above, pp. 135, 142.

Charles I. Whereas the confederates, anxious that a united front should be presented to the English parliament, had arranged peace with Ormonde, Rinuccini had raised the clergy against it. Aided by Owen Roe O'Neill, whose influence had been great after his victory over the Ulster Scots at Benburb (June 1646), he carried out a *coup d'état* by which a new general assembly had been convoked. This body had promptly repudiated the treaty, whereupon Ormonde had handed Dublin over to the English parliament, in whose name Michael Jones had become governor.

The Irish at that time had been divided into factions. O'Neill and Preston, the leaders of the two field-armies, had been jealous of each other and had rarely combined, and the extreme pretensions of the clerical group about Rinuccini had given umbrage to the old Anglo-Irish gentry. After Preston's overwhelming defeat at Dangan Hill by Michael Jones, it had proved possible to arrange a paper treaty at Kilkenny (January 1649) between the confederates and the royalists. Ormonde had returned and in the king's name had agreed that the penal laws should be abolished and an independent parliament established. For a moment the prospect had looked fair for this royalist-catholic alliance, and soon only Dublin, Drogheda, and Derry held out against it. However, Ormonde's defeat by Michael Jones at Rathmines ruined the only field-army that might have opposed the new forces Cromwell was bringing from England.

Cromwell, who had been entrusted by parliament with the reconquest of Ireland, landed in Dublin in August 1649 at the head of a well-equipped army of about 12,000 men. He at once determined to strike northwards at Drogheda, into which Ormonde had thrown some of his best troops. He summoned the garrison, about 3,000 strong, to surrender, and meeting with a refusal ordered the town to be stormed. The garrison made a stout resistance and twice repulsed the attackers. But the third assault, led by Cromwell in person, was successful. What followed is described by the victorious general: 'Being thus entered, we refused them quarter; having, the day before, summoned the town. I believe we put to the sword the whole number of the defendants, I do not think thirty of the whole number escaped with their lives. Those that did, are in safe custody for Barbadoes.'[1] Cromwell writes, in explanation of his

---

[1] Letter CIV, in Carlyle, i. 464–5.

harshness: 'I am persuaded that this is a righteous judgment of God upon these barbarous wretches, who have imbrued their hands in so much innocent blood; and that it will tend to prevent the effusion of blood for the future.'[1] Unfortunately for this defence of his severity, Cromwell was in error in supposing that the garrison was composed of those who had participated in the massacre of 1641. On the other hand he might have pleaded that the usage of war sanctioned putting to the sword those who persisted in defending an untenable town after being summoned to surrender.

From Drogheda Cromwell marched a month later to Wexford, and there too the garrison was slaughtered. God in his providence, said Cromwell in a letter, had caused the defenders 'to become the prey of the soldier, who in their piracies had made preys of so many families and [were] made with their bloods to answer the cruelties which they had exercised upon the lives of divers poor protestants'.[2] Other towns surrendered rather than risk a storm, but the approach of winter saved Waterford.

The position at the end of the year is thus summed up by Cromwell in writing to the Speaker of the house of commons: 'Although God hath blessed you with a great tract of land in longitude alongst the shore, yet it hath but a little depth into the country.'[3] Cromwell left Ireland in the following spring, entrusting to his son-in-law, Henry Ireton, and his successors, Edmund Ludlow and Charles Fleetwood, the completion of the conquest. They did not have to face the Irish army in the field, for neither Ormonde nor the earl of Clanricarde (who followed him in command) could unite the Irish factions. The war of sieges and forays lasted until the surrender of Galway in May 1652. The attempt of the Irish to throw off the English yoke had met with a terrible retribution, but their failure had been due more to their own divisions than to the superior strength of England. As a contemporary Irish poet wrote:

> The Gael are being wasted, deeply wounded,
> Subjugated, slain, extirpated,
> By plague, by famine, by war, by persecution.
> It was God's justice not to free them,
> They went not together hand in hand.[4]

---

[1] Letter cv (ibid., p. 469). [2] Letter cvii (ibid., pp. 486–7).
[3] Letter cxvii (ibid., p. 517). [4] C. H. Firth, *Oliver Cromwell* (1909), p. 264.

The decade of warfare had wrought havoc throughout Ireland, and what the sword had spared famine and pestilence had devoured.

Bad as the condition of the native Irish undoubtedly was, parliament soon proceeded to make it worse. Except for the comprehensiveness of their scheme for the settlement of Ireland, there was nothing novel about it, for it was based upon the plantation system that had commended itself to all rulers of Ireland from the time of Philip and Mary. Indeed a step in that direction had already been taken in 1642, when an act had been passed confiscating two and a half million acres of the holdings of Irish rebels, and allotting this land to those who would 'adventure' money for the reconquest.[1] To these original creditors were now added the merchants and others who had advanced cash or goods, and the soldiers whose heavy arrears of pay were to be satisfied from forfeited Irish land. Thus the parliament hoped at one and the same time to punish Irish rebels, reward English soldiers, and 'plant' an honest people. The act for the settling of Ireland (12 August 1652) exempted from pardon for life and estate those who had had any part or lot in the early stages of the rebellion beginning in 1641, together with about a hundred Irish leaders mentioned by name (Ormonde being the best known), and all who had slain Englishmen except in open warfare. The leaders of the Irish armies not comprehended in the first category were to be punished and to lose two-thirds of their estates, and those who had not manifested 'constant good affection' to the English parliament were to forfeit one-third of theirs and to be liable to transplantation.[2] By a later act those in the last class were to transplant themselves into the province of Connaught, or the county of Clare, before 1 May 1654, under penalty of death as spies and enemies.[3] As a result of this legislation, it is said that two-thirds of the land of Ireland changed hands. But, as happened in the case of Ulster fifty years before, the native Irish were normally not transplanted, because the new owners of the soil wanted them as labourers.

Apart from the permanent grievance of the land settlement, Cromwell treated Ireland with an enlightenment far in advance of his time. Free trade between the two countries was estab-

---

[1] 16 Car. I, c. 33, *Statutes of the Realm*, v. 168–72.
[2] *Acts and Ordinances*, ii. 598–603.   [3] Ibid., p. 750.

lished, and Ireland was allowed equal access to foreign and
colonial markets. In addition she secured representation in the
parliament of the three nations and, like Scotland, was allotted
thirty members. Other benefits were the administration of
impartial justice and the maintenance of law and order. The
religious policy of the government had been explained by
Cromwell in advance. In reply to the demand that liberty of
conscience for the inhabitants of a garrison town should be the
condition of surrender, he had said: 'If by liberty of conscience,
you mean the liberty to exercise the mass, I judge it best to use
plain dealing and to let you know, where the parliament of
England hath power, that will not be allowed of.'[1] Although
catholics were not compelled to attend protestant services,
priests were hunted down and exiled. As a compensation the
government endeavoured to establish a godly ministry and even
provided preachers who could talk to the Irish in their native
language.[2]

A critic observes, somewhat unjustly, that it was sad to
'observe how garrisons are placed in every quarter where the
Irish inhabite, ministers in none; as if our business in Ireland
was onely to set up our own interess and not Christs'.[3] He
might have added that private interests also had prevailed over
national. He notes that those in favour of enforcing the transplantation scheme to the utmost argued that if the Irish were
allowed to remain 'the English may degenerate, and turn Irish
unless a separation by transplanting one from the other be
observed; and to this purpose experience of former ages has
urged'.[4] These fears proved justified, for the Cromwellian
soldiers in two generations tended to become Roman catholic
in religion and Irish in sentiment. The government foresaw the
danger, however, and prohibited mixed marriages. The soldiers
were forbidden, under heavy penalties, to take Irish women to
wife unless there was clear proof that the latter had been converted to protestantism. But the order was ignored.[5] The result
was that the large landlords remained protestant and became
divided from the small farmers and peasants, who remained

---

[1] Letter cx, in Carlyle, i. 493.
[2] R. Dunlop, *Ireland under the Commonwealth* (1913), i, p. clx; ii. 517, 654–5, 660–1.
[3] Vincent Gookin, *The Great Case of Transplantation in Ireland* (1655), p. 3.
[4] Ibid., p. 18.
[5] John P. Prendergast, *Cromwellian Settlement of Ireland* (1875), pp. 232–5; Dunlop, op. cit. ii. 711–12, 363.

catholic, by religion, language, race, and a memory of the Cromwellian settlement.

The commonwealth also encountered a stern opposition nearer home, from the Scots. Six days after the execution of Charles I, the Scottish estates proclaimed his son, Charles II, king of Great Britain, France, and Ireland. Their envoys in England demanded that Charles II should be there recognized, whereupon the Long Parliament expelled the envoys and declared that they had laid 'the grounds of a new and bloody war'. More than a year elapsed, however, before actual fighting began in earnest, the delay having been due partly to Cromwell's preoccupation with Ireland but more especially to the reluctance of Charles II to accept the terms under which the Scots would acknowledge him as their king. In the spring of 1649 the Scottish commissioners visited him in exile in the Netherlands and demanded that he should accept the covenant and presbyterianism and impose them throughout Great Britain and Ireland. He refused, hoping that Montrose,[1] whom he commissioned to call the Scottish royalists to arms, would emulate his former triumphs and thus make the Scottish covenanters more reasonable. If Montrose failed, he thought Ormonde in Ireland might prove a better champion than Argyll in Scotland. But Cromwell's successes in Ireland ruined all hope that she might be made the base for the conquest of England, and Montrose, whom the king was forced publicly to disown, was defeated and executed. Charles therefore gave way, though he refused to sign the covenant until he was actually at sea on his way to Scotland. He struggled hard against the importunities of the Scottish commissioners, but they compelled him to swallow the bitter pill. They made him, said one of them, 'sign and swear a covenant, which we knew, from clear and demonstrable reasons, that he hated in his heart. . . . He sinfully complied with what we most sinfully pressed upon him.'[2] When he landed, he found that he had gained little by his sacrifice, for he was treated as a prisoner and fresh humiliations were heaped upon him. He was forced to issue a declaration in which he desired to be deeply humbled before God, because of his

---

[1] During 1644-5 Montrose, with a mixed force of Highlanders and Scotch-Irish, had won many notable victories for Charles I against the presbyterians in Scotland, but he had been overthrown at Philiphaugh in the autumn of 1645 and forced to flee the country.

[2] *Diary of Alexander Jaffray*, ed. John Barclay (1833), p. 32.

father's opposition to the works of reformation, and to the Solemn League and Covenant; and because his mother had been guilty of idolatry, the toleration of which in the king's house could not but be a high provocation to a jealous God, visiting the sins of the fathers upon the children.[1] Charles is reported to have said that he would be ashamed to look his mother in the face hereafter.

Covenanting zeal found further opportunities for this intolerance in the appointment of a commission to purge the army raised to restore Charles II. It is said that the commission set to work with such good will that it cashiered three or four thousand old soldiers and left in the ranks only those who were 'ministers' sons, clerks, and such other sanctified creatures, who hardly ever saw or heard of any sword but that of the spirit'.[2] To such bigots as these Cromwell's appeals for a peaceful outcome of the differences between England and Scotland fell on deaf ears. In vain he pleaded that they should ask themselves whether all that they had done was infallibly agreeable to the Word of God. 'I beseech you', he said, 'in the bowels of Christ, think it possible you may be mistaken.'[3]

Having appealed fruitlessly to the covenanters to abandon Charles II, Cromwell determined to compel them by war. He led a fine army across the border, but for a time was unable to force his elusive enemy, Leslie, to fight on a fair field. Indeed it looked as if his invasion of Scotland would end in complete failure. At the beginning of September 1650 he was hemmed in at Dunbar by the Scottish army on the hills, and there seemed nothing to do except to embark on board the fleet, which had followed him offshore on his march northwards. Nevertheless Cromwell said, 'We have much hope in the Lord; of whose mercy we have had large experience.'[4] Fortunately for Cromwell the Scots, fearing his escape, descended from the hills in order to be near enough to prevent his embarkation. They intended to fight at their convenience, but instead they were surprised by Cromwell's attack at dawn and completely routed. Some three or four thousand of the Scots were casualties, and ten thousand prisoners—and this at a cost of less than thirty English lives.

The effect on the Scots of the news of Dunbar was over-

---

[1] Sir Edward Walker, *Historical Discourses* (1705), p. 171.   [2] Ibid., pp. 162–5.
[3] Letter CXXXVI, in Carlyle, ii. 79.   [4] Letter CXXXIX (ibid., p. 92).

whelming. They had been so confident of the righteousness of their cause that its utter overthrow produced much heart-searching. Many felt they could no longer withstand 'the dreadful appearance of God against us at Dunbar after so many public appeals to him'.[1] About fifty or sixty ministers held an open discussion of the reasons for the Lord's controversy with Scotland, and certain of the Scots at least (like Jaffray) began to realize that perhaps the intolerance of the kirk was a sinful mistake.[2] An English soldier noted that most Scots 'do idolize and set up their ministers, believing what they say, though never so contrary to religion and reason, and they stand more in awe of them, than a schoole boy does of his master'.[3] After Dunbar, however, the presbytery never recovered the position it had enjoyed during its golden age from 1638 to 1650. Moreover Dunbar shattered at a blow the policy embodied in the Solemn League and Covenant—the attempt to thrust upon Englishmen an extreme form of presbyterianism. As Newburn had been the Valmy, so was Dunbar the Waterloo, of the stricter covenanters.

The immediate result of Dunbar was the creation of further divisions among the Scots. The more rigid covenanters laid the blame for that disaster upon ungodliness in high places. Some even drew up a remonstrance in which they declared that they would refuse to acknowledge Charles II until he had given full proofs of the sincerity of his adhesion to the covenant. This was condemned in a resolution of the committee of estates, and the two documents gave names to the opposing factions—remonstrants (or protesters) and resolutioners. The former were sufficiently strong in the south-west to make the latter relax their hostility to the 'malignants', so that an alliance was formed between covenanter and royalist. Charles II was crowned at Scone, the Act of Classes[4] was repealed, and the king shook himself free from the shackles Argyll had set upon him. His enjoyment of the kingdom was short-lived, however, for Cromwell, having overrun the lowlands, advanced to Perth and threatened to cut off the royal army about Stirling from its source of supplies. By this manœuvre he had purposely left

---

[1] *Jaffray Diary*, p. 44.   [2] Ibid., pp. 38, 40.
[3] *Charles the Second and Scotland in 1650*, ed. S. R. Gardiner (1894), p. 137.
[4] Passed in 1649 to exclude all except sincere covenanters from all public offices or military commands.

the road to England open. Charles seized his opportunity and marched south as far as Worcester, but found that few Englishmen would join a Scottish invading army. Cromwell, on the other hand, had no difficulty in enlisting the English militia, who fought at Worcester side by side with veterans of the New Model. This 'crowning mercy' left Charles a wandering fugitive, who after many hairbreadth escapes found a boat to carry him to France. Scotland was too exhausted to raise another army, and Cromwell's lieutenant, George Monck, speedily conquered the land. A royalist insurrection, under first Glencairne and then Middleton, took place in 1653-4, but received no active support from the lowlands and came to an end after one defeat, at Dalnaspidal.

Scotland, like Ireland, was now united to England, and was allotted thirty representatives in the parliament at Westminster. In addition she enjoyed free trade with England and the colonies. By the maintenance of garrisons and posts, the highlands were kept in excellent order. Justice was administered by commissioners, of whom the majority were Englishmen, and their impartiality extorted the reluctant admiration of the Scots. Although the estates of noblemen who had fought for Charles I in 1648, or Charles II later, were forfeited, tenants or vassals were pardoned for their participation in the wars. No attempt was made to interfere with the religious services of the presbyterians, but the general assembly was forbidden to meet and all coercive jurisdiction taken from the presbyteries. On the whole Burnet's tribute is deserved: 'We always reckon those eight years of usurpation a time of great peace and prosperity.'[1]

Yet Cromwell's government was bitterly hated. The garrisons in Scotland entailed a crushing burden of taxation, and the clergy remained resolutely hostile. As Monck confessed in 1657, 'The Scots are now as malignant as ever they were since I knew Scotland.'[2] They felt that whatever material benefits they might enjoy from the union were too dearly purchased by the loss of their independence. 'As for the embodying of Scotland with England', wrote one, 'it will be as when a poor bird is embodied in the hawk that hath eaten it up.'[3]

Cromwell had now thoroughly conquered the domestic

---

[1] *History of My Own Time*, ed. Osmund Airy (1897), i. 61.
[2] *Scotland and the Protectorate*, ed. C. H. Firth (1899), p. 347.
[3] *Life of Mr. Robert Blair*, ed. T. M'Crie (1848), p. 292.

enemies of the commonwealth and could at last turn his attention to the problems of peace. The form of government established after Charles's execution could not be regarded as other than temporary, for it consisted of a mere remnant of the Long Parliament, dependent for its authority upon the army. Cromwell saw as clearly as any lawyer that a veiled military despotism was not likely to find favour in the eyes of most Englishmen. He must have realized that the existing republic could not long survive his own death—if it lasted till then—and that the sole hope for its permanence was to broaden the narrow base of support on which it stood. To do so it was essential to reconcile victors and vanquished, and to attract the large middle group that had been more or less neutral during the civil wars. This ultimately proved impossible, and must have appeared exceedingly difficult to the most sanguine in 1651. It is true that the Scottish invasion that ended at Worcester had aroused the national pride. However, elation over the army's success against the Scots was likely before long to yield to resentment at the high taxation necessary to pay the soldiery. Meanwhile it seemed possible to maintain or enlist popular support by a threefold programme: reducing taxation, granting an amnesty to royalists, and initiating reforms. Unfortunately, in none of these projects could Oliver Cromwell count on the cordial co-operation of parliament. The commons readily passed a resolution to disband certain regiments and reduce the number of companies in others, thus effecting a saving of £35,000 per month and enabling a reduction of the monthly assessment from £120,000 to £90,000. But the foreign policy of the council of state, and in particular the war with the United Provinces, soon destroyed this boon and restored the assessment to the old high figure.

As for the royalists, there was undoubtedly a tendency among them to submit to the powers that were. Not a few gladly salved their consciences with some such argument as occurs in Hobbes's *Leviathan*, that allegiance is due only so long as the sovereign affords protection. This view, said Clarendon,[1] prevailed for a number of years and extinguished all visible fidelity to the king, so that Hobbes could brag that he persuaded many to submit to the usurper. However, the royalists' attitude to the republic ultimately depended more upon their treatment

---

[1] *A Briefe View and Survey of the . . . Leviathan* (1676), pp. 92–93.

by their conquerors than upon Hobbes's political philosophy. It was soon obvious that they could not expect leniency. After much delay and with considerable reluctance, parliament eventually passed what was called an ordinance of general pardon and oblivion.[1] Its introductory sentence boasted that it was enacted in order that all people might enjoy their just rights and liberties; but, actually, the bill was too clogged with exceptions to carry out these ideals in their entirety. From the general indemnity for all offences committed against the state prior to 3 September 1651 (the date of the battle of Worcester), high treasons and rebellious acts—mere words being pardoned —committed since 30 January 1649 were excluded, as well as sums due to redeem sequestered lands. For the most part the act was received with derision. The little effect it might have had in reconciling royalists to the republic was speedily undone, later in that same year, by another act, providing for the sale of estates forfeited for treason. The number of individuals concerned was more than six hundred, who, said Cromwell, were driven like flocks of sheep, forty in a morning, to the confiscation of goods and estates.[2] The economic necessities of the state sufficiently explain this treatment of the losing side as irreconcilable and therefore to be ruined, but some members may have shared the opinion Ludlow afterwards set down in his *Memoirs*,[3] that Cromwell was merely cultivating popularity in urging clemency for royalists, and they may have derived a measure of satisfaction from thwarting him.

The commons were just as difficult on three other questions in which the army was vitally interested—reform, religion, and a general election. Although the primary causes of the puritan revolution were political and religious, economic and social factors, which were by no means insignificant at the beginning, were now growing in importance. The open attack of levellers and diggers upon the commonwealth—one section demanding far-reaching democratic changes in the constitution, and the other, smaller but equally vociferous, advocating socialistic measures—could not be met with a policy of mere negation. The attitude of parliament towards legal reform may be cited as an example of its attitude towards reform in general.

---

[1] *Acts and Ordinances*, ii. 565–77.
[2] Ibid., pp. 623–52; S. R. Gardiner, *Commonwealth and Protectorate* (1903), ii. 200; Speech III, in Carlyle, ii. 370.   [3] Vol. i, pp. 344–5.

The need of some change in legal procedure, as well as alterations in the law itself, hardly admitted of debate. The dilatoriness and costliness of proceedings in all courts practically denied justice to a poor man. The court of chancery, in particular, excited the indignation of all reformers. In Barebones' Parliament a speaker alleged that there were twenty-three thousand cases depending in that court, some of which had already lasted ten, twenty, or even thirty years, and that in some of them five hundred orders or more had been issued. After this it is not surprising to read that certain members did not hesitate to call chancery 'a mystery of wickedness and a standing cheat'.[1] In all courts the pleadings were technical, prolix, and conducted in a language not spoken or even comprehended by any but lawyers, and documents for different courts were written in different hands which no one but the initiated can read now or could then. Fees and costs were excessive, and there were not a few in debtors' prisons who owed their ruin, like Sam Weller's acquaintance in the Fleet, to disputed legacies. As for the law itself, then, and for the next two hundred years, reform was urgently needed. There were, as Cromwell said, 'wicked and abominable laws',[2] by which a man might be hanged for stealing a trifle, or, indeed, for almost any felony.

The remnant of the Long Parliament did little to remedy any of these abuses. At least two committees proposed admirable reforms, but the commons were content to waste their time by interminable debates. Many excellent sentiments were uttered, but, said Cromwell, 'we know that many months together were not enough to pass one word, called "incumbrances"'.[3] Such legislation as was passed tended, for the most part, to make matters worse instead of better. The draconic law, which made adultery punishable by death (10 May 1650), was definitely a step in the wrong direction, and, like most statutes with exorbitant penalties, was nullified by the refusal of juries to convict.

The religious chaos that existed after the abolition of episcopacy and the failure of the presbyterian system to win general acceptance, continued. The one contribution the commons made that was undoubtedly popular with the army was the abolition of the old statutes imposing penalties on all refusing

---

[1] *Parliamentary History*, iii. 141-3.
[2] Speech v, in Carlyle, ii. 541.   [3] Speech i (ibid., p. 283).

to attend their parish churches on Sunday. Otherwise the commons were unable to agree on any positive enactment. Members with presbyterian sympathies were anxious to impose certain fundamentals before a man should be free to propagate his opinions, while others, like Vane, were against any form of established church. Cromwell was as anxious as Vane or Milton that there should be no revival of religious persecution, but he saw more clearly then either of them the folly of disestablishing the church, and consequently abolishing tithes, without first making some provision for the stipend of ministers.

To these causes of disagreement between the army and the commons was added the dispute about the dissolution of the Long Parliament. After some hesitancy the army had been persuaded not to turn it out in 1648 and to be content with Pride's Purge. Since that time the army had sought in various ways to induce the remnant, or Rump, to name a day for dissolution. With infinite difficulty the members at length were brought to agree that 3 November 1654 should be the last day of their session. But as the incapacity to effect reform, the corruption and complacency of members, gave more and more offence, Cromwell and others exerted every effort to advance the date of a general election. The Rump, however, clung like limpets to their seats. Though they were frightened into preparing a bill for a new representative, as it was called, it soon became apparent that the bill was merely a scheme for perpetuating the present members in power, for they were to keep their seats without the necessity of re-election and to be the sole judges of other persons chosen; and these provisions were to apply to all future parliaments. This was too much for Cromwell and his officers, who summoned a conference with the parliamentary leaders and evidently urged them to suspend the bill. However, next morning it was being hurriedly rushed through parliament when news was brought to Cromwell of what was happening. Hastily summoning a few files of musketeers of his own regiment, he went down to the house. He listened for a brief while to the debate, until the Speaker was about to put the question that the bill be passed. He then rose and, after praising the good work that parliament had done formerly, upbraided members individually for corruption, evil living, and so on. At length he summoned his soldiers, and the house was cleared. Later in the day, he told the council of state that their attendance would be required no longer, for parliament was dissolved. John Bradshaw spiritedly rebuked him: 'Sir, we have heard what you did at the house this morning, and before many hours all England will hear it; but you are mistaken to think that the parliament is dissolved; for no power under heaven can dissolve them but themselves: therefore, take you notice of that.'

The supreme authority on this period comments that 'Bradshaw was right: the ideal of constitutional government which the Long Parliament represented would prove stronger in the end than Cromwell's redcoats.... With its expulsion, the army flung away the one shred of legality with which it had hitherto covered its actions.'[1] It is certainly true that military force appeared 'naked and unashamed', having cast aside the transparent veil of constitutionalism. For the moment, however, the populace greeted with hearty approval the ignominious ejection of the Rump. Its members had become so odious that contemporaries eagerly listened to, and repeated with exaggerations, the reproaches Cromwell had hurled at offending members.[2] Also, there was a certain poetical justice that the Rump, which owed its supremacy in the commons to the military *coup d'état* of Pride's Purge (just as the earlier presbyterians owed their majority to the expulsion of royalists), should at length fall a victim to military violence. Nevertheless the 'interruption', as the expulsion of the Rump was called in parliamentary circles in 1660, was a grievous mistake, for it divided the civilian and military supporters of the republic. The bitter hatred the rigid republicans felt for the Cromwellians was never appeased, and wrecked the successive parliaments Oliver and Richard Cromwell summoned. It survived the downfall of Richard Cromwell and was fatal to the compromise hastily arranged with the army leaders in the spring of 1659. Not even the shadow of the approaching Restoration could make men like Hesilrige, Scot, and Vane forget or forgive the ignominy they endured on 20 April 1653.

Having expelled the Rump because it refused to dissolve itself, the army leaders could hardly delay in substituting some kind of representative body. It must be confessed that they were grossly inconsistent, inasmuch as their nominees were not

---

[1] Firth, *Cromwell*, p. 324.

[2] For a severe condemnation of the Long Parliament, see 'The Digression', in Milton's *History of Britain* (*Works*, x. 317–25).

elected at all. Letters were sent round to the congregational churches in each county, asking them to name persons they considered fit to be members of the new representative. When the replies were received, the council of the army sat from day to day and finally picked out 129 representatives of England, to which were added 5 for Scotland and 6 for Ireland. The writ of summons stated that 'divers persons fearing God, and of approved fidelity and honesty'[1] were chosen by the army officers. The 140 have sometimes been called the Nominated Parliament and sometimes Barebones' Parliament (after one of its members).

The Nominated Parliament was a great disappointment to its conveners. Its members' enthusiasm was at least equal to the ecstatic fervour of Cromwell's opening speech, but their lack of experience of public affairs could not be overcome by mere zeal for righteousness. They might declare that 'they looked for the long-expected birth of freedom and happiness', but of the few acts they managed to pass only one is remembered today (that establishing civil marriage),[2] and this caused much unpopularity. With little debate the abolition of the court of chancery was voted and a committee appointed to codify the law— some hoped so to simplify it that it might all be contained in a volume no bigger than a pocket-book. Ecclesiastical questions were tackled as vigorously as the law. A resolution was passed abolishing patronage, and indirectly members voted for the disestablishment of the church instead of for its reformation. A small majority was against tithes, believing that a better method of providing ministers' stipends could be found than the way by which many a good soul got but £20 or £30 a year to maintain himself and family, while others received £300 or £400.[3] This evident intention to change radically the existing ecclesiastical system convinced the army leaders that they had not found a fit instrument for their needs. They therefore induced their supporters in the Nominated Parliament to meet early one morning and agree to resign their powers into Cromwell's hands. Their action was a surprise to him, for he had taken no part in the intrigue, which had been mainly the work of Major-General John Lambert. The latter now urged Cromwell to

---

[1] *Old Parliamentary History*, xx. 151.   [2] See below, pp. 203–4.
[3] 'An Exact Relation of the Proceedings and Transactions of the Late Parliament', in *Somers Tracts*, vi. 266.

accept the constitution some of the officers had drawn up, which is known as the Instrument of Government.

This, the first written constitution in English history, provided that legislative authority should be in the hands of a lord protector (Cromwell) and parliament, and that the executive should be controlled by the lord protector and the council. During the sessions of parliament it should share in the control of the military and naval forces (during its abeyance the council was to take its place) and should have power to make new laws or amend old ones and to prevent any tax unless with its consent. In the interim before parliament met, the protector and council might make laws and ordinances. Parliament must be summoned once every third year and not be dissolved until at least five months had elapsed from the first day of meeting. England was to be represented by four humdred members, Scotland and Ireland by thirty apiece; the redistribution of seats was made by abolishing many small boroughs and giving counties more representation. All who had fought against parliament were to be disabled from voting or election for the first four parliaments, and Roman catholics were to be debarred permanently. Otherwise all possessed of an estate, real or personal, of the value of £200 might become voters. The protector was to have a suspensive veto only, and any bills presented to him by parliament might become law in his despite after twenty days. Constant revenue should be raised to maintain an army of thirty thousand, as well as a convenient number of ships, plus £200,000 per annum for the expenses of the government. Professing Christians, except papists and prelatists, should be protected in the exercise of their religion.

The new constitution made a complete breach with the immediate past. It showed the army's distrust of the omnipotence of the house of commons, in the establishment of which they had acquiesced so heartily in 1649. Similarly it completely ignored the dreams of Harrison, and the like, that the saints should rule the earth, and marked a return to common sense after the ecstatic hopes evoked by Barebones' Parliament. The Nominated Parliament had disillusioned all but the most fervid believers in a fifth monarchy, and its complete failure even to get into touch with realities ensured that no such body would be trusted with supreme power again. Instead, the army officers tried the plan of checks and balances. In place of an omnipotent parliament sitting all the year round was substituted a parliament that was to meet only occasionally and whose sessions might be short. The new features were: the lord protector, whose power was circumscribed by the necessity of securing the consent of parliament or, when it was not sitting, of the council; and the council, which was no longer nominated by parliament —its fifteen members were named in the Instrument. Except for its partial control of the purse, which could be exercised only once in three years, parliament could not prescribe to the executive. There were thus three authorities established, with no provision for their co-ordination, and no machinery was established for amending the Instrument if it should be found defective.

The results of the elections to the new parliament were not very promising from Cromwell's[1] point of view. The Irish and Scottish representatives formed a solid bloc of officers or their dependants, but their adherence to the protectorate was offset by the return of prominent republicans and by the election of numerous presbyterians of moderate views—the £200 qualification for county voters, instead of the former 40-shilling freehold, probably helped them because many possessed real or personal estates of the required value. The protector seems to have realized the need for conciliation, for his opening speech called for a policy of 'healing and settling' and denounced the levellers in language likely to appeal to the representatives of the upper classes before him. He accused the levellers of seeking to destroy the classes into which society was divided: noblemen, gentlemen, and yeomen, a distinction worthy to be preserved. They wanted, he said, to reduce all to an equality which would give the tenant as liberal a fortune as the landlord. He then was equally vehement in castigating those guilty of excesses in religion—their blasphemies and wantonness, their desire to destroy the established church as anti-christian by abolishing tithes, and their constant itch to overturn everything. The protectorate had been established at a time of great danger and suffering. There were wars with Portugal, Holland, and France, and the trade of the nation was ruined and the manufacture of cloth was at a standstill for want of a market. For all these ills a remedy had to be supplied by the present government, which in addition had this further claim to their support: that it had been

---

[1] Usage prescribes that Cromwell be called by his surname, although as protector he signed himself 'Oliver P.'.

instrumental in calling a free parliament—'I say, a free parliament'.[1]

Cromwell's appeal for co-operation did not receive a very cordial answer, for members soon evinced a zeal to discuss all sections of the Instrument of Government, as if they were at liberty to make any amendments they desired. The licence they allowed themselves induced Cromwell to summon the house before him and to inform members bluntly that they were not to meddle with what he called the fundamentals of the new constitution. He was determined, he said, that these should be handed down to posterity as 'the fruits of our blood and travail'. They were: that the government should rest in the hands of a single person and parliament; that parliament should not make itself perpetual; that there should be liberty of conscience; and that neither protector nor parliament should have absolute control of the military forces. These, he declared, had been 'so owned by God, so approved by man', that sooner than yield them he would be willing to be rolled into his grave and buried with infamy. He ended by telling members that he had a pledge they must sign, to accept a government by a single person and parliament before they could be suffered to re-enter their house.[2]

All but about thirty members signed the pledge Cromwell demanded, but there was still no harmony between parliament and protector. The former continued to act very much as if they were a constituent assembly, and made some important amendments to the Instrument. In the first place, they tried to make the executive responsible to parliament by providing that, after a new parliament had met, old members of the council of state should continue to sit only forty days unless a vote approving them was passed. The question of the degree of toleration to be permitted was a more awkward stumbling-block, for parliament wished to exclude those guilty of certain blasphemies or heresies, of which it should be the judge.

The irreconcilable differences, however, developed over the control of the armed forces. Parliament wished to restrict the joint control by protector and parliament to the lifetime of the present protector, and an important debate took place on this point. On one side it was argued that to deprive the protector of the command of the standing army would be to surrender the cause for which they had so long fought, 'for such

---

[1] Speech II, in Carlyle, ii. 339–59.   [2] Speech III (ibid., pp. 366–90).

parliaments might hereafter be chosen as would betray the glorious cause of the people of God'.[1] To this it was answered that, if any cause was more glorious and precious than another, parliament was the most worthy body to be entrusted with it. In this brief argument the fundamental, and insuperable, difficulty of any adjustment between the views of Cromwell and those of the parliament was revealed. Cromwell and the army were convinced they had a sacred cause to defend, even against a majority of their fellow countrymen. His attitude on this point had not changed a particle since 1647, when he had said that what really mattered was not what the people wanted but what was for their good. The interpreters of 'goodness' were to be the general and his army.

There is something artificial, therefore, in discussing Cromwell's failure to maintain cordial relations with the parliament, for concealed beneath discussions of minor issues was the knowledge of disagreement about the all-important question—whether England should continue to be ruled by military dictatorship. Actually the final breach between Cromwell and his parliament occurred when it became evident that the house contemplated a reduction of the army from about 57,000 men to the 30,000 mentioned in the Instrument of Government, and did not intend to provide funds for the larger establishment. Accordingly Cromwell dissolved parliament, after telling members that their bickerings had caused more discontent and division in the nation during the five months they had sat than had existed for years past.

Proof of the truth of his words was soon forthcoming, for in March 1655 occurred Colonel John Penruddock's rising in Wiltshire. Although the royalists were easily subdued, Cromwell seems to have regarded this insurrection as proof that they were irreconcilable, and he abandoned his policy of 'healing and settling'. Some of the insurgents were transported to Barbados to serve for five years as labourers; those who remained in England were subjected to severe restrictions, for whose enforcement a new type of local military organization was devised. Cromwell attempted to consolidate his position by dividing England and Wales into eleven districts and nominating eleven officers, with the rank of major-general, to command them. Nominally these new posts were created to supervise the

---

[1] *Diary of Thomas Burton*, ed. J. T. Rutt (1828), i, p. lxxiii.

reorganized militia, but, in fact, that was the least arduous of their many duties. They performed the functions of tax collectors, policemen, and guardians of public morality. They were charged to exact from royalists a tax of 10 per cent. on their rentals and to deprive them of all weapons. The official defence of this discrimination was that the royalists clearly intended to keep themselves apart from the well-affected of the nation and even to entail their quarrel upon their posterity. Therefore it was only reasonable that those who threatened danger to the state should pay for the means adopted for its security. Furthermore the major-generals were ordered to suppress horse-racings, cock-fightings, bear-baitings, and any unlawful assemblies (on the ground that these were convenient meeting-places for hatching plots). They were to enforce the laws against drunkenness, profanity, and blasphemy, to prohibit plays and interludes, to close gambling-dens and brothels, and to diminish the excessive number of alehouses.

The major-generals threw themselves into their work heart and soul, and for the first time many parts of the country experienced the full rigour of puritanism.[1] The experiment was too short-lived to have any permanent effect upon the morality of Englishmen, but lasted long enough to leave behind it an abiding hatred of militarism. Hitherto, between the royalists and the parliamentarians had been a large body of neutrals who bore some resemblance to the modern non-party man. By 1655 the pressure of taxation had already begun their transformation into enemies of the army. The austere régime of the major-generals completed their conversion. Henceforth there was no doubt at all that the majority of the nation was hostile to the domination of military force, however discreetly veiled. This feeling was clearly shown by them at the election of 1656 and in the ensuing parliament. The results of the election were certainly surprising, and exhibit a remarkable revulsion of feeling as compared with the years of the first civil war. The areas in the south-east and east of England, which had then been the main bulwark of parliament, were now chiefly represented by determined opponents of the protectorate, while its supporters found seats, in the west and north of England, in the former strongholds of royalism (whose adherents were, of course, excluded from voting).

[1] See below, p. 306, for further particulars about the major-generals.

As soon as the election was complete, the council of state, at the instigation of the army officers, examined the list of members carefully and issued tickets of admission to parliament only to such of them as they approved. Those who did not receive certificates were excluded from the house by a strong military guard. In all, about a hundred members were forcibly debarred, and, as a protest, some fifty or sixty others absented themselves when it became evident that the majority of the remnant was prepared to acquiesce in such a constitutional outrage. The illegality of this *coup d'état* was too obvious to need demonstration. The point of view of its perpetrators seems to have been that, since some kind of parliamentary approval of the existing constitutions, or of co-operation in amending it, was necessary to placate public opinion, the only thing to do was to secure a majority by some means or other. It is a testimony to the hold that the very name of parliament had upon the people, that the army leaders should have thought it worth while to secure a majority by the simple expedient of excluding a third of the total membership.

An analysis of the constituencies represented by the members not allowed to take their seats reveals that more than seventy were counties, and especially those counties which had been centres of puritanism. Thus the seven counties comprising the old Eastern Association were represented by fifty-seven members, of whom twenty-nine were excluded. Similarly the West Riding of Yorkshire, which had been a kind of parliamentary oasis in the midst of royalism, now lost four of its six representatives. The explanation would seem to be that the new qualifications for voters, by enfranchising many hitherto unqualified, had resulted in the return of members hostile to military rule. It is difficult to believe that the property-owners worth £200 or more elected so many republicans for any other reason than that these republicans had become the most determined opponents of the army since the expulsion of the Rump in 1653. Certainly the county voters must have been actuated, not by the desire to establish a republic, but by the desire to curb such militarism as the major-generals had delighted in. In any case there can be no doubt at all that the exclusion of the hundred members, legally elected, made permanent the quarrel between the republicans and the adherents of the protectorate, and destroyed in advance whatever prestige the protectorate might otherwise have expected to derive from parliamentary approval.

When parliament met, the results were not at all in accordance with the hopes of the army leaders. The majority was willing enough to accept Cromwell's denunciation of Spain and to vote money for the war,[1] and to set up a high court to try those plotting the protector's death—the secretary of state explaining that it was safer to try conspirators thus than by the ordinary juries.[2] On the other hand the militia bill, which proposed to continue the decimation tax on the royalists in order to support a militia, aroused violent opposition. A dread of the continuance of the rule of the major-generals soon became evident. The anti-military sentiments of the house found powerful advocates, who deplored the tendency to divide the state into cantons and to hand over the laws to be executed by a power too great to be bound by any legal restraint. The soldiers answered defiantly that it was blows, not fair words, that must settle the peace of England, and that the quarrel was between light and darkness. When a member spoke of indemnifying the major-generals for any illegalities they might have committed, the officers boasted in reply that their swords would indemnify them. The debate made it quite clear that members were less afraid of a royalist rising than they were of a continuance of the rule of the major-generals. Another point that emerged was that Cromwell was out of sympathy with his officers.

The same hostility to military rule that was responsible for the rejection of the militia bill caused that revision of the constitution usually called the Humble Petition and Advice. The primary objective of its framers was to change the present arbitrary form of government for one long familiar to the English people and restricted by usage. They therefore, in the first clause, asked Cromwell to assume the title and dignity of King. Thereupon the anger of the opponents of monarchy knew no bounds. It is somewhat ironical that the army officers who were responsible for the exclusion from parliament of the civilian opponents of government by a single person, whether called protector or king, should now have had to bear the burden of the opposition to the proposal to make Cromwell king. Lambert stated the position of his brother officers very

---

[1] See below, pp. 231-4.
[2] C. H. Firth, *Last Years of the Protectorate* (1909), i. 42.

clearly—that the re-establishment of kingship was contrary to all the oaths and protestations they had made and to the principles for which they had taken up arms and shed so much blood.[1]

On his side Cromwell wavered for a long time. He had become extremely dissatisfied with his position in the state. He told[2] a meeting of a hundred officers of the army that they had made him their drudge upon all occasions; they had forced him to dissolve the Long Parliament and call the Nominated Parliament; they had wanted the first protectorate parliament to be dissolved. They had introduced a militia bill into this parliament and it had been defeated; he had been against calling the present parliament, but they had been confident they could get men chosen to fulfil their desires. After these many failures it was time to come to a settlement and to lay aside arbitrary proceedings unacceptable to the nation. By the proceedings of this parliament the need was clear for a check, or balancing power, such as the house of lords or a body so constituted, for the case of James Naylor[3] might happen to be their case. This speech explains very clearly Cromwell's attitude towards the Petition and Advice. As he said, the title of king weighed with him no more than a feather, but the Instrument was already revealed as a very defective constitution and must be amended. Ultimately he declined to become king in name, although he was given the right to nominate his successor.

He never explained the reasons for his self-denial, but they were probably two: he knew that many of the senior officers, including his own relatives Fleetwood and John Disbrowe, were unalterably opposed; he knew, too, that most of those he was fond of referring to as the peculiar people, who were to God as the apple of his eye—the honest interest of the nation—were opposed to his becoming king. His hold over the army was so strong that there was little doubt that, if he had wanted to accept the title, he could have done so and dismissed the dissentient officers without provoking mutiny. So long as the army remained loyal he could have disregarded the protests of the more sober elements of puritanism—their remonstrances would hardly have been heard amidst the current denunciations of the fifth-monarchy enthusiasts and levellers. Cromwell refused the

---

[1] *State Papers, Venetian, 1657–1659* (1931), p. 22.
[2] Carlyle, iii. 487–8.   [3] See below, p. 196, n. 1.

title because he felt that it would be an offence to the noblest elements of puritanism. He knew that those who had followed him from Edgehill or Naseby to Dunbar would regard him as an apostate, and he knew that the 'people of God' would regard him as one who had disgraced the cause. Therefore, in spite of the insistence of parliament, he refused the crown.

Once the question of the headship of the state had been dismissed, it proved comparatively easy to complete the new constitution. According to the Humble Petition and Advice, parliaments, which were to meet at least once every three years, were to consist of two houses. The house of commons received an important concession: it was given the sole right to admit or exclude those who had been legally chosen by the constituencies. The house of lords was to contain from forty to seventy members, nominated by Cromwell and approved by the commons. In other respects such differences as existed between the Instrument and the Humble Petition mainly concerned the council of state, which was now designated the privy council: its members were to be nominated by the protector, with the consent of the council and the subsequent approval of parliament, and removed only if parliament agreed. The new protectorate was obviously more like a monarchy than the old, but still was merely a kind of half-way house, and it was clearly an insufficient breakwater against the strong current of opinion that was running in favour of the restoration of a known form of government—namely, a monarchy. Indeed Cromwell's installation as protector was conducted with such ceremony that, but for the absence of a crown and the omission of anointing, it might have seemed like an ancient coronation.

The six months that elapsed between the first and second sessions of parliament were mainly occupied, so far as domestic history is concerned, with the selection of members to sit in the second chamber. When the actual list was compiled, it contained the names of sixty-three persons, of whom only forty-two were sworn in. Of the remainder some were kept away by their official duties, but most refused to obey the summons to sit. Of the new lords seven were members of Cromwell's family and seventeen were officers commanding regiments. These two groups could outvote the officials, ex-officers, and country gentlemen who formed the remainder. Probably the list was as representative as Cromwell could make it, although the military element was unduly prominent. The impression it made upon the nation at large seems to have been adverse. The opinions of the austere republicans were well expressed by Mrs. Hutchinson, that at last Cromwell 'took upon himself to make lords and knights, and wanted not many fools, both of the army and gentry, to accept of and strut in this mock title'.[1] Another point of view is furnished by Ludlow, who says that the principal part of the new lords were such as had procured their present possessions by their wits, and were resolved to enlarge them by selling their consciences for the purchase of the protector's favour.[2] A more serious defect was Cromwell's failure to secure the presence of men of property or of the old nobility.

When parliament met, the only obstacle to the return of excluded republican members was an oath to be true and faithful to the protector, and not to contrive anything against his lawful authority; and this they took without hesitation. The presence of these determined opponents of the protectorate was the more grave inasmuch as some thirty of its supporters were lost to the commons through their transference to the upper house. The consequence was that the Cromwellians lost control, and day after day slipped by in fruitless debates on whether the second chamber should be regarded as the 'other house' or the 'house of lords'. This difference in nomenclature marks a distinction of great importance, for, if the former title were adopted, it would imply that the powers of the second chamber would be limited to those specifically conferred on it by the Petition and Advice, whereas if it were called the house of lords it would seem to have become the heir of the body abolished in 1649 and coequal with the commons. The arguments are of interest as showing current views about the second chamber, and about the sovereignty of the people. Referring to events in 1649, one republican claimed that the people of England were by the providence of God set free from any negative. What was fought for, he asked, but to be able to make your own laws without restrictions? The old house of lords had been abolished because it had become a hindrance to the passing of good laws. Other arguments were that the new lords had not enough landed property to enable them to act as a balance.

[1] Lucy Hutchinson, *Memoirs of the Life of Colonel Hutchinson*, ed. C. H. Firth (1906), p. 299.   [2] *Memoirs*, ii. 31.

They had no stock in the country, no interest, 'not the forty-thousandth part of England'.

To such contentions a major-general replied that there were better qualifications than land or riches, such as religion, piety, and faithfulness to the Commonwealth, and these virtues the new lords had. A major added, significantly, that they had a balance more potent than territorial possessions—namely, the sword. The commander of a regiment had as good a balance as could be devised, and could do more than most men. Cromwell intervened to call attention to the need for harmony and constructive legislation amid foreign and domestic perils. But Hesilrige and Scot, and the like, were deaf to all reason. Come what might (and the gallows awaited Scot and the Tower Hesilrige), they were determined to pull down the protectorate. They were busily engaged upon negotiating an alliance with disaffected officers in the army, fifth-monarchy men, and fanatical preachers, and had a petition prepared for presentation to the house of commons. They passed the word round for their supporters to be present there, and hoped to carry a snap vote to restore the republic and recall the Long Parliament. Unfortunately for them Cromwell heard of their designs and, on the morning fixed for the presentation of the petition, hurried to parliament and dissolved it, seeking no man's advice, and rebuking Fleetwood, who remonstrated with the phrase, 'You are a milksop.' Thus ended Cromwell's last parliament. The rupture seemed to prove that he could not govern within the limits of a constitution, whether drafted by the army leaders or drawn up by parliament.

In the speech that preceded the dissolution Cromwell accused members of playing the king of Scots' game, but, as it happened, Charles II was unable to profit by the occasion. The small army he had equipped in Flanders for the invasion of England was ill paid, the vessels to transport it were blockaded, and the older generation of royalists in England were apathetic. Moreover, in spite of the incitements of republicans and fifth-monarchy men, the army remained loyal. Indeed only one regiment showed obvious signs of disaffection, and that, strangely enough, was the protector's own regiment of horse, which was the true descendant of the Ironsides Cromwell had raised in the first civil war. Its commander, Major Packer, explained to parliament in 1659 how he had served Cromwell for fourteen years but had been, without any trial or appeal, cashiered because he would not acknowledge the other house to be a house of lords. But Packer, and the five captains who suffered with him, found no open support, although it is probable that a good many officers in the army sympathized with them.

The abrupt dissolution of parliament, however successful in checking disaffection, had one great drawback. It aggravated a disease that, unless checked, threatened to gnaw away the strength of the protectorate—the chronic want of money. The Petition and Advice had contemplated a revenue of £1,300,000 per annum, but the expense of the government was at the rate of £2,500,000. To make good some of the deficit, parliament voted with great reluctance that £600,000 should be raised by a monthly assessment—a tax that had been levied in varying amounts since 1643, but remained as unpopular as when first imposed. Part of the £500,000 still wanting was to be secured by a final assessment lasting only three months, another part by a tax on new buildings within ten miles of the walls of the City of London. The shortcomings of Cromwell's financial advisers may be gauged by the income from the latter tax, which produced little more than a tenth of the expected amount. Moreover the yield from the other taxes fell short of the anticipation. The excise tax, always odious, became even more abhorrent when farmed out. Therefore the contractors could not afford to offer so much for the right to collect the duties, with evasion and even resistance apt to be widespread. The customs duties were similarly disappointing to the treasury, for the new rates recently fixed were too high and interposed a barrier to trade. Altogether the revenue was nearly £500,000 less than the expenditure. Unfortunately this was not the whole story, for there was already about £1,000,000 owing, partly a legacy from the commonwealth but mainly the price of the ambitious foreign policy pursued during the protectorate. The bulk of the debt was due to the armed forces, about £540,000 to the navy, £300,000 to the army. The consequences of this indebtedness threatened to be unpleasant. In the case of the navy the device often adopted, of keeping ships at sea when there was no money to pay them off, could not be continued indefinitely. The army was also in difficulties, for soldiers would soon be compelled to live at free quarter, which they themselves loathed and which was certain to intensify the hostility already felt towards the military. It was imperative, therefore, to make some move to avoid bankruptcy.

The civilian members of the privy council turned their thoughts once again to a parliament, although their military colleagues, who were becoming more prejudiced against parliamentary government as each legislature in turn was found wanting, favoured raising money by force of arms. There was no question but that the protectorate would adopt the constitutional policy, but before parliament could profitably be summoned it was imperative to decide what answer should be given to the petition (which was inevitable) that Cromwell should accept the title of king and what steps should be taken to ensure the acquiescence of the army in the decisions of parliament. Although positive knowledge is lacking, it is probable that Cromwell had made up his mind that this time he would not disappoint his supporters in parliament and would accept the crown. It is even more probable that he had decided that a drastic purge of the army was necessary and that he would have replaced the would-be politicians among the higher ranks by men content to obey the orders of the civil power that commanded them. Before steps could be taken towards fulfilment of either of these tasks, Cromwell fell ill and died (3 September 1658).

During his last hours Cromwell was heard to murmur that the Lord had made him, though most unworthy, a mean instrument to do His people some good. To serve the minority of the nation that seemed to him to be the people of God had been the guiding principle of his life. To try to secure for them their civil liberties as men, and their spiritual liberties as Christians, he had fought to destroy the old monarchy and the ecclesiastical system associated with the name of Archbishop Laud. For their sake he had fought the Scottish presbyterians when they had tried to force upon Englishmen a yoke too grievous to be borne. For their sake, too, he had not hesitated to disregard civil rights when they seemed to conflict with freedom of conscience. For forms of church government or for sectarian creeds, he cared as little as for constitutional forms. To him the essence of puritanism was the good life. And he hoped to see the day when it would be shameful to see men bold in sin and profaneness. The mind is the man, he said, and if that be pure the man may signify something. Otherwise what difference between a man and a beast?[1]

The attempt to translate these ideals into practice, especially by means of major-generals, was fatal to any chance of the permanency of the protectorate. In a negative way he had succeeded, and, in spite of the Restoration, absolute monarchy and Anglican exclusiveness could not become powerful again after the hard blows he had dealt them. Of all his achievements, he would probably have found most satisfaction in his share in establishing puritanism. Thanks, in large measure, to his greatness, nonconformity had time to grow so strong and flourishing that neither its own excesses nor the coming persecution could uproot it. Nevertheless he had not succeeded in making England puritan, or even in making puritanism admirable to the majority of Englishmen. Indeed puritan austerity and inquisitorial morality had become repugnant, and the feeling was already widespread that even religious freedom might be too dearly purchased if secured at the sacrifice of civil liberty. In fact there was a strong reaction in favour of the old constitution and the known laws of the land. The wave of conservatism might have dashed in vain against a united army, but, as it proved, only Cromwell could keep the army from disruption. So long as he lived he could rely upon its loyalty and trust it to close up the ranks in response to his appeal. But even in his lifetime its solidarity was in appearance rather than in reality, and after his death it was soon seen how deep the divisions were. Of all the unsolved problems Cromwell bequeathed to his son Richard, none was more serious than the position of the army in the state and its internal dissensions.

[1] Speech v (Carlyle, ii. 541).

VIII

RELIGIOUS HISTORY, 1640-60

WHEN the Long Parliament met in November 1640, its attitude towards religious questions was parallel to its attitude towards politics. Just as there was a large majority to condemn Strafford and other agents of despotism, so Laud and the bishops found few defenders. In each instance unity prevailed so long as the house was content with a negative programme. Yet from the very first it was apparent that there was no real agreement whenever any fundamental changes in the church were under discussion. Thus the London petition that demanded the abolition of episcopacy, 'root and branch',[1] was introduced on 11 December, but was kept in abeyance until the following February. Then an animated debate ensued during which episcopacy itself was warmly attacked and defended. It is noteworthy that even the supporters of episcopacy had no good word to say for the present bishops. For a time the parliamentary leaders, having experienced the strength of the party in favour of episcopacy, were content with a measure 'to restrain bishops and others in holy orders to intermeddle with secular affairs', but it was rejected in the house of Lords. Meanwhile a bill had been introduced into the commons to abolish bishops, deans, and chapters, 'root and branch'. Its preamble stated that long experience had shown that these church officials had hindered the perfect reformation and had been very prejudicial to the civil government. During the debates, Vane moved as a substitute for the prelates the appointment of a body of commissioners, lay and clerical, to exercise ecclesiastical jurisdiction in every county. During the summer, however, the bill was dropped. An attempt was made to introduce into the Grand Remonstrance a clause about the Book of Common Prayer, but the church party was too strong and it had to be laid aside.[2] At the beginning of 1642, when the popular indignation at the attempt to arrest the five members was so strong, a bill to remove bishops from the house of lords passed the two houses and received the royal assent. Next year, when the civil war

---

[1] Gardiner, *Constitutional Documents*, pp. 137-44.
[2] W. A. Shaw, *History of the English Church, 1640-60* (1900), i. 116.

had begun and parliament had already started the practice of dispensing with the royal assent, the work of destruction proceeded apace. One ordinance declared bishops, deans, and chapters abolished, and, later, another confiscated their lands, which were to be sold. The heads of the church had now been removed, but the organization to be substituted for episcopacy gave almost infinite trouble. In this new task parliament soon found that it had no free hand, for it became necessary to try to please, first the Scots, and then the army.

Experience had already suggested the difficulty of satisfying the Scots, for during the negotiations preceding the treaty (August 1641) that ended the bishops' wars, they had pressed the English to adopt uniformity of religion in the two kingdoms as the best preservative of peace, but had received nothing more than a vague promise that the houses would proceed in due time to such a reformation of church government as would conduce to the glory of God and the peace of the church. Even when civil war had become inevitable, parliament was still unwilling to accept Scottish aid at the cost of enforcing unity of religion in the two kingdoms, and refused to go farther than to announce its determination to abolish episcopacy and to consult with godly and learned divines.[1] Consequently the Scots remained neutral until the following summer, when the serious defeats the parliamentarians sustained, both in the north and the west, induced a change of heart at St. Stephen's. Then the parliament passed an ordinance to establish an assembly famous as the Westminster Assembly. Its membership consisted of representatives of both houses, and English divines, to whom eight Scottish commissioners were joined. It was directed to confer about such questions relative to the liturgy, discipline, and government of the church of England as should be referred to it by parliament.[2] Shortly afterwards a committee of the two houses was named to proceed to Scotland to prevail upon the brethren there to assist the common cause of the defence of protestantism.[3] The upshot was the Solemn League and Covenant, by which the contracting parties, described as noblemen and commons of all sorts in the kingdoms of England, Scotland, and Ireland, pledged themselves to endeavour to preserve the church of Scotland; to reform religion in England and Ireland, in doctrine, worship, discipline, and government,

---

[1] Ibid., p. 130.   [2] *Acts and Ordinances*, i. 180–4.   [3] Ibid., pp. 197–202.

according to the Word of God and the example of the best reformed churches; to bring the churches of the three kingdoms to the nearest possible uniformity in faith and government; and to extirpate popery and prelacy.

When the Scottish commissioners arrived in London, they found great reluctance there to accept a full-blown system of presbyterianism, and soon were longing for the arrival of their army on English soil to spur on their dilatory colleagues. Weeks were spent in debating such a question as, Were elders of divine or human institution? The independents in the assembly were especially concerned to deny scriptural authority for an exclusively presbyterian system, for they well knew that, if they yielded this, there was little hope of resisting its general enforcement. That they were willing to accept elders as convenient officials to safeguard the morals of the congregation was far from satisfying the Scots, who loathed the very idea of toleration. 'As yet a presbytrie to this people is conceaved to be a strang monster', complained one of the Scots.[1]

Throughout 1644 the independents were in steady opposition to the presbyterians, and their stubbornness delayed until autumn the resolution to adopt the presbyterian form of church government, and, a little later, the directory for public worship. Parliament was in agreement with the assembly on both questions, for it was essential to present a united front with the Scots during the peace negotiations between king and parliament, which opened at Uxbridge immediately afterwards. After the failure of negotiations the bill to give effect to the proposals of the assembly was dropped, and the summer was almost over before an ordinance divided the province of London into twelve 'classes' and foreshadowed the splitting up of the different counties into presbyteries and the subsequent election of elders. Another ordinance substituted the *Directory* for the Book of Common Prayer for use in all services.[2] A month subsequently the two houses approved the names of the 'tryers' of such as were chosen for the London classes.[3] In spite of this progress the Scots were far from satisfied. Baillie wrote:

Our greatest trouble for the time is from the Erastians in the house of commons. They are at last content to erect presbyters and synods in all the land, and have given out their orders for that end;

---

[1] *Baillie Letters and Journals*, ii. 117.
[2] *Acts and Ordinances*, i. 749–57.   [3] *Lords' Journals*, vii. 607.

yet they give to the ecclesiastick courts so little power, that the assemblie . . . are in great doubt whether to sett up any thing, till by some powerfull petition of many thousand hands, they obtaine some more of their just desyres.[1]

It is significant that the Scots were now relying upon popular support rather than upon their army. In truth, after Naseby the need for the Scottish army had vanished and its plundering had made it unpopular. Parliament, no longer obliged to pay the old deference to the Scots, allowed its Erastianism full range.

The progress made down to that time is defined in the next ordinance dealing with religion: the Book of Common Prayer had been replaced by the *Directory*, episcopacy abolished, and a presbyterian government founded in every congregation, with subordination to 'classical', provincial, and national assemblies, each of these, in turn, subordinate to parliament. All classes and congregations were ordered forthwith to select elders, the electors being residents who had taken the national covenant and were not under age or servants without families. The powers of these elders fell far short of their ambitions, for they could only excommunicate for certain definite causes. Otherwise commissioners were appointed by parliament in every province and only after their decision had been made might the elders suspend from the sacrament of the Lord's Supper a person whose offences were not among those specified. This clause was wormwood and gall to the presbyterians, and they declined to attempt to work the machine that parliament had contrived until an amending ordinance had been passed, although even this permitted an appeal from the elders to a parliamentary committee and thence to parliament itself.[2] Equally unsatisfactory was the treatment accorded to the confession of faith, which never received parliamentary authorization, though its acceptance by presbyterians in general ranks it, together with the catechisms, as the most important and enduring work of the Westminster Assembly.

After some hesitation the presbyterian ministers made up their minds to accept the half-loaf which was all parliament was likely to offer them, and the election of elders in London took place in the summer of 1646.[3] For the country at large the

---

[1] *Baillie Letters and Journals*, ii. 318.

[2] *Acts and Ordinances*, i. 833–8, 852–5. For the assembly's petition against the first ordinance, see *Lords' Journals*, viii. 232–3.

[3] For some curious details see Thomas Edwards, *Gangraena* (1646), pt. 3, pp. 222–3.

record is so defective that it is difficult to estimate the progress made, but in most places little seems to have been done.

The future of this attempt to establish presbyterianism as a national religion now depended largely upon the attitude of the army. Since 1645, when the New Model came into existence, and especially since 1647, when presbyterians either withdrew or were expelled from the army, the majority of the officers were sectaries. Widely as they often differed among themselves in their theological views, they were united in their championship of toleration. They were at one with Milton: 'Give me the liberty to know, to utter, and to argue freely according to conscience, above all liberties.'[1] This sentence might well have served as a motto for Cromwell's army. The history of independency explains the lack of sympathy between the ideals of parliament and of the army that fought for it.

One of the most astounding features of the period is the growth of sectaries from a negligible handful before 1640 to a body strong enough to have gained control of the army, executed the king, and founded a commonwealth, in ten years. Although 'great awakenings like that which characterize the commonwealth era always present . . . an element of surprise and mystery',[2] yet it is possible to suggest factors that contributed to this sudden outburst of sectarianism. The meaner sort, who had saved protestantism during the Marian persecution by contributing the bulk of the martyrs, had long been dissatisfied with the Elizabethan settlement. Their longing for a more spiritual and less political reformation was fostered by their reading. They were happy in that they had at hand the Authorized Version of the Bible. But their devotional literature was by no means confined to the Scriptures or the Book of Common Prayer. A remarkable feature of the sixty years or so which closed in 1640 is the enormous output of devotional literature. Books of pious aphorisms, prayers, sermons, and devotions literally poured from the press. Arthur Dent's *Plaine Mans Path-Way to Heaven*[3] went through twenty-five editions between 1601 and 1640. Thomas Egerton's *Briefe Method of Catechizing* reached its thirty-ninth edition in 1631, and John

---

[1] *Areopagitica*, in *Works*, iv. 346.
[2] Rufus M. Jones, *Mysticism and Democracy in the English Commonwealth* (1932), p. 4.
[3] One of the two books that formed the dowry of Bunyan's first wife. The other was Lewis Bayly's *The Practice of Piety*.

Norden's *Pensive Mans Practise* claimed forty impressions by 1627. Reading these manuals made men feel independent of bishops and priests: they naturally differed widely in the conclusions they reached after their reading. While the middle classes were united in opposition to episcopacy, they became divided about all else. Whereas the upper-middle-class man tended to adopt an Erastian form of presbyterianism, the lower-middle-class man often became a separatist.

The presbyterian and the sectary had many grounds of difference, apart from their denominational opinions. Undoubtedly the merchants and moneyed classes who formed the backbone of presbyterianism despised the upstart mechanics,[1] who now took upon themselves, male and female alike, to preach, and who often seemed totally devoid of all dignity and restraint —especially in scenes of adult baptism by immersion. Other causes of offence were their arrogating to themselves the name of the godly party or saints, their frequent interruption of services and assumption that ministers of other persuasions were mere time-servers, their mission-like zeal (which was aided by their gifts of popular oratory), their claim to revelations (which are said to have led some to deny the Scriptures to be the Word of God, and to have earned for themselves the epithet, 'anti-Scripturists'),[2] and the strange excitement—even ecstasy—that often attended their meetings. The self-sufficient presbyterian, who had a hatred of enthusiasm which would not have been out of place a century later, never realized that, during the upheaval caused by the civil war, many found formulae insufficient, and that the most exact observance of religious duties gave no comfort to soldiers like Paul Hobson or to gentlewomen like Mary Springett.[3] They felt that they derived no benefit from ceremonial and rebelled at the conception of the sufficiency of the Scriptures. The result is well described by William Penn, in his preface to Fox's *Journal*:

. . . many left them [puritans], and all visible churches and societies, and wandered up and down, as sheep without a shepherd, and as doves without their mates; seeking their beloved, but could not find

---

[1] According to Edwards, 'Needie, broken, decaied men, who know not how to live . . . turn independents' (*Gangraena*, pt. 2, p. 152).

[2] Edwards, *Gangraena*, pt. 1, p. 82. Others are reported to have said that, now that 'they were all taught of God, and needed not that any one should teach them', men in black clothes were no longer necessary (ibid., pt. 3, p. 90).

[3] Ibid., p. 90; W. C. Braithwaite, *The Beginnings of Quakerism* (1912), pp. 13-15.

Him (as their souls desired to know Him) whom their souls loved above their chiefest joy.

These people were called Seekers by some, and the Family of Love by others; because, as they came to the knowledge of one another, they sometimes met together, not formally to pray or preach, at appointed times or places, in their own wills, as in times past they were accustomed to do; but waited together in silence, and as anything rose in any one of their minds that they thought savoured of a divine spring, so they sometimes spoke.

Although it cannot be proved that George Fox and other early 'publishers of truth' derived their message directly from the seekers, yet this sect supplied the most congenial soil for their teaching.

George Fox, the greatest religious leader the puritan revolution produced—the son of a weaver and the apprentice of a shoemaker—like many another at this time failed to derive any spiritual consolation from the existing creeds. For four years he wandered about England, seeking rest and finding none, until at last he felt that the truth had been revealed to him. The great discovery he had made was that the human soul might enjoy immediate contact with God and a man's life be guided by an inner light, the working of the holy spirit in the heart of man. From 1647 onwards he was unwearied in spreading the message he had received. He was fortunate in his hour and appeared to many as the prophet of a new age. The quakers readily absorbed the majority of the seekers and attracted many whose religious beliefs had been upset by the revolutionary times and had not found any satisfactory substitute. They were soon strong enough to survive persecution and the discredit due to Naylor's extravagances at Bristol.[1]

It is an amazing tribute to Fox's gifts that the sect he founded should have made headway, for the quakers had nearly everything against them. Their refusal to accept many of the social habits of the time or to recognize the authority of magistrate or minister made them unpopular with the ruling classes.[2] The lowly position they assigned to the visible church, their irrever-

[1] In 1656 Naylor entered Bristol after the manner of Christ's entry into Jerusalem. For this he was condemned by parliament to be whipped twice, to have his tongue bored through, and to be branded.

[2] Evelyn's impression is probably typical: 'I had the curiosity to visit some quakers in prison; a new fanatic sect, of dangerous principles, who show no respect to any man, magistrate, or other, and seem a melancholy, proud sort of people, and exceedingly ignorant' (*Diary*, 8 July 1656).

ence towards 'steeple houses' (as they called churches), and their reliance upon 'openings' rather than the Scriptures, generally antagonized the regular members of any congregation, of whatever denomination. Moreover, although Cromwell had the greatness to realize the value of the faith that was in them, usually the military were bitterly hostile to them, principally because they were fundamentally pacifists, but also because some stayed in the army, drew their pay, and did their utmost to convert their fellow soldiers—at least, officers said they did. Politically the quakers were unimportant and did not interfere directly in the party struggles of the time.

The two parties in politico-religious strife were the presbyterians and independents. The fundamental cause of the quarrel between these two groups was their completely divergent views on toleration, but there were also many other causes.

The presbyterian was usually a man of property and detested and feared the radical views often expressed by the sectaries. In the main, extreme opinions on religious affairs were often accompanied by revolutionary doctrines in politics. Indeed, the levellers' programme had a Christian origin. If men were equal in the sight of God, they should be equal before the law. It was God's will that tyranny should be resisted. The fundamental law, declares Lilburne, was the perfection of reason, agreeable to the law eternal and natural and not contrary to the word of God. How these novel doctrines appeared to a presbyterian is illustrated by a quotation from Thomas Edwards, one of their publicists:

That seeing all men are by nature the sons of Adam, and from him have legitimately derived a naturall propriety, right, and freedom, therefore England and all other nations, and all particular persons in every nation, notwithstanding the difference of lawes and governments, rancks and degrees, ought to be alike free and estated in their naturall liberties, and to enjoy the just rights and prerogative of mankind, whereunto they are heirs apparent; and thus the commoners by right, are equall with the lords. For by naturall birth all men are equally and alike born to like propriety, liberty, and freedom; and as we are delivered of God by the hand of nature into this world, every one with a naturall innate freedom, and propriety, even so are we to live, every one equally and alike to enjoy his birthright and priviledge.[1]

[1] *Gangraena*, pt. 3, p. 17; D. B. Robertson, *The Religious Foundation of Leveller Democracy* (1951).

Most of the levellers were political rather than social reformers, but there were enough socialists to produce a crop of
manifestoes and pamphlets to alarm the well-to-do citizen.
Gerrard Winstanley, the creator of the digger movement, is described by his biographer[1] as 'mystic and rationalist, communist
and social reformer'. His communism involved ploughing up
the common and waste land throughout England, regardless
of the rights of the lord of the manor. 'We have a free right to
the land of England, being born therein', said a digger manifesto; and it is not surprising that the moneyed classes viewed
such claims with alarm or that they tended to make no distinction between the handful of communists and the vast body of
social reformers. Thus the presbyterian was divided from the
sectary by the gravest differences on all the great problems of
the day, religious, political, and social.

Unfortunately the need for agreement was urgent, for the
legislation passed up to 1648[2] had led to a kind of ecclesiastical anarchy. As a result of the second civil war, when many
presbyterians had turned royalists, animosity between them
and the independents grew more bitter. The great triumphs of
Cromwell's army at Dunbar and Worcester settled that presbyterianism should not be imposed by force of Scottish arms, and
certainly it would not be imposed in any other way. The position,
therefore, was that there was now no ecclesiastical organization
at all, except in London and a few counties where the presbyterian model had been set up. The greater part of the clergy
was presbyterian and another part independent. According to
the letter of the law, all incumbents should have taken the
covenant, but this was as much a dead letter as the act which
prohibited from preaching all except duly ordained ministers
or candidates for the ministry. One ordinance (27 September
1650) of this period deserves mention—namely, the repeal of
the former statutes imposing penalties for not attending church.
All that the ordinance required was that everybody should
resort to a public place of worship or be present at some other
place where religious exercises were practised.[3] The Instrument
of Government provided that 'the Christian religion should be
recommended as a public profession', to which, however, none
should be compelled by penalties, and that such as professed a

---

[1] L. H. Berens, *The Digger Movement* (1906).
[2] See above, p. 193.   [3] *Acts and Ordinances*, ii. 423-5.

belief in Jesus Christ should be protected in the exercise of their religion; but this toleration was not to be extended to popery or prelacy.[1] All that Cromwell attempted to do during the protectorate was to secure the appointment of one set of commissioners to see that none but fit persons were admitted to livings, and another set to remove unfit and ignorant persons from the livings they held.[2] Hence what he did affected the personnel of the clergy, not the organization or doctrine of the church.

Meanwhile the troubles of the Anglican clergy had been increasing rapidly. With few exceptions they either actively supported, or at least sympathized with, the defeated royalists. The ordinance (27 March 1643) 'for sequestring notorious delinquents estates'[3] concerned such of the clergy as had taken an active part against parliament. The position of others was changed for the worse when parliament began to entrust to local authorities special powers to deal with ecclesiastical offenders. An example of the authority thus delegated is to be found in an ordinance to regulate the university of Cambridge and to remove scandalous ministers in the seven associated counties often referred to as the Eastern Association (22 January 1644).[4] This enactment asserted that the parliamentary cause was hampered, and the souls of the people starved, by the 'idle, disaffected, and scandalous clergy' of the university and counties, and empowered Manchester, the parliamentary commander for those parts, to nominate a committee in every county, with power to remove all university or college authorities and all ministers or schoolmasters who were scandalous in their lives or hostile to parliament. Such persons as the committees found unfit for their charges were to be ejected and their estates sequestered.[5] The provisions of ordinances for other parts of the country were very similar.

Much clearly depended upon the action of local committees, whose sympathies would all be likely to be puritan. It is noteworthy that in the instructions which Manchester sent to the Eastern Association occurs the following: that, because sad experience had shown that the parishioners were not forward to complain of their ministers, many being enemies to that

---

[1] Clauses xxxv–xxxvii (ibid., pp. 221–2).
[2] Ibid., pp. 855–8, 968–90.   [3] Ibid. i. 106–17.
[4] Ibid., pp. 371–2.
A fifth part of the estates might be allotted for the support of wives and children.

blessed reformation desired by parliament and loath to come under a powerful ministry, the committee was required to summon well-affected men, within each hundred, who should be encouraged to inquire into the characters of ministers and schoolmasters. The clerical martyrologist, John Walker, alleged that these informers deliberately manufactured cases against the clergy; and, since some at least were rewarded for the information they supplied, the charge may occasionally have been justified. Certainly there was every opportunity afforded for the gratification of the dislike or envy that a section of parishioners not infrequently felt against their pastor. The most careful examination of the evidence, in recent years, leads to the conclusion that 'numerous examples, to prove the corrupt practices of accusers and the injustice of the parliamentary committee, may be found in Walker's *Sufferings of the Clergy*'.[1]

The causes of ejection were many. As a rule political grounds had at least as much weight as ecclesiastical with the local committees, and instances are known of clergymen who were deprived of their livings for disaffection alone. It is quite certain that charges of disaffection to parliament claimed far more victims than accusations of vice. The commonest vice alleged against the clergy was tippling, but accusations of immorality are not uncommon.

The ejected clergy probably formed about a third of their whole number. The fates of these three thousand or more were varied. Some hundred and fifty, including such men as Morley or Cosin,[2] preferred voluntary exile to any compromise with the victorious party in England. They were often exceedingly poor and sometimes in danger of actual starvation. Yet they continued to study and write so that 'the Interregnum became in fact a golden age of High Anglican theology and apologetic'. Among many works of enduring value were Pearson's *Exposition of the Creed* (1659) and Sparrow's *Rationale upon the Book of Common Prayer* (1657).[3] Of those who remained in England, all who had demonstrated their hostility to the parliamentary cause were not only deprived of their benefices but committed to prison. In the beginning they were shut up in the ordinary

---

[1] G. B. Tatham, *The Puritans in Power* (1913), p. 73.

[2] After the Restoration, George Morley became bishop of Winchester, John Cosin of Durham.

[3] Robert S. Bosher, *The Making of the Restoration Settlement* (1951), pp. 36-37.

London jails, but later were lodged in Lambeth Palace and other sequestered buildings. The remaining two-thirds of the clergy, who were not ejected, were subjected to the same annoyances as the Anglican layman.

All Anglicans were now the victims of severe restrictions. In the first place, the use of the Book of Common Prayer was strictly forbidden, not only in churches and chapels, but even in family worship, under penalty of a year's imprisonment for the third offence.[1] There had been substituted the *Directory*, whose use during the protectorate was made optional according to the wishes of the parishioners. In one parish, therefore, a rigid presbyterian might be following the liturgical forms enjoined in the *Directory*, and in another an independent might be using no set forms of prayer or of service. Both independent and presbyterian, however, combined to prohibit the old liturgy of the church of England and to prosecute those who attempted to use it. Thus the Anglicans were denied the right to organize a church on a voluntary basis—a privilege enjoyed by other protestants outside the church of England. Consequently a permanent obstacle was erected against any reconciliation between the victors and the vanquished of the civil wars. This was not a grievance that affected only the hierarchy or even the clergy, but one that touched the life of the laity in a number of different ways. The Anglican layman, during the commonwealth and protectorate, never ceased to regret the issue of the war, for he had a permanent grievance set before his eyes, at least once a week, in the prohibition to worship as he and his fathers had worshipped.

It is difficult to obtain any reliable information as to the extent of the success attending the effort to suppress the old liturgy. Apparently, except in a few favoured districts where the use of the Prayer Book was connived at by the authorities, a churchman had either to rest content with a new liturgy hateful to him, both as objectionable in itself and as a symbol of defeat, or with no liturgy of any kind. Some, certainly, braved the penalties of the law in their own homes. Lady Falkland's biographer records that, when she was warned of the probable consequences of saying the prayers of the church daily in her house, she produced Foxe's *Book of Martyrs*; and the story of Lady Knevit's persistence in using the Prayer Book of Edward VI

[1] Ordinance of 26 Aug. 1645 (*Acts and Ordinances*, i. 755-7).

during the Marian persecution was read aloud and commended as an example to be followed.[1]

Certain of the clergy, too, defied the law, sometimes with the connivance of the authorities, sometimes without. In the heart of London was at least one church where John Evelyn, the diarist, could go and find a liturgy still in use.[2] At other times he attended his parish or another church, where he often found either a presbyterian or an independent officiating. On one occasion he was surprised to see a mechanic step up into the pulpit, the purport of his sermon being that the saints were now called to destroy temporal governments and other 'such feculent stuff'. Frequently he stayed at home on Sunday afternoons to catechize and instruct his family, for speculative and political sermons and discourses had quite replaced the old catechism. The result, said the diarist, was that 'people had no principles, and grew very ignorant of even the common points of Christianity'. He records, from time to time, that he attended services in private houses, and notes, of one, that 'we had a great meeting of zealous Christians, who were generally much more devout and religious than in our greatest prosperity'.[3]

The prohibition of the use of the Book of Common Prayer, in addition to depriving the churchman of the services he liked to hear, inflicted three especial grievances—that the rites of baptism, marriage, and burial could not lawfully be celebrated as he wished.[4] By an ordinance of 24 August 1653, births and burials were to be registered before a civilian appointed for the purpose, who might charge a fee of fourpence but no more. A father, therefore, who wished his child to be baptized according to the Book of Common Prayer, had to find a minister willing to risk the penalties prescribed by law for using it. Since the ceremony could take place in a private house, this presented no insuperable difficulty.

It was obviously much more difficult to arrange for the reading of the Anglican burial service, since an interment was in a public place. When the body of Charles I was taken to Windsor for burial, the royalists accompanying it were anxious that Bishop Juxon should repeat the church service, but this was

---

[1] John Duncon, *The Holy Life of Letice, Vi-Countess Falkland* (1653), pp. 43–44.

[2] *Diary*, 1655: 15 April, 16 Sept. The clergyman at the church in question, St. Gregory's, was John Hewitt, executed for conspiracy in 1658.

[3] Ibid., Dec. 1653, 19 Sept. 1655. Cf. 2 Nov. 1656, 3 Aug. 1656.

[4] *Acts and Ordinances*, ii. 715–19.

refused by Colonel Whichcott, the governor of the castle, who forbade the use of any other form than that of the *Directory*.[1] Other authorities were sometimes less punctilious, for Evelyn records that on the death of his mother-in-law he obtained permission that she should be buried with all decent ceremonies, which had not been used in that church for seven years.[2]

Probably the regulations as to marriage were more bitterly resented than any other of these enactments. After due notice had been given, the couple intending to marry were to go before some justice of the peace, where the formalities were of the simplest kind. The man had to declare: 'I A. B. do here in the presence of God the searcher of all hearts, take thee C. D. for my wedded wife; and do also in the presence of God, and before these witnesses, promise to be unto thee a loving and faithful husband.' The woman had to make a similar declaration, except that she was required to promise obedience. Henceforth no other form of marriage was good in law.

This civil rite satisfied few, and most had some kind of religious ceremony. Thus, when the protector's daughter, Frances, was married, in 1657, the registrar of the parish of St. Martin's in the Fields certified that he had duly published the banns on three Sundays.[3] Then Henry Scobell, a justice of the peace for Westminster, 'tied the knot after a godly prayer made by one of his Highness's divines'. Another daughter, Mary, was married to Fauconberg by the Anglican Hewitt according to the forms of the Book of Common Prayer. Joseph Lister, a puritan in a much humbler sphere of life, records that he and his bride were declared man and wife by a justice of the peace, but then parted until his uncle, a clergyman, 'offered to give us a wedding sermon, and if I had not known my wife since the justice married us, he would, after the sermon, marry us again; which he did, and after this we settled in our own house'.[4] Sir James Halkett and Anne Murray were united by a justice; but, she adds, 'if itt had nott beene done more solemnly afterwards by a minister I should nott [have] beleeved it lawfully done'.[5]

There seems no doubt that this ordinance was frequently violated. A debate took place on it in parliament in April 1659.

[1] Sir Thomas Herbert, *Memoirs* (1711), pp. 143-4. [2] *Diary*, 22 Sept. 1652.
[3] Francis Peck, *Desiderata Curiosa* (1779), ii. 500.
[4] *Autobiography* (1842), pp. 47-48.
[5] *Autobiography of Anne Lady Halkett* (1875), p. 103.

One speaker said that not one marriage in a hundred was made according to this act, and both the chief justice and the attorney-general denounced it. One curious fact that emerges from the debate is that a conscientious man might be married thrice to the same wife: once before a justice of the peace; a second time by a minister, according to the *Directory*; and the third time by an Anglican minister. The result was that the clause making invalid all marriages not contracted according to the new form was dropped, and the act itself allowed to lapse the next year.[1]

The declaration that Cromwell issued, 24 November 1655, threatened a heavy blow to the Anglican clergy and, indirectly, the laity. By it no sequestered minister might be employed in any household as a chaplain or schoolmaster; nor might he keep a school, preach publicly or privately, baptize, communicate, marry, or use the Book of Common Prayer.[2] Evelyn notes that he heard the 'funeral sermon of preaching', for henceforth Anglican clergymen would risk imprisonment or exile if they conducted services. 'This was the mournfullest day that in my life I had seen, or the church of England herself, since the Reformation. . . . The Lord Jesus pity our distressed church, and bring back the captivity of Zion!' Yet the declaration was rarely enforced, and Evelyn continued to find in London a service he could attend, even if 'the church of England was reduced to a chamber and conventicle, so sharp was the persecution'.[3]

The sufferings of clergy and laymen alike during the puritan revolution naturally led to an alliance between them. When the Restoration happened, the great activity of the disciples of Archbishop Laud compared with the lethargy of many of the other divines secured the predominance of high Anglicanism in the church. The country gentlemen had been hostile to Laudism in 1640 and many of the country clergy had been of like mind. Yet by 1660 and long afterwards squires, rectors, and vicars were usually high churchmen and supporters of the alliance of church and state associated with Clarendon, Danby, Nottingham, and later statesmen. The future Tory party was in the making.

There was one religious group in England that remained outside the internecine strife of Anglican and puritan—the Roman

---

[1] *Burton Diary*, ii. 67–74.
[2] *Tudor and Stuart Proclamations*, no. 3065; John Walker, *Sufferings of the Clergy* (1714), p. 194.　　　　　[3] *Diary*, 25 Dec. 1655, 3 Aug. 1656.

catholics. They had no direct concern with the outcome of the struggle for the control of the national church, for they did not expect or hope ever to belong to it, but they exercised an important influence upon early Stuart history. By their treatment of the Roman catholics both James and Charles alienated the sympathy of the majority of their subjects.

These two kings held very different views on Roman catholicism from those of parliament. It is remarkable that while James, who prided himself on his learning, looked at the question as a theologian, and Charles, a great patron of the arts, was swayed by aesthetic feelings and admiration for Italian culture in general, both sovereigns entertained hopes of a reunion with Rome. In his first speech to parliament James said: 'I acknowledge the Roman church to be our mother church although defiled with some infirmities and corruptions. No more am I enemy to their church because I would have them reform their errours. . . . My mind was ever so free from persecution.' He then proceeded to divide Roman catholics into two ranks, laymen and clerics. He was anxious to spare laymen, provided they did not stir up sedition, but priests would not be suffered in the kingdom so long as they maintained the supremacy of the pope and his power to depose temporal kings. If the catholic church would lay aside such errors, he would be glad to compromise and negotiate a union.[1]

Charles I was not so fond as his father of parading his theological predilections, but he was very prone to private discussions, particularly with the papal agents resident with the queen from 1634 to 1641. He, too, was anxious to bring about a reunion. According to one of these agents, Con, he once declared, 'At the price of my blood I wish we were united.' On another occasion, he said, 'You must induce the pope to meet me halfway.' He seems to have expected the pope to make certain concessions, such as communion in both kinds, the use of English, and the marriage of priests. Like his father, however, he apparently regarded the power of deposing a heretical ruler as the main obstacle to any approximation to Rome. He demanded the formal renunciation, by the pope, of this power, which was like asking for the moon.[2]

---

[1] *Commons' Journals*, i. 144. Cf. Proclamation, 22 Feb. 1604, in Edward Cardwell, *Documentary Annals* (1839), ii. 50–56.

[2] A. O. Meyer, 'Charles I and Rome', *American Historical Review*, xix. 13–26.

To the mass of Englishmen any idea of a reconciliation with Rome was utterly abhorrent. They regarded the pope as Antichrist and Roman catholicism as idolatrous and superstitious and its adherents as traitors. The mere presence of Roman catholics in England seemed a mark of internal weakness and a constant encouragement to an external foe. Cromwell was voicing a widely held opinion when he said in 1656 that Spain 'had an interest in your bowels. . . . The papists in England—they have been accounted, ever since I was born, Spaniolized. . . . It was so in England, Ireland, and Scotland: no man can doubt of it . . . this Spanish interest at home is a great piece of your danger.'[1] Hatred of Roman catholicism was particularly strong among those classes with political power. Consequently parliament was a steady advocate of penal legislation and its enforcement. Even Milton, who detested persecution in general, felt that reasons of state might justify the exclusion of Roman catholics from toleration.[2] The puritan attitude had at least the merit of consistency, while the policy of both the Stuarts was opportunist and based on no principle at all. They enforced or relaxed the penal laws according to their conceptions of the needs of English foreign policy or the domestic situation.

At the beginning of James's reign a diocesan survey was made which yielded a total of about 8,500 Roman catholics, and which was held to indicate an increase in their numbers. It is likely that only those were included who refused to attend any Anglican services at all, and there were probably at least another hundred thousand who occasionally attended Anglican services to avoid persecution.[3] Accordingly a proclamation was issued for the banishment of priests and Jesuits, and at the same time the recusancy fines were enforced. The reason for this policy was explained by Cecil to the Venetian ambassador—that priests had taken advantage of the king's excessive clemency, to go openly about the country saying mass, that the lives of catholics would be safe provided they kept quiet, but, as regards their property, the laws would be enforced. After all, urged Cecil, wealthy recusants would not find twenty pounds a month a heavy fine, and those too poor to pay this, who consequently

---

[1] Speech v, in Carlyle, ii. 518–19.
[2] *A Treatise of Civil Power in Ecclesiastical Causes* (1659), in *Works*, vi. 19.
[3] The papal agent, Panzani, said in 1635 that the open and crypto-catholics were about 150,000 (A. O. Meyer, *England and the Catholic Church* [1916], p. 64).

lost two-thirds of their property during their lifetime, would now be allowed to rent their estates at a very moderate price, whereas in Elizabeth's reign their buildings had passed to strangers who ruined them by trying to extract as much immediate profit as possible. In answer to the charge that in no country was Roman catholicism so severely persecuted as in England, Cecil replied that this could not be helped, because the object of the laws was to extinguish the catholic religion, for a well-governed monarchy naturally tried to prevent the increase in the numbers of those professing obedience to a foreign potentate. If the pope would surrender his claim to possess the right to excommunicate heretical sovereigns, and papal supremacy were confined exclusively to affairs spiritual, the king would concede liberty of conscience at once.[1]

The Elizabethan statutes re-enacted in 1604 may well have seemed in need of modification. Their general effect was to identify Roman catholicism with treason. Thus the penalties of high treason were pronounced against all Jesuits or seminary priests in England (those harbouring them were the accomplices of traitors), Englishmen in foreign seminaries who did not return within three months, those who converted an Englishman and withdrew him from his allegiance, and those who were willingly so withdrawn. Severe punishments were prescribed for saying or hearing mass, failing to attend the services of the Anglican church, or travelling more than five miles from the usual place of abode without permission. Even this comprehensive code failed to satisfy the bigotry of parliament, and the Gunpowder Plot, of which the vast majority of Roman catholics were entirely innocent, was made the occasion for an increase in penal legislation.

By the first of two statutes passed in 1606, the catholic who so far conformed as to attend Anglican services was now further required to receive the sacrament there or pay a ruinous fine. Moreover an oath of allegiance might be imposed, whose refusal incurred the penalties of praemunire, imprisonment for life, and confiscation of property. The oath demanded the recognition of the sovereign as lawful and rightful king, the repudiation of the papal claim to depose heretical princes, the promise to assist the king in case of rebellion caused by a papal sentence of deposition, and denunciation of the doctrine that princes,

[1] *State Papers, Venetian, 1603–1607*, pp. 327–31.

being excommunicated, can be deposed or murdered, or that subjects can be absolved from their oath of allegiance. The second act reinforced an Elizabethan act, and provided that recusants, except those engaged in business or trade, should depart from the City of London and a ten-mile compass thereof, and should be confined to a fixed abode, whence they could not travel more than five miles without licence from the privy council.[1]

This completed the penal laws affecting catholics, so far as the early Stuarts were concerned. For the most part they were enforced only fitfully and intermittently. Generally speaking, their enforcement coincided with the meeting of parliament. For example, in 1604, 1606, and 1610—years in which there were parliamentary sessions—proclamations for the banishment of missionary priests or for the execution of the penal laws were issued.[2] The extreme penalty of death was enforced in a correspondingly spasmodic manner. The total number of Roman catholics executed for their faith during 1603-60 was about sixty. Of these, eight were laymen and the rest came in equal proportions from the regular and from the secular priests. Rather more than half the executions took place from 1603 to 1625. There were only eight from 1613 until the meeting of the Long Parliament, when about twenty priests were put to death during 1641-7.[3] There was one victim under the commonwealth and one under the protectorate. It is noteworthy that, in court and at the place of execution, the Roman catholics were anxious to proclaim that they would die for conscience' sake, and that the judges and sheriffs were as anxious that they should be branded as traitors or felons.

It is clear that most of those who suffered death might have saved their lives if they had taken the oath prescribed by the statute of 1606. At first there was on this question an acute division of opinion even among the priests, and Blackwell, the arch-priest, actually took the oath. He was deposed in consequence, and Pope Paul V sternly forbade others to follow his example. The impasse thereby created was utilized to the full by an odious breed of informers who for the sake of rewards

---

[1] Tanner, *Constitutional Documents of the Reign of James I*, pp. 94–104.

[2] See *Tudor and Stuart Proclamations*, nos. 981, 1034, 1093.

[3] David Matthew, *Catholicism in England, 1535–1935* (London, 1936), pp. 69, 78, 83–84.

caused many suspects to be haled before the justices of the peace, who tendered the oath. The result was that, at almost any time during the first half of the century, several thousands were confined to prison, where the vile conditions ruined their health and sometimes caused their death. Figures are usually lacking, but at least we are told that, when James ordered the release of catholics in 1622 as a compliment to Spain, the number imprisoned amounted to four hundred priests and about ten times as many laymen.

The new oath, however, gained its importance, not solely as an ingenious weapon against catholics, but also as the cause of a controversy of the first importance which soon spread to the confines of Europe. The controversy began with the briefs of Paul V, forbidding the English catholics to take the oath, and the apology for it, written by James himself, which was published anonymously. The king's argument was that the oath was merely civil, and designed to distinguish between loyal and disloyal subjects. The challenge was taken up by Bellarmine, a Goliath among catholic controversialists. His position was that the English catholics were being required to deny their faith, inasmuch as whatever concerned the papal supremacy was a matter of faith. James was now getting beyond his depth and so contented himself with a declaration addressed to the European sovereigns that the papal pretensions menaced them all. The detailed answer to Bellarmine was left to Bishop Andrewes. He greatly enlarged the issue by dealing generally with the temporal power of the papacy, not merely with the specific question of the oath. By this time the whole of Europe was involved and theologians everywhere took up their pens, including a great continental scholar, Isaac Casaubon, whom James induced to come to England. This controversy was at its height from 1606 to 1620, and it is significant that the last great war of religion was preceded by a paper struggle in which the political activities of the papacy were attacked and defended with unsurpassed knowledge and skill. Probably Andrewes and Casaubon contributed at least as much to the defeat of the Counter Reformation as Gustavus Adolphus.[1]

After the breach between Charles and parliament in 1629, the conditions of catholics in England notably improved. The

---

[1] For a brief but excellent sketch of the controversy, see the introduction to C. H. McIlwain's *The Political Works of James I* (1918).

king no longer felt obliged to try to win protestant support by persecuting Roman catholics, and his uxorious nature made him prone to listen to his wife's appeals to spare her co-religionists. As Clarendon says of this period, the Roman catholics 'were grown only a part of the revenue without any probable danger of being made a sacrfice to the law'.[1] The fines to which they were liable were heavy, and failure to pay them might entail the confiscation of two-thirds of the defaulter's estate. But the law was rarely harshly administered and catholics were even allowed to rent their sequestered estates at a low rate. There would seem to have been a distinct catholic revival in the 1630's, with some notable conversions. The chapels of the queen and foreign ambassadors were crowded, and masses were cele-brated in private houses with only slight danger of interruption.[2] Letters of grace were issued to favoured individuals, protecting them and their families from all persecution.[3] Londoners had to accustom themselves to the sight of papal agents at court (first Con, then Rossetti), and to popish books on sale at the book-stalls. The works of Nicholas Caussin, a French Jesuit, were translated and imported, and at least one of them was printed at Oxford. Native catholics, too, took heart, and John Braids-haigh, for example, wrote his *Virginalia*, comprising sonnets in honour of the Virgin Mary, which was published with licence in 1632.

These halcyon times came to an abrupt end with the meet-ing of the Long Parliament. As one of the complaints most fre-quently made against the personal government of Charles I was the recent toleration of catholics, it was natural that persecution should again become the order of the day. The Irish rebellion served to intensify the popular hatred of papists, and demands for the rigid enforcement of the laws against them appeared in every negotiation between king and parliament, both before and during the civil war. It is not surprising, therefore, that with singular unanimity they fought on the king's side and poured forth their blood and treasure freely in his service. A little book called *The Catholique Apology* (1674) contains impres-sive lists of those who lost their lives fighting for Charles I and of those whose estates were confiscated and sold. A return made by the authorities of the various counties of England and Wales

---

[1] *Rebellion*, ii. 98.
[2] *State Papers, Venetian, 1636-1639* (1923), pp. 69, 217.   [3] Rushworth, ii. 284.

in September 1655 shows that there were just under sixteen hundred recusants whose estates were under sequestration. The case of William Blundell, a Lancashire catholic, was typical. His estates were confiscated early in the civil war, and his wife was granted only a fifth for the support of herself and five children, and she was liable to forfeit half of this if the children refused to be educated as protestants. Some ten years elapsed before the family was allowed to compound for its estates and to repurchase them with the help of friends.[1] The troubles of the catholics began early in the struggle, for they were assessed at special rates of taxation and suffered the seizure of arms and horses without compensation. Two-thirds of their estates, personal and real, were forfeited, in addition to any penalties they might incur as delinquents. To make their discovery the easier a test was devised in the form of an oath renouncing papal supremacy, transubstantiation, purgatory, and other catholic doctrines.[2] A comparison with the earlier oath exacted from recusants reveals that, whereas James had imposed as a test of loyalty an oath which he believed, rightly or wrongly, loyal catholics could take, the Long Parliament devised one that no honest catholic could possibly take.

The hard lot of the catholics was appreciably ameliorated when the presbyterians yielded the reins of government to the independents; indeed, so much so that the latter were frequently accused of being popishly inclined. Probably Cromwell would have been content with some kind of concordat by which the Jesuits were to be expelled, and the temporal claim of the papacy suffered to expire through disuse. A number of English catholics, called Blackloists, would have accepted such a scheme, but it was naturally rejected at Rome. The ordinance of 1650, however, which repealed penalties on those not attending their parish churches, benefited the catholic. Since he was not excluded from the provisions of this act, it was probably intended that he should enjoy the relief it gave, although it was inconvenient to avow that purpose in so many words. In practice, certainly, he ceased to be molested for not going to the parish church, and in April 1655, when it was thought necessary to put the penal laws into force again, the test provided was not evidence of his absence from church but his refusal of the oath established in 1643.

[1] Margaret Blundell, *Cavalier* (1933), p. 18. [2] *Acts and Ordinances*, i. 254–60.

However, this did not mean that the catholic could worship as he liked. The celebration of mass was still forbidden, and a catholic wishing to attend such a service had only two resources—to risk the penalties for attendance in private houses or to go to one of the chapels of the foreign representatives in London. Attendance at these privileged chapels is the great reason why, in spite of penalties, the catholic gentry resorted to London in such large numbers. English subjects had often been prohibited from attending these chapels, and a proclamation was issued in 1655 in much the old form. A number of catholics were arrested for attending service at the Venetian embassy but apparently were merely reprimanded.[1]

When Mazarin interceded on behalf of the catholics, Cromwell himself replied that he had already plucked many from the raging fire of persecution which tyrannized over their consciences and arbitrarily encroached upon their estates, and that he hoped to do more as opportunity occurred.[2] Although he gave his assent to a new act against them, apparently it was not enforced.[3] Indeed the French ambassador reported that the catholics were treated more leniently during the protectorate than under any previous government.[4] This would seem to prove that, excepting presbyterians, puritans were not intolerant even of Roman catholicism. They had fanned the popular hatred of popery in order to discredit Arminianism and Thorough, but proved merciful when actually in power.

No doubt there was still much honest bigotry. For the next century and a half Englishmen were to be found who genuinely believed that their religion and liberty were in danger from popery. But one suspects that others often used religious prejudice for political ends. On the whole the ecclesiastical history of the commonwealth justifies Cromwell's boast, 'I meddle not with any man's conscience.' He claimed that in practice men of all creeds had enjoyed liberty of conscience provided they had not made their religion a shield for rebellion, and boasted that this new freedom was the 'blessedest thing' accomplished under the protectorate.[5] Political reasons caused the prohibi-

---

[1] Gardiner, *Commonwealth and Protectorate*, iv. 18–20; *State Papers, Venetian, 1655–1656* (1930), pp. 54–55, 167, 176, 185, 310.

[2] Letter ccxvi, in Carlyle, iii. 6.   [3] *Acts and Ordinances*, ii. 1170–80.

[4] Gardiner, *Commonwealth and Protectorate*, iv. 19–20; Firth, *Last Years of the Protectorate*, i. 73–79.

[5] Letter cx and Speech v, in Carlyle, i. 493; ii. 537.

tion of Anglican and catholic services by the two constitutions of 1653 and 1657, but at least men were no longer constrained to attend churches they thought heretical. If he had had a free hand Cromwell would have allowed an even greater measure of toleration, but he was in advance of the majority of his fellow countrymen, who still hankered after persecution. Nevertheless it was a good omen that the political grounds for intolerance were being closely examined at the same time that experience seemed to show the futility of rigour and the safety of leniency.

The general spread of rationalism in Europe lies outside the scope of this work; it is not possible to do more than mention a few of the steps towards toleration. The Arminians had shown that the infallibility of the protestant Bible meant little unless there were infallible interpreters of it; the interpretations of the Scriptures admittedly differed even among protestants. By such reasoning they lessened the moral authority of confessions of faith, and the distinctions they drew between fundamental and non-fundamental doctrines, and between things essential and things indifferent, had the same tendency. The small group of liberal churchmen that used to meet at Lord Falkland's house at Great Tew greatly aided the cause of toleration. Chillingworth's book *The Religion of Protestants a Safe Way to Salvation* (1637) argued that protestants disagreed only about matters not necessary to salvation, and that honest seekers after truth were not apt to suffer damnation even if they failed through human frailty. Ten years later Jeremy Taylor published his *Discourse of the Liberty of Prophesying*, perhaps the most important Anglican contribution to the literature of toleration. His position was simply that reason is the ultimate judge of religion as of other matters; since reason is an individual attribute there are likely to be opposing opinions; as no man can be certain that his opinion is right or better than another's, it is wrong to persecute unorthodox beliefs, for there is no demonstrable proof that they are erroneous. Moreover no one can be a heretic who lives a good life. The learned contentions of writers such as these were reinforced by puritan pamphleteers—Roger Williams, Henry Robinson, and John Milton. These all issued vigorous pleas for freedom of conscience in 1644. Milton's best argument is that persecution is unnecessary because truth is strong enough to prevail without the aid of compulsion. Let truth and falsehood grapple, he urged; who ever knew truth to be worsted in a free and open conflict? Moreover the liberty and zeal of sects proved that men were no longer content with 'rigid external formality' and 'gross conforming stupidity'.

There was another group whose members furnish an excellent example of the growth of toleration. The Jews, for two centuries after their expulsion by Edward I, either avoided England or dwelt there in such obscurity as to escape notice. During the sixteenth century the presence of Jews or crypto-Jews attracted attention, especially after the execution for treason of Roderigo Lopez, Elizabeth's physician, who may well have been in some sense the original of Shylock. Their position was improved during the puritan revolution, when they benefited by the intense study of the Hebrew Scriptures and the growth of toleration. Cromwell befriended them, partly through dislike of persecution and partly because he realized that the trade with Spain and Portugal, and to a smaller degree with the Levant, was in their hands. If allowed to settle in England they could assist the mercantile policy that found expression in the Navigation Act. He encouraged the mission of Menasseh ben Israel, a rabbi from Amsterdam, in 1655, and supported his petition. A conference was summoned in which sat members of the council of state, lawyers, soldiers, merchants, and divines, but it was soon evident from its proceedings that Prynne and other pamphleteers had been only too successful in inflaming public opinion against the Jews. So Cromwell derived one benefit alone from the conference—the report of the judicial representatives that there was no legal bar to the Jews' return. Henceforth Cromwell allowed them to reside in England, to trade there, and even to worship in synagogues. Letters of denization were granted to a few favoured individuals, but the rest remained aliens for another two centuries because they were unable to swear allegiance on the faith of a Christian.

IX

FOREIGN RELATIONS, 1630–60

DURING the personal government of Charles I the people of England relaxed somewhat the interest with which they had previously followed events on the Continent. One explanation is their absorption in their own affairs. Another is that, after the meteoric career of Gustavus Adolphus, protestantism was safe, and the Thirty Years War continued in order that the victors might gain territorial compensation. Except as volunteers in the Swedish or Dutch service, Englishmen had no part or lot in the later stages of the war, and the recovery of the Lower Palatinate by the heir of Frederick V, in 1648, cannot by any stretch of imagination be attributed to the diplomatic efforts of Charles I, which excited the contempt of Europe. Apart from this unavailing interest in his nephew's fortunes, Charles can hardly be said to have had any guiding principle in his conduct of foreign relations. Whatever he tried to do on land mattered little, for foreigners recognized clearly enough that he was powerless without a parliament. Perhaps the one chance to strike an effective blow for the recovery of the Palatinate occurred after the battle of Breitenfeld, for then, in return for substantial supplies of men and money, Gustavus was willing to undertake the restitution of both Palatinates. There was one possible source whence a subsidy for Gustavus might be forthcoming, and that was stopped, for the king said the very mention of a parliament was derogatory to his authority.[1] A little previously Charles had moved in a precisely opposite direction in order to help Frederick. In return for the promise of assistance in regaining the Palatinate, a secret treaty was signed at Madrid, in which the kings of England and Spain agreed to make joint war upon the Dutch, by land and sea, and to partition their territory.[2] The treaty was not ratified then, nor in 1634 (when it was again discussed), apparently because at Madrid there was not the slightest confidence that Charles could perform his promises. Nevertheless this friendliness to Spain and enmity to the United Provinces, already envied for their prosperity and

---

[1] Gardiner, vii. 189–93.　　　　[2] Ibid., p. 176.

hated for their haughtiness,[1] were but anticipations of the trend of public opinion, and Charles probably hoped to rally his subjects behind him by appealing to their patriotism through his claims to the sovereignty of the Narrow Seas.

It is noteworthy that, although every attempt had been made under the Tudors (and especially by Burghley) to foster the fishing industry, both by insisting on the observation of Lent and fast days and by checking the importation of fish caught by foreigners, England had remained the great champion of the right to fish freely. Under the Stuarts there was a complete change of attitude towards this thorny subject. James brought from across the border theories about his sovereignty at sea as startling as those about a free monarchy on land. Nevertheless he was content, on the whole, with the assertion that his subjects possessed exclusive fishing rights in the Narrow Seas and with upholding the neutrality of the 'king's chambers' or bays. Judging from the draft treaty of union between England and Scotland of 1604, James would have been satisfied if the subjects of the two kingdoms had shared a monopoly of fishing in waters within fourteen miles from the coast, but the failure of the union prevented the adoption of this reasonable limit. Charles displayed no such moderation, and he put forwrd the most exorbitant claims to dominion over the surrounding seas. He tried to assert the same control over them as over English soil. According to his ideas no other nation might maintain fleets in the Narrow Seas to exercise any of the rights of war (among which the Dutch blockade of the Flemish coast was included), and foreign vessels in these waters were to salute the king's ships, by striking their flag and lowering their topsails. It was to enforce such claims as these that the writs of ship money were issued from 1634 onwards.

The instructions to Lindsey,[2] who commanded the first ship-money fleet in 1635, suggest at least that the king was indifferent whether they led to war with Holland or not. In addition to demanding the salute and to preventing any acts of hostility between ships of belligerents, the fleet was also to compel the Dutch herring busses to accept licences giving them permission to fish. Only the extraordinary patience and tact of the Dutch and French, now allied, averted a naval war. As it was, the

---

[1] *State Papers, Venetian, 1629-1632*, p. 493.
[2] Robert Bertie, first earl of Lindsey.

fleets of both nations kept out of Lindsey's way, and his sole achievement was raising the blockade of the coast of Flanders. The consequence was that the Dunkirkers were able to make a successful raid into the North Sea and to shatter the Dutch fishing fleet off Northumberland.

In no way dismayed at the fiasco of the first ship-money fleet, Charles was determined to persevere. To bolster up his claims to sovereignty at sea, he caused to be printed the elaborate treatise Selden had written in the previous reign in answer to Grotius's *Mare Liberum*. *Mare Clausum* is a monument of misplaced ingenuity and learning, for it attempts to prove that the kings of England had always advanced the claims now put forth. Its series of far-fetched precedents and misapplied analogies delighted the king, who ever loved to have the letter of the law on his side. Full of confidence in the justice of his contentions, he sent Northumberland to sea with the strongest fleet that had ever sailed from English harbours. *Parturiunt montes, nascetur ridiculus mus.* A few Dutch fishermen were persuaded to buy licences,[1] a few merchantmen were convoyed to Dunkirk, and that was all. The next year even less was accomplished, for a strong Dutch fleet convoyed the busses and did not suffer any interference. In 1638 the Scottish revolt against the introduction of the Laudian liturgy found more honourable employment for the fleet than harassing fishermen.

Hence Charles's pretensions had no permanent effects. In England there is no sign that patriotism was gratified by the flattery accorded to it, or that the exaction of ship money was facilitated by the assertion of claims to dominion at sea. The growing jealousy of the Dutch commercial prosperity had not reached such a pitch that Englishmen were anxious to damage their rivals by an attitude of benevolent neutrality to Spain. On the contrary it is probable that the prevalent sentiment was expressed by the country gentleman who exclaimed, when he heard of the sailing of the fleet: 'What a foolery is this; that the country in general shall be thus taxed with great sums to maintain the king's titles and honours! For my part, I am £10 the worse for it already.'[2]

On the other hand the Dutch were naturally incensed at the

---

[1] Specimen of licence in Fulton, *Sovereignty of the Sea*, p. 294.

[2] Ibid., p. 324. Cf. Prynne's *Humble Remonstrance*, p. 17, for the complaint that the navy, being used to convoy Spanish reinforcements to Flanders, neglected the protection of English shipping.

indirect assistance Charles was affording Spain. They were prompt to take their revenge in 1639, when a large Spanish fleet with troops for Flanders appeared in the Channel. A running fight ensued until the Spaniards took refuge in the Downs. Their necessities prompted Charles to offer his help to the highest bidder. He would protect the Spanish fleet for £150,000; he would stand aside and suffer the Dutch to destroy the hostile armament if their allies, the French, would consent to use the army in their pay in Germany to restore his nephew to his hereditary possessions. Meanwhile the Dutch mustered in overwhelming strength, and the accidental discharge of a gun, on board a Spanish ship, which killed a Dutch sailor, was utilized as a pretext to fall on. The Dutch won a decisive victory, and Tromp, after his triumphant violation of English territorial waters, added to the indignity Charles suffered by lowering his flag in mock acknowledgement of English sovereignty at sea.

During the next ten years the question whether the English civil war would be decided without the intervention of any European power was the only one of importance in English foreign affairs. So far as Charles I was concerned his best chances of securing outside assistance seemed to come from dynastic relationships. Unfortunately for him, however, the whole energies of France were consumed by the determination to gain territorial compensation at the expense of the Empire as well as of Spain or by internal dissension. Moreover first Richelieu, and then Mazarin, was not sorry to see England so distracted that there was no further danger of a continuance of that pro-Spanish policy which had so hampered the Franco-Dutch allies. After the first civil war Mazarin's sympathies were with the presbyterians rather than with the independents, and especially with the Scots during the second civil war, and his representative, Montreuil, tried in vain to arrange terms acceptable to both Charles and the Scots. Later, domestic broils, known as the *Fronde*, prevented his striking a blow to save Charles I from the scaffold, even had he been so minded.

The other possible foreign ally for Charles I was the United Provinces. Indeed, in consenting to the marriage (May 1641) of his eldest daughter, Mary, to William, the heir of Frederick Henry of Orange, the king hoped to strengthen his position in England with a political alliance, but was obliged to be content with a present of money. After the outbreak of civil war the house of Orange furnished what assistance it could to Charles, but the oligarchy that governed the Dutch republic remained hostile to his cause. Frederick Henry's influence was strong enough to prevent the formal reception by the states general of Walter Strickland, the parliamentary agent, and to silence his protest against the supply of munitions to Charles I. Moreover, in 1644 a Dutch embassy proposed mediation between the royalists and parliamentarians, and urged parliament to accept the king's terms as outlined in the Uxbridge negotiations; but the sole result of their officious efforts was to create a distrust of their neutrality. In 1647 William succeeded his father, and in the next year he thought he saw prospects of intervening in England when the acknowledgement by Spain of the independence of the United Provinces ended the Eighty Years War. His desire to help his English relatives was so evident that Strickland was sent to Holland again to urge the states general not to furnish aid to the prince of Wales. He was refused an audience, and royalist ships were allowed to refit in Dutch harbours.

The news that Cromwell and the army intended to bring Charles I to trial led all parties in the States General to unite in dispatching an extraordinary embassy to London, where a deaf ear was turned to all pleas for mercy. The execution of the king sent a thrill of horror round Europe, and made both governments and peoples hostile to the new republic. In protestant countries, ministers felt impelled to explain that there was no necessary connexion between protestantism and king-killing; and, in Holland, not only was recognition refused to the commonwealth, but the sympathies of the populace aided the escape of the assassins of its representative, Isaac Dorislaus. Indeed, but for the death of William II at the very hour when he was planing a *coup d'état* to overthrow the Amsterdammers and to substitute personal rule for the bourgeois oligarchy that controlled Holland, he might actively have assisted his brother-in-law.

Spain was the first European power to recognize the commonwealth, but regretted that reasons of state obliged her to adopt this course. In Madrid, as at The Hague, popular sentiment was all on the side of the murderers of an agent of the commonwealth. In France the pronounced dislike of Englishmen caused a merchant at Nantes to beg a correspondent not to address him as *Anglais*, for, he said, his nation was so much hated that he could not pass along the streets in safety.[1] This hostility of the people was soon reflected in governmental acts. The importation of English draperies was forbidden, which was met on the other side of the Channel by a prohibition against French wines and silks. French privateers freely attacked English commerce and evoked the inevitable reprisals, so that for the next six years there was a kind of unofficial war at sea.

It is curious that this unacknowledged state of hostilities with France should have been a cause of the outbreak of war with the United Provinces. At first sight, the substitution of De Witt for William II as the ruling spirit of the United Provinces seemed to suggest possibilities of co-operation between the two protestant republics. Accordingly, early in 1651 Oliver St. John and Strickland were instructed to conclude a close alliance with the States General. Their reception by the public with shouts of 'king-murderers' and the like was but a foretaste of the failure that awaited them. In the beginning the Dutch suggested as a basis for a new treaty the *Intercursus Magnus* of 1496, but they drew back when they found that the English wanted to amplify it (particularly the clauses relative to the reception of rebels, so as to insure the confiscation of the property of the house of Orange in case royalists found refuge with Mary, who was now the mother of the future William III). On their part they were anxious to negotiate a commercial treaty on terms of equality, but were unwilling to go farther towards a political union than an agreement that each would assist the other by arms, provided that the party which received the assistance should pay for it.[2]

St. John's exasperation at the failure of the negotiations at The Hague is traditionally said to have caused him to advocate parliamentary action against Dutch trade, and in October 1651 the Navigation Act was passed. This measure forbade the importation into the British Isles of the produce of Asia, Africa, and America except in British ships or those belonging to the plantations, and required that the majority of the crews should be subjects of the commonwealth. Commodities from a European country should be imported only in ships owned by Englishmen or the people of the exporting country.

---

[1] *Memoirs of the Verney Family*, iii. 403.
[2] See the draft of a treaty, with thirty-six clauses, in *Hist. MSS. Com.*, *Portland MSS.* (1891), i. 605–7; and *Eng. Hist. Rev.* xxi. 320–2, for Thurloe's comments.

The object of this act was undoubtedly to benefit English commerce at the expense of the Dutch. During Elizabeth's reign, it was thought, English merchants had enjoyed a large share of the carrying trade of the world, but of late years they had been supplanted by the Dutch. It was now intended to strike a stout blow at this virtual Dutch monopoly of the carrying trade.[1] Probably the act was never strictly enforced, if only for the reason that there was not enough English shipping available to replace the Dutch. Therefore it is likely that the act did no great harm to Dutch trade, and that it was not, as was formerly supposed, a chief cause of the first Dutch war.

This war between the two republics is to be attributed to a variety of causes. Perhaps the most important arose from the English claim to search Dutch ships for French goods. Since the Dutch were determined to maintain what they called the freedom of the seas, and were prepared to fight if necessary to assert the doctrine that the flag covers the cargo, and had issued orders to their admiral, Tromp, to resist all attempts to visit Dutch ships, this challenge of the right of search may reasonably be regarded as the fundamental cause of the war.[2]

This Dutch war was remarkable both for the propaganda employed by the government to enlist popular support and for its influence upon naval strategy. The difference in outlook caused by the transition from the personal rule of the Stuarts to the more democratic régime of the commonwealth receives no more striking illustration than the anxiety of the government to inform Englishmen of the causes of hostilities in 1652. Whereas the Stuarts had consistently adhered to the theory that the control of foreign affairs was the exclusive prerogative of the Crown, the statesmen of the commonwealth were careful to explain the reasons for the outbreak of war. A study of two pamphlets[3] inspired by the authorities suggests, at least, that there was general exasperation against the Dutch, rather than any particular cause of animosity. Both pamphlets emphasize

---

[1] The ubiquity of Dutch merchants is well illustrated by a letter of Wentworth's from Ireland, 24 April 1634 (*Strafforde's Letters*, i. 233): 'It is true, that in a manner most of the trade of this kingdom passeth to and fro in Dutch bottoms, and it is a necessary devil that we must bear with for a time.' For an earlier example of similar views, see *Works of Sir Walter Ralegh* (1829), viii. 365.

[2] *Letters and Papers Relating to the First Dutch War*, ed. S. R. Gardiner (1899), i. 53.

[3] *A Declaration of the Parliament . . . Relating to the Affairs and Proceedings between This Commonwealth and the States-General* (1652); *The Case Stated between England and the United Provinces* (1652).

the following grievances: Dutch ingratitude for English assistance in gaining their independence; the help given to royalists, and most recently to Charles II, and their many violations of neutrality, which was a mere pretence to get the trade and riches of England into their hands; the affronts to Strickland, and the recent indignities to St. John and him, together with the failure to punish the assassins of Dorislaus; the treacherous massacre in Amboyna,[1] the expulsion of the English from the Spice Islands, and the Dutch monopoly of the trade in nutmegs; and the insolent behaviour of Dutch ships at sea (by refusing to strike the flag), which culminated in Tromp's defiance of Blake in the Downs. One of the pamphlets argues that it is not the bare compliment of saluting which has occasioned the late contests, but it is the absolute sovereignty of the Narrow Seas which is required to be acknowledged by striking the flag, 'and so hath been for many hundred years . . . acknowledged by the nations of Europe'.[2] The Dutch, by refusing to strike, are challenging the English dominion of the seas, and aim at seizing control of the fishing, which they know is

the great staple of their trade and merchandize. . . . And this together with the managing of our trade for our best advantage, held forth in the Act for Navigation; and what else may be found convenient for such an end, may be strongly presumed to be the true grounds of their quarrell against us. . . . The truth is . . . they had not only got a staple of trade as aforesaid; but had almost ingrost all our trade, and thereby spoyled us of our navigation and maritin (*sic*) defence. . . . And because the Dutch see themselves prevented of taking our markets, emptying our pockets, and fishing in our troubled waters, as they had done for many years before, therefore are they offended.[3]

. . . . .

Greater love and assistance then by the English to them hath not been shown to a people. Never was love so ill requited and abused.[4]

The first Dutch war is of great importance in the history of the English navy. Although it lasted just under two years, there were many fleet actions, which, both by reason of the number of ships engaged and of the tactics employed, did much to determine the nature of naval warfare in the future. Moreover, for half a century the English navy had been overshadowed by

---

[1] For John Hall's reprinting of the old pamphlets on Amboyna, see *Huntington Library Bulletin*, No. 6, p. 112.   [2] *The Case*, p. 12.

[3] Ibid., pp. 13–14.   [4] Ibid., p. 19.

the Dutch, and, with the rather slight exception of Rains-borough's expedition against Sallee in 1637, no success had attended English naval operations since 1596. On the face of it a victory by the Dutch might have been anticipated, inasmuch as their mercantile marine was greatly superior to that of England, and hitherto the English navy had consisted of a nucleus of royal ships plus pressed merchantmen. Now, however, conditions were changing, and converted merchantmen were found markedly inferior to warships; and the reluctance of their captains and crews to face constant risks further diminished their usefulness. Therefore the greater number of merchantmen at their command, which the Dutch enjoyed, did not decide the issue of the struggle.

Factors favouring the English were: the strategic advantage conferred by the absence of any very considerable mercantile marine to protect and by a position athwart the trade-routes of the enemy, whose commerce was her very life-blood and had to be maintained at all costs during war; the building of forty new ships in 1649–51, so that the effectiveness of the navy had been practically doubled; and the larger size of the Englsh ships, and their heavier guns.

During most of 1652 the fighting yielded no decisive results. Tromp's failure to bring either of the English squadrons at sea to action, and to protect the herring fleet, caused his resignation in favour of de With and de Ruyter. The latter, following an inconclusive fight near Plymouth with Sir George Ayscue, saved an important convoy. After another drawn battle, off the Kentish Knock, Blake was defeated off Dungeness by Tromp, now reinstated with a fleet twice the size of England's. For three months Tromp rode supreme in the Channel but was beaten in a three-day battle off Portland, suffering severe losses to his warships and to the merchantmen he was convoying. A two-day battle, near the Gabbard, gave the command at sea to England, and for a while a blockade of the Dutch coast was maintained. A desperate effort by Tromp to break the blockade led to his defeat and death (31 July 1653).

These successive reverses had naturally made the Dutch anxious to conclude peace, but they found that the English were still as eager as ever for a union which should transform two sovereign nations into one. In vain Cromwell told the Dutch commissioners: 'You have appealed to the judgment of heaven.

The Lord has declared against you. After the defeat you have undergone, your only resource is to associate yourselves with your formidable neighbour to work together for the propagation of the kingdom of Christ.'[1] However, after the establishment of the protectorate, the fanatical enthusiasm that had permeated the puritan leaders of England during the meeting of Barebones' Parliament cooled down, and mundane considerations recovered their influence. Moreover Cromwell, who had always been dubious about the war, could now, as protector, control the English side of the peace negotiations. Gradually his common sense asserted itself, and the more humiliating conditions formerly proposed were dropped. Even so, the stipulation that each country should expel the enemies or rebels of the other, practically meant that Dutch territory was closed to the Stuarts. Cromwell's attempt to force the States General to decree the perpetual exclusion of the house of Orange from public office was only indirectly granted. The States General agreed that any future captain-general—such as the prince of Orange had been —should be required to take an oath to maintain the treaty; but this was as far as it was safe to ask the States General to go, for the Orangists were strong outside the province of Holland. Holland, however, was willing to go farther, and passed an act debarring the prince of Orange from office under the States General—an act that may have been unconstitutional and was certainly not only inexpedient but also useless, as events in 1672 proved. For the rest the treaty conceded the acknowledgement of the salute in the British seas, and granted compensation for the losses English merchantmen had suffered in the East, for the massacre of Amboyna, and for the detention of their ships in the Sound by Denmark, an ally of the United Provinces.

Meanwhile English prowess at sea commanded the respect of Europe, and, although the hostility of 1649 remained, it was now concealed. Several states now felt the heavy hand of England on account of favours shown to the royalists.

Portugal had begun, in 1640, the war that eventually restored its independence, and its representatives had been warmly received then by both king and people in England. The treaty of 1642 re-established the oldest European alliance and granted important trade privileges to English merchants. The Portuguese ambassador remained in London until 1646 and acted

[1] Gardiner, *Commonwealth and Protectorate*, iii. 41.

as an intermediary for correspondence between Charles I and his queen and others on the Continent. It was natural, therefore, that Rupert should have been kindly received, in 1649, when he took refuge in the Tagus with his small fleet of vessels that had revolted from the English navy the previous year. The prince made Lisbon the base for raids on English commerce, and sold there the goods he seized from merchantmen. Blake established a blockade and captured half the Brazil fleet, but was driven off by a storm that permitted Rupert's escape to the Mediterranean.

The Portuguese soon found they had to pay a heavy price for allowing their neutrality to be violated by the royalists, for, in addition to making restitution of all that English merchants had suffered by Rupert's sale of their cargoes in Portugal, they had to pay a sum of money to meet the expenses of Blake's naval operations against them.

Two years later this political treaty was supplemented by a trade agreement (1654), which gave Englishmen the right of commerce with all the Portuguese colonies and freedom from interference on Portuguese soil on account of religious differences. Other privileges were also granted, so that English subjects dealing with, or residing in, Portugal had the advantage over the Portuguese themselves.[1]

The protestant power that found most favour in the sight of Englishmen was Sweden, and throughout the protectorate efforts were made to form an alliance with her. Unfortunately for Cromwell and those who wished to base international relations upon enmity to popery, the foreign policy of Sweden was now controlled rather by territorial than religious considerations. The possessions, across the Baltic, that Sweden had acquired in the first half of the seventeenth century had incurred the hostility of all her neighbours, protestant as well as catholic, so that her wars were likely to be waged to retain her recent conquests in which England had no special interest. There seemed to be a chance of finding a basis for joint action in 1653, when Bulstrode Whitelocke was sent to the court of Queen Christina. Then Denmark, the hereditary foe of Sweden, was the ally of the United Provinces. It was therefore natural that his instructions should suggest co-operation to open the

[1] Edgar Prestage, *The Diplomatic Relations of Portugal with France, England, and Holland from 1640 to 1668* (1925), pp. 99–132.

Sound to a free trade, which was now obstructed whenever the Danish king or the United Provinces thought fit.[1] Whitelocke found Swedish merchants were already enjoying exemption from tolls at the Sound, and that they were much more concerned about the English exercise of maritime rights. Indeed he learned that *Mare Liberum* was popular, but hoped that the perusal of *Mare Clausum* would efface the impression Grotius's book had made. Actually all that Whitelocke could accomplish was a commercial treaty which, in addition, provided for the mutual expulsion of rebels and traitors and acknowledged that either one of the confederates might trade, during a war, with the enemy of the other, except in contraband.[2]

Cromwell was not dissatisfied, therefore, with the state of foreign affairs in September 1654, when he addressed the first parliament of the protectorate, and he particularly emphasized the cordial relations established with the northern powers. The Sound, previously obstructed, was open to English commerce, he said, and 'that which was and is the strength of this nation, the shipping, will now be supplied thence'. Whereas, formerly, merchants had been glad to obtain Baltic produce second-hand, they could at present engage as freely in trade there as the Dutch.[3] Thus the material interests of England were safeguarded, even though nothing had been accomplished for protestantism.

When Christina resigned her crown in favour of her cousin, Charles X, the prospects of a protestant crusade once again looked bright, for his meteoric career was worthy of a knight errant. He was willing, or professed to be willing, to carry out the war against the house of Habsburg (which to Cromwell seemed the most desirable of all crusades), but he felt that he must first consolidate his position around the shores of the Baltic, and the rest of his reign was all too short for this. Much of his revenue was derived from the customs he levied at the river mouths in his possession, so it was natural that he should try to seize the estuary of the Vistula. Thence he became involved in the interior of Poland and won victories against almost incredible odds, but could not retain his conquests, especially when hordes of Russians appeared in the field against

---

[1] Bulstrode Whitelocke, *Journal of the Swedish Embassy*, ed. Henry Reeve (1855), i. 89–90.

[2] Ibid. ii. 168–75.   [3] Speech II, in Carlyle, ii. 355–7.

him. In the end his position became so critical that he was glad to enter into a series of treaties with the Great Elector and thereby enlist Brandenburg on his side. In spite of this alliance Danzig still held out, and, in the summer of 1656, was relieved by a Dutch fleet, whose mere presence compelled the Swedes to sign a treaty granting the Danzigers the free exercise of their commerce. This pacific demonstration of sea-power ruined Charles's plan to secure the dominion of the Baltic. The Dutch intervention in that sea was dictated by their trade thither, which absorbed half their total tonnage. The schemes of Charles X, therefore, threatened vital Dutch interests; but English merchants were also concerned, so Cromwell refused Charles's demand that an English squadron of twenty ships should be sent to the Baltic to keep the Dutch in check. Permission to raise British volunteers for his army was all that he could secure in return for a second commercial treaty (July 1656), which recognized the principle of the open door as applicable to harbours in Polish Prussia.

In 1657 the situation changed, for on the death of the emperor Ferdinand III, his successor, Leopold, at once sent troops to aid Poland; and, simultaneously, Denmark sought to avenge old wrongs by declaring war against Sweden. The centre of hostilities was thus suddenly transferred from the east to the west Baltic. Charles soon overran Jutland, and only his inferiority at sea prevented a direct attack on Copenhagen. His achievements were neutralized, however, by the desertion of the Great Elector, whose support Poland bought with the grant of full sovereignty over east Prussia. Charles, in his hour of need, appealed to Cromwell for money and ships, but was told that the price of assistance was the cession of Bremen, whose possession the protector coveted as a means of access to the protestant states of north Germany. Charles refused to give up this territory, so the only help supplied was diplomatic: to persuade the United Provinces not to join the coalition against Sweden, and Brandenburg to leave it. Furthermore the protector, long grieved at the dispute between two protestant states at a time when, in his heated imagination, the popish party was arming everywhere, endeavoured to mediate between Denmark and Sweden, but found neither anxious for peace on terms that the other might be expected to accept. Something might have been done if Dutch co-operation could have been secured, but

the commercial rivalry between England and Holland prevented this. During the war now waged against Spain, the
Dutch secretly carried Spanish goods, and the English efforts
to suppress this illicit trade, by stopping and searching Dutch
ships on the high seas, naturally strained relations between the
two countries. Similarly the blockade of Lisbon by a Dutch
fleet, to enforce claims upon Portugal, was indirectly of great
assistance to Spain and hindrance to England (whose navy had
been accustomed to use Lisbon as its base for operations off the
Spanish coast). Remonstrances to the Dutch about the harm
they were doing to the protestant cause fell on ears deaf to all
but whatever advanced their commerce. It so happened that
the ambitious schemes of Charles X threatened their Baltic
trade, and then they were moved to action.

The war between Sweden and Denmark came to a temporary
end in February 1658, when Charles was able by force of arms
to compel acceptance of the treaty of Roeskilde, by which
Scania, Halland, and all other Danish territory in southern
Scandinavia passed into Sweden's hands. More significant
internationally was an article providing for the co-operation
of the two powers in order to close the Sound to fleets hostile
to Sweden. This humiliating peace endured for only a few
months: before the end of the summer Swedish armies were
once again before Copenhagen. Charles X wrote to Cromwell
to justify the renewal of the war on the grounds that Denmark
had neglected to carry out some of the terms of the recent
treaty, had refused to join her fleet to Sweden's in order to keep
the Baltic immune from foreign navies, and was intriguing with
the enemies of Sweden.[1] The unexpectedly stout resistance of
Copenhagen disrupted Charles's plans, but it is likely that he
would ultimately have taken the capital but for the intervention
of the maritime powers, now thoroughly alarmed by Swedish
pretensions in the Baltic and by the evident intention of Charles
to control the Sound and thereby to admit or exclude foreign
shipping at will. This was a dire menace to important international interests. The Dutch had a very extensive trade with
Danzig and Russia, and the English derived the bulk of their
naval stores from the Baltic. Owing to the death of Oliver
Cromwell and the absorption of his successor in domestic problems, the Dutch were the first to act, and sent a fleet, under

[1] Thurloe, vii. 342–3.

Opdam, which forced the Sound, relieved Copenhagen, and confined Swedish ships of war to their own harbours.

However, the settlement of a question that concerned the western powers in general could not be left to one of them alone. The government of Richard Cromwell felt that something must be done, for the continuation of the war would hinder trade, many manufactured goods being transported hither, and hemp, pitch, tar, cordage, and masts being brought thence.[1] Accordingly England, France, and the States General agreed to a convention, signed at The Hague (11 May 1659), that the three powers should jointly mediate to bring about a settlement based upon the treaty of Roeskilde. Two more agreements were later made between England and the United Provinces, to deal with the situation caused by the unyielding attitude of Charles X. The maritime powers now undertook to use their navies to compel Sweden and Denmark to accept a compromise rather less favourable to Sweden than the treaty of Roeskilde. The mediators found that neither party desired peace. Denmark was unwilling to treat alone and wanted to consult at least Brandenburg, the nearest of Sweden's many enemies. Charles, already incensed at the Dutch for ruining his first campaign against Copenhagen, regarded further delay as fatal to his prospects. He was extremely indignant to find that the English and Dutch had already decided on the terms they thought fit and proper. He insisted that he wanted mediators, not judges, and warned the representatives of the maritime powers that, if their projects were based on fleets, he had projects that were based on the sword. When matters were drifting into this impasse, Mountagu's sudden decision to take the fleet back to England[2] reduced her influence to a vestige, and she took no important part in the negotiations following Charles's death in February 1660, which closed the northern war.

Looking back, in respect to both Sweden and Holland disappointment awaited the hope cherished by Cromwell that protestantism might become the ruling factor in his foreign policy. The truth is that he was behind the times in entertaining such a project, for mundane advantages were rapidly rivalling, and even replacing, religious differences as causes of war. He was mistaken in his belief that the catholic nations were girding up their loins for a general attack upon heretical

[1] See Thurloe's speech, in *Burton Diary*, iii. 376–84.   [2] See below, p. 247.

states and that the destruction of the Habsburgs was of prime importance to his co-religionists. In fact Cromwell's foreign policy achieved little[1] when inspired by religion, but was much more successful when based on secular interests. In his dealings with the catholic countries, France and Spain, Cromwell's robust common-sense view of the national interests remained unclouded by dreams about protestant crusades.

At Richelieu's death France occupied Roussillon and Catalonia, Lorraine and Alsace, the passages of the Alps, and Turin, but in the north had gained only Arras, Bapaume, and Landrecies, so that the valley of the Oise still remained open to an enemy for an advance on Paris. However, an invasion by this route was decisively defeated at Rocroi (1643), where the famous Spanish infantry were entirely overwhelmed.[2] Five years later France gained the reward for these triumphs, by the treaty of Westphalia (1648), when the emperor recognized her sovereign rights to Metz, Toul, and Verdun, and to Alsace, then a geographical expression whose exact definition cannot be attempted here. France had defeated the house of Austria, but the triumphant conclusion of a duel that had lasted since the days of Charles V was followed by the confused and humiliating years of the *Fronde*, during which Spain recovered much that she had previously lost. Within a few months of the treaty that attested the victory of Bourbon over Habsburg, the 'day of barricades' in Paris seemed to threaten the very existence of the monarchy. Yet the opposition to the Crown was soon taken out of the hands of the *parlement de Paris*, with which had been associated other *parlements*, by magnates with motives that varied but were all selfish and all dishonourable. There followed four years of civil war and of foreign invasion, when Condé, the victor of Rocroi, led Spanish forces against Anne of Austria, the queen mother, and Mazarin, who governed France during the minority of Louis XIV, and when Bordeaux rebelled and its citizens were invited to adopt the Agreement of the People. Before the end of 1653 the court had subdued or conciliated its enemies, but France had fallen from the triumphant height she had reached in 1648.

The temptation to the commonwealth to fish in these troubled waters was strong, for the French government had refused to

---

[1] For the protection of the Vaudois see Gardiner, *Commonwealth and Protectorate*, iv. 177-94.   [2] *Histoire de France*, ed. Ernest Lavisse (1911), vii, pt. i, pp. 8-9.

recognize the republic and had seized English merchantmen in the Mediterranean. The exclusion of French wines, and reprisals on French shipping, produced an unofficial war at sea, and the outbreak of general hostilities seemed so near that a French agent reported in the autumn of 1650 that if a man wanted to bet he could wager large sums that by spring England would have an army in France.[1] Relations never got so bad that there was fighting on land, but Blake dispersed a French fleet sailing to relieve Dunkirk, and thus helped to ensure the surrender of that port to the Spanish forces (September 1652).

For the next two years the Dutch war served as an exercise for English martial strength, but Cromwell sent trusted agents to report on the numbers of the rebels in France in case a favourable opportunity should arrive of delivering a blow for the Huguenots, whose unprotected state he attributed to their betrayal by Charles I.[2] Obviously the first step to take before openly attacking France was to come to terms with Spain, already at war with her for two decades. During 1654 an Anglo-Spanish alliance seemed probable, but was never made, for Spain had little to offer in money towards the expenses of an English expedition to France and was unwilling to yield the only two concessions that might have sufficed instead—toleration for Englishmen in Spain and liberty for them to trade with the Spanish-American colonies. Rather than give way on these points, Spain preferred not only to forgo the alliance but even to brave English hostility.

Spain's refusal decided Cromwell, who for some time had been turning over in his mind the idea of a raid on the Spanish colonies, after the Elizabethan fashion. He had commended such a project to his council, on the grounds that the Spanish had 'denied you commerce unlesse you be of theire religion' (which was not literally true); that God had called them to work his will in the world at large as well as at home; and that the conclusion of the Dutch war left them with a large fleet on their hands, so that equipping the expedition would cost little more than paying off the ships and laying them up.[3] In the instructions to the commanders of the fleet, the raid is justified because the Spaniards not only made exclusive claims to the

---

[1] *Recueil des instructions: XXIV, Angleterre*, ed. J. J. Jusserand (1929), i. 85.
[2] *The Journal of Joachim Hane*, ed. C. H. Firth (1896), Introduction.
[3] *Clarke Papers*, iii. 207–8.

Americas, but also ill-treated English ships and settlers in those regions as if they were trespassers, and the danger was grave that all the English plantations there would be rooted out. The object of the raid is defined as gaining 'an interest in that part of the West Indies in the possession of the Spaniard'.[1]

The expeditionary force, with Penn as admiral and Venables as general, sailed at the end of 1654 and reached Barbados without mishap. There the 2,500 soldiers who had been either pressed or collected from existing regiments (whose colonels had utilized the chance to purge their ranks of the worst men) were joined by some volunteers from the West Indies. The army was formidable in mere numbers but in no other respect, for the enrolled planters were cowardly and undisciplined, and, with the exception of the marine regiment, the troops from England were little better. When they landed to attack San Domingo other defects were revealed, for the men had no water-bottles and, in the heat, ate too many oranges, which gave them dysentery. The leadership was bad, for Venables was twice surprised in an ambush at the same place. In the end the expedition re-embarked without having ever attacked San Domingo. However, Jamaica was occupied and held, though some time elapsed before the Spaniards, who took to the hills, were subdued.

When news of these events reached Madrid, Cardenas, the Spanish ambassador in London, received orders to ask for his passport, and so an open state of war existed. In a manifesto Cromwell claimed that, in view of the provocation Englishmen had received for years in the West Indies, the recent raid was an act of defence. This plea cannot be accepted, and, at the best, the expedition to San Domingo must be regarded as an armed protest against the Spanish claims to both sea and land in the New World, and against their treating as pirates all aliens who disregarded these claims.

It was natural that the imminence of war with Spain should cause an approximation to France. After Cromwell and Mazarin had co-operated to stay the persecution of the Vaudois, it proved possible to bring to a conclusion negotiations that had lasted several years. One of the points at issue had arisen over Cromwell's anxiety not to sign any clause that might prevent his aiding the Huguenots in the event of their being oppressed.

[1] Granville Penn, *Memorials of Sir William Penn* (1833), ii. 21-22, 28.

A satisfactory formula was at last found by which each country promised not to aid the rebels 'now declared' of the other, and a secret article named Charles II and certain prominent royalists, who were to be expelled from France, and agents of Condé and of the rebels at Bordeaux, who were to be expelled from England.[1] For his part Charles II signed a treaty with Spain (April 1656) by which he was promised the assistance of a Spanish army to aid in his restoration and he himself agreed to the retrocession of Jamaica and to the exclusion of his subjects from the mainland and the islands in the West Indies.[2]

The war at sea opened auspiciously for England, with Stayner's interception off Cadiz of a treasure fleet from the Spanish Main. The galleons were nearly all destroyed, and the loss of specie was enormous, but the English government profited to the tune of only about £240,000, although the captors are said to have plundered thrice as much.[3] This success was followed by one of permanent importance in the development of naval strategy. For the first time in history a blockade was maintained (by Blake) of the Spanish coast throughout the winter of 1656–7. This striking innovation was rewarded when news reached Blake that a second treasure fleet was in the Canaries. On 20 April he destroyed the galleons and silenced the batteries ashore. No prizes were taken, for Blake feared they would hamper his retreat from the Bay of Santa Cruz, and the bullion had been landed and carried into the interior before the action began. Nevertheless the destruction of all the galleons gave England undisputed supremacy at sea and left the precious metals stranded as inaccessibly as if they had remained on the other side of the Atlantic. Blake died on the voyage home, within sight of Plymouth, but the fruit of his great victories survived him. The loss of two treasure fleets fatally crippled Spain, for one of her armies, assembled for the conquest of Portugal with every prospect of success, melted away for want of pay, while the other, in Flanders, was left similarly destitute to face a new combination of allies. By a treaty of

---

[1] Gardiner, *Commonwealth and Protectorate*, iv. 192.

[2] Ibid., p. 234. I suppose the retention of Jamaica after the Restoration might be justified on the ground that Spain failed to provide the Spanish army of the treaty, having no troops to spare because of the progress of the Anglo-French forces in Flanders.

[3] Firth, *Last Years of the Protectorate*, i. 50–57.

13 March 1657 England and France agreed to make a joint attack upon Gravelines, Mardyke, and Dunkirk by sea and land. England was to supply a fleet for blockading these ports, and a contingent of 6,000 men was to be paid by France to assist in the attack by land. When captured, Dunkirk and Mardyke were to be ceded to England.

The first year's campaign was rather disappointing, for only Mardyke was taken and it proved very insalubrious to its English garrison. The war of sieges, so dear to continental generals, proved irksome to the British, whose commander wrote contemptuously, 'Fighting is not the fashion of the country'.[1]

The next year the warfare was brisker. The English contingent joined Turenne in besieging Dunkirk, and covered itself with glory at the battle of the Dunes (June 1658), when the Cromwellians, in a French army, once more prevailed against the royalists, in Spanish ranks. This victory having destroyed all chance of relief, Dunkirk surrendered and was at once handed over to an English garrison. There were high expectations in England of the advantages of Mardyke and Dunkirk. In Thurloe's opinion Cromwell now 'carried the keys of the Continent at his girdle, and was able to make invasions thereupon, and let in armies and forces upon it at his pleasure'.[2]

Cromwell died before much use could be made of the new possession, and his son's brief protectorate coincided with the time when the armies were in winter quarters. Nevertheless the stubborn pride of Spain at length broke down, and a truce was arranged in the spring of 1659 and converted into the treaty of the Pyrenees in the following November. Then both France and Spain slighted their late allies, for France neglected to insert a stipulation that England was to retain Dunkirk and assented to an article that she would not assist England directly or indirectly against Spain, and Spain agreed to the disbandment of the forces under Condé, so that they were not available to aid Charles II, even if he could have found means to pay them and transport them to invade England. Thus the journey Charles II made to Fuenterrabia was entirely fruitless, and he had to abandon hope of a restoration by foreign help to be supplied by the newly reconciled powers.

The study of the foreign relations of England during 1603 to

---

[1] Firth, *Last Years of the Protectorate*, i. 277.   [2] Ibid. ii. 218.

1660 brings out clearly the change of emphasis in the governing factors. At first the personal factor was predominant. The policy of James, during most of his reign, was pacific and pro-Spanish in defiance of public opinion, however ill informed and prejudiced this may have been; and then warlike and anti-Spanish for dynastic reasons. Charles I was under the same influences as his father, in continuing the Spanish war, and may also have been partially actuated by personal pique. The war against France would seem, on the surface, to have been a piece of gratuitous folly, but, whether Charles I realized it or not, there were certain vital English interests involved: the rights of belligerents at sea. For the next twenty years the assertion of English sovereignty of the Narrow Seas and maritime rights had the largest share in determining foreign policy and were mainly responsible for the first Dutch war. During the protectorate Cromwell restored English prestige to the height attained after Agincourt or the defeat of the Armada. Blake's campaigns had revealed to the Continent the terrible strength of England when her sea-power was rightly used. Clarendon, who kept in close touch with European events during his first exile, states that Cromwell's greatness at home was but a shadow of his glory abroad.[1] Nevertheless, in spite of his longing to advance the cause of protestantism abroad, he was never within measurable distance of leading a religious crusade. His foreign policy was largely economic and imperialistic. It included opposition even to Sweden, hitherto regarded as the keystone of continental protestantism, if English trade to the Baltic were threatened; and war with Spain, to end her exclusive claims to the West Indies. It is remarkable that, at the end of the period, the war with Spain, which for fifty years had been looked upon as the natural enemy, should have been unpopular, and that sound puritans who found admission to the national councils should have regarded the care of trade as the principal end of foreign policy. 'We are islanders', said one, 'and our life and soul is trade.' Another declared, about Spain and Holland, that war with the one had not been more destructive than peace with the other. There was an irreconcilable quarrel between Englishmen and Dutchmen. 'We are rivals for the fairest mistress in all Christendom, trade.'[2]

These extracts, which it would be easy to multiply, prove

---

[1] *Rebellion*, xv. 152. [2] *Burton Diary*, iii. 392–4.

that a great change had taken place in the aims of the foreign policy of England. Thurloe, in whose hands the direction of foreign relations mainly rested from 1653 to 1659, fully recognized how their objectives varied with the times. In one of the accounts of foreign affairs during the protectorate, which he drew up after the Restoration, he remarked that, although it was commonly said the interest of England was always the same in reference to other nations and remained unaffected by a change of government, experience proved the contrary.[1] Certainly there were many striking alterations in English foreign policy during 1603-60 and equally remarkable fluctuations in contemporary views of what constituted the true interests of England.

[1] *Somers Tracts*, vi. 329.

X

POLITICAL AND CONSTITUTIONAL
HISTORY, 1658–60

THE protectorate of Richard Cromwell[1] lasted about eight months and falls naturally into two parts, the first lasting from September to December 1658, and the second from the meeting of parliament, at the end of January following, to Richard's resignation in May. Richard was ill fitted by character and training to cope with the difficulties that were largely due to his father's efforts to give the protectorate a more permanent basis than armed force. Cromwell had weeded out the most extreme political and religious fanatics from the higher ranks but had been prevented by death from further dismissals, the object of which would have been to replace such officers as wished to use the army to dictate political policy, by professional soldiers content to serve without questioning the civil government. Monck, the ablest and most trusted of the professional soldiers, who had been for some years commander-in-chief in Scotland, advised Richard to combine every two regiments into one and thus kill two birds with one stone, halve the cost of the army by this reduction in its numbers, and retain only such officers as could be trusted to support the protectorate. Richard's failure to follow this advice almost inevitably entailed his downfall, because his weakness of character and lack of military prestige would certainly prevent his withstanding for any length of time pressure from the army leaders. Signs were soon seen that these officers meant to take advantage of his inexperience and increase the power of the army. The immediate requirements of the officers were that the office of commander-in-chief should be separated from the headship of the state, and that no one should be cashiered except by a court martial. If conceded, these two demands would have taken control of the army out of the protector's hands. Actually the agitation to these ends was quelled before the close of the year, but not before it had become clear that Fleetwood, Disbrowe, and others, commonly called the Wallingford

[1] For details and references see the writer's work, *The Restoration of Charles II* (1955), chaps. i–vi.

House party (from their usual place of meeting), had revealed their desire to make the protector a puppet in their hands, and not before the junior officers—usually referred to as the commonwealths-men—had shown their republican sympathies.

When the parliamentary elections were completed, it was found that the majority of the members were men of moderate views, presbyterians rather than sectaries, and likely to support the protectorate against the army. This group was commonly spoken of as the New Courtiers. It contained a few men who were already cavaliers, and many more, particularly new members who were young men and, while willing enough to support Richard if he resolutely followed in his father's footsteps, would otherwise naturally favour the restoration of the Stuarts in preference to undisguised military tyranny or anarchy. There were also commonwealths-men or republicans, few in number but formidable through the ability of their leaders, Hesilrige, Scot, and Sir Henry (Harry) Vane.

At first, however, the enemies of the protectorate in parliament could only delay by strenuous opposition the measures of the government. In spite of their utmost endeavours a bill to recognize Richard's succession was passed by a substantial majority. Similarly a resolution was voted that the commons would transact business with 'the persons now sitting in the other house, as a house of parliament, during this present parliament; and that it is not hereby intended to exclude such peers as have been faithful to the parliament, from their privilege of being duly summoned to serve as members of that house'.[1] These two votes, settling the two most essential and disputed features of the protectoral government, might have seemed decisive. But once again the destinies of the state were to be controlled, not by parliamentary votes, but by military force.

Apparently the republican leaders in the house were reverting to the tactics they had pursued a year before, when they had tried to incite the army to act against the protector. They revived the very petition whose presentation Cromwell had forestalled by abruptly dismissing parliament in 1658. The petition was artfully designed to attract all types of malcontents. It appealed to republicans because it demanded the restoration of a single-chamber government, unlimited in power by any protector or written constitution. It appealed to the extreme

---

[1] *Commons' Journals*, vii. 621.

sectarians, such as the fifth-monarchy men, quakers, unitarians, and the like by asking that all sincere professors of religion might be provided for (and not merely those included in the present establishment). It made a bid for the support of the army by demanding that officers and soldiers who had hazarded their lives for the nation's liberty should not be dismissed without a legal trial by court martial.[1] This attempt to form an alliance between the republican leaders and the malcontents in the army was much more likely to succeed now than a year ago, for Richard's position was very different from his father's. Both the office of protector and the personality of the new protector were hateful to many in the army. A royalist notes that some of the officers call Richard 'the young gentleman, and say he never drew sword for the commonwealth'.[2] In addition his character, which would have been admirable in a country gentleman, was unequal to the arduous tasks that awaited him. It was very unfortunate for him that, just about this time, two incidents occurred which enabled his opponents to denounce him as a backslider. While rebuking a cornet who complained of the wicked life his major led, Richard is reported to have said: 'You talk of preaching and praying men, they are the men that go about to undermine me', and to have added (turning to Colonel Ingoldsby), 'Go thy way, Dick Ingoldsby, thou canst neither preach nor pray, but I will believe thee before I will believe twenty of them.'[3] Ludlow, himself a stern and unbending republican, notes that thenceforth men who made the least pretence of religion and sobriety thought themselves unsafe under Richard's government, and resolved to separate the military from the civil power. Similarly the quarrel about the other house, between Edward Whalley, a Cromwellian, and Richard Ashfield, a republican, in which the protector took the side of the former, enabled the anabaptists to represent their beloved Ashfield as a martyr to court favouritism.

At the same time that Richard was losing control of the army, parliament also was alienating it. There was a strong anti-militarist tone in all the debates. Nothing was done to raise money to provide for the arrears of pay, now considerable; attacks on the other house often took the form of veiled or even

---

[1] Firth, *Last Years of the Protectorate*, ii. 30–41.
[2] *Clarendon State Papers*, iv (1932), 100.
[3] *A Second Narrative of the Late Parliament* (1659), pp. 30–31.

open complaints against the higher officers of the army, who formed the bulk of its active members; there were denunciations of the major-generals, whose little fingers were said to have been heavier than the loins of the greatest royal tyrants, and many incidental criticisms of all ranks of the army. Perhaps even more serious were the scrutiny of, and censures upon, some of the arbitrary acts of the preceding decade. The anti-militarist sentiments in parliament found vent in the warm welcome frequently extended to victims of military oppression. Robert Overton, committed to the Channel Islands for a military plot against the protectorate in 1654, was released and his imprisonment voted illegal and unjust, in spite of plain warnings from soldiers that votes of that kind would expose all army officers to civil actions for damages. Undeterred, the house next voted the impeachment of William Butler, the most obnoxious of the major-generals, and they even received a petition from seventy royalists saying they had been sold into slavery in Barbados after Penruddock's rising. Notwithstanding admonitions of the inevitable consequences of such an attitude, Hesilrige defiantly said: 'We are likely to be governed by the army. . . . Our ancestors left us free men. If we have fought our sons into slavery, we are of all men most miserable.'[1] Equally tactless was the declaration issued by parliament to observe 18 May as a day of fasting, for it contained a hint to magistrates to use their authority to suppress religious extremists. Even to suggest a revival of persecution was very unwise, for the threat to toleration would be certain to be resented by all sections of the army.

By this time the army was getting out of control. Once more the officers drew up a petition declaring that only their reluctance to meddle with non-military matters had prevented an earlier representation, but that now they felt that all they had fought for was in danger of being lost. They complained that the cavaliers were so encouraged that they often met in or near London, that suits in common law had been commenced against officers who had merely obeyed their superiors' commands, that want of pay threatened to compel soldiers to live at free quarter, and that, in order to get money to buy bread, they were forced to sell at a discount the pay due to them. Therefore they resolved to assist the protector and parliament in plucking the wicked from their places, wherever they might be found.

[1] *Burton Diary*, iv. 262–76.

After this sinister hint, or blunt warning, they concluded by asking that their arrears of pay might be satisfied, that the 'good old cause' should be reasserted in unmistakable terms, and that freedom of worship, 'of late much violated', might again be vindicated.[1] This petition was but one among many signs that the army could no longer resist the temptation to intervene in public affairs. The next step of their leaders was an attempt to get the army council to impose a test that each member of the army and of the council of state should pass—namely, that he should swear that he conscientiously believed that the execution of Charles I was lawful and just. This proposal was defeated for the moment, but showed clearly which way the wind was blowing.

Events were also moving towards a crisis in parliament. Apparently members were unwilling any longer to continue to sit under the shadow of military intervention. Therefore they passed two resolutions of the first importance: that during parliamentary sessions there should be no general council or meeting of the officers of the army without the permission of the protector and both houses, and that no officer should retain his post unless he were willing to promise not to disturb the meeting of parliament. When the protector communicated these resolutions to the army officers, they refused to disband. On the contrary they demanded that he should dissolve parliament. Matters came to a head when Fleetwood, the most prominent among the army leaders at that time, was ordered to come to Whitehall but refused. Instead, he summoned all the regiments in or near London to a general rendezvous of the army at St. James's, while Richard appointed a counter-rendezvous at Whitehall. When the vast majority of the soldiers obeyed Fleetwood rather than Richard, it was clear that he had no option but to submit to the terms of the army. Eventually his resolution gave way to the threats the officers uttered, and parliament was dissolved on 22 April. To all intents and purposes the protectorate was at an end. The country was nominally ruled in Richard's name until 7 May, when the remnant of the Long Parliament (the Rump) was restored. But he had no part or lot in the government, and on 25 May accepted the re-establishment of the commonwealth, an act that may be regarded as his formal abdication.

[1] *Old Parliamentary History*, xxi. 340–5.

The fall of the protectorate was due to many reasons, some personal, some general. Richard's inexperience and weakness, the reckless ambition of Fleetwood, Disbrowe, and other army leaders, and the revived enthusiasm for republicanism among the lower ranks, were among the most obvious causes. In addition there were two factors of great importance: the constitutional position, and the state of the army. Oliver Cromwell had left the protectorate in a very transitional stage, half-way between a monarchy and a republic. He had not progressed far enough to attract those attached to the old constitution, but he had advanced sufficiently to alienate permanently republicans and levellers and all who believed, in the language of the time, that he was setting up what God had pulled down. It was a paradox that, the more he transformed the protectorate into the similitude of a monarchy, the more he was depriving it of its moral justification. Possibly the exceptional services he had rendered to England justified almost any means. But, if the sentimental attachment to the monarchical form of government was essential to strengthen the civil power against the military, there certainly seemed no logical reason for preferring Richard to Charles II.

Similarly Oliver Cromwell had been denied time to complete remodelling the army. He had already dismissed some religious fanatics like Thomas Harrison and some would-be politicians like Lambert; but, as events in 1659 proved, a much more drastic purge was essential if the military forces were to be kept subordinate to the civil authority. Unfortunately this meant the dismissal of many officers who had served faithfully from the formation of the Ironsides, because, from 1647 onwards, they had become so accustomed to control events that their itch to intervene in politics was incurable. To have replaced the politicians in the army by men of the type of Monck or Sir William Lockhart or Edward Mountagu (later first earl of Sandwich), or the ex-royalists lords Broghil and Fauconberg (who were content to serve any *de facto* head of the state), would have converted the army into what all its declarations proclaimed it was not, a mere mercenary body serving for pay. In this respect, too, the elder Cromwell had occupied a middle position. Dismissals had been numerous enough to alarm, but not sufficiently thoroughgoing to render powerless, such officers as felt that the army should be the dominating power of the state. Except for the officers who remained loyal Cromwellians, all sections of the army believed that its influence was threatened by the restoration of parliament in 1659, but here the unanimity ended. That the junior officers should have compelled their leaders to force the protector to abdicate, instead of retaining him as a mere figurehead as their seniors wished, showed clearly the divisions within the army itself. Indeed there was no love lost between the lower ranks and their superior officers. The latter were often absent from their regiments for months, and even years, together, and so were completely out of touch with the men they nominally commanded. Moreover they tended to cast off the role of soldiers and to assume the part of territorial magnates. These 'grandees' had feathered their nests successfully from the public offices they had held; and their affluence, which contrasted ill with the poverty of the lower ranks, was the more unpopular because partly acquired at the expense of the common soldier. Some of them, like Lambert, were said to have made fortunes by purchasing from necessitous soldiers, at a heavy discount, the right to receive their arrears of pay. This cleavage of interest between senior and junior officers, and between the higher and the lower ranks, became more and more important as time went on.

The first task that confronted those who had engineered the military revolution was to decide what form of government should be substituted for the protectorate. The army leaders seem to have been so taken aback by the unexpected overthrow of their plan to retain Richard as the nominal head of the state that they had no alternative to suggest; and again it was the commonwealths-men who insisted upon and secured the recall of the remnant of the Long Parliament whose sitting had been 'interrupted' on 20 April 1653. Meetings were hurriedly arranged with the most prominent members of the Rump, like Vane, Hesilrige, and Ludlow, all staunch republicans.

No detailed account of these conferences has survived, but the demands of the officers of the army were set forth in the petition they addressed to parliament on 12 May.[1] Among the terms were: that the government should be a commonwealth without a single person at its head, or a house of peers; that there should be an act of oblivion for all public acts committed since 19 April 1653; that all Christians should be allowed the

[1] *Old Parliamentary History*, xxi. 400–5.

free profession of their faith, provided this liberty were not extended to popery or prelacy; that all royalists and scoffers at religion should be removed from offices of trust, and not admitted into any such for the future; that members of parliament, in order not to become burdensome by their long sitting, should provide for the speedy election of their successors; that Fleetwood should be made commander-in-chief; that the legislature should consist of the representatives of the people and of a select senate co-ordinate in power; that the administration should be in a council of state; and that suitable provision should be made for the former protector, Richard Cromwell.

From the reception these various demands met with at the hands of the Rump, it is obvious, either that the civilians in their meetings with the army leaders did not realize that the latter believed their requirements would be accepted in full by the Rump, or that (as had happened on 20 April 1653) they made little or no effort to persuade their fellow members in parliament to accept what had been agreed upon. Ludlow, who describes these conferences briefly,[1] shows that the agreement must have been of the vaguest nature on the question of a senate, which was of vital importance. Ludlow, and presumably those acting with him, were willing that there should be a senate but only for a short time. On the other hand the army leaders were as anxious as ever that there should be certain fundamentals which it would be beyond the power of parliament to alter. Since there was no hope that the civilian republicans would agree to anything in the nature of a written constitution, the only way to preserve the fundamentals would be to have a select senate of equal authority with the representative chamber. If the former body were packed with those who accepted the principles the army held dear, it could defeat any measures from the elected house in violation of those principles. In point of fact, however, the Rump at first made not the slightest effort to set up a select senate, but voted that the government should be carried on without a single person or house of lords,[2] and left the question at that until the autumn, when there were debates on the future form of government, and many ingenious and startling suggestions, but no action was taken.[3]

In other respects, too, the Rump disappointed or angered the

[1] *Memoirs*, ii. 76–77.   [2] *Commons' Journals*, vii. 661.
[2] *Ludlow Memoirs*, ii. 99.

army by its measures. It did appoint Fleetwood commander-in-chief, but withheld from him the power (which Fairfax and Cromwell had enjoyed) to name officers. Instead it appointed seven commissioners to nominate officers; but the commissions themselves were to be bestowed by the Speaker in parliament. In this way the Rump hoped to retain complete control over the armed forces. The navy was dealt with in much the same fashion, for nine commissioners, of whom six were members of parliament, were named to control it.[1]

When these parliamentary measures became known to the army, their discontent was instantly manifested. Some officers argued that the promises made to them before the restoration of the parliament were being broken, and others, that the commissions they already had were as good as any the Speaker could give them. Nevertheless the officers thought better of the matter in the end, and during June and July their presence in the house to receive their commissions was a daily sight. Generally speaking, the house cashiered prominent Cromwellians, like Falconberg, Goffe, Ingoldsby, and Whalley, restored officers who had been dismissed by Oliver Cromwell, like Lambert, Overton, and Packer, and renewed the commissions of most of the other officers. However, they displaced some they regarded as of unsound principles, and promoted others without consulting the colonels, whose regiments were thus interfered with. This tactless meddling gave the greatest offence.

Similarly the composition of the new council of state caused dissatisfaction to the army, for of its thirty-one members twenty-one belonged to the Rump, so that the army leaders were certain to be in a minority. Therefore, according to Ludlow, when they did condescend to come they carried themselves with all imaginable perverseness and insolence.[2]

The act of indemnity, on which the officers set much store, was a great disappointment to them. The bill itself gave full pardon for all acts tending to change the government or committed by virtue of authority derived from any assembly commonly called a parliament or from the lord protector or commander-in-chief.[3] On the face of it the bill seemed acceptable enough, but there must have been more in it than meets

---

[1] *Commons' Journals*, vii. 666.
[2] *Memoirs*, ii. 84.
[3] *Acts and Ordinances*, ii. 1299–1304.

the eye, judging by the resentment it aroused in the army. Lambert told Ludlow that, though there was no security by the act to indemnify soldiers for what they had done, parliament had taken care to make them liable to be called in question for whatever they had received. In fact the general said that the bill signified nothing and left soldiers still at mercy. Hesilrige, who had joined the other two, argued: 'You are only at the mercy of the parliament, who are your good friends.' 'I know not', countered Lambert, 'why they should not be at our mercy as well as we at theirs.'[1] Thus the summer passed in a kind of sullen truce. Parliament complacently went its way as if it really represented the people, in whose name it professed to act, and as if it owed the army no special consideration. The army watched the Rump with hostile eyes, willing to wound but afraid to strike. They were certainly not restrained from interfering by any conviction that soldiers ought to obey without question the civil power. Probably they kept quiet only because their leaders had no substitute for the Rump and because the army was divided against itself. The rank and file were already beginning to look askance at the grandees and were by no means certain to submit to orders dictated by the selfish ambitions of their commanders. Just at this moment there was urgent need for unity, as well as an opportunity for closing up the ranks and forgetting the past.

The royalists, who had been getting more and more excited since the death of Oliver Cromwell and especially since the abdication of his son, were now determined to appeal again to arms. The management of their forces had recently been entrusted to six new commissioners, who scoffed at the prudent warnings of their predecessors. Risings were arranged in different parts of the country, in the hope of paralysing the army by distracting its attention hither and yon. On this occasion the old cavaliers were joined by presbyterians, but, whereas the former openly proclaimed Charles II, the latter merely declared for a free parliament and felt that the precipitate loyalty of their allies had ruined their chances of success. There was the possibility, too, that powerful assistance would be available from the sea. The French commander, Turenne, without authority from his government, promised James, duke of York, 2,000 soldiers and arms for twice as many more, with ships to trans-

[1] *Ludlow Memoirs*, ii. 100.

port them to England. Besides, Admiral Mountagu had been listening to an agent of Charles II and suddenly brought the fleet he commanded in the Baltic back to England. The combination was powerful on paper, but all depended on the ability of the enemies of the Rump to keep the field until help joined them from overseas. On the contrary the main force in Cheshire, under Sir George Booth, was easily defeated by Lambert, and the other bands dispersed without striking a blow. Mountagu explained his sudden return on the ground that his fleet needed provisioning, but he lost his command, which was given to John Lawson, an ardent republican.

Most unexpectedly the ignominious collapse of this rising proved a blessing in disguise to the royalists: when their cause looked darkest, a ray of light was seen. Ever since the close of the first civil war they had hoped that their enemies would quarrel among themselves. They had been disappointed time and again, thanks to Cromwell's genius; but now there was no one who could enlist the confidence of all sections of the army. Instead there were Fleetwood, vain and easygoing; Disbrowe, an uncouth bully; and, most dangerous of all, 'honest John Lambert', ambitious, restless, rash, and shortsighted.

It was Lambert who was destined to take the first steps towards upsetting the republican applecart. The officers of his army at Derby drew up and presented to parliament a petition in which they asserted that the proof, afforded by the late victory, that Providence was still on their side, impelled them to insist that His bounty should not be wasted. They therefore asked that the army's petition of 12 May should be no longer ignored, but made the basis of a permanent settlement, and that to preserve the unity of the army Fleetwood should be named commander-in-chief, Lambert second to him, and Disbrowe and Monck, respectively, commanders of the horse and foot. They further demanded that neutrals or malignants should be removed from all offices, corporations regulated, and the magistracy confined to the well-disposed.[1] The leaders in the house, who never lacked the courage of their convictions (however far removed from all contact with reality), promptly voted that to have any more general officers would be hazardous and expensive; and a motion that the petition itself was unseasonable and of dangerous consequence was defeated by only a

[1] Sir Richard Baker, *A Chronicle of the Kings of England* (1674), p. 673.

narrow margin. At the same time Fleetwood was ordered to admonish the officers for their irregular proceedings.[1]

Fleetwood called the officers together, but the results of the meeting were the direct opposite of those intended by the Rump. Instead of resolving to confine themselves in the future strictly to their military duties, the officers determined to support Lambert and the petitioners in his northern army. They therefore drafted a petition of their own, which was presented to the Rump on 5 October. After a vindication of the Derby petitioners, the house was asked to justify them and to punish any one who thereafter should cast scandalous imputations upon the army. The petition asserted that soldiers had not forfeited their liberties as freemen and therefore had the undoubted right to petition; and it insisted that no officer or soldier should be dismissed except by a court martial, that no officer should be appointed until approved by the committee of nomination, and that a commander-in-chief should be named. The stiffness of these requirements was in complete contrast to such ingratiating terms as 'your faithful servants' and 'humble desires',[2] with which the petition abounded.

The Rump, too, was in an uncompromising mood. It had recently learnt that Monck had forbidden the circulation and subscription of the Derby petition among his men in Scotland, and had received his assurances of devotion to the parliament. Thus encouraged the Rump was in no temper to pay excessive regard to the peculiar susceptibilities of the army. While the petition was being debated there was an interruption for discussion of a bill declaring 'in what cases it shall be high treason to levy or collect any tax or assessment, not set or imposed by common consent in parliament; and to make void patents, grants, acts, and ordinances, made since the nineteenth of April 1653, not made by this parliament'.[3] The purpose of such a bill was clear, and its framers must have had in view the possibility of a summary dissolution by armed force. They therefore intended to make it as hard as possible for the army to levy taxes in such an event.

It so happened that, the next day, they were informed that Lambert, Disbrowe, and seven other officers were soliciting

[1] *Commons' Journals*, vii. 785.
[2] *Old Parliamentary History*, xxxi. 460–5; Baker, *Chronicle*, pp. 675–7.
[3] *Commons' Journals*, vii. 795.

subscriptions from all sections of the army to the petition lately presented. Their action was interpreted by the Rump as a sure proof that the petition was designed to unite the army against the civil authority. It was accordingly voted that Lambert and Disbrowe, and their seven co-signatories, should be discharged from all military employment, and that command of the army should be entrusted to seven commissioners, of whom only one, Fleetwood, enjoyed the confidence of the army in the south.

Even the Rump, hitherto ignorant of, or indifferent to, opinion in the army, seemingly did not expect that its last acts would pass unchallenged. It tried to provide for protection against interference by the army leaders, but only two regiments and part of another answered its call. For one day (13 October) there seemed every likelihood that the supporters of parliament and the adherents of Lambert would come to blows. The former occupied Westminster and its approaches, whereupon the latter encircled them and prevented members from reaching the house. The council of state issued orders to the opposing forces to return to their quarters. The orders were obeyed, but Lambert took advantage of the situation to leave soldiers of his faction to guard the houses of parliament. So the Rump was 'interrupted' a second time. A contemporary observed that 'in all the hurly burly the streets were full, every one going about their business as if not at all concerned, and when the parliament sent unto the City to relieve them, they answered they would not meddle with the dispute'.[1] This was the common attitude. At first Milton was almost alone, among spectators of this latest revolution, in his indignation against the army. 'I speak only what it appears to us without doors . . . most illegal and scandalous, I fear me barbarous, or rather scarce to be exampl'd among any barbarians, that a paid army should . . . thus subduc the supream power that set them up.'[2] His voice might have remained that of one crying in the wilderness, but for a reinforcement from an unexpected quarter.

Monck had already made known his views on the relations that ought to exist between the military and the civil powers. In the previous June he had written to the Speaker that he was none of those who seek great things 'haveing had my education

[1] *Clarendon State Papers*, iii (1786), 581.
[2] 'A Letter to a Friend concerning the Rupture of the Commonwealth', in *Works*, vi. 102.

in a commonwealth [Holland] where souldiours receive and observe commands but give none. Obedience is my greate principle, and I have alwaise, and ever shall, reverence the parliaments resolutions in civill things as infallible and sacred.' He now wrote that he was prepared to stand by his words. At once he took measures to consolidate the loyalty of his army, and purged it of all disaffected elements. His own regiment lost its lieutenant-colonel, major, and three captains, and altogether he is said to have displaced 140 officers.[1] In order to secure time for this remodelling of his army, he entered into negotiations with Lambert and spun them out as long as possible. Meanwhile he did his utmost to gain the complete confidence of his men. He called together regularly a council of officers, to which he left the initiative whenever he could, and he organized a systematic propaganda to instruct the rank and file.[2]

The main arguments used to persuade the soldiers to agree with Monck that the remnant of the Long Parliament should be restored were: that the war was begun for the preservation of the protestant religion, the privileges of parliament, and the laws and liberties of the subject; that it could not be lawful for the officers of the English army to expel the Rump after recalling it, acknowledging its authority, accepting commissions in its name, and receiving pay from it, any more than it would be lawful for a servant to rise up against his master; that the military power ought to be subservient to the civil, which was another way of saying that the sword should be in the people's own hands; that if the English soldiers followed Lambert they would be fighting for the selfish ambition of a few officers, who would hazard the destruction of the whole nation rather than lose the commands they had justly forfeited; that these self-same leaders had been raised by the soldiers 'from the meanest mechanicks to lord-like inheritances'; and that in default of a parliament to vote supplies the soldier must live at free quarter and be in danger of losing arrears of pay due to him.

This and similar propaganda were disseminated in England and soon had their effect. Their two main achievements were to intensify opposition to arbitrary rule and to disintegrate the army. Their success in making the soldiery unpopular was much helped by the necessities of the rank and file. There were

---

[1] See the present writer's *Early History of the Coldstream Guards* (1924), pp. 92-97.
[2] See ibid. for extracts from these pamphlets.

now no legal sources of taxation open to the newly formed committee of safety—a body composed of the army leaders, with a few civilians like Vane—and it is not surprising that, when pay was not forthcoming, some of the men took matters into their own hands. Mrs. Hutchinson, wife of a parliamentary colonel and regicide, relates how some troopers came to collect taxes and how the colonel, when he said he would pay only those levied by parliamentary authority, was reviled in the most insulting terms and his house overrun by fifty or sixty men. When he asked them by what authority they came, they showed their swords and said 'that was their authority'. They tore in pieces their captain's letter to Mrs. Hutchinson, in which he utterly disavowed their actions, and sneered at him to his face. Altogether they are said to have taken violently from the countryside, for their own enjoyment, about £25, in addition to the assessments they ostensibly came to collect.[1]

Feeling ran particularly high in the City of London at the employment of soldiers to assist in levying taxes, and often there was resistance. Moreover it is related that, when officers went into the City, they dared not wear their swords, lest they might be recognized and insulted. Public opinion there demanded a free parliament, and a proclamation against petitions to that end led to rioting in which the soldiers sent to restore order killed two or three citizens and wounded many more. The concurrent effect of propaganda and civilian reproaches was that the common soldiers' eyes were at last opened to the true character of their leaders. When it became evident to the forces that had been sent north to oppose Monck that they were being used to gratify personal ambitions, they said frankly they would be neutral but would make a ring for their officers to fight in.

Meanwhile the other side had been active enough in various ways. Some of the old, deposed council of state, including Hesilrige, sent Monck a commission as commander-in-chief of all the forces in England and Scotland, and this greatly strengthened his position. Further they persuaded the governor of Portsmouth to side with them and to declare for the restoration of the parliament. The regiments sent to besiege the town threw in their lot with the garrison. It was even more serious that Lawson, who commanded the fleet in the Downs, came out on the same side. Finally Dublin Castle was surprised and

[1] *Hutchinson Memoirs*, pp. 314–15.

the Irish army in the main induced to join the parliamentarians and Monck.

Amid these accumulating signs of approaching ruin, Lambert in the north, and Fleetwood and the others in London, could do nothing. They and their sympathizers had wasted several months in the harmless game of making paper constitutions. They did not really agree on any point. To many of the army leaders the very name of parliament was anathema. As one prominent officer said, 'he hoped never a true Englishman would name the parliament again, and that he would have the house pulled down where they sat, for fear it should be infectious'.[1] On the other hand the few civilians present demanded the recall of the Rump and were disgusted that the general council of the army preferred to summon a new parliament, 'according to such qualifications and limitations, as are or shall be agreed upon'.[2] There were to be seven 'fundamentals' and twenty-one 'conservators of liberty', to see they were not violated; but the civilian republicans were alienated when the officers named a majority from among themselves. The old vexed question as to whether a senate should be created to act as a check on the house of representatives was answered by the compromise that there should be two elective houses.[3] In all this turmoil political theorists had the time of their lives. James Harrington and his disciples used to meet every evening in a coffee-house to devise the perfect constitution. One who was present remarks that their discourses were the most ingenious and smart that ever he had heard or expected to hear and that parliamentary debates were flat compared with them.[4] Finally the council of officers made up their minds to summon parliament just when events made it evident that the end of their day of power was immediately at hand.

Even Fleetwood could read the signs of the times, and, with the characteristic phrase that God had spit in their faces, once again had recourse to the remnant of the Long Parliament. The soldiers hastened to the residence of Lenthall, the Speaker, and proclaimed their submission. When members reassembled at Whitehall, they soon showed that two expulsions had taught

---

[1] *State Papers, Domestic, 1659-60* (1886), p. 295.
[2] *Ludlow Memoirs*, ii. 171; Bulstrode Whitelocke, *Memorials of English Affairs* (1853), iv. 379.   [3] *Ludlow Memoirs*, ii. 172-4.
[4] John Aubrey, *Brief Lives*, ed. Andrew Clark (1898), i. 289.

them nothing. Instead of a policy of conciliation, which alone might have preserved them in power, they adopted severe measures against all concerned in the military revolution of the autumn. They dismissed probably about 500 veteran officers and non-commissioned officers, whose only offence usually was adherence to the army leaders during the recent troubles. They even depleted their own ranks and expelled Vane and others for sitting in council with the army leaders to discuss what kind of constitution to adopt. Yet they refused to enlarge their number, and denied seats to some of the excluded members, who, with Prynne at their head, demanded readmission. Instead they reverted to their old plan of 1653 of recruiting the house rather than dissolving it. They would retain their own places and would be the judges of the fitness of the newly elected members.

As soon as news of the restoration of the Rump reached Monck, he began his march southwards. Lambert's army, discontented through lack of pay and shattered in morale by recent events, melted away, especially after Fairfax, on behalf of the parliament, had seized York in their rear. During the month that Monck's journey occupied, he received many petitions and addresses in favour of the readmission of the excluded members, which was generally regarded as an essential preliminary to the election of a free parliament. His taciturnity was already well known, and was now of the greatest advantage. Apart from emphatic declarations against kingship or government by a single person, he suffered no hint of his ultimate intentions to get abroad. Probably he hoped that the king would be restored, but for the present he had no definite plans and, like Oliver Cromwell before him, intended to wait on events. As the French ambassador remarked, he was now the most powerful man in England and all parties sought his aid. Uncertainty as to the course he intended to pursue was responsible for his cool reception in London (3 February), when he was greeted with cries for a free parliament, but no other welcome.

The first indication Monck gave of his view of the situation was in his speech to parliament. He told the members that as he marched from Scotland the people everywhere seemed unanimous in desiring a free and full parliament, that the present body should fix a date for its own dissolution, and that the excluded members should be readmitted without any test. Such plain speaking the Rump found hard to swallow, but for the moment managed to dissemble its wrath. Instead its ill temper was vented upon the City of London, where many citizens had decided to defy the Rump and not to pay any taxes until the excluded members had been readmitted. The Rump accepted this challenge, declared the common council dissolved, and ordered Monck to bring the City to terms by destroying its gates and seizing eleven leading citizens. Such an order strained Monck's obedience to the civil authority to the utmost, but of this he gave no sign. When the work of demolition was half completed, he suggested to the parliament that enough had been done but was directed to finish the task. Once again he complied, but the citizens were not overawed and told him they intended to endure the pillaging of their houses rather than pay taxes not levied by a free parliament. Furthermore, the soldiers employed on this expedition to the City cursed those who had sent them on such an odious errand. To Monck and to his men alike, the Rump was revealed in its true colours, and it suddenly became hateful to those who had risked all to restore it.

Monck now had first-hand experience of the perversity of the Rump and found that his officers shared the opinion that the time had come for action. He therefore addressed a peremptory letter to Westminster, setting forth that his soldiers, fresh from their grievous expedition to the City, recalled that they had marched south not alone to promote the restoration of the parliament but also to vindicate the liberties of the people; that he and his army were troubled to find that the house was culpably indulgent to those guilty of the recent disorders; and that it had received the most dangerous petition (from the ana-baptists), which would result in the abolition of tithes and the expulsion of many godly ministers (presbyterians). However, the great cause of the present dissatisfaction in the nation was the non-representative character of parliament, and consequently he must insist that writs be issued forth, by Friday next, to fill up vacancies in the house, and that dissolution must take place in the near future. He concluded by saying that he intended to lodge the greater part of his army in the City in order to beget a good understanding there.[1]

This letter of Monck's at last opened the eyes of the clique at Westminster who claimed to govern as the representatives

[1] *Old Parliamentary History*, xx. 98–103.

of the people of England. They could not disguise their anger at the merited rebuke. The parliamentary leaders, however, were bent on rushing to their ruin, for they deliberately slighted Monck by transferring the command of the army to five commissioners, of whom he was only one and of whom three were his opponents. A proposal that he should be one of the quorum of three was defeated. When Hesilrige left the house in a fury, a well-known quaker seized him by the arm and cried, 'Thou man, will thy beast carry three no longer? thou must fall!'[1] This was the plain truth. The Rump had now alienated all sections of the army, and the general rejoicing at its discomfiture proved that it had very few friends left. The almost universal contempt and hatred found vent in buying and roasting rumps of meat at numerous bonfires. And Monck's soldiers, who twenty-four hours before had been reviled as tyrants, were welcomed in the City with blessings, and more substantial marks of favour, drink and money.

That the City of London should have provoked this crisis, and thus determined that the excluded members should be recalled (which meant that the restoration was now inevitable), was wholly appropriate. Just as their support had enabled the Long Parliament to triumph over Charles I, so their opposition to the Rump made it certain that Charles II would be restored.

Monck was now determined to ensure the conformity of parliament to his wishes. Unlike Cromwell and Lambert before him, he had no need to expel the Rump, but only to withdraw the guard at Westminster so that the members excluded by Pride's Purge could walk in and take their seats. But before he did so he called the excluded members together and secured their assent, in writing, to certain conditions: they must settle the government of the army, raise money to pay it, issue writs for a new parliament to meet 20 April, and dissolve themselves as soon as possible. Accordingly, on 21 February Pepys and other onlookers saw the excluded members return to Westminster. Prominent among them was the indomitable Prynne, whose many pamphlets, by exposing the unconstitutional nature of all governments set up since 1649, had powerfully contributed to the historic event in which he was taking part. As often happened when he was concerned, the ludicrous and the important went hand in hand, for his old basket-hilted sword

[1] Pepys, *Diary*, 11 Feb. 1660.

tripped up Sir William Waller amid laughter. Yet his admission to parliament made it evident that at last the old constitution would be restored; and no fitter representative could have been found of the large and influential group of Englishmen to whom a legal parliament seemed the embodiment of their most prized liberties. The significance of this scene at Westminster was fully grasped by the nation. Pepys that night saw the City 'from one end to the other with a glory about it, so high was the light of the bonfires, and so thick . . . and the bells rang everywhere'. That evening, too, the breaking of Barebones's windows served to emphasize that the day of the saints had drawn to a close.

The hitherto excluded members of parliament adhered strictly to their promise to Monck. They named a new council of state from which republicans were barred, made Monck general-in-chief of the land forces and joint commander with Mountagu of the navy, annulled the engagement to be faithful to a commonwealth without a king or house of lords (previously exacted from office-holders and members of parliament), and dissolved themselves on 16 March. The meaning of these events was clear to all with eyes to see. Pepys went to Westminster Hall the day of the dissolution and found every one joyful and beginning to talk loudly of the king. On the other hand there were those to whom the restoration of Charles II was still abhorrent. For the moment it seemed as if the discontents had found a leader: Lambert contrived to escape from the Tower, where he had been confined by the Rump, made his way to the midlands, and managed to seduce a few squadrons of horse. He was promptly pursued, however, and captured on 22 April near Daventry without bloodshed, for his men refused to fight against their old companions-in-arms. In addition, on two occasions some of Monck's officers wished to interfere with the course of events and to issue a declaration in favour of a commonwealth and against kingship and a house of lords. Monck, however, would not permit their intervention in politics and exacted from all, officers and privates alike, a pledge to accept whatever settlement the forthcoming parliament might make.

Before this time Monck had made up his mind that the return of Charles II offered the only barrier against a threatened chaos. Hitherto he declined to receive royalist agents, but about

18 March he consented to receive a letter from the king. Monck vowed that his heart had ever been faithful but he had never been in a position to serve the king until now. Cautious to the end, he refused to commit anything to paper, but sent some valuable advice orally. He urged that Charles should offer a free and general pardon, confirmation of all sales of lands during the civil wars, prompt payment of arrears due to soldiers, and liberty of conscience. These suggestions were admirably framed to reconcile Englishmen in general to the restoration. Even the army was likely to acquiesce because the matters in which they were vitally interested were specified—indemnity for the past, toleration for the future, arrears of pay, and security of tenure for those who had purchased estates thrown on the market by those raising money to compound for their delinquency. Monck's advice formed the basis of the Declaration of Breda (4 April), but in that document Hyde, now acting as Charles's lord chancellor, caused the insertion of a qualification in each of the concessions—that the king would consent to whatever should be proposed by parliament on each point.[1] Hence the onus of responsibility for any departure from the promises now made would rest on the legislature. The king was thus able at one and the same time to show his attachment to parliamentary government and to provide a means of escape from a strict observance of the conditions of the restoration.

The royalists in England were as prudent as those of Charles's court. They, in turn, issued declarations in order to dispel the false impression many had that they would be implacable to their late enemies. On the contrary they disavowed any feelings of revenge for their past sufferings and expressed the hope that when the fabric of the state was rebuilt it would not, 'like Rome, have the beginning in the blood of brethren, nor like Babel, be interrupted by confusion of tongues: but that we may all speak one language, and be of one name; that all mention of parties and factions, and all rancour and animosities may be thrown in, and buried like rubbish under the foundation'.[2]

Meanwhile the land was in the grip of excitement caused by a general election. There was greater competition for seats than ever before, so that, as a royalist relates, 'the meanest burrough hath five or six importunate pretenders, many fifteen, sixteen

---

[1] Clarendon, xvi. 171–2. [2] Baker, *Chronicle*, pp. 722–3.

and twenty'.[1] It was noticeable that the influence of ministers, lately so potent, was now insignificant, and that republicanism survived as a political force in only a few small boroughs like Hindon, where Ludlow obtained nineteen of the twenty-six electors. The vast majority of the voters, however, chose the candidates most favourable to the prompt return of the king. For example, at Bridgnorth, Monck's letter recommending Thurloe was not even divulged to the public because his local supporters felt that Monck could not have contrived his own election, much less Thurloe's, unless he had declared whole-heartedly for the king.[2] Even the honoured memory of John Hampden could not secure the return of his son Richard for Buckinghamshire.

When the time for parliament to assemble was at hand, the question was not whether the king should be restored, for that was inevitable, but whether any condition should first be imposed. Even before the death of Oliver Cromwell, some of the presbyterian leaders had made the acceptance by Charles II of the Newport Articles[3] the price of their support, and they now reverted to the same idea. The earl of Manchester was the natural head of the presbyterians, and he and the other peers who had continued to sit until their house was abolished in 1649 had expected to re-enter parliament at the same time as the excluded members of the commons, but Monck prevented this on the ground that the army was still opposed to a house of lords.

When the new parliament met (25 April), the all-important question in each house concerned its composition. At first there were present in the house of lords only the survivors of the remnant who had remained faithful to the parliamentary cause up to 1648; the peers who had inherited their titles since that year (the 'young lords') and the peers expelled or created since 1641 (the 'king's lords') were excluded. Similarly, in the commons it appeared as if those presbyterians who shared the views of the lords would have the majority, for more than a hundred members' elections could be challenged on the ground that they were legally barred by the provisions enacted by the late parliament prior to its dissolution—that no royalist or son of a royalist might be chosen. Hence it seemed that those would prevail who wanted to make the king accept the articles establishing presbyterianism, to which his father had agreed while a captive

---

[1] *Clarendon State Papers*, iii. 714.   [2] Thurloe, vii. 888–95.   [3] See above, p. 153.

in the Isle of Wight. All depended, however, upon Monck, and, after hesitation—whether real or feigned, it is hard to say—he let it be known that he favoured the admission of all peers, whatever their intentions, and the retention in the commons of even the royalists who had secured election. This was decisive, and Monck no longer delayed to transmit to the two houses the letters and the Declaration of Breda which the king had sent him. The lords wasted no time in voting that 'according to the ancient and fundamental laws of this kingdom, the government is, and ought to be, by king, lords, and commons'; and the commons promptly agreed.[1] A week later, both houses concurred in the form of proclamation to be used. Its most noteworthy feature was that it emphasized that Charles II, immediately upon the decease of his father, had succeeded, 'by inherent birthright, and lawful and undoubted succession'.[2] Forthwith commissioners were chosen from both houses to attend the king, acquaint him with his proclamation and the great joy and enthusiasm that were accorded it, and beg him to make a speedy return to his parliament and to the exercise of his kingly functions.

Charles accepted the invitation to come back to England, and was everywhere greeted with the warmest acclamations. He is alleged to have made the sardonic comment that it must have been his own fault that he had been absent so long, for all he saw protested that they ever wished for his return.[3] The feelings that animated many royalists when they witnessed Charles's entry into London were well expressed by the diarist, John Evelyn:

> I stood in the Strand and beheld it, and blessed God. And all this was done without one drop of blood shed, and by that very army which rebelled against him: but it was the Lord's doing, for such a restoration was never mentioned in any history, ancient or modern, since the return of the Jews from their Babylonish captivity; nor so joyful a day and so bright ever seen in this nation, this happening when to expect or effect it was past all human policy.[4]

Evelyn was right in describing the Restoration as unprecedented, inasmuch as it was brought about by an army raised to fight, first against Charles I and then Charles II. That an army which had often protested with all sincerity against

---

[1] *Commons' Journals*, viii. 8.   [2] Ibid., pp. 16–17.
[3] Clarendon, *Rebellion*, xvi. 246.   [4] Evelyn, *Diary*, 29 May 1660.

government by a single person, and especially against the return of Charles Stuart, should eventually acquiesce in the triumph of a cause they had so often defeated, was mainly due to George Monck.

But, if he must be given most of the credit for the peaceful restoration, he must also bear much of the responsibility for an unconditional restoration. He was a stern disciplinarian, and proved himself, after Cromwell's death, the only general able to control the soldiers committed to his charge. In his contest with Disbrowe, Fleetwood, and Lambert he could count on the unquestioning obedience of the rank and file, while they could not. This advantage, though it might have sufficed to enable him to defeat these officers in the field, would not by itself have sufficed to secure a bloodless restoration. To bring that about he mainly relied on the force of public opinion. He realized clearly that, if he could secure time for this to influence the common soldier, an army like Lambert's, which was acting in direct opposition to the general will, would slowly disintegrate. On the whole he did little more than allow public opinion full vent, occasionally holding it in check, occasionally giving it new direction. He saw so plainly that the mass of Englishmen were bent upon Charles's return that he cut short the attempt of the presbyterian leaders in parliament to impose conditions. It may be that, with experience of the futility of paper constitutions and of every kind of oath—to be faithful to the covenant, the 'negative oath', the English 'engagement', and what not— he had no faith in any promises to observe the constitution that might have been extorted from Charles II. It is more likely that he was aware that the coincidence that parliament took the steps immediately antecedent to the king's return, and that the king, on his part, had been careful to make the various provisions of the Declaration of Breda subject to parliamentary approval, ensured the future of parliamentary government in England. Be this as it may, it is certain that the enhanced prestige and increased authority that parliament enjoyed after the puritan revolution were far stronger guarantees of constitutional government in England than any paper constitution that could have been evolved amid the threatening chaos of the spring of 1660.

XI

SOCIAL AND ECONOMIC HISTORY

IN certain respects, to attempt to write a social and economic history of England under the early Stuarts is like making bricks without straw. Our knowledge of many fundamental facts is imperfect, and of some it is likely to remain so. There are additional difficulties due to the failure of economic periods to coincide with political.

A serious defect in our knowledge is the lack of any satisfactory data about population. It is not known how many people were living in England in the reign of James I, or how they were distributed between the north and the south or between town and country. Yet it may be assumed that there were between 4,000,000 and 4,500,000 inhabitants and that a large majority lived in the country, in parishes with only a few hundred inhabitants.[1] It is likely that a large proportion, perhaps as many as six-sevenths, of the people of England lived south of the Humber, and that the eastern half of the country was more densely populated than the western (with the exception of the clothing areas in Wiltshire, Somerset, and Gloucestershire). Similarly, although England has, with trifling exceptions, remained constant in size and therefore contained about 32,005,000 acres in 1603 as at present, it is not known how many of those acres were cultivated. This has an important bearing upon such a question as the extent of inclosures. A great scholar[2] has calculated what proportion of the total area was inclosed, but that information, though valuable, does not indicate what proportion of the land under cultivation was affected.

The year 1603 is not an outstanding date in economic history, except that probably the woollen industry had by then almost reached the peak of its prosperity and London had attained a supremacy over all other towns and ports greater than before or since. Even in 1603, however, there were signs that the

---

[1] If the population be taken as 4,500,000 and the number of parishes as 10,000, the average would be 450 people per parish. As the urban parishes were more thickly populated than this, the country parish probably did not average more than 300 people.   [2] E. F. Gay. See below, p. 279.

supremacy of each was to be challenged: the one by the growth of newer industries which, although individually looking insignificant alongside the woollen industry, were to be progressively important and ultimately were in some cases to outgrow it; the other by the outports which, largely through colonial trade, in later centuries collectively surpassed London. The colonies supplied an important new feature in trade, and it is remarkable that within half a century of their foundation they exercised a definite influence upon English policy, both foreign and economic.

One of the chief factors, however, does not belong exclusively to, or even originate in, the years 1603–60, but is common to the previous century. The rise of prices, which still continued during this period, is perhaps the most significant economic fact. It affected all classes from the king to the peasant. It made the former revenue of the Crown inadequate and thus was a leading cause of the struggle between king and parliament. It worked hardship on all with fixed incomes, those dependent on customary rents, such of the clergy as held livings where the tithes were commuted, the small farmers whose few acres were not quite self-sufficing and yielded no surplus to sell, the wage-earners (unless a bench of magistrates would change the wage assessments), and institutions like hospitals and other charitable foundations, schools, and colleges. On the other hand certain classes benefited. The landlords who could rack-rent their tenants, the up-to-date farmers who could produce for the town markets, the large-scale merchants, and the upper middle class in general all enjoyed high prosperity so long as prices soared.

There were, therefore, many movements at work that, even under normal circumstances, would undoubtedly have brought about a great change in the social and economic situation of England. But circumstances were destined to be anything but normal under the early Stuarts, and the new economic forces that were coming to light were deflected from their natural course, partly by the royal policy and more especially by the civil wars.

The puritan revolution, unlike the French Revolution, was not primarily a social movement but a political and religious movement. Nevertheless a revolution which, in its varied phases, lasted twenty years could not fail to shake the fabric of society. Indeed, at times during the civil wars, it seemed as if the very foundations would be uprooted, for the diggers and some levellers clamoured for far-reaching social changes. The superstructure was actually altered when monarchy and the house of lords were declared abolished, and when many of the natural leaders of society either went into exile or suffered impoverishment at home from the fines they had to pay to compound for their delinquency. These alterations were temporary, for king and nobility enjoyed their own again at the Restoration. Similarly the attempt of the puritans to impose their moral code upon their fellow countrymen was short-lived. Parliament could reinstate the pre-civil-war constitution and repeal ordinances, and so destroy the visible signs of the great rebellion, but there is no doubt that domestic life and social intercourse were markedly different in 1660 from what they had been in 1603 or even 1642.

The extent to which social life was affected by the court cannot be exactly estimated, but, whereas Elizabeth contrived to make her court the centre of national life, the early Stuarts were by no means so successful. Her court, though not without some scandals, was outwardly dignified, impressive, and sober, and its frequent progresses gave opportunity for all classes to see their queen and for the few to entertain her. The court of James I, on the other hand, was extravagant and disorderly, frivolous and indecorous, with hard drinking common and immorality winked at. The solemn progresses of Elizabeth gave way to the hurriedly arranged hunting parties of which James was inordinately fond, and thus the influence of the court was less widespread. Moreover James's partiality for Scots, and his extraordinary infatuation for successive favourites, alienated the English nobility. Besides he had none of the arts of popularity—he despised the middle classes, disliked crowds, and never looked every inch a king. He was not, personally, an enthusiastic supporter of the entertainments then regarded as pre-eminently courtly. He had no special liking for plays, and did not share his wife's fondness for masques or his son Henry's delight in tilting in the ring. In any case, whatever may have been the contribution of the masques to the development of dramatic art, it is doubtful whether the court gained prestige through Anne of Denmark's interest in them. Sir Dudley Carleton describes the Christmas revels at court in 1604–5, when the queen and some of the noblest ladies painted their faces and arms black in order to appear in the roles of Ethiopians, but their critic thought they looked like 'a troop of lean-cheek'd Moors'. He also disapproved of their apparel, which was rich but 'too light and curtizan-light [like?] for such great ones'.[1] Henrietta Maria followed in her predecessor's footsteps and was herself a performer as well as an ardent if undiscerning patron of the drama. Both James and Charles enjoyed watching the sport of kings, and helped to start horse-racing at Newmarket. James actively encouraged bear-baiting and his son permitted it. They gave their sanction to dancing and to playing games on Sunday. Probably the royal example as well as precept set the fashion in these and other respects, but there were clearly limits to the influence of the court. For instance James's fulminations against tobacco did nothing to check smoking by all classes.

In many ways Charles's court differed from James's. The informality and confusion that the father had permitted were hateful to the son. Early in his reign Charles found time to reorganize his court and household and proved a strict taskmaster. He insisted upon dignity, respect, and regularity, and refused to allow access to his presence by the back-stairs. He set a most praiseworthy example in the encouragement of the arts, had a genuine appreciation of painting, and might have been a Maecenas but for poverty. Such means as he had were used with discrimination, and he did much to introduce the work of foreign artists into England.[2]

The abolition of monarchy in 1649 probably affected social life less than might be expected, for after four years had elapsed Oliver Cromwell was named lord protector and became king in all but name. Whitehall, Hampton Court, and all the other royal palaces were assigned for his use, so he had the first essential of a court. The king's furnishings for his residences were retained when not already sold, or even repurchased in some cases. Paintings and tapestry covered the walls of the public apartments at Hampton Court and Whitehall. The gardens continued to be adorned with statues of Venus and

---

[1] *Memorials of Sir Ralph Winwood*, ii. 44. Cf. *Diary of the Lady Anne Clifford*, ed. V. Sackville-West (1923), pp. 16–17: 'Now there was much talk of a masque which the queen had at Winchester and how all the ladies about the court had gotten such ill names that it was grown a scandalous place, and the queen herself was much fallen from her former greatness and reputation she had in the world.'

[2] For the influence of the court upon the theatre and upon the arts, see below, pp. 394–5, 374.

Cleopatra in bronze, and of Adonis and Apollo in marble, much to the disapproval of the more rigid puritans. A woman otherwise unknown to history wrote to beg Cromwell to demolish these monsters. There is much evil in them, she said, for, so long as the groves and altars of the idols remained untaken away in Jerusalem, the wrath of God continued against Israel.[1]

Much of the former ceremonial of the court was revived; a lord chamberlain, a comptroller of the household, and a master of ceremonies were appointed. Cromwell, though he had no liking for royal trappings, seems to have shared the views of supporters of the protectorate, that the dignity of England required a certain pomp. Opinion is unanimous that on state occasions Cromwell looked the part of a king. Even Mrs. Hutchinson, while bewailing his apostasy from the good old cause, confessed that he had 'much natural greatness, and well became the place he had usurped'. She says that 'his court was full of sin and vanity, and the more abominable, because they had not yet quite cast away the name of God, but profaned it by taking it in vain'. Apparently few agreed with her, or else they were willing to risk the alleged moral contamination, for she acknowledges that almost all the ministers, the City of London, many of the degenerate lords of the land, and the poor-spirited gentry all courted him.[2]

The asperities of puritanism tended to disappear at Cromwell's court, especially after the Humble Petition and Advice made his position hereditary. The marriage of his two daughters, in November 1657, gave rise to entertainments that appeared shocking to the older type of puritans. In addition to music and frivolities, there was mixed dancing, hitherto accounted profane, till five o'clock in the morning. No wonder the French ambassador remarked that 'another spirit appears at Whitehall, dances having been re-established there lately, and the preachers of the old time are retiring because they are found too melancholic'.[3] He further commented that the under-officers of the army grumbled, but he thought this did not matter much because their superiors approved. He was wrong in concluding that the opposition of the commonwealthsmen— called the honest under-officers by staunch republicans—was

[1] *Original Letters and Papers of State Addressed to Oliver Cromwell* [*Milton State Papers*], ed. John Nickolls (1743), p. 115.   [2] *Memoirs of Colonel Hutchinson*, p. 298.
[3] F. P. G. Guizot, *History of Oliver Cromwell* (1854), ii. 584.

immaterial, as events in 1659 clearly proved.[1] Moreover emulation at court divided even the Cromwellians. Much of the tension that eventually overthrew the protectorate arose from personal rivalries. Apparently the womenfolk of Cromwell's household were partly responsible, because, unlike the protector, they were wholly unable to bear their new honours modestly. A royalist reported, early in 1657, that most of the major-generals and their wives were not invited to court on a ceremonial occasion; and, when some one asked where they were, Mrs. Claypole, Cromwell's daughter, answered, 'I'll warrant you washing their dishes at home as they used to do.' It is not surprising to hear that 'this hath been extremely ill taken, and now the women do all they can with their husbands to hinder Mrs. Claypole from being a princess, and Her Highness'.[2] Hence there is probably some justice in Mrs. Hutchinson's caustic remark that for Cromwell's wife and children to aspire to regal state was as ridiculous as to deck an ape in scarlet.[3]

Next to the head of the state in the social scale comes the nobility. When Queen Elizabeth died, the number of lay peers was 59, of whom only 8 owed their titles to her. Her parsimony, although fully in accordance with Tudor policy, was in striking contrast to the profusion of James and Charles, who created peerages wholesale. The former made about 60 peers, so that at his death the house of lords contained some 100 members (certain peerages having become extinct). Charles during the first fifteen years of his reign ennobled about 30 of his subjects, and 'called up' 8 eldest sons of peers. This lavish creation had an important effect socially as well as politically. The peers of ancient lineage naturally looked askance at the parvenus who arrived among them. They were deeply attached to what they called nobility of blood. A curious example of this occurs in connexion with the nineteenth earl of Oxford, a distant relative of his predecessor and an officer serving in Flanders without means to support his honours. In 1629 the peers, therefore, petitioned the king to employ Oxford in his services 'before others of meaner birth and merit', and also to help him to gain

---

[1] See above, p. 243.

[2] *Clarendon State Papers*, iii. 327. This suggests an additional motive for the army leaders' opposition to Cromwell's accepting the title of king.

[3] *Memoirs of Colonel Hutchinson*, p. 298. For an account of Cromwell's court see C. H. Firth in *Cornhill Magazine*, N.S. iii (1897).

a landed estate. At the same time, they urged his Majesty to foster the maintenance of families that had won hereditary honours through virtue and merit, because persons of noble ancestry and good estates would certainly render faithful service to the kingdom.

It must be confessed that most of the peers created by the early Stuarts did not possess the three qualifications thought desirable by the peers in 1629—virtue and meritorious service, ancient family, and broad acres. Cranfield is a good case in point, for he was a London merchant who by sheer merit had forced himself to the front until he became head of the treasury. Perhaps he owed as much to his complaisance in marrying one of Buckingham's relatives as to his distinguished services for the king. Nevertheless his barony and, a year later, his earldom shocked purists and gave a handle to opponents of the court like Sir Anthony Weldon, who complained that Cranfield was of so mean a condition 'as none but a poore-spirited nobility would have endured his perching on that high tree of honour, to the dishonour of the nobility, the disgrace of the gentry . . .'.[1] It could be pleaded on Cranfield's behalf that he had fairly earned his honours, but it would be difficult to justify on this ground other creations, particularly those due to Buckingham. Moreover, about 1615 James began the practice of selling peerages, which were then worth about £10,000 apiece. One of the articles of impeachment against Buckingham was that he frightened a West Country gentleman into paying him £10,000 for a barony. Pym denounced a system which would render men more greedy for money than virtue, when they knew that they would receive titles of honour 'according to the heaviness of their purse, and not for the weightiness of their merit'.[2] Selling peerages had one indirect advantage: it prevented the house of lords from being based solely on blue blood or real estate and, by opening a place for the *nouveau riche*, gave the middle classes representation.

Separated from the nobility by only a title and the privileges it conferred was the country gentry. This class embraced within its ample folds men of gentle birth and breeding, whose worldly possessions might vary from extreme affluence to comparative poverty, but which would include the ownership of land. At

---

[1] *Secret History of the Court of James I*, ed. Sir Walter Scott (1811), i. 452–3.
[2] Firth, *The House of Lords*, pp. 13–14.

the top of the scale would be men of the types of Thynnes of Caurse Castle (Shropshire) and of Longleat (Wiltshire), whose estates were apparently valued at about £40,000 and £35,000 respectively by the committee set up during the civil war for compounding with delinquents,[1] or the Duttons of Sherborne Park (Gloucestershire), whose mansion reminded a traveller of the Banqueting Hall, Whitehall, and whose grounds included a spacious deer park and a race track.[2] At the other end would be men such as the Cornish gentry, few of whom owned estates rated above £10 in the subsidy rolls of 1641.[3] However, the size of a rent roll made little difference to pride in gentility. The country gentlemen stood firm upon the rights of their rank and insisted upon the respect due to their position. One of the finest types, Sir Bevil Grenvile, enforced their legal obligations upon his tenantry. Thus, in 1641 he wrote, 'Make it known to all my neighbours and tenants of the west side of our parish that I shall take it ill if they grind not at my mill, and let the tenants of Northlegh know that if they do it not, as they are bound, I will put them in suit.'[4] Yet he was a kindly landlord and solicitous of the welfare of his tenants. He and most of his class believed in a sort of paternal rule, under which tenants were treated generously provided they were content to follow their landlords' behests. The care of the sick of the village was a regular part of the daily routine of the squire's wife and sometimes even of her superior, the peeress. An admirable example of a local magnate's wife is illustrated by Lady Falkland, who used to visit the sick and read to them, and to keep a regular stock of antidotes against infection and of cordials and other kinds of physic for such of her neighbours as needed them.[5]

The question whether the nobility and the gentry became wealthier or poorer, or whether the one class declined and the other rose, is controversial.[6] It is at least possible that a majority

[1] *Calendar of the Committee for Compounding* (1890), pp. 910–14.

[2] *A Relation of a Short Survey of 26 Counties*, ed. L. G. Wickham Legg (1904), pp. 115–16. Fynes Moryson (*Itinerary* [1908], iv. 168) states that every gentleman with £500 or £1,000 a year from rent had a deer park, but that a prodigal age had compelled many to convert their parks into grazing land.

[3] Coate, *Cornwall in the Great Civil War*, p. 4.

[4] Ibid., p. 96.

[5] John Duncon, *The Holy Life of Lady Falkland* (1648), p. 156.

[6] See R. H. Tawney, 'The Rise of the Gentry, 1558–1640', in *Economic History Review*, 1941; the reply by H. R. Trevor-Roper in *A Supplement* (April 1953); and the rejoinder by Tawney in the *Review* (1954).

in each case was better off and only a minority worse off in 1640 than in 1603. That some of the peers became much better off is evident. Buckingham, after James had given him land worth £80,000, is said to have become second in wealth only to the earl of Montgomery, afterwards the fourth earl of Pembroke. Judging by the amounts some nobles are reputed to have spent on the royalist cause and by the estimates of the value of the estates of delinquent peers which they furnished to the parliamentary committee for compounding, Buckingham would not have been by any means the second wealthiest peer in the 1640's. Yet parliamentary speakers in the 1650's correctly assumed that the nobility had declined relatively to the gentry. Figures obtained from the admittedly defective records of the committee for compounding give £30,000 and £11,000 as the average values of the estates of delinquent peers and of baronets.[1] Because there were more than three times as many English baronets as members of the house of lords, they alone tipped the scales against the nobility. Yet their number, rather less than 500, did not constitute a large fraction of the country gentry. Two explanations why as a group the gentry were richer than the nobility occur at once: the country gentleman may have accumulated wealth more rapidly than the nobleman, or spent a smaller proportion of his income, and the number of country gentlemen may have increased more rapidly than the number of noblemen. Although many landed proprietors were in debt, this fact does not necessarily prove their poverty any more than raising new capital proves a modern company insolvent. This change in the balance of wealth was of the greatest political importance. Because the possession of land—and the *nouveau riche* sooner or later invested his money in land—was becoming recognized as a source of power, the greater wealth of the gentry was to give the house of commons an ascendancy over the house of lords.

On the whole, judged by overt signs, the tenants had not found their dependence so irksome as to make them ready to revolt—except in 1607. The Cornish tenants are said to have had a very dutiful regard for their landlords 'as enured in their obeisance from their ancestors'.[2] Yet even of that time John

---

[1] E. L. Klotz and Godfrey Davies, 'The Wealth of Royalist Peers and Baronets during the Puritan Revolution', *English Historical Review*, lviii (1943).

[2] Quoted in Coate, op. cit., p. 9.

Aubrey writes that 'the nobility and gentry were, in that soft peace, damnable prowd and insolent'.[1] Sir Ralph Verney, in many ways one of the kindest and worthiest of men, and a just and liberal landlord, was nevertheless anxious that his eldest son should keep only the company of his social equals or betters. 'Truly I had rather he should spend five pounds in good noble company then five pence among the meane & ordinary sort of people.'[2] It is difficult to believe that the mean and ordinary sort of people did not resent before 1640 the position of inferiority assigned to them in the category of social values. And probably one reason why the yeomanry and gentry usually fought on opposite sides in the civil war was this class distinction.

Just as it would be possible to divide the squirearchy roughly into the affluent and the fairly well off, so the cultured and educated among them might be distinguished from the boorish and ignorant. At the one extreme would be those who sought to educate themselves in all possible ways. The ideal then entertained of the complete gentleman was: to have many accomplishments rather than to be an expert in one, to be equally versed in the arts of war and of peace, to enjoy sports, to be skilled in music, to know literature, to speak several languages, to be a courtier but withal civil to all classes of men, to have been to Oxford or Cambridge, and to have travelled.[3] Relatively few of the gentry attained this standard and not many approached it. The majority, in all likelihood, deserved the strictures contemporaries passed on them. Thus Samuel Butler in his book of *Characters* devotes one to 'The Bumpkin or Country Squire'. There the squire is derided for his homely education, for his uncouth speech and rough manner of living, for his fondness for holding forth in an alehouse where his chief topics are his horses and his principal entertainment drinking himself and his auditors drunk with strong beer, and so on.[4] In addition the ignorance of the squirearchy was lamentable, and a bishop

---

[1] *Brief Lives*, ii. 317.

[2] *Verney Family*, iii. 90.

[3] See, for examples: Edward Walsingham's lives of Sir John Smith (1644) and Sir Henry Gage (1645); Aubrey, *Brief Lives*, ii. 36–37; *The Poems of Richard Lovelace*, ed. C. H. Wilkinson (1925), pp. lxi–lxiii; and *Memoirs of Colonel Hutchinson*, pp. 27–28.

[4] Samuel Butler, *Characters and Passages from Notebooks*, ed. A. R. Waller (1908), pp. 40–41. Cf. John Earle, *Micro-cosmographie* (1628), xviii, 'An Upstart Country Knight'. The authoress of the *Defence of the Female Sex* [1696], pp. 30–34, repeats, with elaboration, what Butler says.

had to confess: 'our land hath no blemish comparable to the mis-education of our gentry'.[1]

Probably the effect of the civil war was to make things worse. Clarendon denounces in eloquent phrases some of the evils that he regards as directly attributable to those unhappy years. He particularly notes that the woeful vice of drinking had spread very far among the royalists and that the young of both sexes had cast off all moral restraints. Children, he said,

asked not blessing of their parents.[2] . . . The young women conversed without any circumspection or modesty, and frequently met at taverns and common eating houses. . . . The daughters of noble and illustrious families bestowed themselves upon the divines of the time or other low and unequal matches. Parents had no manner of authority over their children, nor children any obedience or submission to their parents; . . . there were never such examples of impiety between such relations in any age of the world, Christian or heathen, as that wicked time, from the beginning of the rebellion to the king's return.[3]

This is exaggerated, for the writer was anxious to throw the blame for the excesses of the Restoration upon the civil wars. Nevertheless there is an important element of truth in the criticism.

The effect of the civil wars on the landed classes is very hard to estimate. Certainly many individual members suffered severely. The majority fought for the losing side, and their estates were at the mercy of their conquerors. A royalist normally had to pay a fine of from one-tenth to one-third of the value of his property (calculated at twenty years' purchase). Originally about seventy prominent individuals suffered the confiscation of their lands, and practically all these may be classed as either peers or gentry. In 1651 their estates were ordered to be sold.[4] Most of these persons were in exile and henceforth had to depend upon

---

[1] Joseph Hall, *Epistles, the Sixt Decad* (1627). Another bishop, Burnet, says much the same of the gentry at the end of the century (*History of My Own Time*, ii. 648).

[2] Cf. *State Papers, Venetian, 1621–1623* (1911), p. 451: 'Sometimes he [Charles I] has left the court for a while on this account, but has returned soon, fearing to lose the daily blessing according to the admirable custom of the country, well worthy of imitation for every child on first meeting his parents each day to kneel and ask their blessing. This happens in the public streets and in most frequented and conspicuous places of the city, no matter what their age.'

[3] *Life of Clarendon*, i. 301–6.

[4] See *Acts and Ordinances*, ii. 520–45. Cf. p. 171 above for other confiscations, and *Calendar of the Proceedings of the Committee for Compounding*, i (1889), Preface.

charity. Even then they had no thought of compounding for their forfeited possessions with those whom they regarded as the murderers of their sovereign. Hyde wrote:

I know no other counsel to give you than by the grace of God I mean to follow myself, which is to starve really and literally with the comfort of having endeavoured to avoid it by all honest courses, and rather to bear it than to do anything contrary to my duty. Compounding is a thing I do not understand, nor how a man can do it to save his life. We must play out the game with that courage as becomes gamesters, who were first engaged by conscience against all motives of temptation and interest, and to be glad to let the world know that we were carried only by conscience.[1]

Some of the dependants of those whose estates were forfeited suffered nearly as severely as the chief delinquents themselves. For example the heir of the earl of Derby (executed in 1651) was granted by parliament £500 a year from his father's lands because, as a member said, his family was in a most distressing condition and, failing relief, would have to go begging.[2]

The humbler royalists, without influence or powerful friends, suffered more than the erstwhile rich nobleman, who usually managed to save something from the wreck of his fortunes. They might have endured the loss of their stock and the plundering of their homes. Forced contributions and taxes might have consumed whatever ready money remained after voluntary gifts of plate and cash to the royal cause had been made. When the fighting was over and it became necessary for the defeated to make terms with the victors, a long and vexatious delay ensued[3] before the amount of the fine was fixed. Then there was great difficulty in raising it, and often the compounder had to sell land when the market was glutted by the action of others similarly situated. How much land actually changed hands the defective state of the records makes it impossible to say, and this is unfortunately particularly true of lands that were permanently alienated by their former owners. At the Restoration the king, the church, and the cavaliers recovered estates previously confiscated and sold. But the royalist who had, nominally, voluntarily mortgaged or sold his property, or part of it, in

---

[1] *Clarendon State Papers*, iii. 23.   [2] *Burton Diary*, ii. 80–81.
[3] Thus the case of the royalist lord mayor of London, Sir Richard Gurney, began in August 1644 and ended in June 1654 (*Calendar of the Proceedings of the Committee for Compounding*, v [1892], xxi).

order to compound for his delinquency, had no redress, and the validity of the sale was recognized. Hence a large class of landed proprietors owed their origin to the puritan revolution. The 'new gentry', as they were called, can be divided into two groups. In the first were the rich citizens and moneyed men who had either advanced money on mortgage to embarrassed royalists or bought portions of their estates outright and in one way or the other supplanted the old squires. The rise of this class was so striking a social phenomenon that it attracted attention as early as 1647, when a satirist describes the upstart gentleman. After lamenting that real gentlemen had been cast aside like a last year's almanac, or like the king, he proceeds:

> I now have liv'd to see the day,
> Wherein a fig-man beares such sway,
>   that knights dare scarce sit by him;
> Yea, I have liv'd to see the houre,
> In which a clothier hath such power,
>   that lords are glad to buy him.

> Thus doe the froth of all the earth,
> A spawne sprung from a dunghill birth,
>   now prince it in our land:
> A people come the Lord knowes how,
> Both fame and nameless till just now,
>   must every one command.[1]

The second class of new landowners consisted mainly of soldiers, who received confiscated lands as payment for the arrears due to them, and creditors of the state, who received satisfaction for their debts from the lands of the Crown or the church. In all parts of England army officers suddenly appeared as the proud possessors of great estates, and seemed on the way to found a new landed aristocracy. Thus Fleetwood became the owner of Woodstock Manor, Lambert of Wimbledon, Okey of Ampthill, Pride of Nonesuch—all Crown lands. Hesilrige picked up cheaply Bishop Auckland and other estates formerly belonging to the bishopric of Durham, and Birch acquired many of the estates belonging to the bishopric of Hereford.[2]

[1] Willis, *Times Whirligig*, sig. B1ʳ. 'Fig-man' seems unknown to the dictionaries. It may mean simply a seller of figs or be a slang term for a grocer.
[2] See *Military Memoir of Colonel Birch* (1873), pp. 154, 197–8, for some interesting particulars.

The effect of the creation of a new class of landlords was profound. While the influence of the old gentry was diminished, their loss of power was compensated for by the influence of the new landowners. In many instances one set of landlords had been substituted for another, but the net result was no great loss of influence by the gentry. The situation has some parallels with that created by the dissolution of the monasteries, when, some say, a sixth of the land of England changed hands. Many of the gentry who lost their lands wholly or in part during the civil wars owed their possessions to their ancestors' compliance with Henry VIII's imperious will. Even the 'new' gentry of the Tudors had succeeded in re-establishing an influence that was feudal in origin and patriarchal in character. On the other hand the new landlords that came into being as a result of the civil wars were generally merchants, or of middle-class stock, and between them and their tenants there was no personal tie— nothing except a cash nexus. To the old squire the manor and those dependent upon it had been almost the 'be-all and the end-all here', the subject of his constant care and major interest. To the new-comer from the city the purchase of an estate meant social prestige and political influence. Eager to enjoy the privileges conferred by the ownership of land, he was often negligent of the duties.

The contrast between the old and the new type of landowner is the constant theme of several generations of writers who agree in lamenting the change. It would be a bad mistake, however, to assume that the new-comer to social life during 1640–60 was the first to incur the censure of the *laudator temporis acti*. Certainly there were more new-comers and they represented a more violent break with the past than was usually the case, but that was all, for even in the sixteenth century there were laments in the countryside that the old order was passing away. One of the most outspoken comparisons between the old squire and the new occurs in a ballad of about 1611–14, 'The Old Courtier and the New Courtier'.[1] The former was a bountiful gentleman with a wife devoted to her household, a study full of books, a hall hung with weapons, good cheer for all at Christmas, and hawks and hounds for sport. The new gallant kept 'a brace of painted creatures', had a wife who cared little about housekeeping but much about her appearance and dress, a study

[1] *Roxburghe Ballads*, ed. J. W. Ebsworth (1889), vi. 756–7.

full of pamphlets and plays, and a new hall hung with pictures and containing a shovelboard, and was a devotee of the new fashion of going to London to enjoy the Christmas festivities. This novel habit of creating a season in London gave general concern. In parliament the demand was heard for a law to compel the nobles and gentry who wasted their substance in 'toys, jewels and clothes' to go and live in the country; and, said one member, if the men plead their wives draw them to London, laws can control wives if husbands cannot.[1] No law was passed, but both James and Charles issued proclamations ordering those whose business did not require their presence in London to depart and exercise the old hospitality[2] on their country estates, and star-chamber proceedings were instituted against those staying in London in violation of such proclamations.[3] It was all in vain: the attractions of London were too powerful.

Perhaps the best proof that the influence of the landed classes was not permanently impaired by the civil wars is to be found by a study of the part they played in local government. After the Restoration, as before, both nobility and gentry carried on the local government of the districts in which they lived. The former supplied the lords lieutenant, and the latter the justices of the peace. The lord lieutenant was usually a nobleman prominent in the county or counties in which he was the official representative of the Crown. He, with his deputies and the sheriff, was responsible for musters of the militia and for levies for service outside the county. He was supposed to exercise a general supervision over the collection of taxes and the suppression of recusancy. He was also expected to keep an eye on the justices of the peace and to see that they enforced the statutes of the realm or the orders of the privy council.

Under the lords lieutenant were the justices of the peace, in whose hands were placed all the details of local government. The appointment of the justices was in the hands of the Crown and was made from the local gentry. They were administrative officials as well as justices, and their co-operation was essential if the machinery of state was to continue to work. Generally they held four quarter-sessions every year, sometimes in the

---

[1] Nicholas, *Proceedings and Debates*, ii. 209–10.
[2] That is, maintain a large household.
[3] Rushworth, ii. 288 ff.; *D'Ewes Autobiography*, ii. 78.

county town, sometimes in four different towns. The large size of the county or the difficulties of communication led in certain cases to subdivisions into three or four areas, each with four quarter-sessions a year. In practice these would be attended by the local justices, but inasmuch as each was appointed for the whole county he might be present at any of the sessions held outside his own district. About the beginning of the century, petty sessions were instituted, in order to avoid the delay of waiting until the next quarter-session. In addition individual justices might act in judicial cases, committing the more serious offenders for trial at the assizes and binding over others for the next sessions. The procedure at quarter-sessions was by present-ment by a jury, who corresponded to the grand jury of the assizes. The judicial and administrative business transacted at quarter-sessions was extremely varied, and the following enumeration should be regarded only as specimens of frequent occurrence in the quarter-sessions records. The commoner offences dealt with included assaults on the person which might cause manslaughter, stealing, rioting, trespassing, recusancy, bastardy, and playing unlawful games, such as cards or bowling 'by the meaner sort'. The more interesting of the administrative duties were regulating trade, fixing wages, licensing alehouses, relieving the poor, maintaining roads and bridges, and dealing with emergencies such as a scarcity of grain or an epidemic of plague. To fulfil their orders the justices of the peace had at their disposal constables and surveyors of highways in towns, petty constables, church wardens, and overseers of the poor in the parishes, and the higher constables in the county. All these positions might involve many unpleasant and unpopular duties, such as collection of taxes and rates, enforcing service in road-making, looking after the impotent poor or moving them to the parish in which they were born[1] or to the place of their last legal settlement, inflicting punishments, like whipping or sitting in the stocks, that the justices might decree, reporting to the high constable offences committed in their locality, and attend-ing quarter-sessions. The occupants of these arduous positions were usually selected in turn from householders and served for a year.[2]

[1] See *Surrey Quarter Sessions Records, Order Book and Sessions Rolls, 1659–1661* (1934), p. 14, for a typical example of the removal of aged persons likely to be a charge on the parish to which they have just come.

[2] The above is mainly based on the excellent introduction to James Tait's

Both the nobility and gentry derived the bulk of their incomes from land, although affluent and intelligent members of each group not infrequently invested in joint-stock companies or other enterprises, or made big loans, secured by land, to members of their own circles.[1] Next to them in the social scale in the country were the yeomanry. But before discussing this group it is necessary to deal with the condition of agriculture in general, from which both gentry and yeomanry derived their incomes.

Agriculture, then even more than now, was mainly determined by geographical factors and particularly by the nature of the climate, soil, means of communication, and so forth. Since the western half of England contains all the mountains and much of the hilly country and consequently has the wetter climate, while the eastern half is drier, flatter, and has many navigable rivers with easy access to the sea, it is natural that the west should be predominantly pastoral and the east arable. This generalization, however, should not be allowed to conceal the existence of mixed farming everywhere. The arable farmer needed cattle and sheep both to supply meat for his family and to manure his land (for he had no other fertilizer except marl, and this was dear and hard to transport). Therefore he could not be solely a corn-grower. Likewise a grazier or sheep farmer had to plant sufficient cereal crops for himself and his household.

Although in many parts of England farming was still largely for subsistence,[2] there had long been an important export or coastwise trade from the east coast. Moreover the growth of London and of a few other large towns must have made the supply of food for their markets the first consideration of the farmers in the vicinity. As means of communication improved, they could devote themselves more exclusively to supplying meat to neighbouring towns or to raising sheep in order to sell their fleeces.

Lancashire Quarter Sessions Records (1917). Other valuable accounts are Hilary Jenkinson's introduction to *Surrey Record Society, Number XXXII* (1931); and J. W. Willis Bund's introduction to *Worcestershire County Records, Quarter Sessions Papers*, vol. i (1900).

[1] The extent and importance of these transactions among members of the landed classes deserve study.

[2] Thomas Powell, *Tom of All Trades* (1631), p. 4, says that it was true of most gentlemen living upon the revenue of lands 'that the height of their husbandry amounts to no more than to clear the last halfe yeeres booking, and borrowing at the rent day'.

While there were considerable areas in the north, west, and south-east that have sometimes been called the 'old inclosures' and that had never, so far as is known, been cultivated as champaign land, the more general method of cultivation was the open-field system. This usually took the form of a three-field system, though there were many places where a two- or even a four-field system prevailed, and not a few where there were more fields than four. What may almost be called the traditional description gives a rotation of wheat, barley or rye, and fallow. This is accurate enough, provided the impression is not conveyed of too great rigidity. To take an example, it did not necessarily follow that, because, in a field, a sowing of wheat was due, the whole of its area should be so used. Part of it might be hedged off for peas or beans or vetches, as was also true of the second field under cultivation at that particular time. Of course, where the four-field system was followed a greater degree of elasticity was possible, and a crop of beans might intervene between two kinds of cereals. Sainfoin was not unknown, and the field cultivation of such vegetables as turnips and potatoes found advocates but few practitioners. As for grazing, the common meadow was closed while the hay was growing, and the cattle and sheep were turned out on the fallow or commons. When the harvest had been reaped, the animals were pastured in the stubble. The chief difficulty confronting the grazier was to keep his animals alive and fit during the winter, for he had no roots or artificial feeding stuffs available, but had to rely almost exclusively on hay or straw.

In most areas the arable fields were divided into numerous strips, which were separated from each other by balks, and the number of sheep or cattle a villager might graze in the common fields was limited by custom, the size of his holding, or in some other way. This system is well described in the case of Daventry, which towards the end of Elizabeth's reign was said to stand in open country, to be a market town, and to have a fertile soil suitable for corn and grain, with reasonably good pastures for cows and sheep. The fields were three in number, two containing about 375 acres each, and a third 1,275. Each field was subdivided, and these subdivisions were in turn split up into many holdings, several of which might be in the hands of a single individual. For instance one subdivision of 37 acres contained 96 holdings, owned by 17 different persons. In addition there were common pastures amounting to 300 acres; on a certain day the common fields were thrown open, and for each 28 acres of his holding a tenant might pasture 50 sheep and an unlimited number of cattle.[1]

A fundamental and extremely difficult question in the history of agriculture in the seventeenth century is the extent of inclosures. In order to generalize accurately it is necessary to know, first, their extent up to 1603 and then their extension from that date to 1660. Unfortunately the available evidence is inconclusive. What may be called the literary evidence is almost all on one side, and would indicate that a great deal of land was inclosed and that the process caused widespread distress. The well-known laments of St. Thomas More and Latimer the martyr were repeated in one form or another for over a century. Ballad-mongers, pamphleteers, and preachers all united in condemnation. On the other hand an examination of the statistical evidence, available for twenty-four counties, leads to the conclusion that less than 3 per cent. of the total area of England was inclosed by 1607.[2] Even granting that the material on which this calculation is based is defective, it is difficult to believe that the total percentage can have been more than 5. At first sight, at least, the loud outcries and fierce denunciations of the inclosure movement would seem inexplicable. Indeed no single explanation will suffice. To begin with, the proportion of land inclosed to land under cultivation (and not to the total area of England) was greater than one in twenty, and considerably more in the nine counties in the midlands,[3] where the bulk of the inclosed land was situated. In Stuart times these counties were the great wheat-growing areas, and an inclosure there of between 8 and 9 per cent. would be serious, since the object in view was for the most part to transform arable land into pasture. This would involve most of the evils of which contemporaries complained—the decay of villages, diminution of population when a shepherd or two sufficed instead of a score of labourers, and the creation of a class of

[1] E. M. Leonard, in *Trans. Royal Hist. Soc.*, N.S. xix. 104–6.

[2] See A. H. Johnson, *The Disappearance of the Small Landowner* (1909), pp. 42–44, for a convenient summary of the conclusions of Professor E. F. Gay, 'Inclosures in England in the Sixteenth Century', *Quarterly Journal of Economics*, xvii. 576–97.

[3] Leicester, Northampton, Rutland, East Warwickshire, Bedford, Buckingham, Berkshire, Oxford, and Middlesex. Next to these come Huntingdon and Cambridge.

unemployed, some of whom became 'sturdy beggars'. Furthermore the nibbling at commons or waste threatened the wellbeing of any village where the old system of agriculture was still in use, for such unoccupied lands were essential. Then, too, men of conservative views felt instinctively, or saw dimly, that a new order was arising in the countryside and that, instead of the old semi-communal life, in the future it would be a case of each man for himself and the devil take the hindmost. Fear of the unknown magnified the extent of the reality. Also, contemporaries complained that the old hospitality of the countryside was disappearing and giving place to a grasping, commercial spirit.

These evils would be felt all the more severely in districts in the midlands where the displaced labourers might not find near at hand alternative means of employment. Although industries were springing up around the fringes of this area—coal in Leicestershire, coal and iron in Staffordshire, salt in Worcestershire, and ironware in Shropshire and in and around Birmingham—the absorption of labour was at first small. And even when work was available, labour was immobile and shackled by the poor laws. A contemporary laid his finger on the spot: 'I complaine not of inclosure in Kent or Essex, where they have other callings and trades to maintaine their country by, or of places near the sea or City, but of inclosure in the inland countreys which takes away tillage, the only trade generall they have to live on.'[1]

Many customs, such as pasturing on the common, although long enjoyed unchallenged, might on appeal to the courts turn out not to be legal rights at all. The tenant, contented with the privilege he was enjoying, had not worried about a grant from the lord of the manor, and, consequently, was often wholly unable to furnish any kind of legal proof. That many of the inclosures were now being made by an award in chancery rendered it difficult for the small holder to offer any resistance. Moreover a farmer who fondly believed that he had a copyhold of inheritance and that his land would pass as a matter of course to his heir on his death, and who often paid a rent which, thanks to the fall in the value of money and other causes, bore little proportion to the value of the land he occupied,

---

[1] John Moore, *A Scripture Word against Inclosure,* Introduction, quoted in *Trans. Royal Hist. Soc.,* N.S. xix. 139.

suddenly found that his landlord was no longer content with the customary payments but was bent upon substituting a rack rent, and also sought to supplant the copyhold of inheritance by a mere copyhold for life. An example of what was happening is supplied by a petition from 186 inhabitants of a barony in Cumberland to Oliver Cromwell. Their respective tenements, they said, had descended from ancestor to heir, paying only a two- or three-penny fine at the most—that is, two or three years' ancient rent of their tenements as it fell due, upon the death of the lord of the manor or upon change of tenant by death. They performed suit of court and border service, and owed one boon or day's work at harvest, or fourpence in case of default. They paid a penny for liberty to cut wood growing on their tenements and 'four pence at Michaelmas for land serjeant fee, and no other rents, monies or services whatsoever'. Now a new landlord, who had purchased these manors from the Crown, endeavoured to break their ancient customs and to exact arbitrary, unreasonable fines—forty pence, fifty pence, and even more—and those refusing to pay he ejected from their lands and thus depopulated much of the barony; or else he wasted the tenants' sustenance by suits at law in order to compel them to become tenants at will.[1]

Nevertheless, before our period ends, inclosures find defenders, who argue that progressive farming is impossible in the old communal villages, with their countless strips, common pasture, and obsolete methods. And, as population slowly grew, towns became larger, and employment in industry increased, improved methods were necessary. These considerations made inclosed farms essential.

Of particular importance during the seventeenth century was the draining of fens and marshes. In all, well over half a million acres were added to the cultivated land in England. The outstanding example is the draining of the Great Level of the Fens, which had stretched through six counties, from Lincoln to Cambridge—a vast morass, with a few islands here and there. Transportation was in punts or on stilts. A contemporary[2] described the fen population as a 'rude and almost barbarous

---

[1] John Musgrave, *A True Representation of the State of the Bordering Customary Tenants in the North* [*c.* 1654].

[2] Sir William Dugdale, quoted in E. Lipson, *The Economic History of England*, ii (1931), 375.

sort of lazy and beggarly people'. Nevertheless, however scanty a livelihood the fens afforded, their inhabitants offered a prolonged resistance to the various undertakers who, in return for a portion of the land, contracted to drain it. The reason for the opposition is admirably summed up by Thomas Fuller. Tell the fenmen, he says, of the large benefit to the public of fattening a bullock or sheep where formerly a pike or duck fed, and they will reply 'that if they be taken in taking that bullock or sheep, the rich owner inditeth them for felons; whereas that pike or duck were their own foods only for their pains of catching them'.[1]

Next to the nobility and gentry in the social scale of the landed classes comes the yeomanry, who occupied in rural society much the same position that the middle class occupied in the towns. There were the yeomen of ample means who had freeholds that had long been in the possession of their families, and there were many more qualified to vote at the election of the knights of the shire by the possession of 40s. freeholds. In addition copyholders and leaseholders were often, if rather loosely, called yeomen. The term was thus extremely elastic, and can be applied to what Bacon called the 'middle people' between gentlemen and cottagers.[2]

According to the statistics compiled by Gregory King at the time of the revolution of 1688, there were 40,000 freeholders of the better sort, 140,000 of the lesser sort, and 150,000 farmers.[3] It is likely that freeholders would include copyholders and leaseholders and that the farmers were tenants at will. Since King's are the only estimates available for the seventeenth century, there is no statistical information to show whether the numbers of the yeomen were declining. Perhaps if figures were in existence they would tend to prove (as in the case of inclosures) that the lamentations of contemporaries over the supposedly disappearing yeomen were much exaggerated. It is likely enough that inclosures, by making large-scale farming more profitable, diminished the number of small landowners. The very fame of the yeoman, the reputation he had acquired

---

[1] *Worthies of England*, ed. P. Austin Nuttall (1840), i. 221.

[2] Bacon, *History of King Henry VII*, in *Works*, vi. 95. It is noteworthy that Bacon says that cottagers 'are but housed beggars'.

[3] See the table in G. Chalmers's edition of King's *Observations* (1804).

in the middle ages as the backbone of the strength of the military force, and his good name as a cheerful provider of hospitality, all combined to make writers sing dirges over the alleged decline of his class.

In so far as the yeomen did suffer a reduction in numbers, it is probable that the reasons were both economic and social. It is rather paradoxical that, at the time when the political importance of the yeomen was increasing, their numbers were diminishing. The explanation is that the progressive, rich yeoman was absorbing the land of his poorer, backward brother. Therefore, the number of yeomen decreased at both the top and the bottom of the social ladder. The poorest members of the class sank down into the peasantry and the richest often passed into the ranks of the gentry. William Harrison, in the second half of Elizabeth's reign, noticed that some yeomen 'do come to great welth, in somuch that manie of them are able and doo buie the lands of unthriftie gentlemen', and, often sending their sons to the university and inns of court, leave estates that enable them to become gentlemen.[1] Probably this tendency to secure a coat of arms and set up as a gentleman became more marked under the early Stuarts. Nevertheless, although some yeomen were anxious to step out of their class, others were full of pride in it. They were proud of their moderate estates, which might have been in their family for three or four hundred years, and they had no desire to exchange the substantial comfort and unostentatious dignity of a freeholder for the more extravagant and pretentious rank of a gentleman. So far as the south, and particularly the south-east, is concerned, they were normally puritans in religion, or, if Anglicans, strong protestants, and were opposed more or less instinctively to Arminianism and sacerdotalism. In politics they were warm supporters of parliament against the Stuarts. Probably the adherence of the gentry to Charles I's cause influenced the decision of the yeomanry to fight on the other side, for there seems to have been a considerable amount of class feeling between gentlemen and yeomen. When Henry Oxinden, a Kentish gentleman, wished to marry a yeoman's daughter, he found that his relatives frowned upon the match. It was in vain he pleaded that the father had educated his daughter at school among children of gentle birth, that he mixed with gentlemen

[1] *Description of England,* ed. F. J. Furnivall (1877), i. 133.

in sports, and that his estate was of great antiquity although diminished by the custom of gavelkind. The very fact that Oxinden said defiantly that he preferred a man of low degree who was virtuous, rich, wise, or powerful to the greatest lord of the kingdom, who was inferior in these qualities, proved that in the eyes of members of his own class he would be marrying beneath himself.[1]

Next to the yeoman, and not always distinguishable from him, was the small farmer, often called the husbandman. He usually had a modest holding, at a customary rent, with rights of grazing on the common. He lived an arduous life, in which all the family shared. Nevertheless independence and sufficiency seem to have been regarded as adequate reward for so much toil. One of the finest passages in Dorothy Osborne's *Letters* refers to this class:

about sixe or seven a clock, I walke out into a common that lyes hard by the house where a great many young wenches keep sheep and cow's and sitt in the shade singing of ballads; I goe to them and compare theire voyces and beauty's to some ancient shepherdesses that I have read of and finde a vaste difference there, but trust mee I think these are as innocent as those could bee. I talke to them, and finde they want nothing to make them the happiest people in the world, but the knoledge that they are soe. most comonly when wee are in the middest of our discourse one looks aboute her and spyes her cow's goeing into the corne and then away they all run, as if they had wing's at theire heels.[2]

Generally the husbandman found it necessary to work for wages, at harvest time, to secure ready money to purchase what was not produced on his little farm. The women and children of the family, in addition to the help they gave out of doors, were busy indoors spinning thread which a weaver might make into cloth for their own use or for sale to a clothier.

England in 1603 was still largely an agricultural country, and four-fifths of the population lived on the land. Nevertheless there were evident signs that industry was gradually becoming more important. By this time most of the elements necessary for an industrial society were present. If the four main stages in the evolution of modern industry are labelled the household,

---

[1] *The Oxinden Letters*, ed. Dorothy Gardiner (1933), pp. 278–9.
[2] *The Letters of Dorothy Osborne*, ed. G. C. Moore Smith (1928), pp. 51–52.

the handicraft, the domestic or commission[1] or putting-out,[2] and the factory, the third stage had already been reached by 1603. There were, certainly, some survivals of the first and many examples of the second. Then, as now, but to a much greater extent then, a family often depended upon the labours of its members for its clothing. A well-to-do gentleman like Oliver Cromwell might appear in the house of commons clad in homespun. Even in medieval times, however, some of the needs of the family could not be satisfied within the household and it had been necessary to have recourse to the craftsman. He dealt directly with his customers and tried to fulfil their wants by the labours of his own hands. He still survives today in the local butcher or baker, cobbler or carpenter. The craftsman's organization was the gild, and so long as the medieval town remained relatively self-sufficing this system worked well enough. But as soon as the economic unit became enlarged so as to include wider areas, which gradually grew until they became coextensive with the nation and, as the seventeenth century advanced, its possessions beyond seas as well, the deficiencies of the gild system were revealed. Although there was an unwillingness openly to admit it, the gilds had outlived their usefulness and were being pushed into the background. They did not give up the ghost without a struggle. It is a true saying that during 1550–1750 the old and the new systems of industry were at grips—and the new was capitalism.[3] The Elizabethan statutes were intended to restore the gilds to their former preeminence, and the gilds themselves in many boroughs amalgamated in order to 'strengthen the ramparts of town privileges against the assaults of unrestricted competition'.[4] The movement was generally sponsored by the local authorities, who hoped thus to retain or regain the virtual monopolies their gildsmen had enjoyed in the late middle ages. But the attempt to maintain the old industrial order did not succeed: the new economic forces were too strong. Therefore control of industry by the gild was in places non-existent, in others obsolete or imperfect. The handicraft stage was replaced by the putting-out system. The characteristic feature of this was that the work

---

[1] The late George Unwin's term.
[2] The most expressive term, preferred by Professor E. F. Gay.
[3] T. H. Marshall, 'Capitalism and the Decline of the English Gilds', in *Cambridge Historical Journal*, iii. 23.   [4] Ibid., p. 25.

was done for an employer or putter-out who had the wool distributed to the spinners or the thread to the weavers; and spinners and weavers were employees as much then when they were working in their homes as later under the factory system.

So soon as the capitalist employer began to produce on a large scale for a wide market, the division of labour was inevitable. The craftsman had, as it were, taken five parts—workman, foreman (superintending his journeymen and apprentices, if any), employer, merchant, and shopkeeper. Gradually these five functions were performed by different individuals. First of all, the artisan became separated from the master, and this marks the beginning of a permanent classification of industrial society into employers and employed. At the bottom of the scale was the journeyman, the lifelong wage-earner. Next to him came the small merchant, or shopkeeper, who often made with his own hands what he sold. Finally there were the capitalist manufacturer, the employer who was also a merchant, the shopkeeper who bought what he sold, and the shipping merchant.[1]

Not novel in the seventeenth century, but powerfully developed then, was the company. There had been plenty of companies before, such as the regulated companies for foreign trade, but the rapid growth of the joint-stock company was a new phenomenon. Its evolution can be illustrated by the history of the East India Company, founded in 1600. At first its capital, or stock, was raised for each voyage separately. This was found inconvenient in practice, so the governor and directors began to raise a joint stock for a number of years—four, at first. Finally, terminable stock was abandoned and permanent capital was raised. Even before the last stage was reached, shares in the common stock were bought and sold, and both the word 'stockjobber' and the speculator himself were in existence.

Apart from the professional classes, the industrial system just outlined absorbed the bulk of the middle classes. There was, however, very great divergence between the richer and the poorer members of this category. At the top were the merchant princes like Sir Thomas Smith, the governor of the East India Company, or Edward Backwell, a goldsmith banker, who helped to finance Cromwell's expeditionary force in Flanders;

---

[1] This paragraph is mainly based on the Introduction to George Unwin, *Industrial Organization in the 16th and 17th Centuries* (1904).

and at the foot were the small shopkeepers and tradesmen. As was the case with the country gentry, the lower degrees contained by far the greater number. Relatively speaking there were more small employers then than now. Most of them had started as apprentices and served as journeymen. Formerly all or most of the journeymen might, legitimately, have expected to become masters, but times were changing. With the growth of capitalism, the richer merchants were ceasing to confine their interest to one trade or craft and were becoming entrepreneurs, and the journeymen were becoming lifelong wage-earners.

Early in the eighteenth century Swift and others attracted attention by contrasting the moneyed interest with the landed interest, much to the disadvantage of the former. Nevertheless a century earlier there was much capital, in the dual significance of the word—the stock of a company, and the accumulated wealth devoted to production. However, there were few capitalists pure and simple, and most who dealt in high finance had some other business. There were no specialized bankers, but there were a number of men who did the work of bankers. The word itself was in use, and seems to have been synonymous with a dabbler in exchanges. In addition to the exchange specialists, who were usually merchants as well, there were brokers, scriveners, and goldsmiths, whose transactions involved many of the activities of bankers today. They received deposits and lent out money at interest.[1] Previous to the civil wars, however, merchants used to deposit their spare cash in the mint at the Tower; but, after Charles threatened, in 1640, to seize the bullion there, they began to utilize the strong-rooms of goldsmiths. This habit grew so rapidly that a London goldsmith wrote in 1660 that the goldsmiths in Lombard Street were just like the bankers at Amsterdam, keeping the cash of a great many London merchants. Nevertheless, even if there were no banks in the technical sense, many of the services performed by banks today were commonly available in the seventeenth century. The use of credit was general, both in the metropolis and in the country. Frequently, perhaps usually, the jobber (badger or brogger) gave out wool to the spinners or weavers on credit, just as he himself often bought wool from farmers on credit. Apparently, in the latter case at least, formal agreements were

---

[1] An act of 1624, which limited interest to 8 per cent., indirectly endorsed acceptance of interest.

drawn up containing a promise to pay a specified amount at the expiration of a given time. Much the same course was pursued, on a national scale, in financing the civil war. Parliament made many of its purchases on credit, and induced citizens to advance or adventure money for such purposes as the conquest of Ireland, and rewarded its creditors with grants of Irish lands, &c. It is curious, however, that the government lagged behind the individual, and that England was behind Holland. Cromwell's government was severely hampered by a debt of a million and a half pounds, which would not have been a real source of weakness if some system of funding the national debt had been used.

In considering industry, it is natural to select for discussion the most important—namely, the woollen or textile branch. 'Divide your exportable commodities into 10 parts', said Coke, 'and that which comes from the sheep's back is nine parts of the ten'.[1] Throughout the Stuart period men extolled the golden fleece: the woollen industry was the chief employer of labour at home and the stoutest prop of foreign trade. It was the earliest of manufactures and the most widespread. It provided full-time employment for many, and enabled small farmers to supplement their meagre profits by the spinning of their families at home. It permitted both large- and small-scale production, although the tendency in most localities was to concentrate the control of cloth-making into few hands.

One feature of the textile industry in the seventeenth century must not be overlooked—the new drapery. The religious refugees from the Netherlands in the 1560's had introduced the manufacture of fustian, a coarse cloth made of cotton and flax. The main centre for this was Lancashire, particularly Manchester and Bolton, and before the end of James's reign a petition stated that there were at least forty thousand pieces of fustian made every year. The flax used came from Ireland, where its growth was much stimulated by the efforts of Wentworth, and the cotton (or cotton wool as it was then called) came from the Levant. It is doubtful whether any pure-cotton fabrics were manufactured in England at this time.[2]

The textile industry by 1603 had reached the point at which the handicraft system had been overtaken by the putting-out

---

[1] Speech on 14 Feb. 1621. *Commons Debates 1621*, ii. 76.
[2] George W. Daniels, *The Early English Cotton Industry* (1920), chap. i.

system. Yorkshire and Devonshire were two counties where the former was still prevalent. During a debate in the house oi commons in 1614, one of the members for Yorkshire said there were 13,000 men employed in the cloth industry within ten miles of his home, of whom 2,000 were householders with stock (or capital) worth not more than £20, in many cases not more than £5.[1] A few years later a writer on Devonshire tells of the husbandman's sending his wool to the market, where it is bought by the spinner. The latter brings the yarn back the following week to sell to the weaver, who in his turn sells the cloth to a clothier ('who sends it to London') or merchant, 'who (after it hath passed the fuller's mill and sometimes the dyer's vat)' exports it.[2] These two descriptions of the old method of cloth-making incidentally reveal its weaknesses. The crafts-man's small capital compelled a quick sale, and thus not only wasted time by enforcing attendance at the market each week but put the seller at the mercy of the buyer, for the former had to sell the product he had finished before he could buy the raw materials for another week's work. The prices, therefore, were low, and there seems to be no evidence to prove that the spinner was better off under the handicraft or gild system than under the putting-out.

In striking contrast to the poverty that attended the crafts-man was the affluence of the clothier. He was the capitalist of the clothing industry, and was often a large employer.[3] State-ments to the effect that a clothier gave employment to several hundred or even a thousand workmen are not uncommon, and the wealth some of them amassed proves that they engaged in large-scale operations. A fortune of many thousands of pounds, even of a hundred thousand pounds, awaited the entrepreneur who was bold and successful. Such a man had no resemblance to the medieval gildsman, who had himself been an apprentice —perhaps a journeyman—before becoming a master. The en-trepreneur was a product of a new age, who might never have been engaged in any branch of cloth-making, but who never-theless might control all the stages through which the wool passed before it was ready for sale as cloth. He or his agents visited the local markets, bought up the wool, and distributed

[1] Commons' Journals, i. 491.
[2] Thomas Westcote, A View of Devonshire in MDCXXX (1845), p. 61.
[3] Here and elsewhere the meaning of 'employer' is 'one who gives out work'.

it among the cottagers, whose spinning-wheels turned it into yarn. The yarn was then collected and taken to weavers, who owned their own looms and wove it into cloth at piece rates. Others might be employed to finish, bleach (by washing), and dye the cloth before it was ready for the market. In cases where a single clothier did not control all the different processes of the industry, there were middlemen ready to undertake one or more of the stages, and to take their percentage of profit.

The middlemen who were the objects of much undiscriminating criticism were the wool-brokers. In the late middle ages they had performed an essential task and had been organized as a society of staplers, with their staple at Calais. After the loss of this town in Mary's reign, the staple had been moved, first to Middelburg and then to Bruges, but was abolished altogether by a proclamation in 1617, on the ground that the whole process of the manufacture of wool should be completed at home. Staples were accordingly to be established in London and twenty-two other places; and staplers, notwithstanding any previous regulations, might buy wool anywhere in England and sell it at any staple.[1] They seem to have taken full advantage of the privileges thus afforded them and to have performed the useful function of supplying clothiers with wool from districts far from their immediate neighbourhoods. Thereby they contributed to the breaking down of the provincialism that hampered the expansion of industry. On the other hand charges were freely bruited abroad that they 'engrossed' most of the wool and were consequently able to sell at their own rates. Moreover the fact that they bought in different areas resulted in a mixture of wool of varying qualities, which was naïvely thought to result in poor cloth—in reality much of the reputation of English woollens rested on skill in mixing different wools. The most famous centre for the buying and selling of cloth was Bakewell (or Blackwell) Hall, near the Guildhall. It served both as a warehouse and as a market-place, and was supposed to have a monopoly of all sales within the capital. However, the monopoly was avoided by another kind of middleman known as the factor, who was an intermediary between the clothier and his customer, the draper or wholesale dealer. Like the staplers, the factors were denounced as aiming at their own

---

[1] Steele, no. 1197.

profit and forcing up prices, but some of them, at least, were useful agents for clothiers in distant parts of England, who could not afford the time to go to London themselves.[1]

It is impossible to state categorically whether the woollen industry expanded under the early Stuarts or not. Probably it did, but there is no doubt that it nevertheless suffered from two severe depressions, one in the twenties and the other during the civil wars. A committee of the privy council was nominated to inquire into the causes of the earlier depression, and apparently questioned all and sundry engaged in the clothing trade. The committee eventually reported that the diminished trade was due to the increase in the manufacture of cloth abroad and to the wars on the Continent (which hampered the trade thither), the restrictive policy of the merchant, the changing fashions in England (which dictated the wearing of silks and foreign stuffs instead of woollen cloth), and the deceits and impositions in making or dyeing English cloth.[2] Some of the evidence presented to the committee underlines the points in its report. The drapers, for example, complained that bad cloth was made, and, through the corruption and remissness of the alnager, was disposed of privately and not offered for sale in the public markets, where it could be checked. Their particular remedy was that clothiers, dyers, weavers, and so on should be restricted to their proper trades (and that, in particular, the first-named should not be allowed to control all branches of the industry) and that the cloth should be examined and sealed before sale. Merchants had their own special grievances in the monopolies of trade, in certain areas, that were enjoyed by the different chartered companies. The Merchant Adventurers asserted that the Dutch had taken advantage of the English regulations for dyeing and dressing cloth to make their own cloth, which, though coarse, was used in Germany. They and others complained of the export of wool. One fact occurs over and over again in the records of these years: the clothiers everywhere had larger stocks on their hands than they could sell. There was evidently a glut in the market, probably caused by the reduction of exports and possibly by an increase in manufacture. The obvious measure of relief seemed to be that the clothiers should dismiss their workmen and cease to make cloth

---

[1] Both the staplers and the factors are discussed in Lipson, *The Economic History of England*, ii. 26–31.   [2] *State Papers, Domestic, 1619–1623* (1858), p. 410.

until existing supplies were exhausted. The paternal government of James I, however, viewed with disfavour this simple, if cruel, method of adjusting supply and demand. The privy council, therefore, wrote round to the justices of the peace to urge the clothiers not to discharge their workfolk, who, 'being many in number and most of them of the poorer sort', were likely to disturb the public peace by their clamours if deprived of their means of livelihood. Similarly the justices were to prevent any wool-grower from engrossing the wools and keeping them two, three, or more years to enhance the price. They then proceeded to lay down a golden rule for wool-grower, clothier, and merchant alike: whoever made a profit during the prosperous years of the reign must, now, in the decay of trade, bear such a share of the public loss as might best conduce to the general good and the maintenance of trade.[1]

The woollen industry shared in the prosperity that attended English trade in the 1630's, but during the last twenty years of the period suffered severely. During the civil wars there were complaints from all parts of the country of the decay of trade in general and particularly of the clothing trade. Some of the causes were directly attributed to the war. There was much plundering in order to secure cloth for the soldiers, and a certain amount of destruction of wool through the use of woolpacks as alternatives to sandbags. Then there was the interruption of communication between different parts of the kingdom owing to the presence of hostile forces. This was the more serious because many localities were dependent upon others, at a distance, for the supply of wool or half-finished cloth. The heavy taxation drained away much of the ready money available and, combined with the uncertainty of the times, made merchants unwilling to buy more than a bare minimum. There was also much danger in trying to export cloth, for pirates were very active and were reinforced, during and after 1648, by Rupert's royalist privateers. Once again, however, the main cause of the falling off of exports was alleged to be the poor quality of the cloth. In 1642 Sir Henry Vane reported, from a committee concerned with the diminishing sales of Suffolk cloth, that, out of fourteen or fifteen thousand cloths, nine or ten thousand were falsely made[2]—a complaint that meant little

---

[1] *Acts of the Privy Council, 1621–1623* (1932), pp. 131–3.
[2] *Commons' Journals,* ii. 528.

more than that clothiers were adapting their goods to a changing demand—and there is ample evidence that the control of
the manufacture of cloth had broken down. Moreover the
foreigners made cloth for themselves—because, as old-fashioned
critics alleged, they could no longer depend upon a high standard in the English product—and undersold their English
rivals. In this they are said to have been much helped by
clothiers and workmen who had gone abroad.[1]

Among the more popular remedies proposed was the revival
of regulation. A number of bills were introduced into the Long
Parliament for preventing this or that abuse, but it proved
easier to denounce evils than to find cures for them. Among
the ordinances actually passed were those prohibiting the exportation of wool and exempting wool from the excise imposed
on it in 1653. In 1650 there was passed an act for regulating
the making of stuffs in Norfolk and Norwich, which set up a
corporation of master weavers who were to enforce the use of
a common seal, see that worsted yarns maintained a certain
quality and length, and examine all stuffs before they were
sealed.[2] On the whole, therefore, the commonwealth and protectorate did little for the woollen industry except to keep the
peace at home, but even the benefits thus conferred were
neutralized by the war against Spain, which cut off one of the
clothiers' best customers. It was unfortunate for the industry
that the difficulties caused by wars both at home and abroad
came at a time when the old system of national regulation was
breaking down. Actually, with the gild system outgrown, there
was no efficient machinery available to enforce a high standard
of craftsmanship.

The length of the foregoing treatment of the textile industry
can be justified on two grounds: that this industry was easily
the most important of the time, and that it was the most advanced in business technique. But, on these very accounts, it
cannot be accepted as typical of industry in general. Moreover
it was by no means the only industry to merit consideration. In
the aggregate there were signs (somewhat obscured, it is true,
by the political and religious ferment agitating England) that
foreshadowed, sometimes faintly and sometimes distinctly, the
beginning of a new era in the economic history of England. In

---

[1] *State Papers, Domestic, 1650* (1876), pp. 21–22, 178–81.
[2] *Acts and Ordinances*, ii. 451–5; cf. ibid., pp. 775–80.

the first place there was no likelihood of any further expansion of the older branches of the textile industry—indeed, they were hardly holding their own—although some of the newer fabrics were already experiencing a healthy growth. In the second place there was increased specialization and localization. Thirdly certain industries, most of which were not new, grew in importance. It was already clear that they were destined to flourish in the future. It was equally obvious that they were going to be increasingly organized on a capitalistic basis—that the liquor of the housewife was to be replaced by the beer of the brewery, that the making of salt was likely in time to be confined to a few suitable districts, that glass made in England would supplant the imported article, and that mining would go on thriving until it had become one of the leading industries. Already there was a very considerable coal trade, some of it coastwise, especially to London, some of it abroad. Indeed England was even then the largest producer of coal in Europe. These and other indications pointed to a rapid industrial growth in England as soon as the course of politics promised internal peace.

The condition of the working classes in the seventeenth century was largely determined by the Elizabethan act of 1563, frequently called the Statute of Apprentices or of Artificers.[1] That famous act had attempted to reduce into a coherent whole many former statutes. It enacted that those engaged in certain employments[2] should be hired by the year, and that single persons of any age, and all persons under thirty, not possessing lands or tenements worth 40s. per annum or goods of the value of ten pounds, should labour in the crafts in which they had been brought up, and that persons not otherwise employed, and without property of the annual value of 40s., should labour at agriculture. Such labourers must not leave, without a licence, the place in which they had been employed. Merchants should take as apprentices only those whose fathers possessed a 40s. freehold,[3] and should bind them to serve for seven years. In

---

[1] 5 Eliz., c. 4, *Statutes of the Realm*, iv (1819), 414–22.

[2] Which included all those concerned in the textile industry, shoemakers, bakers, brewers, smiths, butchers, and millers.

[3] This applied to the inhabitants of a corporate town—otherwise the sum was three pounds. There were exceptions in favour of smiths, carpenters, rough masons, plasterers, bricklayers, &c.

specified occupations every master was to employ one journeyman, if he had three apprentices, and an extra journeyman for
every additional apprentice. Disputes between masters and
apprentices were to be settled by the justices of the peace. These
magistrates were empowered to fix the rates of wages, at the
Easter quarter-sessions, and to enforce their schedule by fine
and imprisonment. The hours for artificers, and labourers hired
for wages, were to be from 5 a.m. until between 7 and 8 p.m. in
the summer, and from daylight to dusk in the winter, with an
allowance of not more than two and a half hours for meals.
This statute was continued by another passed at the beginning
of James's reign, with the added stipulations that the power of
the magistrates to establish wages was extended to all labourers,
weavers, and spinners, and that the clothier was not to act as a
justice when rating the wages of weavers and spinners.[1]

During the fourteenth and fifteenth centuries wages had
largely been settled by the gilds, although from the time of the
Ordinance of Labourers (1349) the state had not hesitated to
try to fix the remuneration of unskilled workers. From the
sixteenth to the eighteenth centuries the central government
endeavoured to regulate wages through the agency of the justices of the peace. The Statute of Artificers laid down the
principle that wages should conform to the dearness or cheapness of living. The difficulty was to keep the justices up to the
mark, and the privy council not infrequently applied the spur.
Thus, in 1614 the justices of Wiltshire were ordered to call the
neighbouring clothiers before them and find out whether it was
true that they were paying their weavers only what was given
them forty years ago, in spite of the fact that prices of all kinds
of foods were almost double what they had been then. The
justices were required to see that the weavers' wages were in
proportion to the dear times.[2] The wage-earners seem to have
recognized the benefits they derived from the wage assessments,
inasmuch as they are found petitioning the council to compel the justices to issue a schedule of wages. It is also significant
that, of the surviving wage assessments, there are more for the
years of personal government (1629–40) than for any period
of corresponding length.

As to the amounts of the wages, a recitation of figures would

---

[1] Jac. I, c. 6, *Statutes of the Realm*, iv. 1022–4.
[2] *Acts of the Privy Council, 1613–1614* (1921), pp. 457–8.

mean little without greater knowledge than is at present available of how the labourer spent what he earned and of what additional sources of income he had. Moreover it rarely happens that there are sufficient assessments for any one county to permit a useful comparison of rates of wages fixed at different times. Wiltshire is an exception, for assessments are extant, for that county, for 1603, 1635, and 1655. In the first year wheat was cheap; in the second, dear; and the third includes a harvest when the price of wheat was the lowest of the century.[1] The curious thing is that, whereas the skilled labourer's rate was considerably more (about 50 per cent.) in 1655 than in 1603, the common day labourer's was precisely the same. In the last year, as in the first, he was rated at 3*d.* a day, with meat and drink, or 7*d.* a day without—and an additional penny in each case during the summer months. If rates for piece-work are considered, the increase in wages between 1603 and 1655 is found to be 22 per cent. It may be that, if account were taken of the fact that the last wage assessment was made in a time of great cheapness, the rise of real wages would be considerably greater. Such other assessments as exist tend to confirm the evidence of those from Wiltshire and would suggest that economic conditions, particularly demand and supply, had as much weight in determining wages as the action of the state. Probably the explanation of the rising wages of the skilled, and the stationary wages of the unskilled, is the relative scarcity of the former type of labour and the abundance of the latter. The commonwealth accepted the principle that had been laid down in the Elizabethan statute and ordered it to be put into effect,[2] but it is doubtful whether the republican council of state was as anxious to enforce the law about wages as the king's privy council had been.

It seems obvious that the wages paid were not expected to be the sole income of a family, for the labourer with a wife and children could not have supported them properly on his own earnings.[3] He must have relied on their defraying part of the household expenses, and have contrived to make both ends meet with the help of the pennies they received. In those days women often toiled in the fields like men (although paid less),

---

[1] J. E. Thorold Rogers, *History of Agriculture and Prices* (1887), v. 184, 200, 210.

[2] *Commons' Journals*, vi. 180-1.

[3] See Alice Clark, *Working Life of Women in the Seventeenth Century* (1919), pp. 69–73.

and their children with them. Otherwise, they stayed at home spinning monotonously for hours on end. There seems to have been a curious reluctance on the part of the government to admit that there had come permanently into existence a labouring class dependent solely upon wages, and without any land at all on which to raise their daily bread. There is this excuse to be advanced—that outside the larger towns there were relatively few labourers. On the other hand there were many artisans employed in the textile industry. The fewness of the former and the multitude of the latter explain why there was a distinction made in the wage assessments—a maximum wage was fixed for the ordinary labourer, with penalties to punish the employer who exceeded the established rate, but for the textile artisan there was a minimum wage, with liberty to the employer to pay as much more as he thought requisite.[1] It is clear that there was a scarcity of labourers but an excess of artisans. The legislation dealing with wages was in conformity with the economic tendencies of the age, but other laws were in contradiction, and their enforcement was often in the hands of those most interested in seeing them remain a dead letter. Acts of parliament, or proclamations, might try to maintain the husbandman, but actually the growth of capitalism and farming for profit were creating a large class whose means of existence was entirely derived from wages. And economic forces proved stronger than the early Stuarts.

Throughout the seventeenth century the relief of the poor depended upon the famous Elizabethan statute of 1601.[2] According to that enactment, the churchwardens of every parish, together with substantial householders, were to be nominated yearly by two or more justices of the peace as overseers of the poor. The overseers were charged with setting to work the children of paupers and all without adequate means and daily employment, with raising by taxation such sums of money as they thought necessary to provide a convenient stock of flax, hemp, wool, thread, iron, and other wares for the employment of the poor, with granting relief to the lame, impotent, old, blind, and such others as were poor and not able to labour, and

[1] For the whole question of the assessment of wages, see R. H. Tawney, in *Vierteljahrschrift für Sozial- und Wirtschaftsgeschichte*, xi (1913).

[2] 43 Eliz., c. 2, *Statutes of the Realm*, iv. 962–5. This statute was a re-enactment of that of 1597, with slight changes. The latter is reprinted in J. R. Tanner, *Tudor Constitutional Documents* (1930), pp. 488–94.

with apprenticing pauper children. In the event of the able-bodied poor refusing to perform the tasks allotted to them, they might be sent to the house of correction. In order to provide dwellings for the poor, the overseers might erect houses on waste or common land within their parish (with the leave of the lord of the manor). With exceptions for certain deserving classes begging was strictly forbidden. By another act the justices of the peace were to cause to be erected one or more houses of correction in every county or city in order that all rogues, vagabonds, and sturdy beggars might, after being whipped, be sent to a house of correction, unless the place of birth or residence for one year of the culprit was known, in which case he or she was to be sent from parish to parish until reaching the place of birth or last legal residence.

Probably a mistake was made in fixing so small an area as a parish as the unit of poor relief, because the overseers were often more concerned to save their neighbours' pockets by restricting relief than to afford proper aid to the needy. Certainly the anxiety of overseers of the poor that new-comers should not become a charge on the parish often worked great hardship. Thus a labouring man born in a parish and working there all his life might find, on marrying a woman living elsewhere, that the overseers would not permit her to reside in the parish lest the expected family should become a charge on the poor rates. Sometimes the overseers would not allow a couple to continue to dwell in their own village after marriage.[1] Such actions might well create vagrants out of hitherto self-supporting men and women, but the parish responsible for the social crime might be able to avoid maintaining them. More reasonable was the attempt to prevent the settlement of strangers by fining heavily landlords or lodging-house keepers who provided a roof for intruders. In fact the first regulations against overcrowding were inspired as much by fear of increased poor rates as by dread of visitations of the plague in insanitary tenements.

The enforcement of statutes in the seventeenth century mainly depended upon the attitude of the justices of the peace and on the success or failure of the privy council in goading them into activity. So far as a partial examination of defective materials enables a judgement to be pronounced, it is probable that the enforcement of the statutes regulating poor relief was somewhat

[1] Alice Clark, op. cit., pp. 80–83.

spasmodic in the reign of James I (except during 1621–3) and much more systematic under Charles I, particularly during the years of personal government. The years of scarcity between 1621 and 1623 gave a temporary stimulus to the relief of the poor, and those of 1629–31 had a more permanent effect. During the first period, the danger of famine and the fear of the rioting that it might cause made the government unusually active, and they in their turn influenced the local authorities. Among the remedies put into force were the severe limitation of the quantity of malt that might be used for brewing—'barley is in time of scarcitie the bread-corne of the poore'[1]—and the suppression of unnecessary alehouses, even up to 50 per cent. In some places local authorities or individuals bought wheat and sold it to the poor at less than the market price. In London, during 1630–1, the most elaborate measures were taken to help the destitute. The population was numbered and found to be 130,000; hence it was calculated that 5,000 quarters of wheat would be necessary to serve the inhabitants presumably for two weeks, and each liveried company was ordered to provide its quota and to sell it cheaply to the needy. If a farmer was detected in profiting by a time of scarcity to obtain a high price for his corn, the usual penalty imposed was that he should now sell it well below the market price.

Other calamities which severely exercised the local authorities were the plague and fires. During visitations of the plague an attempt was made to isolate the victims, and this naturally compelled their support. The alternative method was to erect pesthouses, as they were called, and local records show much activity in this direction. In some places a physician was hired to look after the poor. At a time when houses were still largely built of wood, disastrous fires were frequent. Sometimes a whole town would be practically razed to the ground. In this event, too, attempts were made to board the poor at neighbouring residences. In cases of especial calamity the council might authorize the use of circular letters or church briefs to permit collections to be made for the destitute.

In addition to these more or less compulsory measures of relief, philanthropy did a great deal to mitigate hardship. Almshouses and endowed charities existed in nearly every town,

---

[1] Proclamation of Oct. 1622, quoted in E. M. Leonard, *The Early History of English Poor Relief* (1900), p. 145.

some being survivals from medieval times, some more recent foundations. Among the latter the most notable was the Charterhouse, endowed by Thomas Sutton, who left a large sum of money to establish a hospital for pensioners (not to exceed 80) and a school to maintain and educate 40 boys. Sometimes charities took the form of pensions or gifts of small amounts. Occasionally the overseers of the poor imitated the charitable and granted what is called today outdoor relief, paying the impotent poor a weekly amount, or billeting them. These varied methods, whenever local authorities were energetic, should have sufficed to look after the aged or maimed.

For pauper children the favourite device seems to have been to apprentice them to some trade. Sometimes individuals like Archbishop Laud would provide funds for apprenticing a number of children; or local authorities would have recourse to a special tax. This way of providing for children whose parents could not look after them had an additional merit in the eyes of the seventeenth-century moralists—that children should be taught at an early age the virtues of work. For those of more tender years provision might be made that they be taught knitting or spinning.

During the civil wars the condition of the poor deteriorated rapidly. The destruction of trade threw many out of work; the excise, being levied on many of the necessities of life, was an added burden; the income of charitable institutions fell off so greatly that they could maintain fewer sufferers (although they were freed from taxes);[1] and there were a marked decrease in charity and a slackness of local agencies, now that they were no longer spurred on by the privy council. In addition, the advent to power of the middle class unduly aggravated the sufferings of the poor, inasmuch as the former were inclined to regard material success as the reward of righteousness, and poverty of sinfulness, particularly laziness. To work hard and to get rich were thought worthy ambitions, but to be poor and out of work appeared disgraceful rather than unfortunate. From the time of Hugh Latimer onwards, preachers were fond of quoting St. Paul's remark that 'if any would not work, neither should he eat',[2] and of emphasizing the greater opportunities

[1] By a series of ordinances beginning 16 Nov. 1644.
[2] Thess. iii. 10. Cf. L. B. Wright, *Middle-class Culture in Elizabethan England* (1935), chap. 6.

of service that the rich enjoyed as compared with the poor. Consequently, when the authorities were moved to action, especially during the brief ascendancy of the major-generals, they were more anxious to suppress vagrancy than to relieve the impotent poor or to provide work for the unemployed.

There was nothing very novel about the legislation for the relief of the poor passed during the commonwealth and protectorate. There was urgent need to deal with the question of the high price of corn, for 1646 had been the first of six bad harvests, with the result that the average price of wheat during these years was nearly 60s., and for the years 1647–9, 65s.[1] On the whole the act of 1650 followed traditional lines. A licence was necessary before wheat or other grain could be purchased in order to be sold as meal or flour, all material had to be sold in the open market, and offenders were denied the writ of habeas corpus. Other measures were the provision of coal cheaply, a renewed attempt to stop corn-engrossing, permission to export all kinds of corn when certain fixed prices were not exceeded in the home market, and the establishment of the London Corporation for the Poor. In addition to these measures actually adopted, the pamphlets of the time propounded many remedies to cure unemployment, some of which seem strangely modern. Among the latter the most interesting is an anticipation of the labour exchange, by a proposal to establish a poor man's office where masters might meet and engage servants.[2]

On the whole the evidence confirms a recent verdict that the poor-law policy of the interregnum leaves a general impression of 'harshness coupled with failure'. This lack of success contrasts very unfavourably with the improvement effected by Charles I and the privy council between 1629 and 1640. A pamphleteer in 1648 indignantly denied that a man might do what he liked with his own,[3] but in practice there was less disposition to check ruthless exploitation during the puritan régime than during the personal government of the Stuarts.

Among the most unfortunate classes in England was the debtor. The law permitted a creditor to cause the imprisonment of his debtor,

---

[1] Rogers, *History of Agriculture*, v. 205.

[2] Margaret James, *Social Problems and Policy during the Puritan Revolution, 1640–1660* (1930), p. 278. My obligations to this book are much greater than a few references might suggest.   [3] Ibid., p. 265.

> Tear forth the fathers of poor families
> Out of their beds, and coffin them alive
> In some kind clasping prison, where their bones
> May be forth-coming, when the flesh is rotten.[1]

If, however, a creditor had a debtor imprisoned, no other mode of execution was open to him.[2] An act passed in James's reign[3] was more concerned with the interests of the creditors than with the unhappy plight of the debtor, because it merely stated that, as divers persons owning both real and personal estate had wilfully chosen to live and die in confinement rather than to pay their just debts, their lands and goods were liable for a new execution after their death. When incarcerated, the debtor's lot varied directly according to his means. As a petition in 1660 stated, prisons were sanctuaries for the rich and able debtors, but murdering dens of cruelty to poor men and women.[4] Those with money in their pockets could hire comfortable quarters, but the poor debtor was left dependent on alms for the barest necessities of life, and received nothing at all from the authorities except a place of confinement, which was usually filthy and overcrowded. In 1649 a petition of many thousand poor distressed prisoners for debt stated that they were destitute of any means of support for themselves or their families and were about to perish, as many had recently done, for want of bread. They asked that those who had some means might be allowed to compound with their creditors, and that those who had nothing and were likely to be buried alive in prison might be released.[5] A few months after the petition, an act was passed ordering the release of prisoners whose worldly goods did not exceed five pounds (4 September 1649). Other acts of a similar nature were passed from time to time, and a more comprehensive measure was framed (5 October 1653); and a number of persons were named to see that the debtors were not overcharged by the prison authorities.

Most prisons in which debtors were confined, such as the Fleet, were virtually the property of the wardens, who held the office in serjeanty. The warden had to make a living and to pay his assistants from the fees and rents which were extorted

---

[1] Ben Jonson, *The Fox*, Act I, sc. i.
[2] Holdsworth, *History of English Law*, viii. 231.
[3] 21 Jac. I, c. 24, *Statutes of the Realm*, iv. 1233.
[4] *Hist. MSS. Com., Seventh Report* (1879), p. 141.   [5] Ibid., pp. 113–14.

from the inmates. The servility to the well-to-do and the harshness to the poverty-stricken which such a system engendered were graphically described by a great novelist in the eighteenth century, and his picture would have been equally true to life one hundred years before.[1]

It is ironical that the lot of the criminal in jail was, in one respect at least, superior to that of the unfortunate debtor. It was the business of the responsible authority to provide food for the criminal in prison, and there are cases known in which a physician was provided to look after him when sick. Regular levies seem to have been made for the maintenance of felons in jail, though the penny a day provided can have supplied only the most meagre diet.[2] Occasionally references are found to acts of kindness on the part of jailers, but normally brutal severity was displayed towards prisoners. An example of the treatment meted out to them is that of Thomas Laycoke, whose only offence was travelling without permission: a lock and chain were fastened on one of his legs and he was shut up in a damp room at a bridewell for ten days, without fire or candle, and stripped and inhumanly lashed. It is apparent, too, that women sometimes fared as badly.[3] In addition to the brutality of jailers, the prisoner was exposed to the diseases bred by insanitary conditions and insufficient diet, and the rate of mortality was shockingly high. The penalty of death was awarded for scores of felonies, and executions were frequent, but the fevers which were endemic produced more effective jail deliveries than any hanging judge.

One social evil which caused much concern to magistrates, especially to those of puritanical dispositions, was the large number of people who lived by their wits. Both the countryside and the towns seem to have swarmed with rogues and vagabonds, sturdy beggars and sharpers, or cony-catchers, as they were then called. In London, in particular, every device was employed to trap and cheat the gull.[4] Bowling alleys, brothels, gaming-houses, and taverns were full of cheats looking for some innocent to be fleeced, and, if they spared their victim

[1] Henry Fielding, *Amelia*.

[2] *Warwick County Records*, vol. i (1933), ed. S. C. Ratcliff and H. C. Johnson, pp. 6, 14–15, 20, &c.

[3] *Extracts from State Papers Relating to Friends*, ed. Norman Penney (1913), p. 17.

[4] Many examples are recorded in *County of Middlesex, Calendar to the Sessions Records*, N.S., ed. W. Le Hardy, i (1935).

anything, there were plenty of pickpockets and highwaymen to take what was left. At the end of the civil wars these parasites seem to have multiplied, and during the commonwealth severe measures were adopted against them. Thus, on 26 June 1657, it was enacted that all wandering, idle, loose, dissolute, and disorderly persons were to be flogged as rogues and sent to a house of correction, and another ordinance of the same date was levelled against persons living at high rates, with no visible calling to maintain them in their licentious and ungodly practices. Moreover, anyone caught winning money at cards, dice, or by betting was to forfeit double the sum gained. There is no sign, however, that it was found possible to enforce these ordinances, and in default of an adequate constabulary they must have been, for the most part, a dead letter.

There remain for consideration the changes the puritans tried to make in the social habits and customs of Englishmen, and the extent of their accomplishment.[1] Thanks to their military success against Charles I and the cavaliers, the puritans had, during 1642–60, their one opportunity in English history to enact inhibitory laws,[2] and to try to enforce their moral code. They were inspired by an intense conviction of a common responsibility for sin. They thought an emphatic affirmative should be given the question, 'Am I my brother's keeper?', and believed that it was possible by legislation to remedy the existing social system and to cure the evils to which flesh is prone. They over-estimated the power of laws and the effectiveness of legal punishments. They did not distinguish between vice and crime, and theological considerations exercised great influence in determining their views of crime and punishment. Accepting the Scriptures as an absolute rule of life, they wished to remodel the laws of England upon the code delivered by Moses to the Israelites. In this respect they were very like their brethren in Massachusetts, who, in the Epistle prefixed to *The Laws and Liberties of Massachusetts* (1648),[3] wrote:

So soon as God had set up politicall government among his people

---

[1] This section owes much to some unpublished lectures which the late Sir Charles Firth most generously placed at my disposal.

[2] There had been, of course, plenty of laws against immorality or other vices under the early Stuarts, but they had been less draconic, less frequently enforced, and never put into operation by major-generals.

[3] Reprinted by the Harvard University Press, 1929, for the Huntington Library, with an Introduction by Max Farrand.

Israel hee gave them a body of lawes for judgement both in civil and criminal causes. These were breif and fundamental principles, yet withall so full and comprehensive as out of them clear deductions were to be drawne to all particular cases in future times.

As an example of the adoption of biblical law in both countries may be cited the punishment of adultery with death. In 1650, in England, an act to this effect was passed, but its severe penalties nullified its authors' intentions. A careful inquiry[1] has revealed only three, or perhaps four, cases in which the conviction of a culprit was followed by the infliction of death. Between 1651 and 1659 twenty-three persons were indicted for that offence before Middlesex juries, but with one exception the verdict was always 'not guilty'. As it is improbable the evidence was so often insufficient, it is clear that the jurymen would not convict in view of the extreme penalty. In fact the consequence of making the law so severe was that the evildoer escaped scot-free.

On the other hand legislation was more successful in repressing practices generally abhorred. At the beginning of this period duelling was very prevalent and threatened to become more so. Thanks to the civil wars, London was infested with disbanded soldiers, cashiered officers, and young bloods known as Hectors, and all these were constantly picking quarrels about punctilios. Accordingly an ordinance was issued that any person sending or receiving a challenge and not informing the authorities within twenty-four hours should be imprisoned for six months. Any person fighting a duel and killing his antagonist was declared guilty of murder and was to suffer the legal penalty therefor. Even when no death took place, both the principals and their seconds were condemned to banishment for life. This legislation was fairly successful, for public opinion supported it and a jury did not hesitate to convict a duellist.[2]

Equal zeal was shown in an attempt to repress minor offences against morality, such as drunkenness, swearing, and gambling. Of these, the first was naturally the most widespread and the most difficult to suppress. Even under the rule of the puritans the judicial records of the period supply evidence of the drinking habits of all classes.[3] Moreover men rather gloried in their

---

[1] F. A. Inderwick, *The Interregnum* (1891), pp. 33–38.   [2] Ibid., pp. 28–31.
[3] For earlier conditions, see H. G. Hudson, *A Study of Social Regulations in England under James I and Charles I: Drink and Tobacco* (1933).

excesses than felt ashamed of them. One boasted that he had been drunk so often in the last year that the magistrate could hardly find pens, ink, and paper enough to record all occasions. The government, and those legal authorities who shared the views of the government, tried every kind of device to cure this evil. Thus, from time to time justices would prohibit the conversion of barley into malt, partly because of the scarcity of wheat and partly because 'sober people abhorred the multitude of ale-houses'. At Nottingham some burgesses presented a petition to the Corporation against the excessive number of ale-houses in the town: 'Your petitioners (by sad experience) have observed that by permitting soe many unnecessary alehouses and tipling houses within this towne, the name of God is much dishonoured, his day profaned, and his cretures abused.'[1] But their championing of temperance was rendered suspect by their petition that henceforth none but burgesses should be permitted to brew beer.

Another way of dealing with the problem was to close all public houses on Sundays and fast days, to draw up a report on the number of ale-houses necessary for each parish, and to refuse to grant any new licences on the death of the present innkeepers till such time as the number should be reduced to the quota thought needful for each parish. Generally speaking, the justices of the peace showed little energy in the work of reformation. Hence, in 1655, when Cromwell divided England into districts and appointed a major-general to undertake the policing of each district, their instructions strictly charged them to suppress unnecessary ale-houses.[2] They carried out their instructions with singular vigour. Thus one major-general in a few months closed a third of the ale-houses in Warwickshire. Another was equally energetic and declared that the suppressed houses had been cages of all uncleanness and wickedness, and that the object of the law in licensing inns was not to set up houses to tipple in but to make provision for entertainment of strangers and travellers. However, the rule of the major-generals ended at the close of 1656 and most of the justices did not imitate them.

Severe measures were taken, too, against swearing. By an act of 1650 a scale of fines was imposed, graduated according to the rank of the offender. A duke paid 30s. for his first offence,

---

[1] *Records of the Borough of Nottingham*, v (1900), 250.
[2] D. W. Rannie, 'Cromwell's Ma:or-Generals', *Eng. Hist. Rev.* x. 495-6.

a baron 20*s.*, and a squire 10*s.*, and inferior persons 3*s.* 4*d.*—
double fines were imposed for a second offence. Women were
charged for expletives according to the rank of their fathers or
husbands. Those who could not pay their fines were to be set
in the stocks for from three to six hours. Some magistrates
enforced this act with great severity. Not only did they exact
the maximum fine for each oath, but they punished singularly
mild asseverations. Thus one man had to pay fines for saying
'God is my witness' and 'I speak in the presence of God', and
another had to pay his 3*s.* 4*d.* for saying 'Upon my life'.[1] In fact,
apparently any kind of interjection might be costly.

   Some of the legislation passed by the Long Parliament was
inspired both by rigid theology and by zeal for pure morality.
Thus the observation of certain church festivals was abhorrent
to puritans, but they were all in favour of prescribing other days
to be strictly observed as fasts. For example the traditional
method of celebrating Christmas was thought by parliament
to give 'liberty to carnal and sensual delights'. Accordingly, in
1644, 25 December was ordered to be kept as a fast day, in order
that all might call to remembrance their own sins and those of
their forefathers in transforming a day sacred to the memory
of Christ into an occasion of revelry. Three years later, it was
forbidden to observe Easter, Whitsuntide, and other festivals.
These regulations met with much opposition in many parts of
England. Even in London, members, as they walked down to
Westminster on Christmas Day in 1656 to attend parliament,
could not but observe that the tradesmen had shut up shop and
were keeping the day as a holiday. There was a debate on the
subject that morning. 'The house is thin', commented a colonel,
'much, I believe, occasioned by observation of this day. I have
a short bill to prevent the superstition for the future.' A major-
general continued the debate: 'If ever bill was well timed this
bill is. You see how the people keep up these superstitious
observances to your face; stricter, in many places, than they
do the Lord's day.' Another member complained: 'I could get
no rest all night for the preparation of this foolish day's solem-
nity. This renders us, in the eyes of the people, to be profane.
We are, I doubt, returning to popery.'[2] The bill was read once,
and then passed into oblivion.

---

[1] Hamilton, *Quarter Sessions*, p. 154.
[2] *Burton Diary*, i. 229–30.

Instead of festivals, the puritans prescribed as a fast day the last Wednesday in every month, in addition to a number of extra fasts for special occasions. With rigid puritans, a fast day meant abstinence from every kind of food. A youth complains, 'Not one of us, young or old, ate so much as a morsel of bread for twenty four hours together, which was a great weariness to me and went much against my carnal heart.'[1] What made these fast days the more obnoxious to the generality was that the soldiery was used to enforce their observance. Thus, on a Christmas morning, a little before dinner-time, soldiers were sent round London to search all kitchens and ovens and to carry away any meat they found being cooked.

The observance of the Sabbath was equally rigid.[2] No less than three acts were passed to this end, each stricter and more detailed than the last. All agreed in prohibiting any kind of sport or pastime on Sundays and fast days. These rules were rigorously enforced. Moreover the common rights of Englishmen were violated in the interests of Sabbatarians when constables were authorized to search private houses without warrant if they suspected the inmates of profaning the Lord's day. Work of any kind was prohibited in the same thoroughgoing fashion. Not only was buying or selling or any outdoor work connected with industry or agriculture strictly forbidden, but all domestic labours which could be considered unnecessary. The words of the act were that 'no worldly labours or work of their ordinary calling' were to be done. Accordingly domestic servants became very fastidious and refused to cook the Sunday dinner or to clean their kitchens on that day. Indeed they were wise in their refusal, for there is an instance of a girl who worked on Sunday and was reported to the local minister. He demanded that she should pay ten shillings as a penalty if over fourteen, or, if younger, receive corporal chastisement. As soon as the minister went away, she was given two or three taps on the back with a branch of heather, 'such gentle touches on her cloathes', exclaimed the angry minister, 'as would not have hurt an infant of two dayes old'.[3] Another remarkable instance is afforded by a girl whose good deeds later earned for her the

---

[1] *The Autobiography of Joseph Lister*, p. 6.
[2] This subject is treated in W. B. Whitaker, *Sunday in Tudor and Stuart Times* (1933).
[3] *The Life of Adam Martindale*, ed. Richard Parkinson (1845), pp. 124–5.

honourable title of 'the Quaker Saint of Cornwall'. For mending her dress on Sunday she was denounced to the magistrates and, being unable to pay the fine, was set in the stocks. It was pouring with rain, which created a rivulet that ran over her. Nevertheless her brothers joined the crowd to jeer at her and taunted her that she must be proud of her legs, so to exhibit them to the public.

Travelling, by land or water, on Sunday was also denounced. Except going to church, every kind of locomotion was forbidden. Some benches of magistrates enforced these rules as strictly as possible. Thus a man and his wife and a pair of young persons described as sweethearts were convicted for walking abroad on the Sabbath. Another was condemned to pay ten shillings for walking into a neighbouring parish to hear a sermon. There were members of parliament for whom this prohibition of travelling did not go far enough. During a debate, one of them wanted to add a penalty upon all who idly sat at gates or doors or elsewhere. The zealot remarked that sitting on doorsteps as was usual could not be a sanctification of the Lord's day. Another thought this was not sufficiently comprehensive. 'Some persons', he said, 'have not conveniency to sit at doors, so I would have you add some to it, viz. leaning or standing at doors.' The clause was lost by only two votes.[1]

The zeal of the puritan to reform anything and everything was all-embracing. He was as ready to wage war against prevalent fashions as against fashionable vices. In fact the puritan revolution was in some respects a protest against social customs as well as against political or religious grievances. Quakerism, for example, might be regarded as one manifestation of the revolt of democracy against ceremoniousness in dress and speech. In one of the most interesting of quaker diaries, Thomas Ellwood, Milton's amanuensis, tells us that he began by giving up the vanities of worldly dress—'trimmings of lace, ribbons, and useless buttons, . . . by mistake called ornament'. Next he abandoned the use of the vain phrases that were the ornaments of discourse. Other renunciations followed, as, for instance, 'the giving of flattering titles to men between whom and me there was not any relation to which such titles could be pretended to belong. This was an evil I had been much addicted to, and was accounted a ready artist in; therefore this evil also was I

---

[1] *Burton Diary*, ii. 264–5.

required to put away and cease from. So that thenceforward I durst not say, Sir, Master, My Lord, Madam (or My Dame); or say Your Servant to any one to whom I did not stand in the real relation of a servant, which I had never done to any.'

Ellwood goes on to say that he abandoned the vain practice of uncovering the head or bowing the knee in salutation, but found many obstacles. As he insisted on not removing his hat in his father's presence, as a protest against 'hat honour', his father destroyed all his hats, one after another. When he addressed his father in the second person singular, his father fell upon him with his fists, saying, 'Sirrah, if ever I hear you say "thou" or "thee" to me again, I'll strike your teeth down your throat.'[1]

Others besides the quakers turned their attention to the vanities of this world. A preacher, for example, wrote a treatise on the loathsomeness of long hair.[2] As a matter of fact the habit of wearing long locks was giving way to a custom which puritans regarded with even greater aversion—namely, the wearing of wigs. 'These periwigs of false-coloured hair', says the preacher, 'are utterly unlawful and are condemned by Christ himself, who says "no man can make one hair white or black".'

From male attire, preachers turned to female fashions and found them evil. Englishwomen were said to be most immoderate, both in their tastes and their expenses, and many a sermon, pamphlet, and ballad treated of their vanity and exorbitances. The puritan objection to 'painting, patching, spotting, and blotting' is well summed up by Hamlet's remark to Ophelia about women, 'God has given you one face, and you make yourselves another'. To improve on nature argued dissatisfaction with God's work, and was held to be proof positive of sinful lusts. Face-repairers were reminded of the fate of Jezebel, who on Jehu's approach painted her face and sat at an upper window; but, when the king saw her, all he said was, 'Throw her down'; and dogs ate her flesh.

Accordingly parliament thought the time opportune for a revival of the old sumptuary laws to regulate the manners and dress of all classes of the community. The hopes of men with expensive wives or daughters ran high. For example the English agent in Switzerland, John Pell, wrote home to his wife that,

---

[1] *The History of Thomas Ellwood*, ed. C. G. Crump (1900), pp. 18–19, 37–38.
[2] Thomas Hall, *Loathsomenesse of Long Haire* (1654).

on their daughter's approaching marriage, the cheapest trous-
seau would suffice, because parliament was about to impose a
severe penalty on all guilty of displaying excessive pride in their
clothes. If the bride's dress went beyond what the expected
statute permitted, and her husband's purse was made to smart
for it, 'let him thank himself, not blame the dotage of his wife's
mother, who loved to see her chickens decked in peacock's
feathers'.[1] This prudent father was doomed to disappointment,
however, for the bill was never passed.

The puritans' attitude towards amusements was influenced
partly by their fear lest, if people ceased to labour diligently
at their calling, the devil would find mischief for their idle
hands, and partly by the knowledge that the only leisure most
of them had was on Sunday, so that if they played any games
at all they would almost inevitably be guilty of profaning the
Sabbath.

The first amusement to be forbidden was the stage, whose
suppression is described elsewhere.[2] Bear-baiting and cock-
fighting were easily stopped, inasmuch as soldiers were employed to shoot the bears and twist the necks of the cocks. The
reason alleged for stopping these pastimes was that they were
commonly accompanied by betting, drinking, swearing, and
other dissolute practices. The same reasons justified, or attempted to justify, the prohibition of athletic sports. Thus parliament thought all who played such games as bowls or football
on Sunday[3] might justly be excluded from the sacrament of the
Lord's Supper. Various country recreations were frowned upon,
particularly maypoles and May games, on the ground that they
were habitually practised on Sundays. Maypoles, said an ordinance, were 'a heathenish vanity generally abused to superstition and wickedness'. That they were usually the occasion for
dancing made them especially objectionable. What was called
mixed or promiscuous dancing was regarded as indecent and
sinful, and before, during, and after the puritan revolution
furnished the theme for much pulpit oratory.

The general effect of the repressive measures of the puritans,
their inhibitions and prohibitions, was exactly what would be
expected—that they imposed a yoke heavier than most English-

---

[1] *The Protectorate of Oliver Cromwell* [letters of John Pell], ed. Robert Vaughan
(1839), ii. 418. Cf. Inderwick, p. 45.
[2] See below, p. 398.   [3] *Acts and Ordinances*, i, 791.

men would bear. In some respects the position at the beginning
of the puritan revolution was similar to that obtaining in 1789.
At both times there was profound dissatisfaction with the *status
quo*, and a firm determination to change it. The champions of
puritanism,[1] like the champions of 'liberty, equality, fraternity',
were full of enthusiasm and confident that they could, as it
were, make a new heaven and a new earth. No evil seemed too
malignant to be cured, no injustice too gross to be remedied.
Men in 1640 as in 1789 felt that

> Bliss was it in that dawn to be alive,
> But to be young was very heaven! Oh times,
> In which the meagre, stale, forbidding ways
> Of custom, law, and statute, took at once
> The attraction of a country in romance!
>
> .　　.　　.　　.　　.
>
> What temper at the prospect did not wake
> To happiness unthought of? The inert
> Were roused, and lively natures rapt away![2]

For a time success smiled upon the reformers. They were able
to prevail against their open opponents because their enthusiasm was contagious and attracted to their side the great mass
of people who were normally without strong political or religious convictions. The English puritan and the French revolutionary retained the fervent support of this sort of middle party
during the comparatively brief period when abuses or privileges
were being swept away. So soon as the destructive side of each
revolution gave place to the constructive, doubts began to arise
in the minds of many who were alarmed at the growing fanaticism of the revolutionary rank and file. In England, as in France,
the extremists were checked by a military leader in whose rule
many acquiesced lest a worse thing befall them.

In England, whether the protectorate should be permanent
or transitory depended on its ability or failure to secure the
adherence of the non-party man. The opposition of the cavaliers was likely to endure, but events proved that it was too
weak to overcome Oliver Cromwell and the army. Moreover
there are no clear signs that, in the early days of the republic,

---

[1] It should be recalled that in 1640 the word *puritan* signified an opponent of
personal government as well as of Laud's ecclesiastical policy.

[2] Wordsworth, *The Prelude*, bk. xi.

the majority of Englishmen wished to overthrow it. On the other hand there is abundant evidence that in 1659–60 most men were eager for the restoration. This marked change in public opinion had many causes, but it is certain that among the most potent—perhaps the most potent—was the general detestation of puritan repressive legislation and inquisitorial morality. The nation had become disillusioned. Many of those who in 1640 had been swept off their balance by the moral fervour of puritanism and had rallied to its banners, had first gradually returned to their lukewarmness and then become hostile. There were still plenty of missionaries of the New Jerusalem, but they had ceased to attract disciples. Men had started to ask who had benefited by the political and ecclesiastical changes that had impoverished and harassed the nation. The almost unanimous answer was: only the soldiers and the clergy —the redcoats and the blackcoats, as contemporaries called them.

The puritan clergy had neglected the precept, 'Be not righteous overmuch', and suffered the penalty of having their zeal attributed to the basest motives. The most forcible expression of the prevalent belief that ministers were self-seekers who used their religion to cloak their sordid ambition occurs in a poem, published in 1655 and entitled *A Satyr against Hypocrites*. In it the minister and his flock, the service and the sermon, are held up to ridicule. There are satirical accounts of a puritan Sunday, fast day, and the feast that follows compulsory abstinence. The minister recalls Dickens's Mr. Chadband. He, too, lays about him prodigiously at table, and greedily swallows all the liquors within reach. From time to time he interrupts his gluttony to point a moral:

> Then quoth the priest, 'The cheere that here we see
> Is but an emblem of mortality.
> The oxe is strong, and glories in his strength
> Yet him the butcher knocks down, and at length
> We eate him up. A turkie's very gay,
> Like worldly people clad in fine array,
> Yet on the spit it looks most piteous,
> And we devoure it as the wormes eate us.'

This picture is, of course, a complete caricature, but it nevertheless reflects what many thought. It is the more significant because it was drawn by one who had been born of puritan parents and brought up in a puritan household—by John Phillips, the nephew of perhaps the greatest of all puritans, John Milton.

Traces of this anticlerical spirit, this hatred of the Paul Prys of the period, can be found everywhere. The election to parliament for the county of Norfolk, in 1656, furnishes two excellent examples. The opponents of Sir William Doyley, the successful candidate, attempted to get him disqualified as ungodly. It was said that he had suffered a rascal in his house to imitate the puritan preachers, holding up his hands and lifting up his eyes in derision of them, in order to make mirth at a great feast.[1] At the same election Edmund Chillenden was reproached for voting for a candidate who was not a godly man. 'Pish', answered Chillenden, 'Let religion alone; give me my small liberty.'[2] The importance of this remark is that it emanates from one who had been an officer in the Ironsides, one of the agitators elected by the army in 1647, and afterwards a preacher and an independent minister.

Because so pronounced a puritan had decided that the establishment of a puritan church system would be too dearly bought if it involved the sacrifice of political liberty, it follows, *a fortiori*, that Englishmen in general had arrived at the same conclusion. Indifference to the various questions at issue, and dislike of the new bustling ministers who had succeeded the old easy-going clergy, were undermining the ecclesiastical system and the code of morals established by law. After a bitter struggle, a minority of the nation had succeeded by force of arms in transforming church and state according to its liking, but it failed to overcome the passive resistance of the ordinary citizen who was not primarily a royalist or a parliamentarian. It had been possible to overthrow institutions but not fundamentally to change habits. The attempts to interfere with daily social customs met with little success and irritated men beyond endurance. The consequence was that the puritans, in their endeavours to compel men to be good (as they understood goodness), defeated their own ends. The Laodicean was converted into an active enemy. As the puritan code of morals was essentially the creation of the secular power, this hostility turned against the government, undermined it, and helped ultimately to overthrow it. Chillenden's demand, 'Let religion alone; give me my small

---

[1] Thurloe, v. 371.   [2] Ibid., p. 287.

liberty', became in 1660 the cry of most Englishmen. Accordingly, the puritan revolution was followed by the bloodless restoration of Charles II. England had repudiated the puritan attempt to enforce strict morality by the use of an army, and had answered the preacher as Sir Toby answered Malvolio: 'Dost thou think, because thou art virtuous, there shall be no more cakes and ale?'[1]

[1] *Twelfth Night*, Act II, sc. iii.

XII

FOREIGN TRADE AND COLONIES

ENGLISH seventeenth-century economic theory about foreign trade was permeated by the belief that it was essential to have an excess of exports over imports. It is true that some writers were inclined to emphasize bullionism and others what has come to be called mercantilism. The former tended to magnify the importance of exchange transactions and of restrictions on the export of coin and bullion, and of regulation through supervision of individual transactions. James I and Charles I were both bullionists. For example a proclamation was issued (25 May 1627) that the exchange of money was a royal prerogative, and goldsmiths were forbidden to intermeddle with foreign money or bullion, or to melt current coin. More influential, however, was the theory that in the case of a country like England, with no gold or silver mines to speak of, the only way to increase its stock of precious metal was to export more of commodities than was imported. When this happy state of things was brought about, England enjoyed what much later was called a favourable balance of trade. The best-known of all the mercantilist treatises is Mun's *England's Treasure by Forraign Trade*. Mun laid down as a maxim that 'the ordinary means therefore to encrease our wealth and treasure is by *forraign trade*, wherein wee must ever observe this rule; to sell more to strangers yearly than wee consume of theirs in value'.[1] One reason why the mercantilists so strongly urged the accumulation of bullion was that they tended to confuse wealth and money. Although it would be unjust to state that they looked upon precious metals as the sole wealth of the country, their over-emphasis upon the accumulation of gold and silver often made them act as if they did.

It has been well said, however, that, so far as the abler mercantilists were concerned, more important 'than the absolute identification of wealth with gold and silver was the attribution to the precious metals of functions of such extreme importance to the nation's welfare as to make it proper to attach to them a

[1] p. 5 of the reprint published for the Economic History Society by Basil Blackwell (1928).

value superior to that of other commodities. These functions
. . . were to serve as state treasure, as private stores of wealth,
as capital, and as a circulating medium.'[1] The question of state
treasure was of little importance under the early Stuarts, but
saving the precious metals fitted in so admirably with current
theories of the virtue of thrift that it was much stressed. The
puritans were never tired of urging that diligence and saving
and passing a toilsome and modest life were highly commendable virtues, while even the nobility and gentry, many of whom
themselves were extravagant and idle, thought that the middle
and lower classes should be content to work hard and spend
little. The failure of mercantilists to distinguish capital from
specie used as circulating medium confused the arguments that
the accumulation of bullion would stimulate industry and trade,
but it did enable them to make out a very plausible case for the
view that the only way to add to capital was to secure a favourable balance of trade. As for the use of gold and silver as means
of exchange, the mercantilists often argued that a greater supply
of money meant a greater circulation thereof, and that more
circulation meant more trade and therefore greater production
and accumulation of wealth. Certain of them saw correctly that
an abundance of money made commodities dear, and some at
least were convinced that there was some arithmetical relation
between the amount of money in circulation and prices; but
they nevertheless failed as a rule to see that, if the supply of
money were increased, its chief effect would be to raise the
prices of commodities rather than to increase the physical
volume of sales and of output.

In addition to these arguments, which are largely based on
the importance of bullion in the economic life of the nation,
the mercantilists had another, making a stronger popular appeal, that the greater the volume of exports and the smaller the
volume of imports the greater the amount of employment available in England. This type of argument probably accounts for
the complacency of the country in the face of such wild projects
as that propounded by Alderman Cockayne in the middle of
the reign of James I to dress and dye all cloth before export.[2]

[1] Jacob Viner, 'English Theories of Foreign Trade before Adam Smith', *Journal
of Political Economy*, xxxviii. 270. His two articles contain the most searching examination of the writings of early English economists within brief limits. For a more
elaborate account see Eli F. Heckscher, *Mercantilism* (1935).

[2] See below, pp. 332–3.

Superficially it did seem a great waste to send undressed cloth abroad to be dyed and finished, thus paying foreign workmen for doing what it ought to be possible to do in England. The sequel showed not only that the English product was unsatisfactory in quality, but also that, whereas the foreigner would be willing to buy undressed cloth, he was much less willing to buy it dressed. This is a clear example of one of the great weaknesses of mercantilism, the neglect to consider the consumer's point of view. Theorists and merchants were liable to concentrate their attention too exclusively on supply without concerning themselves sufficiently about the existence or non-existence of an effective demand. None the less it is only fair to acknowledge that the abler writers realized the handicap they were under in not having adequate statistical information at their command. A good example of this occurs in connexion with the East India Company. The frequent attacks on its exclusive rights were usually inspired by the knowledge that it exported bullion as well as commodities to India and imported only commodities. The defenders of the company argued that it was true there was an apparent unfavourable balance of trade, but that if it were possible to trace to its ultimate destination each of the commodities imported from India it would be found that, thanks to re-exports and the substitution of Indian for French luxury articles, the trade yielded a far greater national gain than if so much gold and silver had been directly imported from the East. But this line of argument led nowhere, because there was insufficient knowledge available as to what did become of the company's cargoes, how much of them was re-exported, and to what extent they obviated buying similar commodities from foreign countries.

To put such a mercantilist policy into effect necessitated an elaborate and intricate system of regulating trade. The endeavour to control trade took many forms—duties, both export and import, prohibitions, monopolies, and regulation of quality and of measures. Control was the more feasible because the bulk of the trade at the beginning of the seventeenth century was in the hands of various companies. All these, whether short-lived or of long duration, were alike in aiming at exclusive rights to trade with a specified locality. Thus the Russia Company tried to engross trade with Russia, and the Eastland Company with the Baltic seaboard, both importing flax, hemp, pitch, tar, tallow, furs, cables, and ropes, for which they exchanged coarse cloth and salt. The Merchant Adventurers attempted to monopolize the north-German and Dutch trade, dealing, for the most part, in textiles. The African Company traded with the west coast of Africa south of Barbary, sending such commodities as textiles, bracelets, and glass beads, and bringing back ivory, dyes, hides, and spices. The Levant Company controlled the eastern-Mediterranean commerce, carrying thither lead, fine cloth and other textiles, and fish. The East India Company aimed at a monopoly of trade with the mainland of India and the Spice Islands. And, finally, the Virginia Company took to itself much of the trade with America.[1]

The principal change in overseas trade under the early Stuarts came from the new plantations overseas. Elizabethan statesmen, in framing a mercantile policy, did not need to take cognizance of any of the problems that were later presented by colonies, because in 1603 England did not possess a single colony. Nevertheless, by 1660 the foundations of the British Empire had been well and truly laid. Newfoundland, much of the east coast of the present United States, and a number of West Indian islands had all passed into English hands; in India several trading stations or factories had been acquired; and a precarious footing was maintained in the East Indies. In this expansion all classes participated: the nobleman and the squire took an active share in promoting companies to form plantations; the merchants did likewise, and provided a large proportion of the funds necessary to defray the heavy initial costs. The hope of reaping their reward in large dividends doubtless induced individuals to subscribe; but the underlying and motivating force was the conviction that the nation as a whole would benefit greatly if it might depend on its own possessions across the seas for its stocks of raw materials and thus be no longer dependent upon foreign sources.

The colonists themselves were in the main drawn from the lower ranks of society. The motives that led many thousands of English men and women to leave their native land in order to emigrate, during the first half of the seventeenth century, were most varied, and often almost imperceptibly merged into one another. Perhaps the most important was the economic. Accord-

---

[1] The last two companies founded colonies; details of their trade are therefore given below.

ing to a recent authority 'the largest number of those who settled in North America' were influenced by 'the desire for land and an opportunity to make a home for wife and children'.[1] Certainly the inducement of land grants was frequently held out in the propaganda of the early promoters of colonization.[2] At first sight it is very surprising that there should have been an acute land-hunger in England at the beginning of the seventeenth century, for the population then was little more than an eighth of what it is today. Nevertheless there seems to have been a surplus population and in particular a growing landless class. Moreover, the old copyholder of the middle ages was gradually being transformed, or was in danger of being transformed, into a leaseholder or tenant at will. Therefore the chance of making a fresh start in a new country where land was plentiful appealed strongly to all whose status was changing for the worse in a transitional period.

It was not only those whose prospects were poor if they remained in England that emigrated. The lure of the unknown and the extravagantly eulogistic descriptions of newly discovered lands attracted some adventurers of the type that found an outlet for their energies in privateering so long as the war with Spain lasted. Then, some were inspired by missionary zeal to convert the poor savages from idolatry to Christianity. An early ballad called 'Newes from Virginia' says of the new plantation:

> To glorifie the Lord 'tis done,
> And to no other end;
> He that would crosse so good a worke,
> To God can be no friend.

Others were moved rather by the hope of establishing a purer church for themselves than they could enjoy in their native land. A ballad entitled 'The Zealous Puritan' (1639) pointed out these advantages, apparently sarcastically:

> There you may teach our hymns,
> Without the laws controulment:
> We need not fear the bishops there,
> Nor spiritual-courts inroulment;
> Nay, the surplice shall not fright us,
> Nor superstitious blindness.

[1] Charles M. Andrews, *The Colonial Period of American History* (1934), i. 54.
[2] Cf. John Rolfe's letter from Virginia in 1616, *Hist. MSS. Com., Eighth Report* (1881), App., pt. ii, p. 31.

Some were more worldly, and wished to bestow English civilization upon the natives.

> And so Virginia may in time,
>   be made like England now;
> Where long-lovd peace and plenty both,
>   sits smiling on her brow.[1]

There were not a few who had little choice in their emigration. Transportation of the vagrant and the criminal appealed to the authorities as an easy way of getting rid of undesirables. James in 1617 issued a proclamation for the more peaceful government of the border and ordered that notorious malefactors should be sent to Virginia or to the wars.[2] Political prisoners were also sent overseas. During the civil war Scotch, Irish, and English enemies of the commonwealth were transported, chiefly to Barbados and Virginia. Also, since it was difficult to induce enough servants to emigrate, a regular trade in kidnapped or trepanned persons of both sexes grew up.[3]

The history of foreign trade is inextricably bound up with colonial history during 1603–60. Then, certainly, traders planted the flag instead of merely following it. They made their way to most quarters of the known world, and settled or tried to settle colonies. The importance of the interdependence of foreign trade and colonies entails their treatment side by side, so far as possible. Therefore the plan for the rest of this chapter is: first, to describe the colonies founded in the reign of James I (but, once a colony is mentioned in the chronological order of its founding, its history is carried down to 1660); secondly, to give an account of trade, divided into chronological sections; then, to consider colonies founded under Charles I and Cromwell; and, finally, to discuss the constitutional and economic relations of the colonies with the mother country.

The reign of James I was a period of great colonial expansion, and plantations were made or attempted in India, the East Indies, Newfoundland, Guiana, Virginia, and Massachusetts.

The beginning of British dominion in India is entirely due

---

[1] *An American Garland*, ed. C. H. Firth (1915), pp. 13, 24, 25. Cf. the verses prefixed to Thomas Gage, *The English-American* (1648).

[2] Steele, *Proclamations*, no. 1202. Cf. *Acts of the Privy Council, 1621–1623*, pp. 206, 356, for examples of the transportation of reprieved criminals.

[3] There are many indictments for stealing children, in order to convey them on shipboard, calendared in *Middlesex County Records*, iii. 181, 185, &c.

to private enterprise. During the last twenty-five years of the sixteenth century, Englishmen, like Dutchmen, had been endeavouring to break down the Portuguese[1] monopoly of trade with the Far East. A few intrepid sailors and several travellers by land had reached the mainland of India and even the Malay Peninsula, but there was little definite information available by the end of the century, when a number of merchants were incorporated, on the last day of 1600, as 'the Governor and Company of Merchants of London trading into the East Indies'. The task before the company was formidable in the extreme. The certain rivalry and probable hostility of the Portuguese and Dutch—already in the field—had to be encountered, and no active assistance would be forthcoming from the Crown. The voyage was long and hazardous, with no friendly ports *en route* or at the end of the journey. The seas were largely uncharted and the land unmapped. Even under favourable circumstances, the length of the voyage caused great delay between the investment of capital to equip merchantmen and the distribution of profits.

Fortunately for the company the first voyages were very successful. Nine voyages were made up to 1612, during which time the English acquired no permanent station on the mainland of India. In that year permission was gained from Jahangir, Akbar's successor, to build a factory or trading station at Surat, at the mouth of the Tapti River, north of Bombay. The ensuing twenty years of intermittent hostilities with the Portuguese came to an end only when the English president of Surat and the Portuguese viceroy of Goa agreed to keep the peace and permit their nationals to trade with each other in India. This agreement was incorporated in a treaty between England and Portugal in 1642, two years after Portugal had begun her war for independence from Spain. The treaty that Cromwell extorted from Portugal in 1654 secured freedom of trade with all the Portuguese lands beyond the sea. Henceforth the relations between the two nations, in India, were harmonious and the East India Company was once for all insured against the menace of Portuguese hostility.

The Dutch proved much more serious rivals in the Far East than the Portuguese. They, too, had had their struggles with the Portuguese, had ejected them from the Spice Islands, and,

[1] The crown of Portugal was personally united with that of Spain, 1580–1640.

before our period comes to an end, had taken Ceylon from them. The main interest of the Dutch centred in the Malay Archipelago, and there they succeeded in seizing Pulo Run and Amboyna from the English, who retained only a few stations of minor importance, such as at Bantam and Bencoolen. The East India Company, therefore, was thrown back, as it were, upon the mainland of India. There their fortunes largely depended upon their relations with the native rulers and, in particular, with the mogul emperor. Realizing this, they sent to India, as their representative, a traveller already well known for his explorations of the Amazon—Sir Thomas Roe. His penetrating insight, solid judgement, and practical sagacity, combined with a charm of manner that few could resist, enabled him to secure not only the confirmation of the privileges the company already possessed at Surat, but also permission for Englishmen to travel freely into the interior for purposes of trading. Perhaps even more important was his enunciation of the policy the company followed for more than half a century. He was emphatically opposed to the use of force to extort trade concessions. 'A war and traffic are incompatible', he wrote, '. . . Let this be received as a rule that if you will profit, seek it at sea, and in quiet trade; for without controversy, it is an error to affect garrisons and land-wars in India.'[1] This policy yielded most satisfactory results so long as the mogul empire held together. Gradually other stations were established, including Fort St. George, which soon became Madras. In the early 1640's settlements were made in Bengal, and a factory was set up at Hughli but did not immediately rival either Surat or Madras.

The chief imports from the East were spices, calico, raw silk, indigo, and saltpetre. Of these, contemporaries attached the greatest importance to spices, of which pepper was most valued, cloves and nutmegs ranking next. Calico encountered some opposition at first, because its use would compete with that of English textiles. Woven silk did not become a very profitable commodity until Indian weavers had been instructed by Englishmen. Indigo had then a value out of all proportion to its worth today, and for a long time was one of the staples. Supplies of saltpetre were the more welcome in view of the great difficulty in securing an adequate supply elsewhere. This com-

[1] Cited in W. W. Hunter, *The History of British India* (1900), ii. 241-2.

modity naturally became more prized with the advent of the civil war, since it is one of the main ingredients of gunpowder.

England's main exports to the East were textiles, lead, tin, and coral (from the Mediterranean). Unfortunately for the English producer, it proved impossible to sell in the East enough of these articles to pay for the exports thence. Accordingly it was necessary to export bullion.[1]

During the 1640's the East India Company's fortunes touched their nadir, and there were times when total abandonment of the factories in India seemed inevitable. The shareholders were divided in their sympathies during the civil wars; the royalist members were obliged to withdraw when subscription to the Solemn League and Covenant was enforced. Trade in general suffered many violent interruptions, and the company had to face the additional handicap of the Courteen[2] Association's continued activity in the East. The great unfairness of this rivalry was that not only did it cost the company part of their trade but that it was held responsible by the native authorities for the misdeeds of the interlopers. The situation was so bad that raising a joint stock proved almost impossible, and parliament made matters worse by exacting a loan.

However, the clouds began to lift during the commonwealth and protectorate. A kind of coalition was arranged with the Courteen Association, which restored more or less normal trading relations with India. The Dutch war, and Cromwell's insistence that the Dutch should compensate Englishmen for the injuries inflicted upon them in the East, at Amboyna and elsewhere, and should return Pulo Run, showed that, for the first time, the company could rely upon governmental support. Even so, prosperity did not come, for the company was divided against itself on the question whether the joint stock should be abandoned and members allowed to trade with their own capital and ships in whatever manner seemed good to them. At length, in 1657, Cromwell granted a new charter, which marks the beginning of a new period in the company's history. Trade with the East was reconstituted on a joint-stock basis, and the freedom of the company was thrown open to anyone who cared to subscribe £5. The effect was immediate: despite the pressure of taxation and lean times, nearly three-fourths of a million

---

[1] Shafaat Ahmad Khan, *The East India Trade in the 17th Century* (1923), chap. i.
[2] See below, p. 335.

pounds were eagerly subscribed for fresh capital. As has been well said, the company 'cast its medieval skin, shook off the traditions of the regulated system, and grew into one united, continuous, and permanent joint stock corporation in the full sense of the words'.[1]

Turning to America, it is uncertain how early European fishermen first visited the banks of Newfoundland, but at least it is known that, throughout the sixteenth century, Portuguese, Spanish, French, and English fishermen crossed the Atlantic and brought back cod, mackerel, and herring. They had made no attempt to set up a permanent habitation on land, and merely needed a base where they could mend their nets and dry, salt, and store their catches until they were ready for the voyage home. In 1583 Sir Humphrey Gilbert had landed in St. John's harbour, hoisted the English flag, and taken possession of Newfoundland in the queen's name. But no colony was founded as the immediate result of his action. Nearly thirty years elapsed before the incorporation of the company of adventurers and planters of London and Bristol for the colony of Newfoundland. The first voyage (1610) was unusually quick and the mild winter gave promise of a prosperous settlement; but the fair hopes thus aroused were not fulfilled. In spite of several determined efforts, of which Lord Baltimore's endured the longest, it proved impossible to found a colony. The weather was too inclement, and the soil too barren to make agriculture profitable. Moreover the powerful fishing interests in England had no desire to see a colony in Newfoundland acquire rights in territorial waters, or along the foreshore, because its privileges might conflict with their practices. They wanted merely settlements on shore that would provide a few months' shelter for their fishermen, and therefore small communities of this type were all that were established on the coast of Newfoundland in the seventeenth century. They prevailed because they were supported at court, because fishing both supplied the training school for English mariners and fitted in ideally with mercantilism—the sale of fish to Spain and the Mediterranean countries yielded a 'favourable' balance of trade.

Even more short-lived were the settlements made as a consequence of the grant to Sir William Alexander of the land to be

[1] Hunter, ii. 135.

known as New Scotland or Nova Scotia. James issued a charter conveying all the territory now included in Nova Scotia and New Brunswick, and much besides, to Alexander, and even instituted an order of Nova Scotian baronetcies in imitation of the device for raising money for the plantation of Ulster. Although the Scots, in general, were not attracted by the scheme, expeditions were dispatched and landed at Port Royal, on the Bay of Fundy. It was soon found, however, that these projects conflicted with those of Richelieu, who had plans for the extension of French influence in Canada, and, when Charles I made peace with France in 1629, the settlement was abandoned.

Equally unfortunate were the first English attempts to colonize Guiana, which lay between the Spanish settlements on the Main and those of the Portuguese in Brazil. When Raleigh returned from his expedition against the Spanish possessions in South America in 1595, he wrote a book called *The Discoverie of Guiana*, describing explorations along the Orinoco River in search of a gold mine at Manoa. His narrative attracted much attention and led to several attempts at further exploration and settlement. Sir Thomas Roe sailed up the Amazon and spent over a year (1610–11) ranging over the country between that river and the Orinoco, without finding any trace of the gold supposed to abound in that region. Six years later came the most famous Guiana expedition, headed by Raleigh himself, who had been released from the Tower in order that he might renew his search for the gold mine he had failed to find twenty years before. He was strictly commanded by the king not to invade Spanish territory. When Raleigh arrived at the mouth of the Orinoco, he decided to remain there while a trusty lieutenant proceeded up the river in quest of the gold mine. On the way the Spaniards at San Thome were attacked, but not defeated decisively enough to permit the English to continue to advance. There was nothing to do, therefore, but to return to Raleigh, who had perforce to abandon the expedition and return home ignominiously. The Spaniards made angry complaints to James about the attack on San Thome, and he sacrificed Raleigh in order to appease those whose political alliance he was seeking. Accordingly he had Raleigh executed under the sentence passed on him in 1603.[1] In spite of the failure of this Guianan expedition, several settlements were

---

[1] See above, p. 3.

made at the mouth of the Amazon, but each was crushed by the Portuguese.

The first permanent American colony founded by England was in Virginia, and its early history shows on every side marks of its origin in trade. In 1606 two Virginia companies were incorporated, one for London and one for Plymouth, and they were authorized to form settlements in that part of North America lying between latitudes 34° and 45°.

The initial expedition sent out by the Plymouth company formed a settlement in south Maine. These colonists were very unprosperous and soon abandoned the undertaking. After their experience no Englishmen except fishermen were to be found on the coast of Maine for many a long day.

The expedition from London was more fortunate, although it, too, had its trials and tribulations. It sailed into Chesapeake Bay, entered the James River, and disembarked on the site of the future Jamestown. The colonists were soon in trouble, and by the time the first supplies reached them from England their numbers were reduced from 143 to 38. Thus one establishment was already abandoned and another in grave danger of a like fate.

Moreover an expedition under Sir George Somers, sent out in 1609, was wrecked on some islands nearly six hundred miles from the American coast. As it happened, this disaster was a blessing in disguise, for the salubrious climate and rich supplies of ambergris induced the company to secure a royal grant of the Somers Islands, or the Bermudas. A subsidiary group was immediately formed, and within a few years had planted six hundred people. Fortunate in avoiding the fate of the older organization, the Bermuda Company was not dissolved in 1624 but survived another sixty years.

Meanwhile the Virginia Company had been given a new charter (1609), creating a joint-stock company, with Sir Thomas Smith as its treasurer. A great effort was made to enlist the help of all classes by such methods of propaganda as were then available—sermons, pamphlets, and ballads—but with rather unsatisfactory results. A third charter, in 1612, gave the company better chances of succeeding, for its territory was extended and its authority increased. It was now able to make regulations likely to promote a permanent settlement. In particular it laid down rules establishing the private ownership of land, and permitting the retention in private hands of the profit from its cultivation. Great improvements followed because the planters now had every inducement to till the soil, and to depend upon steady labour for a livelihood. The dreams of easily acquired fortunes that had attracted many had to be abandoned, but in their stead a resource was discovered that promised a permanent reward to the owners of land—tobacco. Once the suitability of Virginian soil for the cultivation of this plant was recognized, the future of the colony was practically assured. From 1614, when the first shipment was made to England, tobacco became the great staple commodity, and easily survived the attempts of the company's directors to insist on a more diversified economy.

By this time the Virginia Company was nearing its end. It had succeeded in founding a colony strong enough to survive the Indian massacre of 1622, when about four hundred of the colonists were slain. It had not, however, achieved the purpose for which it was formed, financial gain. It was bankrupt and rent by internal dissensions. It closed its chequered career when, as a result of *quo warranto* proceedings instituted in the king's name, its charter was declared forfeit. The next year (1625) Charles I issued a proclamation that, inasmuch as the colony had not hitherto prospered, it should, together with the Somers Islands (Bermuda) and New England, form part of the empire and be under his direct rule.[1]

One legacy from the days of the company must be mentioned —the legislative assembly. The introduction of popular government into the colony was a novelty at the time, and may be due to the influence of Sir Edwin Sandys, a prominent member of the Virginia Company as well as the leader of the parliamentary opposition to James I. Be this as it may, the first legislative assembly to meet in an English colony and on American soil was apparently chosen by all the male adults in Virginia, where the franchise was clearly far more liberal than in the home country. The delegates met in Jamestown in 1619, and it was at once obvious that the instinct for self-government was already strong. After the dissolution of the company the constitutional position of the house of burgesses was uncertain for more than a decade. In 1639 and 1641, however, the instructions to the

[1] Rymer, *Foedera*, xviii (1726), 72–73.

respective governors directed that, once a year or oftener, they were to convene the burgesses, who, together with the governor and his council, were empowered to make laws (which should correspond as nearly as possible to the laws of England)—the governor having the right of veto.

During the years 1625–41 the plantation made steady progress. Perhaps the greatest obstacle to rapid growth was the high mortality among the early colonists. It is said that, of those embarking in English harbours, three out of every four, perhaps five out of every six, died prematurely, some during the voyage in small, crowded ships, more from malaria and other diseases prevalent in and around Jamestown, and from Indian attacks. Nevertheless the survivors persevered, and even prospered. Most of the settlers were either small landowners or indentured labourers who had contracted to serve a master for four or five years. When they had completed their time, they might become small landowners or hired workers. Land was either leased or bought, subject to a quitrent to the king, which at the time, however, was rarely paid. Apart from the building of houses and a few ships, there was little or no industrial life. The early attempts to make glass, &c., had completely failed and the sole dependence was now upon agriculture. The two staple crops were Indian corn and tobacco, the former for consumption at home, and the latter for export.

The second permanent English colony in America was made by the Pilgrim Fathers. They were a body of separatists who had sought on foreign soil the freedom of worship denied them at home. A group of them had been in the habit of making Scrooby Manor, in Nottinghamshire, their headquarters, but in 1608 a number, from Nottinghamshire, Lincolnshire, and Norfolk, thought it prudent to emigrate to Amsterdam. There they found other separatists, but, because of the prevalence of many contentions, they moved to Leyden within a year. At that place they remained for another eleven years, when some of them decided to move once again. On the whole, though unmolested by the tolerant Dutch authorities, they had been disappointed in the spiritual results of their sojourn abroad. They had not flourished as they had hoped and they were conscious that their children were losing their English heritage and becoming foreigners. After much heart-searching, the determination was finally reached that some of the refugees of

Leyden should combine with merchants in England to make a plantation across the Atlantic. Unlike the Virginians, they were never incorporated but remained a voluntary joint-stock company. Actually, when the *Mayflower* set sail in September 1620, thirty-five of its passengers were from Leyden and sixty-six from London and Southampton. Those directly from England were not separatists and were not inspired by religion so much as by hope of material improvement. The Pilgrims landed at Plymouth in December and lost half their number the first winter, mainly from scurvy contracted during the voyage. The mortality rate continued high, and in spite of considerable immigration the population increased so slowly that it is said to have amounted, in 1637, to only 549.

The colony was agricultural, with maize, wheat, and cattle as the staples. Fishing helped to provide means of trading, but the Pilgrims were too far south of the best-stocked waters, and their attempt to establish a base farther north was never really successful. Shipbuilding proved rather beyond their resources. Their trade with the Indians provided them with furs, which, together with maize and timber, formed the bulk of their commerce with England, and enabled them to buy out the adventurers in England who had been their partners in the original enterprise.

Their form of government was extremely simple. On board the *Mayflower* a covenant had been drawn up in order to bind the signatories to unite in a political and religious society and to obey whatever laws should be made. Annually the governor (who was William Bradford during 1621–56, except for five years) and his assistants were chosen by the freemen. They joined with representatives of the freemen to form the general court that acted as the legislature. The colony retained its separate identity until 1691, when it was annexed to Massachusetts.

The effect on trade of the great colonial expansion during James's reign is hard to evaluate. Generally speaking, times were prosperous until about 1620 (except for 1607), and then bad. Little credit for the good years can be given to James I, and he must bear much of the responsibility for the bad times, because 'few sovereigns have restricted and disorganized trade more than he did, by the numerous and ill-considered burdens he laid upon it'.[1] The expanding trade can be attributed to the

[1] W. R. Scott, *The Constitution and Finance of English, Scottish and Irish Joint-Stock Companies to 1720*, i (1912), 133.

peace with Spain, to a number of new enterprises, and to the success attending the East India Company and the Russia Company during the first half of the reign. Moreover the incorporation of the Virginia Companies (1606), the settlement of the Bermudas (1611), the revival of the African Company (1618), and the beginning of Scottish colonization in Nova Scotia (1620), all gave a temporary stimulus to trade.

When the depression came, towards the end of the reign, contemporaries blamed the shortage of specie, mistaking effect for cause. The slump seems to have been due mainly to the impecuniosity of the Crown and the measures taken to alleviate it; to the monopolistic system pursued both in domestic manufactures and foreign trade; and to causes beyond the control of English statesmen, such as the outbreak of the Thirty Years War. Throughout his reign James was in debt, and the unsoundness of the national finances reacted upon private fortunes. Unlike Elizabeth, James rarely repaid the money he borrowed, and thus inflicted losses upon individuals out of all proportion to the sums he himself had received. He lived in a kind of vicious circle, because his failure to settle his accounts promptly was offset by the exorbitant charges of merchants who risked supplying him with goods. The king's pennilessness had other unfortunate consequences because, when unable to reward his favourites with presents of money, he often granted them monopolies or permitted them to accept bribes in order that others should secure monopolies.

Monopolies were among the most prominent economic phenomena of the time, and powerfully influenced both the industrial life of the nation and its foreign trade. They may be grouped into three categories: (1) sole right of supervision, such as the right to license ale-houses or that given the duke of Lennox to act as alnager of the new drapery; (2) the sole right to use a process of manufacturing that was asserted to be either new or revived after disuse—this would correspond to the modern patent; and (3) the exclusive right of trading either in some commodity or with certain foreign countries or localities. All these were liable to serious abuse, were the subject of great contention at court and in the City, and were critically examined in every parliament in James's reign.

The first great attack on monopolies, and in many ways the most interesting of them all, occurred in 1604, when a bill was brought into the house of commons and passed with only forty dissentients that all merchants should have full liberty to trade with all countries.[1] The committee appointed to consider this bill made a most interesting report, in the course of which they asserted that, although there might be five or six thousand persons free of the several trading companies, the real control of the mass of the trade of the realm was in the hands of two hundred persons at the most. They further alleged that monopolies in restraint of trade were against the laws of the land, contrary to the example of other nations, and a hindrance to the more equal distribution of wealth, which tended to be accumulated in London to such a degree that the customs collected there came to £110,000 a year, and at the outports to only £17,000. The bill was dropped after a conference with the lords, but at the next session a measure with more limited purpose was placed on the statute book—namely, to throw open the trade with Spain, Portugal, and France to all subjects.[2]

Inasmuch as trading companies were exempted from the Statute of Monopolies, passed in 1624, it would seem as if there was a change of heart. After all, some sound arguments could be adduced to support the exclusive rights of trading companies. When dealing with areas where the government was unstable or hard to deal with (such as Russia, Africa, India, or Turkey), a company was in a much stronger position than an individual would have been to enforce the observance of any agreements made. Often capital expenditure was necessary to bribe ministers or to erect warehouses, and the maintenance of consuls was a permanent expense. So long as the English government was not in a position to foster foreign trade, it seemed necessary to delegate power to a company. Perhaps a fair conclusion would be that monopolistic trading companies were a necessary stage in the development of some sections of foreign trade, but that their privileges were often too extensive and maintained long after the circumstances justifying their creation had passed away.

Probably trading monopolies in themselves would have been much less objectionable but for the financial needs of the Crown. The worst example of an attempt to increase the royal income was that in connexion with the cloth trade, which has already

---

[1] *Commons' Journals*, i. 183, 218, 253.
[2] 3 Jac. I, c. 6, *Statutes of the Realm*, iv. 1083.

been mentioned. At this time the cloth was exported either partly finished or undyed, with the result that all the finer cloths were dressed and dyed abroad. William Cockayne, an alderman of the City of London, proposed that he and other promoters should be granted a patent to finish all cloth in England before exportation. They calculated that from £600,000 to £700,000 a year would be added to the value of the cloth exported, and James was to receive £300,000 of this. Lavish bribes are said to have enlisted the support of many courtiers, and the king yielded to the temptation. It may be that he failed to perceive the real motive of Cockayne and his associates— to break the monopoly of the Merchant Adventurers. At any rate the privileges of the Merchant Adventurers, who had hitherto exported much of the cloth, were suspended, and a new company formed in order to deliver the cloth abroad. The exportation of undyed and undressed cloth was prohibited in 1614. This ambitious scheme was a disastrous failure and seriously injured English export trade of cloth. The new company was unable to dye much of the cloth available, and what it did dye was so badly done that foreigners would not buy it. The Dutch, angry at the threat to their dyeing industry, prohibited the importation of dyed cloth, and began themselves to manufacture cloth. In the end, James found it necessary to dissolve the new company and to re-establish the old, but by this time part of the foreign market had been lost. The natural consequence was that while a few favourite courtiers filled their pockets, the textile industry suffered a severe, if not incurable, wound, and the regular channels of trade were disorganized.

In many regards the reign of Charles I was similar to that of his father. Apart from a sharp though brief depression about 1630, trade flourished until the late 30's, when there was another depression, which reached its most acute stage in 1640. Again the Crown must bear much of the blame for the gradual darkening of fair trading prospects. Like his father, Charles I endeavoured to increase his revenue by monopolies. The weakness of the statute of 1624 was that it contained no provisions against granting monopolies to companies. The method actually employed was simple. A monopoly was granted to a corporation which promised a substantial annual sum to the Crown. An example is provided by the coal trade. The hostmen of Newcastle controlled the export of coal from that town, and some of them obtained from Charles the sole right to sell to colliers coal for the London market. This, as has been pointed out, was a monopoly within a monopoly, for only a hostman might sell coal for shipment and now only an inner ring of the host-men could supply the London market.[1] The consequence of this and many other grants of exclusive privileges to corporations was really a system of indirect taxation which violated all the canons of sound finance. The Crown received relatively little, but owing to its interference the price of commodities was raised, their quality often deteriorated, and the progress of industry was hampered.[2] It is calculated that in order that the Crown might receive £80,000 a year gross from the monopolies in starch, coal, salt, and soap, the consumer had to pay between £200,000 and £300,000 a year more for those articles.[3]

The attitude of the Crown to the monopolistic trading companies was a curious medley of inconsistencies. It would seem as if there were only two logical courses to pursue—to throw trade open to all merchants or to respect the exclusive rights granted to companies. The early Stuarts, however, followed no consistent policy of any kind relative to the companies and, while causing merchants heavy losses by interfering, neither threw open the trade nor secured a substantial increase of revenue by maintaining existing monopolies or granting new ones. A brief statement of the relations between the Crown and the East India Company will illustrate the ineptitude of the course pursued.

The charter of 1600 granted the East India Company 'the whole entire and only trade and traffic' in all places, between the Cape of Good Hope and the Straits of Magellan, not in the possession of friendly powers, yet James in 1604 licensed Sir Edward Michelborne to trade in China and elsewhere in the East, and the East India Company suffered in reputation, for the native rulers naturally made little distinction between one English ship and another. Legitimate traders, therefore, were penalized for the misdeeds of freebooters. Again, although James solemnly confirmed the exclusive privileges of the East India Company in 1609, soon afterwards he was persuaded to establish a Scottish East India Company with powers so

---

[1] Scott, op. cit., i. 208–9. Cf. J. U. Nef, *The Rise of the British Coal Industry* (1932), ii. 279–80.   [2] George Unwin, *The Gilds and Companies of London* (1908), p. 327.
[3] Scott, op. cit., p. 214.

extensive that the charters of the East India Company and the
Levant and Russia Companies were all infringed. This time the
threatened companies were put to the expense of buying out their
rivals. Worst of all, Charles authorized a courtier, Endymion
Porter, to fit out privateers to sail in the Red Sea, and soon
there was formed the Courteen Association, so called from the
name of its leading capitalist, Sir William Courteen, a wealthy
merchant with interests in London and Middelburg. Authorization was now given to the new group to establish factories or
trading stations in all places in India where the East India
Company had none. The new association, however, was after
quicker returns than were likely to be obtained from legitimate
trade, and soon began to import base money into India and
thus dealt a heavy blow to the credit of the older company.
Furthermore, in 1640 Charles bought on a kind of instalment
plan the East India Company's stock of pepper, sold it at a loss,
and therefore depreciated the market for future sales, but never
made any payments.[1] The history of other companies would reveal similar, though usually not so extensive, grievances against
the Crown. Therefore it is not surprising to find that the London
merchants, after suffering such infringements of charter rights
and heavy losses needlessly inflicted to enrich courtiers, were in
general hearty supporters of the parliamentary cause.

The depression which developed in the late 30's reached a
crisis when Charles I seized the bullion in the Tower, for,
although it was restored, confidence was undermined. A proposal to debase the coinage, which was abandoned before being
put into execution, further weakened confidence. During 1640–
50 the depression continued. The civil wars violently interrupted
trade. The attempt of the king to cut off supplies from London
was most serious, in view of its prominence as the commercial
centre of England. Heavy taxes increased the distress caused by
the fighting. The parliamentarians spent annually about three
times the revenue enjoyed by Charles I prior to the civil wars,
and deficits ran high. So far as parliament had a definite policy
with regard to trade, it seems to have been to suppress monopolies in England but to encourage companies with exclusive
rights to trade abroad. Thus an ordinance (12 October 1643)
was passed in favour of the Merchant Adventurers forbidding

---

[1] William Foster, 'Charles I and the East India Company', *Eng. Hist. Rev.* xix.
456–63.

any to trade with the regions assigned to the company and confining members to those who had been bred merchants and were willing to pay a heavy fine.[1] In order to win the support of parliament these companies had to make considerable contributions towards carrying on the war, and, in a sense, their grants were as pernicious as the former bribes to courtiers, for in each case the company was deprived of much-needed capital.

So far as trade is concerned, the most important event that happened under the commonwealth was the passage of the Navigation Act.[2] However, so far as the immediate future was concerned, the act should rather be regarded as a gesture or as an indication of economic policy than as effecting a revolution in shipping circles. In any event it could not have been carried out in its entirety without inflicting severe losses upon English merchants, for the English mercantile marine was not large enough to carry all the trade hitherto carried in foreign vessels.

There was at first apparently a revival of trade during the protectorate, but the Spanish war hampered it severely. In fact the war against Spain, which a half-century before had been regarded as a profitable source of wealth as well as a righteous crusade, now became unpopular in the very cities where anti-Spanish feeling had hitherto been so strong. The losses merchants suffered made them become hostile to the protectorate, and one reason why the City of London was so bitterly opposed to the army in 1659 was the depression in trade. Merchants made formidable adversaries, for nothing is more remarkable in the economic history of this period than their success in permeating the country with a knowledge of, and belief in, the supreme importance of trade. The merchants were quick to profit by the opportunities for propaganda the times afforded, and were so successful that trade rivalled and even prevailed against religion as a guiding principle in the conduct of foreign policy.[3]

During the first fifteen years of the reign of Charles I, the intense activity in founding colonies of his father's reign was well maintained. There were new plantations in the West

---

[1] Another ordinance, upholding the Levant Company, was passed 7 March 1644.
[2] For a brief description and an estimate of the effect on Anglo-Dutch relations of the Navigation Act, see pp. 220-1.　　[3] See quotations at end of chap. ix.

Indies, and many additional areas were occupied on the Atlantic Coast of North America.

In the West Indies, Spain had taken possession of Cuba, Hispaniola, Porto Rico, and Jamaica, although she had concentrated her efforts rather on the mainland of Mexico and Peru than on these islands. Nevertheless she claimed exclusive rights to navigate the Caribbean Sea. The Elizabethan sea-dogs had made many raids into these forbidden waters, but the first English settlement, at St. Christopher (or St. Kitts), did not occur until 1624. The colonists were soon joined by some Frenchmen, who lived peaceably with their neighbours. The Spaniards ejected the settlers in 1629, but they later returned and continued their dual occupation until after the Restoration. Englishmen also occupied Nevis, Montserrat, and Antigua (1628–36). Meanwhile Charles I had granted the earl of Carlisle, a courtier and a Scot, a patent for the colonization of the Caribbees, and this grant proved most prejudicial to one of the earliest English colonies in the West Indies, Barbados.

In 1625 an English ship, homeward bound, touched at Barbados, found the island uninhabited, and took possession of it in the king's name. Sir William Courteen at once realized the rich possibilities of the island and sent out several ships. Within a few years there were from 1,600 to 1,800 people on the island, who were fed and supplied with the necessary equipment by their employer, Courteen, who naturally received the profits from the sale of the cotton and tobacco that were cultivated.

Meanwhile Carlisle, heavily in debt, leased ten thousand acres in Barbados to his creditors, who thus threatened to reap where Courteen had sown. The latter, therefore, had recourse to the earl of Montgomery, afterwards of Pembroke, one of the 'incomparable paire of brethren' to whom the first folio of Shakespeare's works was dedicated in 1623. Montgomery, too, was a courtier and succeeded in persuading Charles to grant him Trinidad, Tobago, and Barbados to hold in trust for Courteen. In the end, however, Carlisle, whose interest was the greater, proved the more agile courtier, and his claim to Barbados was upheld.

The colony suffered severely during the years when the proprietorship of the island was in dispute, and there were times when the cessation of the supplies of provisions Courteen formerly sent threatened famine. There was, too, another burden to be borne by the settlers: the governors nominated by Carlisle were autocratic, quarrelsome, and self-seeking. Nevertheless one of them summoned a parliament, which started for the Barbadians the representative form of government that they have never lost. Also, in spite of harsh treatment, they flourished and by 1640 were engaged in a profitable export trade in tobacco, cotton, and indigo.

The next colonizing effort in the West Indies was the formation of a company to settle the district lying between 10 and 20 degrees latitude and 60 and 83 degrees longitude. The leading members were puritans, such as Lords Saye and Sele, Warwick, and Brooke, and John Pym, and they hoped to establish a sanctuary where their coreligionists would be free from oppression and able to worship according to their own consciences.[1] For a project of this kind, however, the West Indian islands occupied, Providence and Association, were wholly unsuitable, because they were situated in the very heart of the Spanish settlements. The Spaniards made short work of the colony in Association, but their first attacks on Providence were beaten off. Realizing the futility of their original plans, the directors of the company turned their thoughts more and more to an anti-Spanish crusade in the Caribbean Sea. They were determined to persevere, they said, because the island might be made the means of intercepting the treasure of the Spaniard, whereby he has 'troubled and endangered most of the states of Christendom and doth foment the wars against the professors of the reformed religion'.[2] The Spaniards realized the threat to their treasure fleet, and concentrated sufficient strength to overwhelm the settlers in 1641, and thus brought to an end the short career of the puritan colonists in the West Indies.

The first settlements in New England were made with a view to promoting the fishing industry. During the sixteenth century, Englishmen had been in the habit of crossing the Atlantic Ocean to fish and had returned at the end of each season. However heavy their catches may have been, their cargoes were restricted by the necessity of taking the fishermen as well as the crew to and fro, and of carrying extra provisions. Moreover, since the

---

[1] A. P. Newton (*The Colonizing Activities of the English Puritans* [1914], p. 121) draws an interesting parallel between the motives of these puritans and those of the founders of Massachusetts.   [2] Ibid., p. 248.

fishermen had to land, in any event, to salt and pack their fish, it would have been convenient to establish a permanent base on the coast. The early attempts to set up permanent posts failed, both because a good harbour with fertile land in its immediate vicinity was not found and because fishermen, when they were not at sea, made poor agriculturists, and also poor traders, so that they failed to utilize their opportunities of acquiring furs from the Indians in exchange for baubles. The settlement which seemed the most promising was that made at Cape Ann by a group sent over from a company formed at Dorchester. Their exclusive right to the cape was challenged, in vain, by the Pilgrims, who were also anxious to have a base near the best fishing waters. Nevertheless the settlement did not prosper and most of its survivors returned home. A few decided to try their luck elsewhere along the coast and became the founders of Salem.

However, the failure of the Cape Ann project did not daunt the Dorchester company. Being unable to continue to bear by themselves the expense of colonization, they looked about for partners and found them in London and the eastern counties. The New England Company that was organized in 1628 was drawn from three separate areas, each strongly puritan. Dissatisfaction with the ecclesiastical policy then being adopted, which was Arminian in theology and rigid in discipline, made puritan gentlemen and members of the middle classes intensely interested in any scheme that might provide a refuge for the persecuted, and give promise of economic improvement. Among those instrumental in forming the new organization were John Venn, later a regicide, and Hugh Peter, hanged at the Restoration for his share in the execution of Charles I. The sole achievement of the company was the dispatch of provisions and recruits to the 'old planters' at Salem. Almost at once it was transformed into the Massachusetts Bay Company, which was apparently granted the same territory as the old company, but received much greater authority to govern it. The headquarters remained in England, where the members were naturally anxious to receive a dividend on their investments. But most of those who crossed the ocean were, or believed themselves to be, religious refugees. They had left England profoundly dissatisfied with both the political and the ecclesiastical government and anxious to breathe the free air of a new country. They had sought to escape the laws of their native land, and did not intend to exchange one form of control, that by a king, for another, that exercised by shareholders eager for profits. Accordingly, almost immediately they began to agitate for shifting of control from England to America, and in 1629, at a general meeting of the shareholders, 'twenty-seven members being present out of a total generality of one hundred and twenty-five',[1] a vote was carried to transfer the government of the plantation to New England. In the spring of the next year John Winthrop, a prime mover in the latest developments, in company with some seven hundred emigrants, took the charter to New England and formed the vanguard of what is usually called the 'great puritan migration'.

It has been calculated that, during this movement, some 60,000 people left England—about a third of them bound for New England. Between 1630 and 1643 nearly 200 ships carried 20,000 men, women, and children thither at an estimated cost of £200,000.

This rapid influx of immigrants, many of whom had left their mother country because of unwillingness to submit any longer to a hateful government, gave a powerful impetus to the feeling of independence that animated the leaders of the Massachusetts Bay Company. It is important that the charter had been transferred to America because the puritans in the company were able to establish control of the colony. In the form of government that was devised, the intention of the founders was to establish a Christian commonwealth in which puritan ideals would find full recognition. Almost at once the momentous decision was taken that none should be admitted to the privileges of a freeman unless he should first be accepted as a member of a church. Inasmuch as the freemen were to choose the assistants, as vacancies occurred, and the assistants to name a governor from among themselves, power was put into the hands of a sifted group. The right to rule the many was entrusted to the few—the elect of God. In the oath that was imposed, there was no mention of loyalty to the king—merely an acknowledgement that the taker was subject to the government of Massachusetts. These provisions were in violation of the charter. Moreover little regard was paid to the interests of those subscribers of the company's stock who stayed in England, and they probably never received anything except some land in the plantation. The treatment the subscribers to the Massachusetts Bay Company

[1] Andrews, op. cit., p. 391.

received compares unfavourably with the scrupulous satisfaction the Pilgrims gave all their financial backers.

Even with the best intentions, it would have been difficult for the settlers in Massachusetts to reimburse the investors, because they had no staple commodity to export. They sent furs to England, but the quantity was far too small to cover the cost of the manufactured articles they needed. So long as there was a large emigration all went well, for the new-comers were glad to exchange the manufactured articles they brought with them for land or food. When the immigration suddenly dropped, in the early forties, after the downfall of the personal rule of Charles I, an acute crisis occurred in New England, for means were lacking to pay for imports. Of necessity, a reorganization of the economic life of the colony took place. Henceforth exports were prepared, not with an eye to the English market, but to trading with the West Indies, where were sent increasingly large cargoes of fish, grain, and lumber. Inasmuch as this purely intercolonial trade was not advantageous to the English mercantile interests, it was frowned upon from the start. Its continued existence gave umbrage to England, and the persistent efforts to suppress it were powerful factors in fostering that spirit of independence that led to the Revolution.

The oligarchical government set up by Winthrop and his associates did not pass unchallenged, and in 1632 the inhabitants of Watertown protested against a levy on the ground that the right to impose taxes was vested in the general court of freemen, not solely in the governor and his assistants. The upshot was the establishment of a representative assembly (the second on the mainland of America), but the right to vote for the election of deputies was still confined to church members, who were about one-fifth of the total number of male adults.

The determination of the ruling body to preserve the colony from moral or schismatical contamination was shown by the severe punishment of sinners and by the expulsion of the heterodox. The most famous instance of intolerance concerned Roger Williams. He was a pastor at Salem and refused to admit the right of magistrates to control consciences or beliefs. He wished each congregation to preserve its separate existence and not to be associated with other churches, and denied the validity of the grant of Indian lands to the company, holding that a settler was morally bound to pay the Indians for the land he occupied. For these and other unpopular opinions, he was expelled from Massachusetts. Acts of intolerance of this kind led to the founding of Rhode Island and, largely, of New Hampshire and Connecticut.

Williams, on his banishment, went to Narragansett Bay and established Providence (Rhode Island). He bought land from the Indians and set up a free commonwealth based on a compact, which confined the majority's power of making laws to 'civil things', thus averting religious persecution. Other towns were founded, and remained little independent states until 1643, when the Long Parliament joined three of them together —a fourth was added in 1647.

Connecticut, with its fertile soil, was settled by men coming from a variety of homes. The Pilgrims sent exploring and trading expeditions thither, and purchased lands of the Mohicans, whose chief, Uncas, is well known in story. Massachusetts also contributed her quota of early arrivals, and the Council of New England made a grant of territory to Lord Brooke, in consequence of which New Haven was established. In 1635–6 some dissidents from Massachusetts came and began other townships. Thus there originated a number of tiny states, each independent of its neighbours. This movement can be regarded as part of the expansion of Massachusetts.

The need of unity in the face of the dangers threatened by possible wars with the Indians, the Dutch in New Netherland (later New York), and the French in Canada, was responsible for what is usually called the New England Confederation. In 1643 delegates from Massachusetts, Connecticut, New Haven, and Plymouth met to frame articles of union—neither Maine nor Rhode Island was represented. According to the articles of confederation, the constituent colonies entered into a firm and perpetual league of friendship and amity for offence and defence, for propagating the gospel, and for furthering mutual safety and welfare. There was to be no interference in the internal affairs of each colony. To administer the common interests, eight commissioners were to be appointed annually—two from each colony—of whom at least six must act together before business could be transacted. Among the powers delegated to the commissioners was authority to decide questions of war or peace, to manage Indian affairs, and to provide for the return of fugitive servants and criminals.

Although the confederation was a loose league rather than a definite union, the adoption of the federal principle of equal representation of colonies very unequal in population and wealth was remarkable. That this was premature was revealed as early as the first Dutch war (1652-4), when Massachusetts was unwilling to join the other colonies in raising troops, justifying her refusal on the ground that the general courts of the several colonies must be guided by conscience and had full liberty to judge whether the acts of the commissioners were just and according to God and to be obeyed or ignored. Owing to internal stresses the confederation did not long survive the Restoration. Although the different colonies joined together to conduct the fiercest Indian war of the century (1675-7), they united because they had to face a common danger, not because they were members of an existing confederation. Nevertheless, the constitutional innovation was of importance, both on account of its experiment with federation, however imperfect, and of its having raised, in immature form, several fundamental issues, such as nullification and undelegated sovereignty, that were destined to be of the greatest moment in the later history of the United States.

The founding of Maryland was mainly due to George Calvert who, after serving the Crown as secretary of state during 1619-25, retired from office, declared himself a Roman catholic, and was created Lord Baltimore in the Irish peerage. For some time he had been interested in colonization. He had sent some settlers to Newfoundland and obtained the grant of a province there, which he called Avalon. Thither he migrated in 1627, but found the climate too cold and, consequently, sought the warmer shores of Virginia. He could not remain, because, as a Roman catholic, he was unable to take the oaths of allegiance and supremacy. Returning to England he was granted a patent in 1632 for the land north of the settlement of Virginia—being restricted to land hitherto unsettled and unoccupied by Europeans. The colony was called Maryland after the queen, Henrietta Maria.

The first Lord Baltimore died before the charter was sealed, but his heir, Cecilius, entered eagerly into his father's project. He was given a province free of all obligations to the Crown (except loyalty and the yearly payment of two Indian arrows) and was empowered to make laws, provided the advice and consent of the freemen or representatives were first obtained. In addition, he received the patronage of all churches built, and was enabled to exercise an all-too-rare liberality towards different religions.

The first expedition started in 1633 and is said to have consisted of about twenty gentlemen and three hundred labourers.[1] Among the former were Leonard Calvert, the proprietor's brother, and governor of the new province, and other catholics, together with two Jesuits. The new settlers finally arrived in the Potomac and founded the city of St. Mary's in March 1634. They were fortunate in escaping many of the trials and tribulations that befell most other colonies, such as disease, scurvy, famine, and Indian attacks. They profited by the experiences of the settlers in Virginia and Massachusetts. In fact they prospered so well that their first crop of Indian corn allowed a surplus for export to New England, where it was exchanged for salt fish. Also they were fortunate in that they could profit by the experience of the Virginians and plant tobacco, which became their staple product as well as their currency. They developed a rural or agricultural society, with scattered plantations instead of the urban civilization of New England. Some of their estates were large, were known as manors, and even had the courts baron and courts leet of English feudalism. However, these manors gradually lost their early characteristics and became plantations worked by slaves.

During the civil wars, the colonies sided with the king or remained neutral, and even New England, though sympathetic with the puritan cause, stood aloof. They did not wish to become entangled in a struggle the outcome of which was doubtful. They perceived that if they adopted the losing side some of their privileges might be curtailed. When the second civil war was over and the republic was established, the Long Parliament was not able to give immediate attention to the colonies, where Virginia and Barbados had recognized Charles II as rightful king. It was not until 1651 that Sir George Ayscue was sent with a fleet to the West Indies, where its mere presence sufficed to induce the Barbadians to expel Lord Willoughby, the royalist leader, and to acknowledge the commonwealth. Similarly, without recourse to arms, parliamentary commissioners persuaded

---

[1] So Baltimore told Wentworth (*Strafforde's Letters*, i. 178–9). The number of emigrants looks large in view of the tonnage of the two vessels chartered.

Virginia to disavow its royalist governor, Sir William Berkeley, and they also received the submission of Maryland. During the Dutch war the council of state in London hoped that the colonies would attack the Dutch settlements in New Netherland, but very little was attempted until 1654, when a small expedition was sent to New England. With this aid in sight even Massachusetts, which had hitherto refused to join the New England Confederation in an attack on New Netherland, permitted a levy of five hundred volunteers, and the other plantations were more zealous. The treaty of peace with the Dutch was concluded before their settlements in America could be attacked, but the little fleet Cromwell had sent out was not wasted, for it proceeded to attack Acadia and capture it. It is curious that the territory so easily won should have been retained without French protest during the Anglo-French alliance under the protectorate but that its surrender was demanded by the French after the Restoration.[1]

It is clear that the Crown had taken a smaller share in the founding of colonies than it had in the voyages of Drake and others, in the previous century. Neither James nor Charles had funds to invest in hazardous colonial enterprises. Therefore these were left to private individuals, inspired by hope of gain or desire for religious freedom. On the other hand the Crown did endeavour to exercise some control over colonies as soon as they were planted. The amount of this control varied considerably, and, in any case, was applied far more to the trade than to the internal development of a colony. One explanation is that there was no constitutional machinery adapted to colonial government. Another is the weakness of the Crown, which had few weapons at its disposal to enforce its decrees. Unquestionably there was from the first a sturdy opposition in the colonies to dictation from England. It is significant that the delegates who met at Jamestown in 1619 and inaugurated parliamentary government in America petitioned that the laws they might pass should be put into force at once, without waiting for approval or disapproval from England (although they might ultimately be annulled) and that they should have the right to object to any of the Virginia Company's decrees on their behalf.

[1] Keith Feiling, *British Foreign Policy 1660–1677*, pp. 70–71.

The royal council for Virginia was too short-lived to reveal the merits or demerits of such a body, but it would seem certain that, as colonies multiplied in number, there could not have been a separate council for each. Henceforth the privy council exercised such supervision as existed, and it is likely that much of the business it did transact was delegated to its committee for trade. In 1634 the first standing committee for foreign plantations was named, with Archbishop Laud as its most prominent member. It was given very large powers over all the colonies, including the right to make laws for them. The immediate purpose of the committee was to regulate the affairs of New England, but Massachusetts either evaded or defied its orders. As Charles soon had his hands full of troubles in Scotland, he was helpless to enforce the decrees of the committee. All that could be done was to endeavour to control emigration, but there is no reason to believe that the proclamation restraining subjects from leaving the realm without a licence was ever efficiently enforced.[1]

It proved simpler to regulate trade than to define constitutional relations between the Crown and the colonies. Almost at once the colonial export trade was subject to regulations in the interest of the English merchant, who would thus reap the reward of the sacrifices he had made in helping to found the plantation. Undoubtedly the most important commodity the colonies produced for export at this time was tobacco. Various experiments in regulation were made, but nearly all had this in common—that the tobacco should be sent directly to London[2] and there sold to commissioners, or others named for the purpose. In return the colonies received two concessions—that tobacco-growing in England should be prohibited,[3] and that foreign tobacco should be either excluded or imported in only small quantities.

Although, with respect to Massachusetts, Charles I had been unable to enforce his desires, a fairly definite policy, both political and economic, was discernible under the early Stuarts. There was a conscious effort to create an empire that should be commercially self-sufficient. At the same time, an attempt

---

[1] Rushworth, ii. 298.

[2] As early as 1621 the privy council ordered that all the colonial products were to be first landed in England, and the customs paid thereon, even if their ultimate destinations were foreign ports.   [3] From 1619 onwards.

was being made to curtail wide privileges granted in the early charters and to establish a larger measure of control. As usually happened then, these two policies were not pursued consistently, or with much regard for logical development. Nevertheless a start had been made with the erection of a framework into which the old colonial system could later be fitted.

It was impossible for either king or parliament to pay much attention to colonial affairs during 1642–9, when whatever had already been accomplished in establishing greater control over the plantations was completely undone. Moreover colonial trade fell into the hands of foreigners, especially the Dutch, who established a virtual monopoly of commerce in the English West Indies and who were granted the right to trade with Virginia, by an act passed by the house of burgesses in that colony.

After the execution of Charles I the remnant of the Long Parliament that was now the supreme power in the land made its attitude towards the plantations as clear as daylight, in three ordinances (1 August, 3 October 1650, 9 October 1651). The first appointed Sir Henry Vane, the younger, and fourteen others, commissioners for regulating trade, and authorized them to investigate the English plantations in America, and elsewhere, and to advise how they might be best managed and made most useful to the commonwealth, and 'how the commodities thereof may be so multiplied and improved, as (if it be possible) these plantations alone may supply the commonwealth of England with whatsoever it necessarily wants'. The second ordinance was directed against the colonies that refused to acknowledge the newly established republic, and declared that, having been planted by the people of England, they 'are and ought to be subordinate to and dependent upon' her. The third, the celebrated 'Navigation Act', decreed that no goods should be imported from Asia, Africa, or America, except in ships owned by Englishmen or colonists.[1]

Taken together these three ordinances established the theory of the relations between England and her colonies that was destined to endure. The rules prescribed for the subordination of the colonial trade to the advantage of English merchants survived the Restoration and in a more stringent form lasted until the American Revolution. Parliament, however, made no attempt to push its policy too far, and the colonies were left

---

[1] See pp. 220–1, 336, for other references to the Navigation Act.

free to regulate their internal affairs with little interference. If they infringed the Navigation Act, however, there was likely to be trouble. Evasions of it by New England merchants were winked at because of the natural sympathy felt by the leaders in England for their co-religionists across the Atlantic. But in the southern colonies foreign ships were liable to seizure and confiscation. In the West Indies, and particularly in Barbados, as a correspondent informed Cromwell, English merchants were neglected and free trade established with foreigners, even with the Dutch,[1] so recently at war with the English. Here too, therefore, the intruding alien saw his ships captured and their cargoes declared forfeited for illegal trading.

When Cromwell became protector at the end of 1653, he was the first Englishman who had both the will and the power to pursue an imperial policy.[2] He was anxious to enlist the help of the existing colonies, particularly New England, in order to extend the bounds of the empire. He was not likely, therefore, to enforce too harshly the colonial regulations drawn up during the commonwealth period, and he himself made no striking contributions to either the statutes or the theories governing the relations between the colonies and the motherland. On the other hand he bequeathed to a succession of statesmen the principle that, in a European war, England should employ her navy to despoil her enemies of their colonies. Sea-power had begun its great career as empire-builder.

The most promising field for the expansion of English colonies seemed to lie in the West Indies. Although an inroad had already been made upon the Spanish monopoly there, the English colonies owed their continued existence rather to the impotence than to the good will of Spain. Cromwell therefore assembled the large expedition whose fortunes have already been traced.[3] It sailed in December 1654. The results seemed very disappointing. The attack on Hispaniola was a disgraceful failure, and, at the time at least, the capture of Jamaica was not regarded as an adequate recompense. Nevertheless Cromwell was determined to retain the island. To try to secure settlers, he strongly urged the people of Massachusetts to send

---

[1] Thurloe, iii. 249.

[2] This imperialism seems to me the best justification for the late S. R. Gardiner's statement that Cromwell, in the world of action, was what Shakespeare was in the world of thought, 'the greatest because the most typical Englishman of all time' (*Cromwell's Place in History* [1902], pp. 115–16).   [3] Above, pp. 231–2.

emigrants to Jamaica, but few adopted the advice. Yet, in spite of every obstacle, including a high rate of mortality among soldiers and settlers in the early years, the island remained in English hands. Although this conquest was the only permanent territorial gain due to Cromwell, his West Indian policy was far from being the failure it appeared. He did not live to witness the full reward of the blood and treasure he had poured forth; but he had won for England a naval supremacy in the West Indies that insured the permanence of English settlements there.

XIII

EDUCATION AND SCIENCE

THE profound effects of the Renaissance in English education had by no means spent themselves by the beginning of the seventeenth century. New ideals of scholarship vibrated powerfully through the realm of thought, and fresh material for study was available in abundance. The highest in the land became men of letters or their patrons, and the middle classes were imbued with 'the modern faith in education as a means to cure all social ills, to induce happiness, and to make mankind generally wiser, wealthier, and more godly'.[1] The Reformation had hampered in some ways, and helped in others, the cause of education in England. The destruction of monasteries, nunneries, and chantries swept away most of the facilities for teaching the boys and girls of England, and the grammar schools founded out of the spoils by no means filled the void. Moreover, although teaching the young was taken out of the hands of what had been primarily religious institutions, the church retained a tight grip over education. Not only must every schoolmaster have a licence that attested his orthodoxy, but also it was forbidden, under the severest penalties, that any child or youth should be sent abroad to be educated. The very choice of subjects of study was largely dictated by theological considerations. No doubt it was a great benefit that the artisan or the labourer should try to learn his letters in order to read the Bible in his native language, but it is by no means certain that education in England did not suffer, in the long run, through confining the teaching of boys at the grammar schools mainly to Latin, Greek, and Hebrew, the three languages essential for biblical study and theological controversy.

The general interest in education can be illustrated in a variety of ways. There were many writers on methodology, of whom John Brinsley, who published his *Ludus Literarius* in 1612, and Charles Hoole, who issued his *New Discovery of the Old Art of Teaching Schoole* in 1660, are the most important for the curriculum of a grammar school. There were many pamphleteers

---

[1] Wright, *Middle-Class Culture in Elizabethan England*, p. 44.

and social reformers who wanted education to be made more practical and who were not slow to advocate their particular panaceas, which ranged from Milton's proposal to establish academies up and down the country, each to accommodate 150 students from 12 to 21 years old who should be given 'a compleat and generous education', to plans for preventing idle children from becoming beggars or thieves, by placing a schoolmaster in every parish.[1] Moreover the middle-class triumph during the puritan revolution seemed to offer the brightest prospects for educational extension and reform. In 1641 both Manchester and York petitioned parliament to establish a university in the northern parts;[2] and a college was actually established at Durham during the last years of the protectorate but did not survive the Restoration.[3] In addition, during 1641–2 John Amos Comenius, whom many regarded as the leading educationalist in protestant Europe, was invited to England by an influential group, including Pym and Selden, to set up a great college for scientific work, which was also to take part in the reform of existing institutions.[4] There seemed some likelihood that the state might assume part of the responsibility and expense of the education of its citizens, and the Grand Remonstrance (clause 187) announced the intention to reform and purge the foundations of learning, the universities, in order that the streams flowing thence might be clean and pure. The house of commons resolved that the lands of deans and chapters, which they proposed to confiscate, should be employed to the advantage of learning and piety.[5]

Actually, nothing came of the scheme with which Comenius was associated, and only very occasional grants were ever made for educational purposes out of the sequestrated revenues of ecclesiastics, as, for example, at Chester, where £36 per annum was granted to the headmaster of the free school and £9 to his usher.[6] The engrossment of the parliament in the civil wars and, when they were over, the costliness of the army, prevented

---

[1] Foster Watson, 'The State of Education during the Commonwealth', *Eng. Hist. Rev.* xv. 63–64.

[2] *Fairfax Correspondence*, ed. George W. Johnson (1848), ii. 271–80.

[3] *Victoria County History: Durham*, i (1905), 380–1.

[4] *Comenius in England*, ed. Robert F. Young (1932), pp. 11, 16.

[5] *Commons' Journals*, ii. 176.

[6] Ordinance of 1 Oct. 1646. In the same city, three preachers were granted salaries of from £150 to £100 each. In certain schools the headmaster might keep the fees—sometimes only for extras—and make a profit from boarders.

the state from interfering in the existing educational system except by ejecting royalist fellows of colleges or schoolmasters.

There were three main classes of schools at this time. In the petty schools children were taught for two or three years to read and to spell. At seven or eight years of age they were ready to proceed to a writing school or a grammar school. At the former, additional instruction was given in English by reading at least a chapter once a day, but the two main subjects taught were writing and arithmetic, with which were associated 'such preparative arts, as may make them [the pupils] compleatly fit to undergoe any ordinary calling'.[1]

For anyone wishing to enter one of the professions, an education at a grammar school was customary. The grammar school attained its greatest importance during this period. It was richly supported by the middle classes, which poured their wealth into the endowment of education between 1560 and 1660, probably to a greater extent relatively than during any other hundred years in English history. The number of endowed schools founded in the first half of the seventeenth century was as large as of those founded in the whole of the previous century.

At the grammar school, the usher taught the first three forms Latin grammar from Lily's *Brevissima Institutio*, whose use was first made compulsory in 1540 and authorized again in 1604. Forms four to six were under the direction of the headmaster, and studied rhetoric and Greek and, finally, Hebrew. This insistence on the study of language to the neglect of other subjects was a remarkable illustration of the puritans' acceptance of the Bible as the supreme rule of life. They naturally urged that the young should be taught the languages of the Old and New Testaments and of the patristic writings. The value of this narrow education largely depended on the ability of the schoolmaster to broaden it by such devices as prescribing themes requiring a knowledge of subjects not included in the curriculum. Those Etonians fortunate enough to be entertained at the table of the provost, Sir Henry Wotton, may have found, in his lively conversation about historians and poets, compensation for the aridities of grammar.[2] On the whole, however, although

---

[1] Hoole, *New Discovery* (1912 reprint), p. 56.
[2] See L. Pearsall Smith, *The Life and Letters of Sir Henry Wotton* (Oxford, 1907), i. 203–4.

a contemporary pleaded that there was no calling more serviceable to church and state than that of a schoolmaster, even
he admitted that teaching was a despised occupation.[1]

Another schoolmaster acknowledges the grievous complaints
made, in almost every place, that children who were put to
school either altogether wasted their time or at most learned
very little. As a rule students of fifteen or sixteen years of age
had not 'so much as anie sense of the meaning and true use of
learning, for understanding, resolving, writing, or speaking,
but onely to construe and parse a little'.[2] Even when they had
derived some benefit, they had to lead toilsome lives and endure
overmuch severity.[3] Another frequent complaint was that the
schoolmasters were brutal. There were many like Adam Martindale's teacher, who used to whip boys unmercifully for trivial
causes or even for no faults at all.[4] The usual hours of working
were, in the summer, from 6 to 11 o'clock, and from 1 to 6
o'clock; in the winter the school day began an hour later and
ended an hour earlier. A contemporary authority on both the
theory and practice of education advocated that children should
have part of the afternoon set aside once a week for recreation,[5]
but not infrequently the founder's statutes stood in the way of
any such indulgence.

Of the two universities, it is natural to deal with Oxford first
as the older.[6] Oxford seemed to be flourishing during the first
forty years of the seventeenth century. Towards the end of 1602
the new library that Sir Thomas Bodley had constructed out
of the earlier libraries associated with Cobham and Humphrey,
duke of Gloucester, was ready for use. Its progress was extraordinary. At its opening there were some 2,000 volumes, which
had increased to 6,000 three years later and to 16,000 by 1620.
Later gifts, which added greatly to its treasures, came from men
of such diverse character as Laud, Selden, and Cromwell. The
Stationers' Company in London agreed to give a copy of every
book printed—a generous act, which became a statutory obligation in Charles II's reign. The university press received a new
impetus when Laud secured for it letters patent (1632) authoriz-

---

[1] Hoole, *New Discovery* (1912 reprint), pp. 13, 3.
[2] John Brinsley, *A Consolation for Our Grammar Schools* (1622), p. 8.
[3] Ibid., pp. 1–2.
[4] *Life of Adam Martindale*, p. 14; Brinsley, *Ludus Literarius*, pp. 276–7.
[5] Brinsley, *Ludus Literarius*, pp. 300–1.
[6] For its recognized precedence see *Parliamentary Diary of Robert Bowyer*, pp. 55–56.

ing three printers, each with two presses and two apprentices, and a royal charter (1636) authorizing the printing of 'all manner of books'. Two colleges were founded in the reign of James I, Wadham, a new foundation, and Pembroke, which incorporated Broadgates Hall. Scholarship was not neglected. Sir Henry Savile founded the professorships in geometry and astronomy that still commemorate his name; William Camden, the most famous antiquary of his time, endowed a professorship of ancient history; and the earl of Danby gave the university five acres of land, opposite Magdalen College, for botanical gardens, and spent a large sum in raising and enclosing them in order to promote the study of physics and botany. When the universities were entrusted with the appointments to church livings in the gift of Roman catholic patrons, Oxford received the patronage in the south and west, and Cambridge in the east and north-east.

In spite of this outward appearance of prosperity, all was not well with Oxford. The few surviving narratives of undergraduates agree that drunkenness, licentiousness, and idleness were common.[1] Consequently, when Laud, then bishop of London and afterwards archbishop of Canterbury, was elected chancellor in 1630, he felt impelled to reform the university. It was typical of him that he should have set himself first to ensure the strict observance of formalities, 'the outward and visible face of the university' but then 'utterly decayed'.[2] He was as anxious that students should cap their seniors in the street as that the preacher of an offensive sermon at St. Mary's should be banished the university.[3] In addition he was eager to reform the statutes of the university, which, he said, 'had lain in a confused heap for some ages, and [were] extremely imperfect in all accounts'. In 1636 the Laudian statutes were adopted and remained in force for more than two centuries.

The Laudian code made only such changes in the medieval statutes as were felt to be essential. Instead of introducing radical modifications, it stereotyped and rendered compulsory tendencies that had been growing during the previous century. Its general effect was to strengthen the position of the colleges and to increase the power of their heads. The old 'democracy' of the middle ages disappeared from Oxford. The hebdomadal council, which consisted of the vice-chancellor, the proctors

---

[1] *Autobiography of Thomas Raymond and Memoirs of the Family of Guise*, ed. Godfrey Davies (1917), pp. 116–17.   [2] See *Works*, v. 13.   [3] Ibid., pp. 48, 56–59.

(now no longer elected by vote of all masters of arts but nominated by the colleges under a rotatory system[1]), and the heads became the governing board. Similarly much of the freedom that formerly prevailed was replaced by cast-iron rules. The lectures to be delivered by the various professors and the readers, and the members the university required to listen to them, were all prescribed; it was even stipulated that the lectures should be taken down by students who had not yet attained a master's degree. The disputations that had formed so important a feature in the life of a medieval student were still retained, but with diminished importance, and were supplemented by more regular examinations.

The history of Cambridge is less eventful. Apparently licentiousness and intellectual sterility were as prevalent here as at Oxford. The statutes of 1570 had done for her very much what the Laudian code did for Oxford. They had greatly strengthened the powers of heads of houses, who chose the vice-chancellor and his advisory board, the *caput*. The heads also fixed the times and subjects of lectures, and had veto over the elections of fellows, scholars, and other officers in their own colleges. In fact the former liberal constitution of the university was replaced by an oligarchical rule.

Both universities were very different institutions, under the early Stuarts, from what they had been a hundred years before. They were far less democratic, politically and socially. The heads of colleges had become a distinct body, and the fellows were often divided into seniors and juniors and were at loggerheads; they were now sharply differentiated from the resident bachelors and masters of arts and even more so from undergraduates. The bachelors wishing to become masters were no longer encouraged to reside at the university, and their absence removed a strong link between the governing bodies and the students. This division was the more serious for the undergraduates, since they were often very young.[2] Consequently these lads, surrounded by a multitude of rules, as if they had been schoolboys, seem to have delighted in breaking them with more or less impunity. Apparently the only efficient

[1] It should, however, be noted that the effect of the rotation was to enable the smaller colleges to choose proctors from their own bodies. Without it they would always have been liable to be outvoted by the larger.

[2] The average age at which undergraduates entered Cambridge was about 16 (J. B. Mullinger, *The University of Cambridge* [1884], ii. 398).

check upon them came from their tutor, who was expected to be a kind of guardian as well as instructor. The undergraduate spent his first year on rhetoric and the second and third on logic. Thus there appears to be good ground for Milton's complaint that it was the old error of the universities, not yet well recovered from the scholastic 'grossness of barbarous ages', that they presented their novices with the most intellectual abstractions of logic and metaphysics, with the result that, having had their unbalanced wits tossed in fathomless controversies, the students, for the most part, grew into hatred and contempt of learning.[1] However, this might be said in favour of Cambridge, at least: it was receptive of new ideas upon logic and did not disregard the assault Ramus had made upon Aristotle and his scholastic commentators. In addition, after about 1640, there was a great wave of Platonism, and Cartesianism attracted many disciples. At each university theology was the most important subject, but the exclusion of both Roman catholics and puritans meant that the study was now 'conceived in a more and more narrow, intolerant spirit'.[2]

An example of the sensitiveness of the authorities to any unorthodox views is afforded by the very brief career of Isaac Dorislaus at Cambridge. This former member of the University of Leyden was appointed to a newly founded lectureship in history, but was silenced, ere he had well begun, because when discussing the excesses of Tarquin he was thought to have spoken too warmly in favour of liberty.

Mathematics was wholly neglected by the undergraduates, and the lectures of the mathematical professors were attended, if at all, by bachelors of arts or the possessors of higher degrees. This neglect was not undeserved, for the textbooks used were quite out of date and the lectures showed no signs of contact with the 'new philosophy'. Ptolemy was deemed sufficient as a guide to the celestial system, as was Plato for cosmic theory. On the whole, therefore, it is difficult to dispute Bacon's judgement that the curricula of the two universities were unsuitable to develop the intellect or to extend existing knowledge, although affording good training for the memory.[3]

Oxford and Cambridge, alike, were vitally affected by the civil wars and by the triumph of the puritans. Both contributed

---

[1] *Works*, iv. 278–9.　　　　[2] Mullinger, op. cit. ii. 415.
[3] See, for example, the quotations, ibid., pp. 437–8.

freely to the king's cause and sent most of their plate to be melted down and coined to pay Charles's army, although Oliver Cromwell prevented part of the donation of Cambridge from reaching its destination. Although there was no actual fighting in its streets, Cambridge, as a garrison town, suffered somewhat from the measures taken to fortify it. More serious was the visitation of William Dowsing to enforce an ordinance for the destruction of monuments of superstition, because then much damage was done to college chapels. The real trials began, however, when the earl of Manchester was entrusted with the enforcement of an ordinance (22 January 1644) for regulating the university. The covenant was to be tendered to all fellows, and refusal to take it entailed summary ejection. Despite this, in many colleges the fellows were almost unanimous in their refusal to take the covenant, and expulsions were numerous.

Oxford was the royalist headquarters from the time Charles I retreated before the citizens of London on Turnham Green, until June 1646, when the city surrendered to Fairfax. University life was completely demoralized during this period, and books and lectures were neglected for muskets and pikes. Conditions had not become normal when the ordinance of 1 May 1647[1] nominated visitors who were empowered to summon before them all the members of each college, to tender them the covenant and the negative oath (a promise not to assist the king) and to eject the recalcitrants. After the execution of Charles I, an additional test was imposed—namely, the engagement to be faithful to a government without a king or a house of lords. Thus the members of the university had to submit to two tests, one religious, the other political, the one welcome to presbyterians but unacceptable to Anglicans, especially Arminians, and the other obnoxious to both Anglicans and presbyterians. Therefore the members of the university suffered many vicissitudes. An example is provided by the case of Edward Reynolds, who supplanted Samuel Fell as dean of Christ Church in 1648, was himself replaced by John Owen in 1651, restored in 1659, and ejected the next year.

In spite of wholesale expulsions and the distractions of the times, the standard of scholarship at the universities was well maintained and discipline was certainly much improved. Even Clarendon, a loyal son of Oxford, voiced a tribute of admiration

[1] Cf. ordinances of 26 Aug. 1647 and 27 May 1648.

to 'the harvest of extraordinary good and sound knowledge in all parts of learning; the many who were wickedly introduced applied themselves to the study of good learning and the practice of piety'.[1] However, with the Restoration the universities became slacker and noisier than they had been during the protectorate, but contrived to produce many eminent scholars in various branches of learning.[2]

There were many obstacles in the way of female education. Henry VIII, by destroying nunneries,[3] deprived women of their means of education, and did nothing at all to supply a substitute. The two universities were closed to women, and there was no popular interest in providing institutions of higher education for them. Though Lady Falkland was anxious 'that there might be places for the education of young gentlewomen, and for retirement of widows (as colleges and the Inns of Court and Chancery are for men), in several parts of the kingdom',[4] she accomplished nothing. Girls were likewise excluded from most (but not all) grammar schools; even when admitted they were often dismissed at about the age of nine years, when they had learned some English. Only at the petty schools were they on even terms with boys.

The consequence of these restrictions was that girls' schools began to be established during the reign of James I and later. A number were built in London, especially in Hackney, where pupils of good family were boarded. Apparently, however, more attention was paid by the teachers in such schools to fashionable accomplishments, like music and dancing, than to subjects taught in a boys' grammar school. These seminaries were therefore condemned by many for their encouragement of frivolity.

Most of the learned ladies of the time seem to have been educated by their parents, by a resident chaplain, or by tutors. Lucy Apsley, afterwards the wife and biographer of the regicide John Hutchinson, probably had an unusual experience, because, as she says, there were eight tutors at one time to teach her languages, music, dancing, writing, and needlework. In spite of these distractions, her genius was averse to all save her

---

[1] *History*, x. 124.

[2] Cf. David Ogg, *England in the Reign of Charles II* (1934), ii. 697.

[3] Fuller (*Church History*, iii. 336–7) comments that, if nunneries were extant, 'haply some virgins of highest birth would be glad of such places; and I am sure their fathers and elder brothers would not be sorry for the same'.

[4] Duncon, *Holy Life of . . .Vi-Countess Falkland*, pp. 29–30.

book, and to please her father she learned Latin so quickly as to outstrip her brothers, who were at a grammar school, even though her tutor, a chaplain, was a 'pitiful dull fellow'.[1] By no means all fathers were anxious to have bookish daughters. Sir Ralph Verney, for example, gently rebukes the girl ambitious to know Latin, Greek, and Hebrew, urges her to be content to read her Bible, and promises her some French novels, plays, poetry, and various household recipes.[2]

On the whole it is likely that most women of the upper classes could read and write (although their spelling was abominable), and, if they wished, their parents were willing to provide opportunities for learning dancing, music, and needlework, and perhaps Latin or French, or both. Certainly the part they took in the management of their husbands' estates, especially during the civil war, suggests that they received, at least, a sound elementary education. Moreover it is probable that a fair proportion of the lower classes, both men and women, could read, and the majority of men, at any rate, could write.[3] The prominent share women of the lower middle classes took in theological disputes and sectarian propaganda during 1640–60 would seem to prove that they were not ignorant, though it is possible that some of them were self-taught.

The sons, as well as the daughters, of a family often were instructed by tutors (if their parents could afford them) rather than in schools, and a distinguished authority on the history of education has shown that many of the improvements in education, especially in the teaching of modern subjects, came from outside the ordinary institutions of learning.[4] The tutors of the sons of the rich might and did teach their pupils many subjects neglected by both schools and universities. Moreover the tour abroad which many young men made under the guidance of a tutor gave them excellent opportunities of learning foreign languages as well as of studying antiquities. As a substitute for foreign travel, or the idleness in which noble youths often spent

---

[1] *Life of Colonel Hutchinson*, p. 14.

[2] *Memoirs of the Verney Family*, iii. 73–74.

[3] In several thousand petitions or receipts of Cromwell's army, usually signed by the men but sometimes by their wives, the vast majority, even of the non-commissioned officers and men, could sign their names; and, in the relatively few documents containing the signatures of all the officers and men of regiments in Cromwell's army, perhaps four-fifths of the men signed their names.

[4] Foster Watson, *The Beginnings of the Teaching of Modern Subjects in England* (1909), Introduction.

their time, it was proposed in 1620 that an academy should be erected 'for the breeding and bringing up of the nobility and gentry of this kingdom',[1] but nothing came of this and similar proposals.

Another supplement to or substitute for a university education was supplied by the Inns of Court, where many men of affairs attended, such as Pym and Cromwell. Selden claimed that, in the least frequented of the four Inns of Court, there were about two hundred students, sons of persons of quality. There was, he says, a sort of academy or gymnasium in the Inns, 'where they learn something of all kinds of music, dancing, and such other accomplishments and diversions (which they call revels) as are suitable to their quality, and such as are usually practised at court. At other times . . . the greater part apply themselves to the study of law.'[2]

Science, like other branches of knowledge, owed much to the Renaissance. This revolt against medievalism assumed many forms. Although ultimately all-embracing, it was slow to touch philosophy, for it had at first more urgent tasks on hand. In the sixteenth century its greatest achievements were the Reformation and the erection of the national state; in the seventeenth, the overthrow of scholasticism. Then there was a spirit of free inquiry abroad in the land, which made men no longer content with the old explanations of natural phenomena. The 'truth' that they now required was the kind that was consistent with their observations. 'Truth' to a scholastic, however, depended on its being in harmony with a certain interpretation of the world which was formulated in the thirteenth century. The synthesis by Saint Thomas Aquinas of Aristotelian philosophy and divine teaching, as revealed in the Scriptures, had powerfully influenced the scholasticism of the later middle ages. It allowed little room for the advance of knowledge and it found no place for the prevalent eagerness to investigate the nature of the physical world. The schoolman was mainly concerned with 'why', the scientist with 'how'. The former was content to formulate a rational and logical theory of the universe and did not test his theory by observation. The later middle ages and the Renaissance were fitly represented at the famous meeting between the Paduan professor and Galileo, when the former

[1] See *Old Parliamentary History*, v. 337.　　[2] Watson, op. cit., pp. xxxi–xxxii.

refused to look through the latter's telescope—apparently because he felt that if he saw anything that appeared to contradict the scholastic theories of the heavenly bodies he would be merely deceiving himself. The scientist tried to discover how nature works and to express what he learned in terms of time and space. He wished to explain phenomena as a result of natural forces, not as examples of the workings of Providence. An illustration may suggest the kind of gap between the old outlook and the new. A scholastic philosopher might have been satisfied with an explanation of sunspots that fitted into their cosmic theory without testing it by observation. Even if he wished to make observations he had no adequate instrument before the invention of the telescope. Modern astronomers claim that observations prove that sunspots are caused by the expansion and cooling of certain gases on the surface of the sun. Their theory is not necessarily truer than a scholastic theory, yet the difference in mental attitude and approach may perhaps exemplify the difference in outlook between the medieval and the modern. What it comes to is this—that the kind of explanation that the medieval philosopher had accepted was no longer adequate for the Renaissance philosopher. The former teleological approach slowly yielded to the empirical, and Aristotelianism gave place to the new or experimental philosophy. To a certain extent this implied a return to Platonism and Pythagorean philosophy that was based on mathematics.

One of the first difficulties, therefore, that had to be overcome by the early scientists was the inheritance from the past. They, the 'moderns', were engaged in a fierce struggle against the 'ancients', who upheld, so to speak, the infallibility of classical philosophers. They had to contend not only against the inertia of ignorance but also against the active opposition of authority. It is true that English scientists were beyond the reach of the Inquisition. They could ignore the condemnation the Roman church pronounced against the Copernican revelations of the motions of the earth as absurd in themselves as well as heretical, and they could not be compelled to assent to this condemnation, as Galileo was, on the ground that the arguments of Copernicus ran contrary to the irrefragable evidence of Scripture. Nevertheless even Englishmen had to tread warily at a time when the Bible was regarded as a manual of absolute truth, for popular writers could refute their scientific arguments with the bare assertion that the sun had been ordered to stand still, and this proved that the sun normally moved[1]—fortunately there were texts that could be adduced on the other side. Moreover, while some resented the new philosophy because it 'calls all in doubt', others, like John Donne, felt that it was impious to try to discover the hidden truths of nature. They would have agreed with Milton that the mind or fancy is apt to rove unchecked until taught by experience

> That not to know at large of things remote
> From use, obscure and suttle, but to know
> That which before us lies in daily life,
> Is the prime Wisdom, what is more, is fume,
> Or emptiness, or fond impertinence,
> And renders us in things that most concerne
> Unpractis'd, unprepar'd, and still to seek.[2]

Furthermore, according to Bacon at least, at schools, academies, and colleges, 'everything is found adverse to the progress of science. For the lectures and exercises there are so ordered, that to think or speculate on anything out of the common way can hardly occur to any man.'[3]

In spite of these handicaps there were men whose desire to know more about the secrets of nature was as profound as that of the early discoverers who crossed the ocean to explore the New World.[4] This zeal to advance the frontiers of knowledge, this burning curiosity to disclose the unknown and, in Bacon's phrase, this striving to enlarge 'the bounds of human empire, to the effecting of all things possible',[5] combined to give birth to modern science.

In discussing the history of science under the early Stuarts, it is natural to begin with Francis Bacon. His services to science were threefold. In the first place, as stated elsewhere, he gave it a wonderful advertisement,[6] though it is important to notice that his influence was not great until science began to become fashionable about the middle of the century, except at Oxford, where his influence began to be important in the 1640's. Secondly he advocated the inductive method and stressed the

---

[1] See John Swan, *Speculum Mundi* (1635), pp. 213–14.
[2] *Paradise Lost*, bk. viii, ll. 191–7. Cf. Donne's poem 'The First Anniversary'.
[3] *Works*, iv. 89.
[4] The comparison occurred to Sir Thomas Browne, who spoke of 'the America and untravelled parts of truth'.
[5] *New Atlantis*, in *Works*, iii. 156.   [6] See below, p. 410.

importance of experiments. Thirdly he obviated one of the great dangers threatening scientists—that their conclusions might incur the condemnation of the church.

According to him, what the sciences needed was a form of induction to analyse experience, and by a process of exclusion and rejection lead to an inevitable conclusion.[1] In order that this conclusion might rest on the solid foundation of experience of every kind, he wished that many experiments should be made and the results carefully recorded, so that ultimately natural laws might be framed. Bacon claimed to have 'established for ever a true and lawful marriage between the empirical and the rational faculty';[2] but it must be admitted that his idea of having a large number of experiments performed more or less haphazard was not likely to be very fruitful. The inductive method by itself rarely leads anywhere. Generally, the great discoveries in science have been made in the study from existing data, and afterwards new tests to confirm or refute them are devised in the laboratory. Moreover, although Bacon insisted so strongly upon the value of experiments, he did not keep pace with the work of other scientists, and particularly his own contemporaries in England, very few of whose names are even mentioned in his writings. He rejected both the old Ptolemaic astronomy, because it was too complicated, and the theories of Copernicus, because they were mere hypotheses. His own theory was largely borrowed from Patrizzi and was really old-fashioned.[3] Furthermore, in his attack on Aristotelianism and his insistence upon experimentation he was often merely pushing at an open door, for he had been anticipated by many Englishmen.

As regards the vexed question of religion and science, he was anxious that things human should not interfere with things divine, and argued that the increase of knowledge about nature would not lead to incredulity about religion. He stated that the understanding, being purged of fancies, would be entirely submissive to the divine oracles, and 'give to faith that which is faith's'.[4] There can be little doubt that Bacon's desire to keep religion and science separate was due to his fear of the conservatism and literalness of theologians.[5] That this fear was not

[1] *Works*, iv. 25.　　　　　　　　　[2] Preface to *The Great Instauration*.
[3] *Works*, iii. 716–23.　　　　　　　[4] *Works*, iv. 20.
[5] Here, and elsewhere in this section, I am much indebted to Basil Willey, *The Seventeenth Century Background* (1934).

illusory may be shown in the case of witchcraft, which the pious were content to accept because it was mentioned in the Bible, and belief in which, for that reason, could not be denounced *in toto*.

The continued existence of scholastic 'truth', without any contact with 'truth' as revealed by experiment and observation, is nowhere better illustrated in the seventeenth century than in chemistry.

Many still held fast to the theory, popular at the end of the middle ages, that the primary elements were qualities rather than substances. What were called the 'principles' of sulphur or fire, mercury or liquidity, earth or solidity, were the primary elements. These elements were presumed to reside in bodies, the first representing that part which was combustible, the second what could be distilled, and the third the residue.[1] According to another view, fire, air, earth, and water were the four elements. So long as such theories prevailed, progress was impossible; but they were not seriously shaken until the closing years of the protectorate. At last Robert Boyle supplied the modern definition of an element as a hitherto undissolved part of a compound, and differentiated between a compound and a mixture. But the main contributions of the 'father of chemistry' were made after 1660.

So far as medicine is concerned, the year 1600 is a convenient dividing line between scholasticism and modern science. Some progress had been made during the sixteenth century, but even then the theories of the ancients—Hippocrates, Aristotle, and Galen—still prevailed. One beneficial effect of the Renaissance had been to supply a more accurate knowledge of what the ancient philosophers had actually written, for previously knowledge of their works had come to a great extent from Arabic sources translated into Latin. As the physician derived most of his knowledge from books, the accuracy of the text was very important. Apparently, anatomical classes then largely comprised readings from Galen, with occasional dissections. Galen's theories of the heart, for example, were almost universally accepted, although the keen eye of Leonardo da Vinci had already questioned them. In 1543 Vesalius published a treatise on the structure of the human body, which the historians of science regard as not only 'the foundation of modern medicine

[1] W. C. D. Dampier-Whetham, *A History of Science* (1931), pp. 81–85.

as a science', but also as 'the first great positive achievement of science itself in modern times'.[1] For the first time, the true facts about the structure of the human body were stated. They were made known to English surgeons by the immediate publication of a compendium which plagiarized Vesalius, and by its later translation into English.[2]

Thanks to Vesalius, Padua became the most famous school of medicine, and it was natural that the Englishman William Harvey should go thither for his medical studies at the close of the sixteenth century. On his return to England, Harvey began his careful dissection of all kinds of animals: it is said that he dissected eighty species. By observation he perceived that the valves of the veins would only permit the blood to flow towards the heart, and the valves of the great arteries would only allow the blood to flow away from the heart. He then saw that the flow was continuous and in the same direction. Since the volume of blood pumped from the heart in an hour was much in excess of the weight of a man, he concluded that the blood must circulate. This discovery of the circulation of the blood is the more extraordinary inasmuch as Harvey had no microscope to aid him in his observations: the lack of it prevented his perceiving the transfer of the blood from arteries to veins through capillaries. In spite of this handicap, with the naked eye he made the most important discovery in the history of physiology and laid the basis for nearly all modern advances in that branch of medicine.

In other respects, however, physiology was slow to progress, being impeded by the general belief in the Hippocratic theory that the body contained four chief 'humours'—blood, phlegm, yellow bile, and black bile. A man's temperament depended upon the prevalent humour, which made him sanguine, phlegmatic, choleric, or melancholic. Nevertheless this terminology often concealed genuine scientific observations of mental disorders. Such improvements as were made in therapeutics were partly due to the importation of new drugs and the increased interest in gardening, both of which enabled new medicines to be concocted. Of equal, or greater, importance was the incorporation of the Society of Apothecaries in 1606, when they were

---

[1] Charles Singer, *A Short History of Medicine* (1928), p. 88.
[2] Sanford V. Larkey, 'The Vesalian Compendium of Geminus and Nicholas Udall's Translation', *The Library*, 4th ser. xiii, no. 4 (Mar. 1933).

united with the Grocers. They received a charter of their own in 1617, at which time they were charged with the examination of apprentices who at the end of their seven years' term wanted to set up as apothecaries themselves, the supervision of all apothecaries within the City of London and a radius of seven miles, and the prohibition of any ignorant or undesirable practitioner or the sale of dangerous or unwholesome drugs. Then apothecaries only dispensed medicines, but they began to prescribe them later in the century. In 1618 the College of Physicians celebrated the centenary of its foundation by issuing the *Pharmacopœia Londinensis*, which went through many editions in Latin as well as in a translation. The College performed other services to medicine by testing the capacity of candidates for a licence to practice, though it is said to have examined rigorously those who proposed to remain in London but to have been more lenient with country applicants.[1] Nevertheless, although the elaborate notes some doctors made of their patients' cases proved them to be careful observers,[2] little advance was made in the modern theory of disease until the time of Thomas Sydenham, who belongs to the later rather than the early Stuarts.

In surgery, the great figure was still Ambroise Paré, whose fame long survived his death in 1590. His works, in Latin, were so much in request in England that they were translated in 1634. Paré made two notable contributions: he showed that gunshot wounds were not poisonous and healed better after the application of ointments than of boiling oil, the common treatment; and he substituted the ligature to stop bleeding, in cases of amputation, for the red-hot cautery.

These and other discoveries were slow to exercise a widespread influence upon medical theories and practices. Proof of this may be found in many places. Here it may suffice to mention three: the failure to control the ravages of the plague, the multitude of empirics and quack medicines that abounded, and belief in the royal touch as a cure for the king's evil. Visitations of bubonic plague were especially severe in 1603 and 1625, but it would be unjust to blame physicians exclusively or even mainly. The real responsibility rests upon the local authorities for their failure to provide adequate sanitation and to enforce

---

[1] *Shakespeare's England* (1916), i. 416–17.
[2] The notes of Sir Theodore Turquet de Mayerne threw much light on the health of James I, his wife, and Henrietta Maria.

royal proclamations to that effect. It is of less importance that the doctors could prescribe nothing more efficacious than lancing the sores—a treatment frequently used, apparently, at the time of the Black Death. It is true that for those who desired a novelty, there was Thomas Lodge's prescription to apply a fowl, after plucking out its tail feathers, to the plague carbuncle. The empirics, or quacks, seem to have moved about from town to town then, much as their successors do now. Their mode of advertisement was to hang out a flag, at the inn in which they were lodging, on which were inscribed the names of the diseases they professed to cure.[1] In addition, honest housewives had old-fashioned remedies of miraculous virtue. As a specimen may be quoted a balsam fondly supposed to cure wounds (inward or outward), broken bones, burns or scalds, bruises or cuts, aches of all kinds, cholera, and the bite of a mad dog, besides granting immunity from the plague and staunching blood.[2]

Belief in such salves is not more surprising than belief in the healing grace of a monarch. It is creditable to James I that at the beginning of his reign he was highly sceptical about the practice of touching for the king's evil. He is said to have remarked that he did not see how a patient could be cured without a miracle, and that nowadays miracles did not happen.[3] This conscientious scruple was apparently overcome speedily, however, for within a year or two of James's accession Shakespeare could write in *Macbeth*:

> *Malcolm:* . . . strangely-visited people
> All swollen and ulcerous, pitiful to the eye,
> The mere despair of surgery, he cures,
> Hanging a golden stamp about their necks,
> Put on with holy prayers.[4]

It is natural that Charles I, with his intense belief in the divine attributes of kings, should have continued the practice. It is equally natural that when he was a prisoner in the hands of the army in 1647 parliament should have attempted to destroy faith in this superstition, and that after his execution cures should have been assigned to handkerchiefs dipped in the royal blood. Charles II found that touching for the evil was one of the kingly powers that he could still exercise during his exile.

[1] Middleton, *The Widow*, Act IV, scenes i, ii.
[2] Margaret Blundell, *Cavalier*, p. 59.
[3] Raymond Crawfurd, *The King's Evil* (1911), p. 84.   [4] Act IV, sc. iii.

In medicine the advance of knowledge was achieved by trained practitioners. In other branches of science, however, the amateur made valuable contributions. The explanation of this is supplied by John Wallis, who said that at school and at Cambridge mathematics was hardly regarded as suitable for academic study, but as the business of traders, merchants, seamen, carpenters, surveyors of land, and perhaps some almanac makers in London.[1] Certainly neither of the two greatest mathematicians of the time, John Napier and Wallis himself, owed anything to academic teaching of their subject. The former was a Scottish laird of very diversified interests. He was an agricultural improver, an inventor of machinery for expelling water from a mine, the inveterate enemy of Roman catholicism, an interpreter of the Book of Revelation, and a mathematical scholar of lasting fame. Unaided, he evolved the theory of logarithms, discovered how to construct them, and calculated a table. He contrived the device commonly called 'Napier's bones', by which multiplication and division could be performed. He also described how these mathematical operations might be done mechanically by metal plates arranged in a box. Thus he anticipated both the slide rule and the calculating machine.

The general adoption of logarithms for astronomical and other calculations was largely due to Henry Briggs, the Cambridge mathematician who became Savilian Professor of Astronomy at Oxford. He convinced Napier that logarithms should have 10 as their basis and toiled laboriously at tables that, when published, claimed to contain the logarithms of 30,000 natural numbers worked to 14 places. Edward Wright revolutionized navigation by applying mathematical principles to it. He was the real creator of the so-called Mercator's chart in use today. Perhaps the man who did most to place the study of mathematics on a firm foundation was a country rector, William Oughtred. He wrote a textbook on arithmetic and algebra and a treatise on trigonometry which settled once for all the elementary principles. To the study of this book the mathematical career of Wallis is said to have owed its inception. Within eight years of perusing Oughtred's work, Wallis published his *Arithmetica Infinitorum*, which, in its turn, inspired Isaac Newton. The

---

[1] See Wallis's autobiographical letter, printed in the *Works of Thomas Hearne*, III. cxlvii.

book is important as containing the germ of the differential calculus. Both Napier and Wallis gave to astronomers gifts of great price, for they reduced to a few days the labour of calculating that had hitherto taken months.

What may be called the mathematical side of astronomy having been provided for, there remained observation and theory. Previous to the sixteenth century, belief was almost universal in the Ptolemaic theory that the earth was the stationary centre of the astronomical system, and that the motions of the sun, moon, and planets were around the earth. Copernicus (d. 1543) held that the planets move in orbits around the sun, not the earth, and his theories were warmly welcomed in England by such men as John Dee and Thomas Digges. The latter made a most important addition to the Copernican theory, arguing that the universe was infinite and that the stars were numberless and distributed throughout space at varying distances from the sun, the centre.[1] This idea took such firm hold in England that, when Kepler tried to disprove the theory of an infinite universe, his arguments were refuted by English scientists, like Harriot, who were using telescopes as soon as, or perhaps sooner than, Galileo.[2] This addition to astronomical theory was the most important English contribution before Sir Isaac Newton's, and is especially noteworthy because, just when our own solar system was explained, it postulated a thesis about the far distant regions, and urged that it should be tested by actual observations. Another important contribution was made by Gilbert, whose work on magnetism confirmed the Copernican hypothesis of the earth's rotation. The task, therefore, which confronted scientists in the half century before Newton was to test by observation the theories of Copernicus and the English additions to them. With the aid of the telescope the moderns gained a decisive victory over the ancients, for the phenomena which could now be seen could not be reconciled with scholastic cosmography, even by the most dexterous logicians.

Side by side with these wonderful developments in science, old superstitions still flourished. The astrologer and the alchemist long survived the advent of the modern scientist. They were greatly aided by the popular notion that stars had much

[1] F. R. Johnson and S. V. Larkey, 'Thomas Digges, the Copernican System, and the Idea of the Infinity of the Universe in 1576', *Huntington Library Bulletin*, no. 5, p. 72.   [2] Ibid., p. 116.

influence upon men's lives.[1] The extent to which the populace was willing to listen to astrologers is demonstrated by Evelyn's comment that their prognostications about an eclipse of the sun had so alarmed the whole nation that hardly anyone worked or stirred out of doors when it occurred.[2] The two best-known astrologers in early Stuart times were John Lambe and William Lilly. The former, a crystal-gazer, enjoyed great popularity in the 1620's, and among his wealthy clients was the duke of Buckingham, whose amorous adventures he was popularly supposed to have aided with love charms. For this reason, among others, he incurred the enmity of the London mob, and was beaten to death two months before his patron's assassination. Lilly had a longer and luckier career and retained the confidence of the credulous to the end of his life. He specialized in cryptic prophesying of both public and private events, and was as ready to claim to have foretold the execution of Charles I as to accept payment for predicting the success of a courtship.

More serious than credulity in impostors was the widespread belief in witchcraft. Probably in all ages such a belief was common among the masses, but in the seventeenth century, at least, it was not rejected by the highest or most learned in the land. The basis of the belief seems to have been the desire to explain what was otherwise unaccountable, together with fear of the malignity of witches. James, who while still king of Scotland wrote a book called *Dæmonologie* to demonstrate the reality of witches and who prided himself on his skill in detecting them, apparently was first convinced of their existence by the unseasonably rough weather that disturbed his voyage when he brought his wife, Anne of Denmark, home to Scotland. The common people likewise (as a contemporary remarked), if they suffered any adverse sickness, or loss of corn or cattle, promptly accused some neighbour or other as a witch.[3] Whenever a misfortune happened in the countryside, someone was liable to recall that an old deformed male, or much more probably female, had once cursed the unlucky individual; since the curse had come true, the curser was bewitched; once that stage was reached, vivid imaginations supplied evidence that the witch was in league with the devil, was visited by imps, and had a

---

[1] See, as an example, Edward Corbet, *Gods Providence, a Sermon Preached before the House of Commons*, 28 Dec. 1642, pp. 12–13.   [2] *Diary*, 5 Apr. 1652.
[3] *The Oxinden Letters*, ed. Dorothy Gardiner, p. 221.

familiar. Those higher in the social scale were often willing to accept the evidence of certain tests—to throw the witch, bound, into the water, when if she did not sink she was clearly a witch, because water was pure and rejected one who had dishonoured her baptism by becoming a witch; or to keep the accused without sleep for two or three days on end and to regard the confession that almost inevitably followed as proof of guilt.[1]

The notoriety attained by the persecution of witches in the century and a half that followed the Reformation would seem, at first sight, to connect it with protestantism. The connexion, if it exists at all, is very slight, for the general acceptance of witchcraft rested on a fear inherited from the dark ages. The protestant's study of the Bible merely supplied him with some texts that bolstered up an already existing belief. Elizabethan and Jacobean statutes against witchcraft, and the works written about it, defined it, and the increased interest in the trials of witches led to their being reported, some at considerable length. These facts explain why the more frequently recorded persecution of witches may have seemed due to protestant fervour.

The figures of executions for witchcraft, although much more numerous, bear some resemblance to those for catholic martyrdoms. In each case there was a considerable number of victims during the first half of the reign of James I, very few under Charles I down to 1642, a large increase during the supremacy of parliament, and an almost total cessation during the commonwealth and protectorate. The worst period of persecution was during 1645–7, when two hundred or more were executed in the eastern counties, chiefly as the result of a crusade of one Matthew Hopkins, who deliberately adopted the mission of witch-hunter.

As early as 1584, Reginald Scot had demonstrated the absurdities involved in the common belief in witchcraft, and had denounced the methods by which evidence was often secured against witches, but there is little to indicate that his arguments prevailed. So long as the existence of witches was accepted as a matter of course, without investigation, this superstition was likely to endure. Fortunately, however, the willingness to adopt traditional belief was being challenged by the new spirit of inquiry. There is a story told of Sir William Harvey's having

[1] Voluntary confessions often seem to have been the hallucinations of crazy old folk whose madness took the form of fancying they had magical powers.

heard of a woman reputed to be a witch and having visited her at her lonely house at the edge of a heath. He overcame her mistrust of him by assuring her that he was a wizard, and said he would like to see her familiar. She thereupon called a toad from under a chest and it drank milk she had brought. Harvey then suggested that, as fellow witches, they ought to drink together. While the woman was absent getting some ale, he cut the toad open, and out came the milk. Thorough examination convinced him that the toad was a 'playne naturall' one, which no doubt the 'melancholly and poore' woman had found, tamed, and finally come to regard as a spirit and her familiar. She was enraged when she found what Harvey had done, and 'flew like a Tigris at his face'; but, by telling her that he was the king's physician sent to find out whether she were a witch and if so to apprehend her, he subdued her sufficiently to be able to escape—fully persuaded that 'there are no witches'.[1]

The advance in outlook of the new philosophy over the old is well illustrated by the comparison between the water test, which was based on the purely arbitrary assumption that water was pure and would reject witches, and the experimental test by Harvey. Fortunately, there were signs that the experimental philosophy was attracting increasing attention. Knowledge of it became more and more available, especially for the citizens of London, for whose benefit Sir Thomas Gresham had endowed seven professorships, at Gresham College, in order that their holders might lecture on the seven 'liberal arts'—divinity, law, physics, astronomy, geometry, rhetoric, and music. Perhaps as important as the education thus provided was the attraction the college had for scientists from all parts. Gradually it tended to become identified with the new philosophy, and about 1645 a group interested in it used to meet weekly in London, at Gresham College and elsewhere, to discuss 'Physick, Anatomy, Geometry, Astronomy, Navigation, Staticks, Magnetics, Chymicks, Mechanicks, and Natural Experiments'. Three or four years later the group was divided, some continuing to meet in London, and others, on their removal to Oxford, meeting there, often at the lodgings of the warden of Wadham College, John Wilkins. These meetings brought together a body of scientists, and those interested in science, who, after the Restoration, were

[1] Wallace Notestein, *A History of Witchcraft in England from 1558 to 1718* (1911), pp. 160–2, citing *Gentleman's Magazine*, 1832, pt. i, pp. 407–8.

incorporated in the Royal Society. One explanation of the scientists' desire to share knowledge and exchange ideas with their fellow workers[1]—of which these meetings were the outward sign—may be that they were beginning to realize the need of specialization. At least it is certain that, whereas in the sixteenth century Englishmen like Recorde or Dee could without presumption write about all branches of science, their successors in the seventeenth century usually found it necessary to restrict themselves to one branch—a Briggs to mathematics or a Harvey to medicine.

[1] It is likely that the stress Bacon laid on scientists' need for co-operation had some influence on the Oxford group at least.

XIV

THE ARTS

In the history of English art, the period 1603–60 is noteworthy for the portrait painters and remarkable for its miniaturists, but is singularly devoid of landscape and decorative artists of considerable merit. It is capable of a threefold division: 1603 to 1632, when Van Dyck settled in England; the decade of Van Dyck; and the twenty years after his death in 1641. During the whole time, the influence and often the presence of foreign artists are very persistent (though in the first quarter of the century the influence of Hilliard the miniaturist was predominant even in oil-painting), while the English painters were frequently the sons or grandsons of immigrants, usually from the Low Countries. During the first of the three divisions enumerated above, the foremost artists were Marc Gheeraerts, Paul van Somer (both in the Flemish tradition), and Daniel Mytens (a Dutch painter), all of whom were primarily portrait-painters and the last appointed picture-drawer for life to the king. The life of English-born Cornelius Johnson (or Janssen) outranges the period at both ends, but he was most active in England during the twenties and thirties. At first we may suspect that he applied himself to painting in miniature, but later he turned his hand to portraits, of which the best are, perhaps, Sir Ralph Verney (1634) and Henry Ireton (c. 1640). In each, much of the inner man seems revealed, and it is clear that the painter is trying to interpret his subjects, not merely to reproduce externals. Both these portraits owe much to Anthony Van Dyck. Although a large part of the life of that great artist lies outside an account of English art, yet the influence of this decade in England was so lasting that it was not displaced for the best part of a century. Some of the qualities that made Van Dyck's work so admired were his fluent draughtsmanship, his grace and ease of pose, the arrangement, his striking design, rich colour, and the silvery tone of many of the portraits. Among those who worked in his studio was William Dobson, of whom it has been said that 'in his most characteristic work he is the most typical exponent of the English temper in seventeenth-century painting'.[1]

[1] C. H. Collins Baker and W. G. Constable, *English Painting of the Sixteenth and Seventeenth Centuries* (1930), p. 46.

Dobson died in 1646, and thus did not feel profoundly the sombre influence of puritanism. On the other hand Robert Walker was permeated by the seriousness of the times, and his portraits of John Hampden and Oliver Cromwell are excellent examples of puritanism as interpreted in art. Although Walker stood aloof from his contemporaries, yet they did not remain untouched by the influence that made so marked an impression upon him. There are few finer examples of the influence of an age upon an artist than is provided by Lely's career. He came to England from Holland the year Van Dyck died, adapted his earlier Dutch style to the more courtly model of the Flemish master, and expressed on canvas the spirit of the romantic cavaliers. When the cavaliers were defeated, however, and Lely painted their conquerors, he abandoned the courtliness and elegance of those early portraits in order to reproduce the spirit of militant puritanism. It is typical of Cromwell to have told the artist to paint him truly as he was and to retain all the warts and pimples or he would not pay a farthing for the portrait, and it is equally typical of Lely that he should have been in need of such a warning.

The distinctively English contribution to technique is modern miniature portrait painting. This had been a natural development from the illumination of manuscripts in England and can be traced to Holbein and the staff of foreign and possibly native limners that he found already at the court of Henry VIII. His English successors in the late sixteenth century and through three-quarters of the seventeenth century developed a peculiarly English technique and brought the art of miniature painting to its perfection. Sometimes large-scale portraits were reproduced in miniature in several copies, in order that these should be available as gifts. And both Isaac and Peter Oliver made many little copies of famous Italian pictures. We are told that Charles II when in Scotland in 1651 had thirteen miniatures made of himself to give to his prominent supporters, and during the protectorate the Swedish ambassador was given a miniature of Oliver Cromwell by Samuel Cooper. The first miniaturist to be noticed is Nicholas Hilliard of Exeter, who confessed that he had always imitated Holbein. But, unconsciously perhaps, he evolved a new technique and a new perception of English life and character. He is the most illuminating interpreter of late Tudor England, and determined the form of English portraiture for his generation.

His best follower was Isaac Oliver, a lively and delicate master. The two John Hoskinses, father and son, covered the reign of Charles I and outlived the republic. They were in no respect the equals of Hilliard or Oliver, in miniature technique or originality of vision, and were far surpassed by Samuel Cooper, who is generally acclaimed as the greatest of all miniaturists. In technique and characterization he did for his age what Hillard had done for an earlier age. He was equally successful with Cromwell (whose best likeness he made), with his supporters, and with Charles II and his courtiers, and has left behind some seventy signed and dated portraits in miniature.

From this brief description it may be clear that, miniatures apart, the first half of the seventeenth century was not a great period in the history of English art, for none of the native artists produced work that approaches the masterpieces of continental painters at this time. Nevertheless English portrait painters had already done sufficient to create a distinctive English temper in art. That temper had an individuality and sensitiveness of its own, so that the student who examines the work of Hilliard, Johnson, Dobson, or Cooper can be certain that he is looking at the portrait of an Englishman painted by an Englishman. It is true that the work of the Stuart painters was amateurish compared with that of their great foreign rivals, and lacked mechanical invention and sureness of touch. They were somewhat insular in technique, but might have profited from a study of Italian and Flemish masterpieces if the civil war had not dispersed or checked the rich collections of foreign art which several nobles, and especially Charles I, were making.

Undoubtedly some of the credit for the high artistic standard attained at this time should be given to the patrons who supported the artists and the collectors who bought their canvases. As a rule patronage and collecting went hand in hand, and this is particularly true of two collectors who deserve special mention, Thomas Howard, second earl of Arundel, and Charles I. The former, who was called by Horace Walpole the 'father of vertu in England', inherited a fine library and a choice gallery from a relative, Lord Lumley,[1] and in order to add to the number of his books and paintings he not only travelled extensively on the Continent himself but also employed agents there. The

---

[1] Mary F. S. Hervey, 'A Lumley Inventory of 1609', *Walpole Society*, vi. 36–50.

inventory[1] of his pictures attests the richness and size of his collection as well as the catholicity and soundness of his taste. He also gathered a celebrated collection of antique marbles, inscriptions, and gems.

Charles I, who inherited the collection of his brother Henry, and, later, the pictures in the royal palaces, amassed an even finer gallery than Arundel, although he had to rely on agents for purchases abroad. The king was especially interested in the Italian masters and was fortunate in securing early in his reign the collection owned by Vincenzo, duke of Mantua, including Mantegna's great tempera series, 'The Triumphs of Caesar', still at Hampton Court. Charles was a genuine connoisseur. He tried in vain to persuade Rubens to remain in England on the occasion of his diplomatic visit in 1630, but profited by his advice to buy the Raphael cartoons (now on loan to the Victoria and Albert Museum), which he intended to have reproduced by the royal tapestry looms at Mortlake. He did actually succeed in inducing Van Dyck to make his home in England. On the whole the eulogy Wotton pronounced on the king is well deserved, that he had so adorned his palaces with pictures and sculpture that 'Italy (the great mother of elegant arts) or at least (after the Grecians) the principall nurse, may seem by your magnificence to be translated into England'.[2] After the execution of Charles I, an ordinance was passed (4 July 1649) for the sale of the goods and personal estate of the late king, and, an inventory[3] having been made, the pictures were disposed of by private sale, which dragged on till 1652–3. Some were bought by Cardenas and found a new home in Madrid, while others were dispersed, and either then or later were taken to Paris, Vienna, or St. Petersburg. Those that were bought by Englishmen, and the Dutch collector Van Reynst, were recovered by Charles II at the Restoration.

The evolution of architecture in England progressed regularly and smoothly from the eleventh century to the sixteenth, and was not subject to any strong foreign influence. The four great periods, called respectively Norman, Early English, Decorated,

---

[1] Mary F. S. Hervey, *The Life, Correspondence, & Collections of Thomas Howard, Earl of Arundel* (1921), App. v.

[2] Sir Henry Wotton, *A Panegyrick of King Charles* (1644), pp. 103–4.

[3] Extracts, with notes, are printed in the *Nineteenth Century*, Aug. 1890, pp. 211–17; cf. *Hist. MSS. Comm., Seventh Report* (1879), pp. 88–92.

and Perpendicular, succeeded one another naturally and harmoniously. The great monuments of this Gothic style are cathedrals and ecclesiastical buildings. Domestic architecture was so dominated by the need for defence against attack that the surviving castles are more interesting as types of medieval fortresses than as dwellings. Monasteries, however, were not built primarily for security, and in them rather than in castles are to be found the origins of the modern house. About the beginning of the sixteenth century an outside influence was felt and the spirit of the Italian Renaissance started to permeate building as it did other activities. It is important to notice that many of the missionaries of the Renaissance were German or Dutch—Holbein being the most famous—and that in the Elizabethan age a very influential book was *Architectura*, by de Vries of Antwerp (1563). Once the new spirit got under way, it spread with such potent force that native characteristics almost disappeared and foreign models were slavishly copied in England.[1]

The new and the old had little in common. The Gothic style in England was flexible, plastic, adaptable, and variable, with a strong tendency towards pronounced vertical lines. The classical style of Italy, on the other hand, was regular and symmetrical, and its trend was towards well-marked horizontal lines.[2] The progress of classical architecture in England was slow; the style in vogue down to 1625 is usually called Early Renaissance, and that of the subsequent period Later Renaissance. The new style came in at a time of great building activity, when the nobility of the Tudors had the means to gratify to the full the spirit of the Renaissance, the love of grandeur and lavish display which characterized the Elizabethan age. They required large mansions or palaces as a setting for their stately lives, and it was in the construction of their homes that the changes in architecture are first noticeable. Knowledge of this new style was acquired partly first-hand from the visits English craftsmen paid to foreign lands, and partly as a result of the invention of printing, which

---

[1] The attitude of Englishmen to the Gothic style is well illustrated by John Evelyn, a cultured gentleman, when he condemns the middle ages for 'mountains of stone, vast and gygantic buildings indeed, but not worthy the name of architecture'. The Renaissance he praises because it rescued architecture from 'a night of ignorance and superstition' ('An Account of Architects and Architecture', in *Miscellaneous Writings*, ed. William Upcott [1825], p. 367).

[2] J. A. Gotch, *Early Renaissance Architecture in England* (1901), pp. 3–6.

enabled men to see in books plans and drawings of recent buildings abroad and to read the rules Italian architects had laid down about the proportions of buildings. These rules had been formulated from the examination of classical ruins and from the study of the great classical treatise on architecture by Vitruvius, the discovery of whose manuscript *De Architectura Libri Decem* in the fifteenth century and its publication in 1486 (and in many subsequent editions) are of the greatest importance in the history of Renaissance architecture.[1] At first English designers felt their way cautiously towards the Renaissance style; they retained the Gothic framework but used Italian ornaments. Their task was difficult, because they had to apply rules which were not devised for the type of building they had to erect, since there was no exact counterpart on the Continent to the mansions of Tudor England. They had to face the problem of adapting the foreign style to native use, and their lack of experience accounts for the rather diversified and experimental types of houses[2] built during the late Tudor and early Stuart periods. It was not until the time of Inigo Jones and Sir Christopher Wren that the problem was solved.

A typical mansion at the end of Elizabeth's reign would be likely to have most of the features described below. The building would be in the form of a rectangle enclosing an open court, with the main entrance in the middle of the north side. Exactly opposite, across the court, would be the hall porch, leading to a passage with screens on either side, the one leading to the kitchens, larders, and winter parlour (a novelty designed for use during cold weather), the other giving on to the hall. During the middle ages the hall had been the centre of the household life, and even now it was only slightly less important. It usually occupied the full height of the building, and was very similar to halls at Oxford and Cambridge colleges, with a dais at the end opposite the entrance and a fireplace at the side, and perhaps bow windows at the ends of the dais so as to provide space for tables for carving. A door from the dais led to the parlour and other living rooms. The two wings of the building held 'lodgings'—sets of two or three rooms, with a door to the court through which the guest would normally pass on his way to the

---

[1] In his *Elements of Architecture* (1624), Sir Henry Wotton writes: 'Our principall master is Vitruvius.'

[2] Sometimes called bastard Gothic.

hall or reception rooms, although the intercommunication of the rooms made it possible to go from one part of the building to another without stepping outside. The windows were narrow and mullioned. The roof was often broken by gables, usually of steep pitch, and sometimes curved, and the chimneys were often massed together into great stacks set at intervals. Novel features might be the long gallery situated in one of the wings of the building and measuring something like 150 by 16 feet, and an open terrace or loggia on the north side of the court, facing the noonday sun.

Among the changes that modified the Elizabethan house were: the conversion of the hall into a vestibule only one story high; the diminution or even disappearance of the inner court and the absence of wings, so that the building became a solid, or nearly solid, rectangle instead of a larger but hollow one or one with a side unbuilt and open; the disuse of gables and the substitution of plain chimney stacks in a single block instead of the ornamental dispersed chimney stacks, with a separate shaft for each flue; and the replacement of the former wide stone mullions by narrow, wooden ones. In addition cornices now surrounded the building and their moulding served to emphasize each story, the top cornice usually being the most pronounced. Pilasters, either square or rounded, with decorated bosses, served to connect the lower and upper cornices and to offer relief to the otherwise plain space between windows.

The first resounding triumph of the classical style in England was the Banqueting House, Whitehall, erected in 1619–22, and now the Royal United Service Museum. This building exhibited no traces of the traditional English style and was at once hailed by contemporaries as a masterpiece of modern architecture; and posterity has fully endorsed their verdict. Its length was 110 feet and its height and breadth each 55 feet. It depended for effect, therefore, upon Inigo Jones's magnificent sense of proportion. That great designer had at one step equalled the finest work of Palladio and others, whose designs the English artist had studied in print and during his visits to Italy. Another gem, started earlier but not finished until more than a decade later, was the Queen's House at Greenwich. Almost as well known were the piazza and St. Paul's Church, Covent Garden, whose portico furnished a model for the entrance to

many an aristocratic home. Both were celebrated in Gay's
Trivia:

> Where Covent-Garden's famous temple stands,
> That boasts the work of Jones' immortal hands;
> Columns with plain magnificence appear,
> And graceful porches lead along the square.[1]

Inigo Jones was as successful with the interiors of houses as
with their exteriors. Fine examples of his designing are to be
found in the state rooms at Wilton, Wiltshire. Indeed the
'double cube' (60 feet by 30 by 30), with its panels filled with
Van Dyck's portraits of the Herberts, and the height of the
walls lessened by coving above a strong cornice, has been called
the finest room in England.[2] An illustration of this room, or of
any state room, will show that internal decoration had developed
marvellously from the day of the baronial hall with its arras.
Now, Jacobean panelling had often displaced the tapestry, and
its carving had almost become an art in itself. The scenes carved
there were much the same as those the tapestry weavers had
depicted. Moreover the plaster work of the ceilings had become
highly decorative, not only with heraldic emblems and scrolls
but with representations of beasts and birds. There were two
further kinds of ornaments which had been rarely seen in a
home before the sixteenth century but which were eagerly
sought far and wide in the seventeenth, pictures and sculpture.
Wotton compared them, in their relation to architecture, to
the gentlewomen who dress and trim their mistress. These arts
had become so fashionable under the early Stuarts that a house
without collections of them would have seemed bare indeed.

Although tapestry lost its dominating position as a decoration
for the state rooms of the wealthy, it was still highly prized.
Indeed the seventeenth century constitutes a famous period in
the history of tapestry weaving, both in France and England.
In the former country Henry IV installed royal workshops in
Paris and Louis XIV organized the Gobelins' factory. In Eng-
land James I started a manufactory at Mortlake. In 1619 Sir
Francis Crane was authorized to establish a manufactory of all
kinds of tapestry in England and allowed to bring from the
Low Countries a number of tapestry weavers. He started his

---

[1] Bk. ii, ll. 343-6.
[2] J. Alfred Gotch, *The English Home* (1919), p. 58, where is a fine illustration of
the double cube.

workshop at Mortlake under favourable auspices, for court
and nobility furnished a rich clientele. One of the most famous
Mortlake tapestries is 'Vulcan and Venus', now in the Victoria
and Albert Museum. Until Crane's death in 1636 the looms
were kept busy, but orders were infrequent during the civil war.
Under the commonwealth the council of state, probably to
encourage native manufactures, showed great interest in the
enterprise at Mortlake and even allowed prisoners captured
during the naval war against the Dutch to be employed as
tapestry weavers there. The revival was short-lived, however,
for Charles II did not share his father's delight in the fine arts.

Furniture was both a decoration and a necessity of the home.
Throughout Elizabeth's reign observers had seen the growing
luxury of all classes, and some thought they detected in it signs
of a decline in English endurance. Certainly, compared with
the furniture of a baronial castle, that of a Jacobean house
might well have seemed effeminate. The rushes, often so noi-
some, which, until towards the end of the sixteenth century, had
served to cover the floor, were giving way to carpets or matting.
Surviving examples prove that there was a 'most remarkable
school of carpet-weaving . . . national in spirit, design, and
colour'.[1] Englishmen also sought eagerly for both Turkish and
Persian carpets. The old trestle table was being replaced by a
table with ornamental legs joined by stretchers, and the benches
by joint-stools, which continued to be used for sitting at table
except by the master and mistress of the house. When a distinguished guest was being entertained, he alone was offered a
chair. As late as 1669, when the grand duke of Tuscany was
visiting Wilton, the earl of Pembroke had provided an arm-
chair at the head of the table for his guest, but the duke insisted
on giving it to his host's daughter, whereupon the earl instantly
drew forth another similar chair for the duke, the rest of the
company sitting upon stools.[2] The chairs used at this time were
of many kinds. The old X-type still survived, but was now often
upholstered with cloth of gold, satin, or less expensive material.
There were oak-panelled arm-chairs as well as plain upright
armless chairs,[3] upholstered in leather (tacked into place with

---

[1] Percy Macquoid and Ralph Edwards, *The Dictionary of English Furniture*, i
(1924), 188.   [2] *Travels of Cosmo the Third* (1821), p. 150.
[3] It is said that the absence of arms was to accommodate the enormous skirts
women often wore.

large-headed nails), and with balustered legs and a stretcher. A piece of furniture that made its appearance towards the end of Elizabeth's reign and became increasingly popular was the buffet of inlaid oak or walnut. Often in the homes of the rich there would be several decorative buffets in the long gallery, serving partly as ornaments in themselves and partly to display china or bronzes. There were usually cabinets and tables of exquisite workmanship standing about the rooms.

In the grand chamber the bed was remarkable. Indeed it was often far and away the most valuable piece of furniture in the mansion. The back frequently had panels carved or inlaid, and at the foot were carved posts supporting a tester with a cornice. From the tester hung rich material, perhaps cloth of gold, which could be drawn completely round the bed at night. Since the foundation of the bed itself was commonly straw or wool, two or three feather beds were superimposed, so that getting in must have entailed a climb. It is no wonder that wooden pins had to be stuck into the sides of the bedstead to prevent the feather beds and clothes from slipping on to the floor.

The improvement in the environment of the house was as striking as in its internal decoration. Although there had been in the middle ages beautiful gardens attached to the palaces of kings or to the richer monasteries, the insecurity of the times and the style of medieval architecture had not been propitious for laying out gardens. But during the sixteenth and seventeenth centuries peace and prosperity encouraged indulgence in what Bacon called 'the purest of human pleasures . . . without which buildings and palaces are but gross handyworks'.[1] As in architecture, the influence of the Renaissance was very potent, especially because those responsible for the architecture of the house were frequently also the designers of the grounds. The garden and the house were regarded as integral parts of a single design and the result was harmony. The development of the flower garden distinct from the orchard and the vegetable garden was the great feature of this period, but of almost equal importance was the arrival, from newly discovered regions, of trees, plants, and flowers,[2] hitherto unknown on English soil. Also notable was the incorporation of the gardeners of London

[1] Essay xlvi.
[2] For a list see Eleanour Sinclair Rohde, *The Story of the Garden* (1932), p. 99.

in 1605, and the prohibition to work as a gardener before a seven years' apprenticeship had been served.

The formal garden at this time was remarkable for the simplicity of its plan. The space available was divided into rectangles or squares, with a broad walk running from end to end, and was situated directly in view of the front of the house to which it belonged. The garden at Wilton, which Evelyn called the finest in England, was laid out by a French architect resident in England, Isaac de Caux, who published plates to illustrate his work and added a description. The garden was 1,000 feet long, 400 broad, and divided into three rectangles, each subdivided by the great walk. The first was again divided by a lateral path, and in each of the four plots were fountains, with flower beds. The second rectangle had the river Nadder running through it and under the great walk, and was remarkable for its groves and two covered arbours 300 feet long, with divers alleys. The shrubs were often clipped and trimmed into ornamental, if unnatural, shapes. In the last rectangle were two ponds with fountains, a lane with walks planted with cherry trees, and a statue of a gladiator in bronze. At the end of the great walk was a portico highly decorated with pilasters and marble figures.[1] Bacon suggests that such statues and other ornaments produced the impression of stateliness and magnificence but added nothing to the true pleasure of a garden; but they were a counterpart out of doors of the collections of marbles inside.

The orchard was clearly intended by the formal gardeners to be an apple garden. Writers recommended that it should be laid out with walks provided with seats of camomile and borders and beds of flowers. Even kitchen gardens were edged with roses and lavender. Clearly the love of sweet-smelling flowers was very strong. Probably one of the greatest differences between the Stuart and the modern garden was the presence in the former of many herbs. Their use to flavour salt meat during the winter and to supply all kinds of home-made medicines gave them an importance they no longer retain. Generally speaking, the gardens contained all the flowers which today are often labelled 'old-fashioned' and the vegetables now in common use, including the then recent importation, the potato.

Formal gardens, like Italian houses, were few and far between in early Stuart England. Most Englishmen lived amid surround-

---

[1] Reginald Blomfield, *The Formal Garden in England* (1901), pp. 54-56.

ings little affected by change in styles of architecture. Manor houses were too diverse to admit of easy generalization, but possibly it would be true to say that the richer the owners the more likely that their dwellings would conform to modern taste in architecture. The citizen in the town usually lived in a wooden or half-timbered house several stories high, with each story overhanging the one below. The object of this device was apparently to provide space and shelter for a stall on which to display merchandise in the narrow street. The ground floor included both shop and workshop, and the master, his family, probably his apprentices, and possibly journeymen, lived in the upper stories. In the country there was no need for over-hanging stories, but here, also, the houses of the middle class were usually wooden or half-timbered unless there was an ample supply of stone but a lack of trees in the vicinity. Prob-ably the famous description William Harrison wrote for Holin-shed's *Chronicle*, at the beginning of the last quarter of the sixteenth century, was still true fifty or even a hundred years later. 'The greatest part of our building in the cities and good townes of England, consisteth onelie of timber, for as yet few of the houses of the communaltie (except here & there in the West countrie townes) are made of stone, although they may (in my opinion) in diuerse other places be builded so good cheape, of the one as of the other.'[1] Confirmatory evidence is provided by the many proclamations issued both by James I and Charles I to regulate building in London. They attempted to confine new buildings to old foundations and to prescribe that their outer walls should be of brick or stone, a brick and a half thick, and that each story should be 10 feet high. James declared that it was his wish that it should be said of him that, while he had found the houses of the city and suburbs of Lon-don of sticks, he had left them of bricks.[2] Harrison goes on to say that, in the Fen district and in the North, houses were built of stakes and wattle and that in many places a few upright and cross posts formed a framework between which clay-covered panels kept out the wind and rain. A foreign traveller, writing about ninety years later, gives the best description of houses then. At Plymouth, for example, he says the buildings were antique and constructed according to the English fashion, being

[1] Harrison, *Description of England*, ed. F. J. Furnivall (1877), p. 233.
[2] Proclamation of 16 July 1615.

tall and narrow, with pointed roofs, and with large glass windows in each of the different stories. These were occupied, he added, from top to bottom. In the West country he noticed that the cottages in the small villages were made of mud mixed with short straws and chips of slate, and were thickly thatched with straw.[1] Another observer, John Aubrey, remarked in 1671 that glass windows were seen everywhere, even in the dwellings of the poorest who lived on alms, whereas before the civil wars the houses of the lower classses had no glass.[2]

The evils of overcrowding were very prevalent, especially in London, where in some quarters a house often contained as many families as rooms. Frequent proclamations against letting cellars to lodgers, or the subdivision of a home into tenements, were ineffective, perhaps through lack of co-operation from local authorities. The result of their slackness was the ever present danger of infection with the plague in congested areas or of fire through the inflammable materials of which dwellings were built. In the country districts, at least, these perils might have been avoided if builders had observed the Elizabethan statute which provided that no cottage might be erected unless four acres of land were joined to it. Probably here, too, the selfish interests or the indolence of the justice of the peace often allowed the law to become a dead letter.

The last years of the sixteenth century and the first thirty of the seventeenth form what is known in histories of music as the 'madrigalian era'. The madrigal—an unaccompanied song for several voices—was so popular then that Henry Peacham prescribed for his *Compleat Gentleman* 'to sing your part sure, and at the first sight'.[3] Simultaneously, sacred music regained the high standard it had been in danger of losing during the Reformation. Perhaps a domestic, amateur nature was the main characteristic of music at a time when it was the recreation of all educated folk. Another feature was that the same man was often both composer and performer. The greater facilities for printing naturally affected music, but even so it is remarkable that, whereas between 1530 and 1587 there was only one collection of secular music published, between 1587 and 1630 there were eighty-eight collections, mainly secular.

[1] *Travels of Cosmo the Third*, pp. 124–8.   [2] *Brief Lives*, ii. 329.
[3] Ed. 1661, p. 100.

William Byrd (?1542–1623), the most representative figure
in Elizabethan music, like most composers of the time was an
organist and a member of the chapel royal. His versatile genius
produced anthems, masses, songs both sacred and secular,
and many pieces for instrumental music, especially for the
virginals, a keyed instrument which preceded the spinet. Orlando Gibbons (1583–1625), his younger contemporary, was
almost equally versatile. He composed some of the finest English madrigals and anthems, and, with John Bull (*c.* 1562–1628),
Farnaby, and Okeaver, has the distinction of being among the
first to compose primarily for viols and the virginals, and thus
prepared the way for the chamber music of the Restoration.
Nevertheless it has been well said that today 'we sing the music
of Byrd and Gibbons because it was written for all time; we
play their music because it recalls to us, as nothing else can, the
transient fashions of a day that is past'.[1]

These composers belonged to a distinctively English school
and were little influenced by the new music which was pervad-
ing Italy at the end of the sixteenth century and which culminated in the opera. During Charles's reign this new influence
began to be potent and made the years 1625–60 a transitional
period. By degrees the old polyphonic music was supplanted by
the homophonic: the several melodies loosely combined, yielded
to the composition in which one melody was predominant. The
madrigal gradually vanished and solo vocal music took its
place, and by the end of the century the victory of the modern
was complete. Nevertheless there was no sudden revolution in
musical composition in England and continuity was preserved.

During the 1630's the masque, which had already become
popular in James I's reign, supplied the main theme for composers. The most famous is *Comus*, set to music by Henry Lawes
(1595–1662); but there were plenty of others. Lawes was probably the most eminent composer of his generation, but it is
likely that he owes some of his posthumous fame to his association with the poems of Milton and Herrick (for some of whose
lyrics he supplied airs) and to their highly eulogistic verses. In
fact, in some respects the history of music resembles that of
the drama, because in each case the reign of Charles I marks a
decline.

During the puritan revolution the development of music

[1] Ernest Walker, *A History of Music in England* (1924), p. 114.

suffered a temporary interruption, inasmuch as its two great
channels were cut off: music for masques was no longer required,
as they were not suffered to be performed; and sacred music
was made almost impossible by an ordinance (9 May 1644)
ordering the removal from churches and the destruction of all
organs. Fortunately this ordinance was not rigorously enforced.
Two other ordinances call for attention, both passed in June
1657: the one declaring that any fiddler or minstrel playing in
an ale-house or entreating any person to hear him play was to
be punished as a rogue; the other enacting that anyone pro-
fanely singing or playing upon musical instruments on the
Lord's day incurred a penalty of ten shillings for each offence.

These injuries to music were not inflicted in hatred of music
as a thing evil in itself. Probably Prynne correctly voiced the
sentiments of the puritans when he said that no Christian dare
deny that music of itself is lawful, useful, and commendable,
but he denounced as unlawful for Christians what St. Basil
called 'effeminate lust-provoking musicke', such as accompanied
stage plays or parts of them.[1] The effect of the puritan dislike
of anthems, and sacred music during church services, is described by Evelyn:

. . . they have translated the organs out of the churches to set them
up in taverns, chanting their dithrambicks, and bestiall bacchanalias
to the tune of those instruments, which were wont to assist them in
the celebration of God's prais, and regulate the voices of the worst
singers in the world, which are the English in their churches at
present.[2]

Nevertheless the leaders of puritanism during the civil wars
were more moderate than Prynne or the rank and file of the
Long Parliament. It is said that Milton had a tunable voice
and that he played on an organ in his house.[3] Though Cromwell was no performer himself, music was one of his favourite
recreations. Not infrequently he provided this kind of entertainment for state functions, and thus has a claim to have
originated concerts. When the Dutch ambassadors were entertained in April 1654, on conclusion of peace, music played all
the while they were at dinner, and afterwards the lord protector
and others joined in listening to more music, some of it vocal,
and to the singing of a psalm. John Hingeston, a pupil of

[1] *Histrio-Mastix*, p. 274.   [2] *Miscellaneous Writings* (1825), pp. 157–8.
[3] Aubrey, ii. 67.

Orlando Gibbons, was appointed organist to the protector and had two organs at his disposal at Hampton Court. When Frances Cromwell was married to Robert Rich, the wedding feast was celebrated at Whitehall with forty-eight violins, which presumably provided the tunes for the mixed dancing which scandalized the straiter brethren. The number of violinists is noteworthy, inasmuch as Thomas Baltzar, the first great violinist that had been heard in England, did not settle there until 1656.[1]

To Cromwell may also be assigned some of the credit for the beginning of opera in England. The puritans who closed the theatres were indirectly responsible for this notable addition to musical entertainment. Sir William Davenant was enterprising enough to produce *The Siege of Rhodes*, with twelve singers and six instrumentalists. Another opera, produced in 1658, *The Cruelty of the Spaniards in Peru*, enjoyed great popularity, for it is said to have been performed every afternoon for some time. In view of the censure occasional critics bestowed upon puritans for their alleged hostility to music, it is ironical to note that, whereas the opera flourished under Cromwell, it suffered an eclipse under Charles II.

Nevertheless, probably the most significant feature in the history of music at this time was its general popularity among all classes. All sorts and conditions of men and women loved music, especially vocal. The compositions that have survived were mostly written for the few, though the poorest may have listened to sacred music in the cathedrals. Certainly the labourer had his traditional airs, to each of which many ballads were sung. The milkmaid and her mother who sang to Isaak Walton's Piscator had their counterparts in real life in the village girls Dorothy Osborne heard singing ballads as they watched the cattle. The puritanism that often characterized the middle classes did not prevent their enjoying music, as the fondness of the Ironsides for psalm singing proved. Probably it was for the more frivolous members of this class that John Playford catered. He was 'the first regular music-publisher in England'.[2] He printed two works that long remained popular and are today, on that account, extremely scarce in any of the score of editions through which each passed—*The English Dancing Master* (1650) and *A Breif Introduction to the Skill of Musick* (1654).

---

[1] *Dict. of Nat. Biog.*, s.v. 'Baltzar'.   [2] Walker, p. 122.

XV

LITERATURE

THE years 1603–60 correspond to no one literary period, for two-thirds of them fall within the period 1580–1642 which historians of the drama loosely call the Elizabethan age, and the remaining third does not contain all the age of Milton. The plan of this series reserves Shakespeare for the preceding volume, but it must not be forgotten that the tragedies, in which his genius reached its supreme height, belong to the reign of James I, and he was influential throughout the years under discussion. Milton, however, is too much the creation of the puritan revolution to be omitted even though his most exalted epics were published later than 1660. Nevertheless, even leaving out the life of Shakespeare, the first half of the seventeenth century has many claims to distinction in literary history. The two greatest publications in English literature fell within its limits—the King James Version of the Bible and the first folio of Shakespeare. The finest comedies of Ben Jonson, and the plays usually assigned to Beaumont and Fletcher jointly, were first performed in the reign of James I. Apart from Milton and Donne and, perhaps, Herrick, the poets were not of the same calibre as the dramatists, but each managed to produce a few gems that have escaped oblivion. The prose was even more notable than the verse, for then appeared Bacon's *Advancement of Learning*, the *Novum Organum*, and the later editions of his *Essays*, and Burton's *Anatomy of Melancholy*. Furthermore it is fitting that the reign of the only learned English king in modern times should be memorable for its scholars. Then England stood at the head of European learning, and a great scholar like Casaubon was glad to find refuge and a spiritual home in the land of his adoption. There he met a kindred spirit in Lancelot Andrewes, whose knowledge of sacred literature was as profound as his own. Coke established for himself a unique position in legal history, and Selden was scarcely less eminent in several fields. Among historians and antiquaries were such giants of erudition as Camden, Spelman, Dugdale, and Prynne; among political thinkers, Hobbes and Harrington. In addition the period produced the forerunners of the newspapers and almost the first diaries and autobiographical writings in England.

Nevertheless the general lie of the land cannot be inferred merely from its prominent features. It is true that the Bible was studied with unexampled thoroughness and that it must have furnished the only reading matter in many poor cottages. However, there were available for people with a few pence to spend a great quantity of ephemeral works, some of which were so popular that they were literally worn out of existence or survive in two or three copies out of many editions. Among them were compendiums which approach as near to the modern encyclopaedia as the existing state of knowledge permitted, almanacs, manuals of self-help of every kind, devotional books, primers of education, sermons by the hundred, and thousands of controversial pamphlets on religion and both foreign and domestic politics.

The importance of the drama is evidenced by the adoption of the year 1642, when the theatres were closed by law, as the end of the Elizabethan age. For the purposes of dramatic history, the period from 1603 to 1660 can be roughly divided into three parts: the reign of James I, the reign of Charles I until 1642, and the period from 1642 to 1660. During the first the romantic drama continued to be the dominant interest, although the realistic and satirical treatment of contemporary themes ran it close. During the second the realistic drama was preponderant, although the romantic and extravagant continued to be written and performed. During the third the theatres were proscribed by puritan ordinances of increasing strictness, but actually some, at least, of them defied the law. During the first two periods the masque was a very popular dramatic form, and afforded opportunity for the lavish display pleasing to an extravagant court and nobility. On the other hand the costliness of staging was severely criticized by puritans.

The first two of these divisions are somewhat artificial, as indeed any treatment must be which has to take as its starting-point the year 1603, which has no significance in literary history except as marking the death of Gloriana. There are the further complications that many of the dramatists began their literary careers in the sixteenth century, and that the romantic and the realistic dramas overlap and writers shifted readily from one to the other to cater to changing tastes. The favourite authors of the first type of play were Beaumont and Fletcher. Others were Dekker, Chapman, Middleton, Heywood, Webster, Tourneur, Ford, and Shirley. The most prominent among the realistic playwrights was Ben Jonson, but there were also Dekker, Chapman, Marston, and Middleton, as well as many minor dramatists.

Ben Jonson supplies the connecting link between Shakespeare and Milton, for he has the former's realistic power and exuberance and anticipates the latter's learned elaboration.[1] He disdained the chronicle play, which had been the most popular form of dramatic art at the turn of the century. In the Prologue to *Every Man in His Humour* (1598), he tells us he will not

> . . . with three rustie swords
> And helpe of some few foot-and-halfe-foote words,
> Fight over Yorke, and Lancasters long iarres.

He was rather in advance of the times, for the chronicle play survived another decade, but then went out of fashion.[2] He became an innovator with a new type of play, the comedy of humours. The characters were each to embody a single humour, or folly, or ruling passion, and the whole play often was designed to expose a particular vice—*Volpone*, greed; *The Alchemist*, trickery.

Jonson was also a determined theorist. He remarked that Shakespeare had no art, meaning doubtless no formal rules, and he himself followed classical practice in his closely constructed plays. His realism is as remarkable as his meticulous workmanship. In the Prologue already quoted he says that he will write about

> . . . Deedes and language, such as men doe use:
> And persons, such as comœdie would chuse,
> When she would shew an image of the times,
> And sport with humane follies, not with crimes.

To his chagrin he found that the four comedies he wrote according to rule attained no great success, so he turned to tragedy. To allow his classicism free range, he chose for subjects, and entitled two plays, *Sejanus* and *Catiline*, but these tragedies in the classical style never won popularity. He found his *métier* in four comedies of 'humour', *Volpone*, *The Silent Woman*, *The Alchemist*, and *Bartholomew Fair* (1605–14). He also

---

[1] Cf. C. H. Herford and Percy Simpson, eds., *Ben Jonson*, i (1925), 127.
[2] See Prologue to John Ford's *Perkin Warbeck* (1634).

achieved during this period his greatest successes with another form of dramatic art, the masque. Aided by the stage settings of Inigo Jones (with whom he eventually quarrelled), Jonson brought these spectacle plays to their highest development.

He did not in his own day and has not since enjoyed great popularity: his own explanation is supplied by the title-page of the works he prepared and published in 1616:

> neque, me ut miretur turba, laboro:
> contentus parvis lectoribus.

Jonson is the first dramatist whose writings were collected and published in folio in his own lifetime. This would appear to attest a certain popularity of his plays, but it is characteristic of the man that he should have proclaimed his contentment with few readers. He seems to have been prophetic, for, while certain choice spirits are ardent Jonsonians in each generation, to many a general reader he is little more than a name.[1] Nevertheless his influence was far greater later in the century than in his own day, for his immediate successors were inclined to be satisfied with types rather than to be willing to take the trouble to create individual characters.[2] This is perhaps the most important reason for the decadence of the drama during the late Elizabethan age.

It is said that Ben Jonson's plays were especial favourites of Charles I, who solaced the last weeks of his life with them and Shakespeare's works. Most Englishmen, however, preferred the more facile productions of Beaumont and Fletcher,[3] whose plays were probably reprinted until 1640 at least twice as often as Jonson's and, like his, embodied in a folio (1647). Popular taste remained constant in this respect for half a century, for Dryden notes that in 1665 the plays of these two collaborators were the most pleasant and frequent entertainments of the stage, and that two of their works were acted for one of Shakespeare's or Jonson's. Their success Dryden ascribes to their authors' great natural gifts improved by study, regularity of

---

[1] G. E. Bentley, *Shakespeare to Jonson* (1945), p. 138, asserts that 'Jonson's general popularity was greater than Shakespeare's from 1601 to 1690'.

[2] One contemporary of Jonson's must be exempted from any charge of hasty workmanship, John Webster, whose tragedies, *The White Devil* and *The Duchess of Malfi*, are second only to Shakespeare's in intensity and power.

[3] *The Cambridge History of English Literature* (vi [1919], 115–16) has an analysis of the authorship of the plays usually passing under the joint names of Beaumont and Fletcher.

plot (especially in the plays with which Beaumont was associated), their intimate knowledge of high society (whose 'wild debaucheries, and quickness of wit in reparties, no poet before them could paint as they have done'), and to their complete command of the English language, which they carried to its highest perfection.[1] In addition they, and likewise Middleton, wrote a number of satirical comedies of London life and approximated to the comedies of manners of the Restoration period. Also they deserved much of the credit for the development of a new type of play, which speedily won the greatest favour—the tragi-comedy, defined as 'a romantic drama involving serious passions, yet ending happily'.[2] Tragi-comedies at their best, of which *Philaster* is an example, are admirably suited for stage presentation, having rapid action, dramatic surprises, original situations, declamation, passion—especially love (requited or unrequited)—and the foreknowledge that the hero and heroine will inevitably live happily ever after. At their worst they become mere melodrama, full of bombast, false sentiment, and improbable situations, with characters lacking individuality and falling into a few types, as the lovelorn maiden or the cowardly debauchee.

Among Fletcher's later collaborators was Philip Massinger, who wrote some fifteen plays on his own account. He was a master in contriving plots and knew the limitations of the stage as well as any man. But in his plays there are few characters to charm or even to interest the reader, for they are mostly conventional. Opinions differ as to whether he was a man of high moral ideals who yielded unwillingly to the prevailing low tastes, but it is at least certain that many of his heroines, even when they seem intended as models of virtue, treated morality as a question merely of outward observance. There is no doubt that taste grew corrupt and depraved towards the end of the Elizabethan age of literature and that the successors of Shakespeare and Jonson catered to it. They seem to have lost their capacity to appeal to society in general and to have aimed at attracting only the court and those who were pleased to imitate it, for courtly influence upon the drama did nothing to raise the prevailing low standard. There was nothing in the frivolous court of James I to maintain a high moral tone, and

---

[1] *An Essay of Dramatic Poesy*, ed. Thomas Arnold (1903), pp. 68–69.
[2] Felix E. Schelling, *Elizabethan Drama, 1558–1642* (2nd ed. [n.d.]), ii. 182.

Charles I and Henrietta Maria failed to exact from their courtiers the chastity they exercised in their private lives.[1] Charles not only suggested the plot of James Shirley's *The Gamester*, but applauded the play as the best he had seen for seven years.[2] Actually it would not be out of place in a collection of the worst Restoration drama.

The decadence of the drama was by no means the only handicap under which the stage laboured in the Caroline period. During visitations of the plague the theatres were ordered to be closed—and this calamity happened in 1625, 1630, 1636, and 1637.[3] In addition the extreme sensibility of the court to criticism might cause any allusions, direct or indirect, to current politics to be harshly punished. Because interest in contemporary events, both foreign and domestic, was strong, playwrights were loath to let slip any opportunities for a scoop. Thus Barnevelt's execution had scarcely taken place before Fletcher and Massinger wrote a play about it, and the return of Prince Charles from Spain without a Spanish wife was celebrated in Middleton's *A Game of Chess*, which was enjoying a remarkable run for those times (nine days) when the privy council interfered and stopped it. During the bishops' wars the exhibition upon the stage of an altar, basin, and candlesticks, and actors bowing before them in ridicule of Laudian church ceremonial, incurred a fine of a thousand pounds on the players and the confiscation of their costumes, whereupon (as a pamphleteer relates), having nothing left them but a few old swords and bucklers, they acted 'the valiant Scot' for five days with great applause, before they were again silenced.[4] The importance of this censorship is that it prevented the dramatists from making a popular appeal to a wider audience than the court. In fact it aggravated the tendency, already marked, for the stage to become less national and more courtly. This was the more serious inasmuch as it facilitated the puritan attack upon the theatre.

The puritans had made a determined assault upon the stage during the late seventies and eighties of the sixteenth century, but, failing to achieve success then, they slackened their efforts for thirty years. About the time of Shakespeare's death they

---

[1] e.g. the case of Henry Jermyn.

[2] *The Dramatic Records of Sir Henry Herbert*, ed. J. Q. Adams (1917), pp. 54–55.

[3] *Middlesex County Records*, iii. 6; *Dramatic Records of Sir Henry Herbert*, pp. 44, 57 n. 1, 64, 65; *Strafforde's Letters*, ii. 56.

[4] *The Second Discovery by the Northern Scout* (1642), p. 8.

recommenced their attack, which culminated in Prynne's *His-trio-Mastix: the Players Scourge, or, Actors Tragædie* (1633). It is impossible to do justice, here, to the thousand pages Prynne devoted to the denunciation of the stage, but his main arguments may be summarized as follows: that God's wrath would be provoked if players were permitted to act in direct defiance of the Scriptures, as happened every time that one of them dressed as a woman[1] or spoke evilly or guilefully; that the plays themselves, with their witty obscenities and adulterous representations, the wanton gestures of the actors, and the ravishing music, kindled a very hell of lusts in the spectators; that no good could possibly come from attendance at the theatre, and the risk of corruption was great for any unsophisticated member of the audience, all of whom came for one wicked purpose or another—the gallant to satiate his love of pleasure, the citizens' wives to laugh at the shameless portrayals of themselves, the country clown to brag after his return of the vanities he had seen, the courtesans to offer themselves for sale, the pickpocket to steal, the knave to be instructed in cozening tricks, and the youth to learn amorous conceits; that the costliness of the theatre, which might be from twopence to five shillings if concomitants be reckoned, meant waste of money that could be better employed and might even involve crime to procure it; that there was a loss of precious time, which could be more profitably spent in crucifying the old Adam; that idle habits would easily be formed and men would cease to labour diligently in their callings, as puritans felt all should do; that the concourse of people, of a Sunday afternoon, to and from a theatre often stopped all traffic and sometimes interrupted divine service; that some difference about a box, a seat, or a place upon the stage was often the cause of quarrels, even duels, and there were haunters who had imbrued their unchristian hands in the blood of two, or even three, of their fellow men and gloried in the number of their murders as the trophies of their valour; and that playgoing corrupted manners so that every fantastical and newfangled fashion for dress or hair, gesture or compliment, was eagerly adopted.[2]

The dramatists retaliated upon the puritans who sought to

---

[1] Called the 'old stale argument against the players' by Ben Jonson, in *Bartholomew Fair*, Act v, sc. iii. Cf. Deuteronomy xxii. 5.

[2] *Histrio-Mastix, passim*, especially pp. 63, 146, 374-5, 390-1, 519, 909.

close the theatres and have actors treated as rogues and vagabonds, by ridiculing them upon the stage. Thus in *The Alchemist*
Ben Jonson introduces Tribulation Wholesome, a pastor from
Amsterdam, where English separatists in exile found a home,
and portrays Ananias as a deacon there. Puritans are painted
as rank hypocrites who under pretence of zeal for the gospel
devoured the estates of widows and orphans. Their real worldliness is exposed by their investing funds of the congregation with
the alchemist, who promises to transmute brass and tin into gold
and silver. This caricature was so popular that Ananias became
the accepted nickname for a puritan. Among the dramatis per-
sonae of *Bartholomew Fair* is the famous Zeal-of-the-Land Busy,
a Banbury man, who sees the mark of the Beast in the most innocent diversions at the fair, and could imagine that a basket of
gingerbread was a 'flasket of idols'. Of course the picture was
vastly overdrawn, but Busy had counterparts in real life in such
puritans as those members of parliament who in the spring of
1645 found time to pass an ordinance to abolish scrambling for
cakes on Easter day at Twickenham parish church. The anxiety
of the puritans about their co-religionists abroad was also ridiculed in court circles. In an unknown play performed before
James I, a puritan having long ass's ears bewails the levity of
the times when the protestant cause was so afflicted in Bohemia
and Germany. 'I will not believe this was entertained with
applause', says a news writer, 'and yet I am told so.'[1] It was
natural that those connected with the stage should rejoice at
the severe punishment meted out to Prynne for his *Histrio-
Mastix*. Shirley wrote a satirical dedication to Prynne for a play
with the title, *A Bird in a Cage*, alluding to the tragedy in which
Prynne was taking part and congratulating him on his retirement—to prison. An opportunity to avenge these and many
other insults came to the puritans during the civil wars.

On the whole there is no sign that the theatre was losing
its popularity during what is usually called the decadence.
From a modern standpoint the plays written between about
1620 and 1640 were markedly inferior to their predecessors, but
contemporaries apparently did not think so. There were only
six theatres in London about 1603, but five were built during
the reign of James I and two during that of Charles I—partly

---

[1] Newsletter of 17 Feb. 1621, in Godfrey Goodman, *The Court of King James*
(1839), ii. 200.

to replace those destroyed by fire. The puritan denunciation of citizens and, especially, their wives for watching plays, and the numerous satirical hits at them in the drama of the time would seem to prove that they continued to attend. The theatres that remained open after 1642 were not those where the audience had been aristocratic but those where it had been plebeian. The conclusion would seem inevitable, therefore, that no 'decadence' was primarily responsible for the success of the puritans' final attack on the stage. Moreover they would have closed the theatres against Shakespeare and Jonson as readily as against Ford or Shirley, because their objection was to the drama as essentially immoral in itself (not merely to immoral plays), and necessarily conducive to the most fatal of all sins, idleness.

The ordinance of 2 September 1642 decreed the closing of theatres on the ground that public sports did not well agree with public calamities nor stage plays with seasons of humiliation. Nevertheless so inveterate was the habit of theatre-going in London that the ordinance was often ignored. Accounts of raids by soldiers supply the names of the theatres that remained open: in October 1643 these were the Cockpit, the Red Bull, and the Fortune.[1] Finding that their first ordinance was not obeyed, parliament passed another, in October 1647, by which all actors were to be punished as rogues. This was as ineffective as its predecessors, for a newsbook reports that, whereas the sermons of the popular preacher Obadiah Sedgwick attracted a dozen coaches, three score carried patrons to the Cockpit. Accordingly parliament tried a new way to suppress stage plays, by directing that galleries, seats, and boxes should be demolished and that spectators should be fined five shillings for each attendance. Nevertheless plays continued much as before, and a series of raids found four theatres open.[2] Thereupon the interiors of three of them were wrecked, but the fourth, the Red Bull, escaped and still presented dramas. When raids made the performance of long plays too hazardous, drolls or short humorous pieces took their place. Later came the moral representations and the operas associated with Sir William Davenant's name. The first English opera was *The Siege of Rhodes*, produced during the autumn of 1656. Davenant, an ex-royalist, was able to ingratiate himself with Cromwell by

---

[1] Leslie Hotson, *The Commonwealth and Restoration Stage* (1928), p. 17.
[2] Ibid., pp. 40–41.

his *Cruelty of the Spaniards* (1658), which was very welcome as propaganda at a time when the Spanish war was becoming unpopular. After the protector's death, the godly fell upon Davenant and put an end to his operas. However, the triumph of the enemies of the stage was short-lived, for soon came the Restoration.

The failure of the puritans to suppress plays even when backed by overwhelming military power and harsh legislation proved how strong a hold the drama had upon Englishmen. Moreover there is abundant evidence of the popularity of the drama in the large number of plays printed, whether in folio or in quarto, during 1640–60.[1] In this, as in so many other respects, the puritans found it impossible radically to alter the social habits of their fellow countrymen.

The transition from Tudor to Stuart times marks a more definite change in non-dramatic poetry than in the drama. At the end of the sixteenth century, poetry, whether sonnet sequence or pastoral eclogue, was often Petrarchan and Spenserian in form and spirit. During the last decade of Elizabeth the Petrarchan tradition began to decline, and although it survived into the next reign it became old-fashioned. The sonnet yielded in popularity to the lyric, which owed much to the outburst of song which made Jacobean and Caroline England, where puritanism was not too morose and powerful, a nation of singing birds. The new generation became surfeited with the oversweet sonnet, and was often both lyrical and sophisticated. Yet the new poets could not recapture 'the first fine, careless rapture' that the Elizabethans had expressed so vigorously, and most of them, having no message to deliver, were content to become experts in form. Romanticism tended to give way to realism. Classicism prevailed over the Renaissance spirit. In Latin writers were found the models for the formal satire and the epigram, which became formidable rivals of the sonnet.

The mantle of Spenser might be said to have fallen on Drayton, best known for his topographical poem, *Poly-Olbion, or a Chorographicall Description of All the Tracts, Rivers, Mountains, Forests, and Other Parts . . . of Great Britain.* This is an excellent example of patriotic poetry, and contains a great mass of learn-

---

[1] L. B. Wright, 'The Reading of Plays during the Puritan Revolution', in *Huntington Library Bulletin*, No. 6 (1934).

ing, including notes by Selden to the first part (1612) but not
to the second (1622), and some fine passages; but most readers
will agree with Ben Jonson that the long verses are unpleasing.
In 1619 he collected into a folio the poems he thought worthy
of preservation (except *Poly-Olbion*). In *The Battaile of Agincourt*
(1627) appeared 'Nimphidia', a charming fairy poem, and *The
Muses Elizium* (1630) has pastoral dialogues in a similar whimsi-
cal style. Samuel Daniel, in his attempts to write a history of
England in verse (as he did in prose), was inspired by the same
patriotic feeling that actuated the writers of chronicle plays.
His *Musophilia* and his epistle to the countess of Cumberland
contain some of the best reflective verse in English. Chapman
also belonged to the old order, and his translation of Homer is
a fine specimen of craftsmanship. He was not a profound Greek
scholar, took considerable liberties with the text, and substituted the spirit of the Elizabethan age for the Homeric atmosphere, yet his clear, lively, vigorous, if unpolished, rendering
won the praise of a long succession of poets from Pope to Swin-
burne. Other Spenserians were the Cambridge divines, Phineas
and Giles Fletcher, who borrowed the allegorical method, ignored the romance which made it tolerable, and treated of
scriptural subjects after the manner of a theological treatise.

To a totally different school belonged the satirists and epi-
grammatists. Joseph Hall aspired to be counted the first English satirist, but incurred the condemnation of Milton because,
among other sins, he failed to strike at the 'most eminent vices
among the greatest persons'.[1] Neither Hall nor Donne (another
satirist) was likely to use satire for veiled attacks on ministers
of state, but both clearly realized its possibilities as a means of
reforming by ridicule some of the foibles of the times. Thus the
former attacked romanticism, then at the crest of its wave of
popularity, and the latter in his third satire did not hesitate to
discuss religion and contrast scornfully the slight effort to understand what was at issue that contented many when adopting
a creed with the stern climb essential to attain truth. The next
generation of satirists satisfied Milton's demands, and the private as well as public life of Buckingham, for example, was
assailed scurrilously, if anonymously.

The epigram, which closely followed Martial in structure,
often merely translating or at least imitating him, had a regular

[1] 'An Apology against a Pamphlet' (1642), in *Works*, iii, pt. i, p. 329.

form and was a short poem leading up to and terminating in a witty or ingenious or surprising turn of thought. Sir John Harington and Sir John Davies were the English pioneers, and Jonson, Donne, and Herrick all left excellent specimens. They became so popular that some fifty collections were printed between about 1598 and 1620, and *Wit's Recreations* (1640) reprinted no less than 660, together with a great many epitaphs. As they were in form the very antithesis of the sonnet and as some of the best ridiculed the old style of poetry, they probably contributed as much as the satire to the new spirit that animated English poets.

The two most potent individual influences that helped to change the prevailing taste were exercised by Ben Jonson and John Donne. Jonson, in epigram, epistle, ode, and song, was a classicist, but his example probably was not more effective than his precept, for he attracted a numerous 'tribe of Ben' that sat at his feet in the Devil tavern and readily adopted his advice about poetry, even if playwrights were less willing to accept it about drama. Among the poets who were his closest disciples were Thomas Carew, Sir John Suckling, and Robert Herrick.

Herrick, a Devonshire vicar who was ejected from his living as a royalist, wrote some of the most charming short poems in the English language. His thought is rarely profound, and his verses lack soul-searching qualities. Within his own range, however, which was village life, he was supreme, and some of his descriptions of rural scenes are masterpieces. The subjects he tried to depict are enumerated in the verse that begins *Hesperides*:

> I sing of *Brooks*, of *Blossomes*, *Birds*, and *Bowers*:
> Of *April*, *May*, of *June*, and *July*-Flowers.
> I sing of *May-poles*, *Hock-carts*, *Wassails*, *Wakes*,
> Of *Bride-grooms*, *Brides*, and of their *Bridall-cakes*.
> I write of *Youth*, of *Love*, and have Accesse
> By these, to sing of cleanly-*Wantonnesse*.

If the later Herrick is the poet of the countryside, Carew remained all his life the unofficial poet laureate and the leading contributor to the amorous poetry that found favour at court. His songs still live, though otherwise his verse is most remarkable for its evidence that the court, whose voice he was, was completely out of tune with the nation. Who but a courtier could have written about the death of Gustavus Adolphus without giving the slightest hint that he was the great protestant hero, or have boldly proclaimed that England had no interest in the Thirty Years War? A comparison between Carew's poems and Sir Simonds D'Ewes's *Diary* would of itself reveal the unbridge-able gap that separated the court from the people. The careless ease the cavalier poets affected is another symptom of their estrangement from the growing seriousness of the age. More in harmony with the times were the sacred poets, Herbert, Cra-shaw, and Vaughan. The success of George Herbert's poem, *The Temple*, which went through nine editions from 1633 to 1660, proved the popular appeal of a deeply religious work which related the spiritual experiences of an Anglican rector. The sacred poems of Herbert and of Donne reflect the more serious side of the court, and illustrate in literature the counter-part to the ritualism of Laud, the attempt to combine beauty with holiness in the life of the national church.

The influence of John Donne was widespread, if hard to define. Born a catholic, he spent his salad days as a young man-about-town and took part in the expedition to Cadiz in 1596. He wrote much of his amatory poetry during this period—in fact, Ben Jonson said[1] he wrote all his best poetry before he was twenty-five—but still found time to steep his mind in medieval-ism. Eventually he yielded to court pressure,[2] joined the national church, was nominated dean of St. Paul's, and became one of the most famous preachers of his generation. His collected *Poems* were not published until after his death, but several of them had previously circulated in manuscript. Carew, one of those he in-fluenced, wrote in an *Elegy* on him:

> Here lies a king that rules as he thought fit
> The universal monarchy of wit;
> Here lies two flamens, and both those the best,
> Apollo's first, at last the true God's priest.

Another poet, Dryden, spoke of his affecting metaphysics, hence the adjective 'metaphysical', which Dr. Johnson later fastened upon a group of poets which included Cowley as well as Donne. Donne was undoubtedly learned: one of his faults was the use of far-fetched 'conceits', incomprehensible or at least repellent

[1] The judgement is very questionable, for Donne's later religious poetry is among his best.

[2] It is likely that his conversion was sincere enough and influenced by the hope of finding a secure refuge amidst the uncertainties that perplexed the minds of the Jacobeans.

to the average reader. In this respect he was a bad example to many servile imitators. This school of wit Pope condemned in his *Essay on Criticism*:

> Some to conceit alone their taste confine,
> And glitt'ring thoughts struck out at ev'ry line;
> Pleased with a work where nothing's just or fit;
> One glaring chaos and wild heap of wit.

Donne, however, was also philosophical, and he shared in the contemporary movement to discover the true nature of things. He was by temperament a rebel against conventions, and he speedily cast aside the accepted rules of Elizabethan poetry. Thus, in his verse, the paragon of the sonneteer is replaced by the fickle woman who is no longer to be worshipped as a kind of ethereal goddess but loved sensually. Like his generation, he was fond of psychological analysis and probed deeply into the hearts of problems and explained the conflicts and doubts that inevitably arise in a nature wherein intellect and feeling were often at war—discord is as often discernible in his poetry as *discordia concors*. After him it was easier for Herbert and the sacred poets to reveal their spiritual emotions. Similarly he was an iconoclast in manner as well as in substance, and helped to destroy that subservience to stereotyped forms which was the bane of the later Petrarchans.

John Milton, who gave his name to the literary age that followed the Elizabethan, stood apart from the main current of contemporary poetry. The one great poet of puritanism naturally had little in common with the various schools of 'wit' that provided most of the verse under the early Stuarts. They were largely of the court, or at least by political and religious convictions opposed to puritanism. Milton was, or became, a republican and an independent of the most advanced type. But, though there was little community of interest between him and his fellow poets (except Andrew Marvell), Milton was no solitary dreamer but an ardent publicist, anxious to advance by his writings the cause he held dear.

Milton's poetry falls into two main divisions: what he wrote before the puritan revolution, and the three long poems on religious subjects which came after it, although to the twenty intervening years belong most of his sonnets. During the first thirty years of his life he wrote relatively little, but the half-dozen longer poems of this period are of the highest quality. They have a charm and sweetness that are lacking in the stern and uncompromising tone of his last works. The self-restraint of his early manhood was deliberately imposed in order that by intense study he might fit himself to write an immortal poem. In *Lycidas* he speaks of fame as a spur that led a noble mind 'to scorn delights and live laborious dayes'. In the same poem, also, occurs a hint of the violent partisanship that marked all Milton's pamphlets, for he fiercely denounces the lazy clergy, the blind mouths who neglect their flock.

This course of self-preparation was interrupted by the civil wars. On the news of the rising in Scotland against Laud's liturgy, Milton returned from his foreign travels to take part in public events. His motives were both political and religious. He was an ardent republican at heart and an intense lover of freedom. Already a puritan of an extreme type, he hated bishops and ritual, and longed to remove every trace of the Roman inheritance from the English church. He saw the struggle as between light and darkness, truth and superstition. He threw himself into the pamphlet war whole-heartedly, albeit with reluctance. He complained that he had not completed the full circle of his private studies and that he would have to write not verse but prose, which would mean that he would have the use, as it were, of only his left hand. Nevertheless there was no hesitation, for he had to express what he felt. It must be stated that he was not a great pamphleteer. Although there are passages of the highest eloquence in his prose (the *Areopagitica* has the finest examples), often the syntax is weak and the meaning only half-expressed. The arrangement is defective, long digressions break continuity, and cumbersome sentences make hard reading. Yet the conviction and sincerity of his writing make him seem like a prophet of old with his message to deliver. As he himself wrote, 'But when God commands to take the trumpet, and blow a dolorous or jarring blast, it lies not in man's will what he shall say or what he shall conceal.' As the civil war went on, he became more and more in favour of extremes. He was virtually the first to defend the commonwealth, in his *Tenure of Kings and Magistrates*, which was designed to show that it was lawful to call to account a wicked king and to depose and put him to death. In his *Readie & Easie Way to Establish a Free Commonwealth*, he uttered, as he said, the last words of expiring liberty, for it was not printed until the Restoration was almost accomplished, and the whole nation was, in his words, 'creeping back to servitude'. As a defender of regicide, he was in great personal danger at the Restoration, but was spared to complete *Paradise Lost*, said by his nephew to have been begun in 1658, and *Paradise Regained* and *Samson Agonistes*. Of the three poems, the last is the one most expressive of the bitterness Milton felt at the return of monarchy and episcopacy. But in *Paradise Lost* there are also echoes of the feelings excited by contemporary events. Milton had the double problem to solve of God's dealings with English puritanism and with the human race in general. It is difficult to believe that, when Milton defined the object of *Paradise Lost* to be 'to justify the ways of God to man', he had not in mind the English situation, for puritans like himself or Cromwell had habitually thought and even spoken of recent events in England as directly ordered by God—and the 'good old cause' was ruined beyond recovery. The only real justification he supplies is in *Samson Agonistes*, and it is justification by faith and not by argument:

> All is best, though we oft doubt
> What the unsearchable dispose
> Of highest wisdom brings about
> And ever best found in the close.
> Oft he seems to hide his face,
> But unexpectedly returns
> And to his faithful champion hath in place
> Bore witness gloriously.

Yet it would be a mistake to regard *Paradise Lost* merely as the product of an age. It certainly owed much to the exaltation Milton had felt at the triumph of puritanism and his bewildered grief at its downfall. But, in the main, *Paradise Lost* would seem to be substantially a personal product and the natural result of Milton's determination so to write something for 'aftertimes as they should not willingly let it die'. It may also be regarded as the supreme achievement of the school of 'divine' poets who from the beginning of the Renaissance had opposed divine to pagan poetry. It is strange that Milton's great epic, like Bunyan's prose allegory, should have been written when puritanism had been decisively rejected by the mass of the people of England. Just as persecution seemed to bring forth all that was noblest in puritanism, so adversity gave birth to its finest literary offerings.

The first half of the seventeenth century is very important in the history of English prose. During the Elizabethan age the English language was in its most plastic state. Every phase of life was expansive in that wonderful time, and language shared in this increase. Contemporaries were fully conscious of this, and feared that the language might be altogether transformed. As Waller complained,

> But who can hope his lines should long
> Last in a daily changing tongue?
> .   .   .   .   .   .
> We write in sand, our language grows,
> And, like the tide, our work o'erflows.

A much greater than Waller, Francis Bacon, spent many of his last days over translations of his works into Latin, because he feared that a modern language like English would in time bankrupt any book. Moreover, so far as the late sixteenth century was concerned, verse was regarded as the medium for the expression of noble thoughts, and when men of fashion did indulge in prose their favourite works were *Euphues* and *Arcadia*. In both, but particularly in the former, there is much fine writing, together with a continual straining after antithesis and epigram; and in the latter there are many far-fetched metaphors and artificialities. Among the antiquaries and scientists Latin was still the language of scholarship. Even when they wrote in English, the tendency of scholars was to use a vocabulary largely latinized. Nevertheless the habit in literary circles in London of slighting the native elements in the language, as of the dramatists to keep prose for comic or vulgar scenes, was counteracted by the growing avidity of the middle class for reading matter, and they preferred homely idiom rather than cumbrous sentences full of words of learned length. Therefore, for their benefit, a group of translators arose of unsurpassed skill. Sometimes they were concerned with foreign classics, as *Don Quixote* (1612–20) or the *Decameron* (1620–5), at other times with the Latin works of Englishmen, such as Camden's *Britannia*, translated by Philemon Holland in 1610.

Another type of literature helped to free the speech of the middle classes from artificialities: the books about travel. The

majority of the narratives included in the great collections of
voyages made by Richard Hakluyt and Samuel Purchas were
written by seafaring men for plain people. The authors therefore avoided the flourishes and rhetorical passages of polite
literature, and their matter-of-fact accounts preserved native
words and idioms. Nevertheless the future of the English
language was by no means assured at the beginning of the
seventeenth century, for the native elements were in danger of
being swamped. The great service the Jacobean age rendered
to prose was to harmonize the forthright, vivid, concrete Anglo-
Saxon element with the sonorous, rhythmic, rich but delicate
foreign elements, mainly Latin. This was easier after the publication of the authorized translation of the Bible in 1611.

In the history of English prose during 1603–60 the King
James version of the Bible stands pre-eminent. This, the first
English classic, has all the requisites of a great book—a theme
of universal interest, and an appropriate exposition. Its language is concrete, not abstract, popular rather than recondite,
energetic but not exaggerated, dignified yet simple. Its vocabulary is ample but not replete, using, it is said, some six thousand
different words as against thrice as many in Shakespeare and
twice as many in Milton. Moreover it has been calculated that
over 90 per cent. of the words used are of English derivation. Ap-
pearing at a time when the language was changing rapidly, it
was of the greatest value in preserving the Saxon elements and
defeating the tendency noticeable among learned men like Sir
Thomas Browne towards an excessive use of latinized forms.
Its victory over other versions of the Scriptures was immediate
and complete. Even puritans of the next generation, like Cromwell, Milton, or Prynne, used the Authorized Version for their
quotations.

Its influence is equally marked on preaching. The school of
preachers, of which Andrewes and Donne were the most eloquent members, crammed their pulpit oratory with verbal conceits of every kind. And their efforts found favour in the eyes of
the pedantic James I, who fully shared Donne's view that the
preacher must never use 'an extemporal and irreverent or over-
homely and vulgar language'.[1] The popular taste, however, was
sounder, and preferred the puritans' extempore preaching, based
on the Bible, to the Arminians' learned discourses full of cita-

---

[1] Donne, *Works*, i. 96.

tions from the classics or the early fathers. At that time Englishmen studied the Bible with an intensity probably never equalled, and it is hardly possible to read a speech or writing of any length without perceiving its indebtedness to the Authorized Version. Moreover, religious literature formed a far higher proportion of the total output of the press then than now,[1] and its style must have been influenced by the source of much of its material, the Bible.

Non-theological prose of the period is too diversified to admit of easy classification, and little more is attempted here than to cite a few specimens of the more important groups. During the seventeenth century, as in the sixteenth, there was much writing of history. Some authors wished to write history in general; some, of their native land or its rulers. In part the motive was patriotic or political, in part moral. Some desired to glorify their country by extolling its past, or to advance some cause they held dear, as John Vicars in his three parliamentary chronicles. Perhaps the other view of history was the more old-fashioned, that its writing should serve some ethical purpose. Raleigh, in his *History of the World*, laid down the principle that it was 'the end and scope of all history, to teach by example of times past such wisdom as may guide our desires and actions'.[2] Statesmen under the early Stuarts were fully conscious of the importance men attached to the precedents of the past, and frowned upon histories that seemed anti-monarchical in tendency. Raleigh's *History* was nearly suppressed because he was too saucy in censuring princes, and Sir Robert Cotton's *Life and Reign of Henry III* was similarly threatened because his exposure of the weakness of that king was supposed to reflect on Charles I. When Edward Hyde left England at the end of the first civil war, he set himself to write a history of the struggle, intended not for publication, then at any rate, but for circulation among prominent royalists as a sort of manual of statesmanship. He hoped that from the faithful record of the errors that had resulted in the great rebellion might be deduced the proper steps to take to bring about a restoration. He devoted much of the two years 1646–8 to this end, and had brought his narrative

---

[1] See Helen C. White, *English Devotional Literature* [*Prose*], *1600–1640* (1931), p. 11, where a classification of the items in the *Stationers' Register* for 1620 proved that of 120 items more than half were religious.

[2] See Sir Charles Firth, 'Sir Walter Raleigh's History of the World', in *Proceedings of the British Academy*, viii (1919).

down to 1644, but another twenty years elapsed before he resumed his historical writings. During his second exile he was more concerned to defend himself than his party, which, in the person of Charles II, had abandoned him in the face of a parliamentary impeachment. Accordingly he wrote an autobiographical record of the years he had spent in political life. Finally he decided to combine his two narratives, and the result is *The History of the Rebellion*. This, the most important single authority for the twenty years it covers, is thus half history and half memoirs, and what began as a means to effect a Stuart restoration ended as a defence of the policy its author had steadfastly advocated from the time he entered the royal counsels in 1641, that of reliance on Anglicanism and the old constitution.

Some of the other historians were actuated more by a genuine spirit of curiosity than by the desire to make the past prove a particular thesis. Their moderation and freedom from violent prejudices made them suspect to eager partisans in their own days, but their usefulness is the greater to the modern historian. Thomas Fuller, an Anglican divine, early regarded the compilation of *The Church History of Britain* as his lifework; but the unsettled times hampered his laudable design to base it upon such documentary evidence as was then available. Nevertheless his book was published in 1655 and is the earliest general history of the church in England that is still worth reading. Because Camden and Speed had described the land, he determined to keep alive the fame of the most notable of its inhabitants. He therefore compiled his *Worthies of England*, which is a kind of early dictionary of national biography, arranged under counties.

Individual biographies appeared at an increasing rate as the century progressed, but at first too often took the form of 'life and times', in which personal details were liable to be submerged by verbose accounts of public events in which the persons described played a part. Clearly something more was required before the commemorative instinct then so strong could produce more than formal biographies. In the general introduction to his *Lives*, Isaak Walton explains that he conceived writing to be 'both a safer and truer preserver of men's virtuous actions than tradition', and that, although he wrote about George Herbert chiefly to please himself, he was also influenced by the hope that posterity would imitate the acts and virtues of his saintly friend. If he had unduly emphasized the ethical purpose of his *Lives*, they would have been of little worth. Fortunately he was content to describe the everyday experiences and the personal characters of five divines, and erected to them a lasting monument. His intimate sketches are still dear to the well-read man; but the large tomes devoted to Williams and Laud are plodded through only by the scholar.

The cynical comment might be made that Walton's avowal of his desire to record 'men's virtuous actions' suggests that their vices would be concealed; but the choice of his subjects saved him from the besetting sin of biographers. The *lues Boswelliana* was kept in check to some extent, in the seventeenth century, by the virulence of party feeling, and scandalous biographies of the first two Stuart kings and of Cromwell are as numerous as eulogistic ones. On the whole, while biographical writing made great strides in the direction of frankness, in this period, it must be confessed that its progress in impartiality was but slight.

Certain of the early diaries, like the biographies, contained little more than a record of events of the time, compiled rather from newsletters or printed sources than from personal knowledge, sometimes with, sometimes without, comments by the compiler. There are often autobiographical details along with notes on public happenings, as in the case of the *Journal* of Sir Simonds D'Ewes. These vary in value with the author and the perspicacity of his observations, but are generally more useful as an index of current opinion than as a storehouse of facts. Moreover they often portray only the outward man, represented, as it were, upon the public stage. They fail to deal with the man in his closet, his inmost thoughts, and the true motives that prompted him on this occasion or that. Pepys's *Diary*, which offers the greatest measure of self-revelation, was only just begun before 1660, but a number of religious journals had anticipated him in disclosing something of the inner lives of their compilers. These authors were under the same impulse as George Fox, who wanted all to know and profit by the recital of the various trials and troubles through which he was led by Providence in preparation for the service to which he felt called.

There is another group of writers, whose purpose was didactic rather than moral or commemorative. These were the philosophers or scientists who hoped to substitute for the theories of the medieval schoolmen a scientific explanation of nature. Of them, Bacon is easily the most famous, for his gift of exposition and his pregnant sentences have preserved his writings from the neglect which has attended the treatises of some of his contemporaries who were much greater scientists. He has been well called the trumpeter of the new age. Statesman, lawyer, essayist, and philosopher, Bacon (it is not difficult to understand) never found time to compose more than a fragment of the great work he had planned, which was to include a history of the general state of learning from age to age, a description of the knowledge which the human race possessed in his day, and a comprehensive scheme for the advancement of science. He did none of these with any fullness; but he did render a great service by insisting on the importance of experiment. That the early scientists in their experimentation had behind them the moral support of Bacon's prestige was of the utmost value, and probably helps to explain the great popularity of scientific writings in general. Bacon, however, cannot be given the sole credit, inasmuch as Elizabethan books about science had sold well.[1] The many editions such works passed through prove the popular interest in scientific treatises when written in English. The spirit of curiosity and love of novelty were shared by the bourgeois as well as by the virtuoso.

During 1603–60 the frequent constitutional changes prompted many writers to propound their theories of the nature of governments. Their works were widely read in the seventeenth century, for they were often topical. Under the commonwealth, constitution-mongering became a popular pastime, and it was natural that the temporary destruction of the old régime and the various experiments with written constitutions during the puritan revolution should inspire many treatises and pamphlets on politics. The most important of these writers was Hobbes, who exercised a permanent influence in curious contrast to the violent animosity excited by his theories on their first appearance. Hobbes, who was interested in science, particularly mathematics, ignored the inductive method recommended by Bacon and deduced from first principles his *Leviathan, or the Matter, Forme, and Power of a Commonwealth Ecclesiastical and Civil.* Unlike many of his contemporaries, Hobbes rejected all schemes for a constitution with checks and balances on the chief power. Instead he logically deduced from a state of nature, which he visualized as

---

[1] L. B. Wright, *Middle-Class Culture in Elizabethan England* (1935), chap. xv; Francis R. Johnson, *Astronomical Thought in Rennaissance England* (1937).

a war of all against all, society binding itself by a contract to yield unquestioning obedience to an absolute sovereign authority. He thus fell foul, alike, of the Anglicans advocating the divine origin of kingship, and of the levellers who argued that to take part in a free government was man's right. King James I wrote and published his *True Law of Free Monarchies* before he ascended the English throne, and although Sir Robert Filmer's *Patriarcha*, usually regarded as containing the orthodox doctrine of the theory of the divine right of kings, was written during this period, it was not printed until 1680. The belief in the divine right of kings, curiously enough, was supported by no prominent treatise both written and published within the period 1603–60. On the other hand, the number of printed pamphlets advocating manhood suffrage and proclaiming that man was born free runs into hundreds.

When the levellers argued in the army council in 1647 that the suffrage ought to be the birthright of every Englishman, the more conservative of the army leaders, like Ireton, countered that the qualification for the franchise should be the ownership of property, thus confining the suffrage to those who had a stake in the country. This thesis found its fullest expression in James Harrington's ideal commonwealth, *Oceana*, in which he argued in favour of a balance of property. He maintained that the nature of the government should depend on the distribution of property. The political importance of the possession of land had long been recognized but had not hitherto been developed into a theory.[1]

Many Englishmen, however, were more concerned about practical politics than about theories of government, and wanted to read the forerunners of newspapers rather than treatises. In the proclamation suppressing Cowell's *Interpreter*, James bitterly complained of the insatiable curiosity abroad in the land and the itching of tongues and pens to leave nothing 'unsearched to the bottom both in talking and writing. . . . Men in this age do not spare to wade in all the deepest mysteries that belong to persons or state of kings and princes that are gods upon earth.'[2] Perhaps the curiosity was the keener because it was difficult to satisfy. The rich might employ the professional writers of weekly newsletters, who retailed such news of public events as could be

---

[1] H. F. Russell-Smith, *Harrington and His Oceana* (1914), chap. iii.
[2] Preface to edition of 1727.

gleaned from the secretary of state's office or court gossip. Those fortunate enough to have friends with access to the ante-chambers of the great might be kept more or less informed of what was happening, by periodical reports. Sir Dudley Carleton and others were indebted to one John Chamberlain for letters throughout the reign of James I. Strafford, when in Ireland, looked to a certain Garrard for knowledge of current gossip. The *bourgeoisie*, however, generally had to be content with such news as was bruited about, told in sermons, or printed in pamphlets. The government did its best to suppress all discussion of public events, but in times of popular excitement, as during the later stages of the Spanish match, proclamations forbidding licentious speech in matters of state proved ineffectual. To acquaint Englishmen with foreign affairs during the Thirty Years War was the motive which inspired the publishers of 'corantos', whose first numbers described the troubles of Frederick of the Palatinate. A dozen or more issues of the *Swedish Intelligencer*, and its continuations, appeared from 1632 to 1639, and enabled English protestants to learn from time to time how their co-religionists were faring in Germany during a critical period of the Thirty Years War. So far as domestic history was concerned, no newsbook or periodical appeared until the meeting of the Long Parliament; thenceforward there were scores of short-lived newsbooks published until Cromwell confined the press to two official publications, each issued once a week.

These forerunners of the modern newspaper exhibited in an immature form most of the characteristics of their descendants: there were reports of news (usually based on letters), leading articles, advertisements, and sometimes illustrations (generally woodcuts of individuals). At the beginning of the civil war, partisanship ran high and both the parliamentary and the royalist newsbooks gave highly exaggerated accounts of victories, real or imaginary, won by their respective armies. The royalist journals improved little, but some, at least, of their rivals became more trustworthy, until the official *Mercurius Politicus* printed reliable reports of battles and other events of public interest. A large proportion of its pages, however, was still confined to foreign news.

In addition to the types of literature already discussed, there was plenty of light reading matter available for all classes. At first much of this fiction was derived from abroad, more often by direct translation than by imitation. Anthony Munday, during the late Elizabethan and the Jacobean periods, started what has been well called 'a factory for the translation of chivalresque romances of foreign origin'.[1] He was strangely up to date in his methods, for he anticipated the Bohns of the nineteenth century with his cheap editions.[2] Furthermore, he knew the value of sequels, and used to divide romances like *Palmerin de Oliva* and issue them in parts. Later the parts were published in a single folio. The kind of reading matter thus purveyed can be judged from the title-page of Amadis of Gaul: '*Discoursing the Adventures, Loves and Fortunes of Many Princes, Knights and Ladies.*'

English writers soon realized the popularity of this sort of fiction, and Thomas Lodge wrote *Rosalynde* (1590), which enjoyed the greatest vogue and furnished the plot for *As You Like It*. Near the end of the period, Roger Boyle composed *Parthenissa* (1654), the best imitation by an Englishman of the French heroic romances. Even the authors of chapbooks followed the same kind of pattern and produced the equivalent of the Victorian novelette. Similar in intent though directly opposite in approach were many pamphlets which described a life of crime that ended with a complete reformation. Robert Greene was especially skilful in his variations on the prodigal-son theme, and his late-Elizabethan pamphlets were reprinted time and again in the first half of the seventeenth century. Those who liked to feel their flesh creep had at hand many works depicting horrors of all kinds, life in a prison, or the plague. Dekker, a singularly vivid writer, gave realistic accounts of London during the visitations of the plague in 1603 and 1625. In the same author's *Seven Deadly Sinnes of London* is a fine specimen of another type of literature, which was devoted to the castigation of the wickedness of the age. Others tried to improve their fellow men by showing that sin never pays. Thomas Beard, Cromwell's schoolmaster, in his *Theatre of Gods Judgements* classified examples of God's judgements under the sins punished. Another writer, John Reynolds, with similar tastes, devoted himself exclusively to murder, and produced a large work that became one of the best-liked books of the century. The example proved

[1] Henry Thomas, *Spanish and Portuguese Romances of Chivalry* (1920), p. 249. This quotation, together with a full treatment of the writings here discussed briefly, can be found in Wright, op. cit.

[2] The importation of cheap paper from Normandy, beginning about 1640, made possible the printing of much popular literature.

infectious, and Henry Burton tried to show that Sabbath-breakers were as invariably punished as Reynolds had shown murderers were.

Nearly all the writings discussed in this last section proclaimed their moral purpose. Sometimes, however, it is hard to avoid the conclusion that certain of the authors were like the pot-poet in John Earle's *Microcosmography*: 'Sitting in a bawdy-house he writes God's judgments.' However this may be, it is of importance that writers appealing to the multitude felt it necessary to pay lip-service, at least, to edification.

There was a class, however, too poor to buy and too ignorant to read the kinds of literature hitherto discussed in this chapter. They were catered for by the ballad-mongers. There were many types of ballads: the long narratives that were usually handed down orally or in manuscript; the poems of professional rhymesters, such as Thomas Deloney, which often gave popular accounts of historical events; and the verses that expressed the attitude of the people towards contemporary events. There were, therefore, ballads to suit all tastes. The child might see the *Two Babes in the Wood* pasted up over the fireplace in the nursery;[1] the rustic might espy on the wall of an inn[2] the story about a countryman's visit to London and his being overcharged for everything; the sentimentalists might read of the constancy of lovers through every kind of trial, and the unexpected good fortune they eventually enjoyed; a young man would find the industrious apprentice extolled as a model to all; the payer of ship money might derive some satisfaction from an account of the building of the *Sovereign of the Seas* in 1637; the sailor might find the hardships of his life sufficiently praised in 'Neptunes Raging Fury'; the adventurer might be enticed to Virginia, or a speculator induced to subscribe to a lottery to raise funds for 'a land of rich increase'. There were ballads awaiting the defeated Wimbledon on his return from Cadiz in 1625, and others ridiculed or praised generals in the civil war. The executions of Strafford and Laud were responsible for some exulting verses: the one was depicted as wanting 'to wear the triple crown of the pope, the other to be as arbitrary as the sultan'.[3]

---

[1] Ben Jonson, *Bartholomew Fair*, Act III, sc. i.
[2] In the *Compleat Angler* (chap. ii) an inn is mentioned as having 'twenty ballads stuck about the wall'. This was probably typical.
[3] C. H. Firth, 'The Reign of Charles I', in *Transactions of the Royal Historical*

This ephemeral literature often offers the sole evidence of what the inarticulate masses thought about current events. John Selden, who formed a collection of ballads which later passed into Pepys's hands, truly said that 'more solid things doe not shew the complexion of the times so well as ballads and libells'.[1]

The years 1603–60 include the most famous decade in literary history, and its classics enjoy enduring fame. Nevertheless other features should not be neglected, and among them are the intensive study of the Bible, the wide diffusion of reading, the growing importance of prose, and the great increase in printing. This sudden outburst of printing was largely due to party propaganda. Hence pamphleteers were forced to adopt a simple and plain style in order to make a popular appeal. Their influence, together with that of scientists and others who were more concerned to set down the truth plainly than to cultivate a rhetorical and ornamental style, helped to prepare the way for the prose of Addison, Defoe, and Swift. Moreover, even if many, indeed most, of these writings relate to events or opinions of very transitory interest, they once formed the reading matter of the majority of homes, and they cannot be neglected in any history of the English people.

Society, 3rd ser., vol. vi (1912). Cf. ibid., vol. v (1911), for a similar article on the ballad history of the reign of James I. [1] *Table Talk*, p. 72.

BIBLIOGRAPHY

THE dates of publication given below are usually those of the editions used by the author.

GENERAL

A general guide to selected sources and later works is supplied by G. Davies, *Bibliography of British History, Stuart Period, 1603–1714*, 1928. Practically a complete list of all contemporary publications is provided by *A Short-title Catalogue of Books Printed in England, Scotland, & Ireland . . . 1475–1640*, 1926, and a work with a similar title for 1641 to 1700, ed. Donald G. Wing (3 vols., 1945–51). Also valuable because it supplies full titles and number of pages is *Catalogue of the McAlpin Collection of British History and Theology*, ed. C. R. Gillett (5 vols., 1927–30). After 1640 G. K. Fortescue, *Catalogue of the Pamphlets, Books, Newspapers Collected by George Thomason, 1640–1661*, 1908, contains four-fifths of the works published during the puritan revolution. A. T. Milne has edited for the Royal Historical Society *Writings on British History*, from the year 1934. There is no adequate guide to the manuscript authorities, but Hubert Hall, *Repertory of British Archives*, 1920, is very useful; M. S. Giuseppi, *Guide to the Manuscripts Preserved in the Public Record Office*, 2 vols., 1923–4, suffices for the Public Record Office. The first part of a more elaborate *Guide to the Public Records* was issued in 1949 with a Preface by Sir Hilary Jenkinson. Julius P. Gilson, *A Student's Guide to the Manuscripts in the British Museum*, 1920, and G. Davies, *A Student's Guide to the Manuscripts Relating to English History in the Seventeenth Century in the Bodleian Library*, 1922, give information about the chief collections in these two libraries. The introductions to the reports of the Historical Manuscripts Commission afford much information about private collections. In general the lives of the most important personages in the *Dictionary of National Biography*, 22 vols., 1908–9, often contain valuable bibliographies, and the same is true of the histories noted below. Addenda and corrigenda to the *D.N.B.* appear in *Bulletin of the Institute of Historical Research*, University of London.

The *Dictionary of National Biography* is, of course, invaluable for this as for all periods of English history. There are a number of other useful works of reference, such as G. E. Cokayne, *Complete Peerage of England, Scotland, Ireland, Great Britain, and the United Kingdom*, 8 vols., 1887–98—a new edition in 13 vols. is complete except for part ii, vol. 12, from Towton to the end of the alphabet; G. E. Cokayne, *Complete Baronetage*, 6 vols., 1900–6; and W. A. Shaw, *The Knights of England*, 2 vols., 1906. For members of the universities valuable lives or lists are given in Anthony à Wood, *Athenae Oxonienses*, ed. P. Bliss, 4 vols., 1813–20; J. Foster, *Alumni Oxonienses, 1500–1714*, 4 vols., 1891–2; and J. and J. A. Venn, *Alumni Cantabrigienses*, 4 vols., 1922–7.

POLITICAL

The most important works for the period are by the late Samuel Rawson Gardiner and Charles Harding Firth. *A Bibliography of the Historical Works of Dr. Creighton, Dr. Stubbs, Dr. S. R. Gardiner, and the Late Lord Acton*, ed. W. A. Shaw, 1903, and *A Bibliography of the Writings of Sir Charles Firth*, 1928, furnish guides. Gardiner's *History of England, 1603–42*, 10 vols., 1883–4; *History of the Great Civil War, 1642–9*, 4 vols., 1893; and *History of the Commonwealth and Protectorate*, 4 vols., 1903, cover the period from 1603 to 1656 with unexampled thoroughness. Even after the lapse of fifty years, it is difficult to add substantially to, or to make more than minor corrections of, this narrative, which is, however, mainly confined to political and constitutional history, with no attempt to treat systematically the economic or social life of the period. Sir Charles Firth continued Gardiner on the same scale in *The Last Years of the Protectorate, 1656–1658*, 2 vols., 1909. He also wrote the best biography of *Oliver Cromwell*, 1900; and his *House of Lords*, 1910, throws much light on the politics of the time and makes clear the importance of the house of peers as often holding the balance of power between king and commons. *The Restoration of Charles II*, by Godfrey Davies (San Marino, California, 1955), covers the years 1658 to 1660. Other histories are G. M. Trevelyan, *England under the Stuarts*, 1904, which has the best and brightest shorter account of the early Stuarts. It opens with a very interesting analysis of the state of England, 1603–40. F. C. Montague's volume (vii) of the *Political History of England*, 1907, is a sound work of the old-fashioned type, dealing exclusively with political and constitutional history. *The King's Peace, 1637–41* (1955), is the first instalment of a narrative history by C. Veronica Wedgwood. In the *Cambridge Modern History*, vols. iii and iv, 1907, various chapters cover 1603–60; those on 'The Reign of James I' by S. R. Gardiner, and on 'Anarchy and the Restoration' by Sir Charles Firth, are the best. David Mathew, in *The Jacobean Age* (London, 1938), *The Social Structure in Caroline England* (Oxford, 1948), and *The Age of Charles I* (London, 1951), surveys some of the general trends.

Of contemporary histories, Clarendon, *History of the Rebellion*, ed. W. D. Macray, 6 vols., 1888, is easily the most important. It has been discussed briefly above (p. 408). A full critical study by Sir Charles Firth is in the *English Historical Review*, xix. G. Wormald, *Clarendon* (Cambridge, 1951), is a provocative study of Clarendon's *History* and his politics and religion. Selected documents are printed in *State Papers Collected by Edward, Earl of Clarendon*, 3 vols., 1767–86. There is also a *Calendar of the Clarendon State Papers*, 4 vols., 1872–1932.

Among the sources for general political history there are several that stand pre-eminent. Rushworth, *Historical Collections* (8 vols., 1659–1701), is mainly a compilation from printed material from 1618 to 1649 which can be found in any large library, but certain portions, such as 'The Trial of the Earl of Strafford', were based on notes Rushworth made in shorthand at the time. *A Collection of the State Papers of John Thurloe*, 7 vols., 1742, contains the official correspondence of the secretary of the council of state and afterwards of the two protectors. It is un-doubtedly the chief authority for the protectorate. The four volumes of *The Clarke Papers*, ed. C. H. Firth, 1891–1901, are invaluable for all that appertains to the army, 1647–60. *A Calendar of State Papers, Domestic Series*, covers the whole period, in about 40 volumes; the portion devoted to the reign of James I is too brief to be very useful, but the later volumes have much material of value. *The Calendar of State Papers and Manuscripts Relating to English Affairs Existing in the Archives and Collections of Venice*, vols. x–xxxii, edited first by H. F. Brown and then A. B. Hind, varies greatly in value according as the Venetian repre-sentative was acute or obtuse. As English relations with Venice during this period were never of primary importance, and often of very little importance, the *Calendar* is mainly serviceable for English domestic affairs, and often has information about Roman catholics that is not to be found elsewhere. After 1640, pamphlets issued from the press in a profusion hitherto quite unknown, and many of them are well worth reading. Broadly speaking, they are more useful as a help to creating atmosphere than as store-houses of facts. In numerous instances they are of great value for social and economic history as well as political. The catalogue of the Thomason collection, already mentioned, is a most serviceable guide. Two good collections have been printed: *Somers Tracts*, 13 vols., 1809–15; and the *Harleian Miscellany*, 12 vols., 1808–11, or 10 vols., 1808–13. For the latter there is the *Contents of the Harleian Miscellany, with an Index*, 1885. For both collections there are lists of contents in the *Catalogue of the London Library*, 1903. More concentrated is *Tracts on Liberty, 1638–1647*, ed. William Haller (3 vols., New York, 1933–4).

Biographies, autobiographies, memoirs, and letters are numerous. For the reign of James I the collected works, life, and letters of Francis Bacon, by J. Spedding, R. L. Ellis, and D. D. Heath, 14 vols., 1857–74, stands first. For current news *The Court and Times of James I*, ed. R. F. Williams, 2 vols., 1848, has many newsletters, but has been superseded by *The Letters of John Chamberlain*, ed. Norman Egbert McClure (2 vols., Philadelphia, 1939). *The Court and Times of Charles I* is a similar work. The gossip, some of it rather unsavoury, about the court is in the *Secret History of the Court of James I*, ed. Sir Walter Scott, 2 vols., 1811.

There are many diaries and lives, both of parliamentarians and of royalists. Sir Philip Warwick, *Memoirs of the Reign of King Charles the First*, 1813; Margaret, Duchess of Newcastle, *The Life of William Cavendish, Duke of Newcastle*, ed. C. H. Firth; and Elliot Warburton, *Memoirs of Prince Rupert, and the Cavaliers*, 3 vols., 1849, are the most notable on the royalist side. For the parliamentarians the following are of particular value: *The Autobiography and Correspondence of Sir Simonds D'Ewes*, ed. J. O. Halliwell, 2 vols., 1845; Lucy Hutchinson, *Memoirs of the Life of Colonel Hutchinson*, ed. C. H. Firth, 1906; *The Memoirs of Edmund Ludlow*, ed. C. H. Firth, 2 vols., 1894 (these are respectively the life and the autobiography of two republicans); and Thomas Carlyle, *The Letters and Speeches of Oliver Cromwell*, ed. S. C. Lomas, with an introduction by C. H. Firth, 3 vols., 1904 (for a complete guide to printed materials, see Wilbur Cortez Abbott, *A Bibliography of Oliver Cromwell*, 1929). W. C. Abbott, *The Writings and Speeches of Oliver Cromwell* (4 vols., Cambridge,

Mass., 1937–47), also contains a vast amount of biographical material. Much information about Charles II and the exiled royalists is to be found in two works by Eva Scott: *The King in Exile*, 1905; *The Travels of the King*, 1907.

For foreign relations the main dependence is upon Gardiner, who was the first English historian fully to investigate them and to demonstrate their influence upon domestic politics. There is no separate work covering 1603–60 on an adequate scale, but Sir John Seeley depicts the broad outlines in *The Growth of British Policy*, 2 vols., 1895. Georges Ascoli, *La Grande-Bretagne devant l'opinion française au xvii siècle* (2 vols., Paris, 1930), is an attempt to show what Frenchmen knew about England. *Recueil des instructions données aux ambassadeurs et ministres de France. XXIV. Angleterre*, ed. J. J. Jusserand, i, 1648–65 (Paris, 1929), is valuable for the period it covers. Among the monographs dealing with one phase or other of foreign policy are: D. A. Bigby, *Anglo-French Relations, 1641 to 1649*, 1933; J. N. Bowman, *The Protestant Interest in Cromwell's Foreign Relations*, 1900; George Edmundson, *Anglo-Dutch Rivalry during the First Half of the Seventeenth Century*, 1911; Guernsey Jones, *The Diplomatic Relations between Cromwell and Charles X Gustavus of Sweden*, 1897; and Edgar Prestage, *The Diplomatic Relations of Portugal and England from 1640 to 1668*, 1925. G. N. Clark, *The Colonial Conferences between England and the Netherlands in 1613 and 1615* (Bibliotheca Visseriana, part ii, Leiden, 1951), is exhaustive, and also contains many valuable generalizations. Part i (1940) of the same work, ed. W. J. M. van Eysinga, prints many documents. John Beresford, *The Godfather of Downing Street, Sir George Downing*, 1925, is a useful study of an able but unscrupulous ambassador at The Hague. For treaties there is the guide by D. P. Myers, *Manual of Collections of Treaties and of Collections Relating to Treaties*, 1922. Many of the treaties and some documents, to 1654, will be found in Thomas Rymer, *Foedera*, 20 vols., 1704–32. A very useful work is F. G. Davenport, *Materials for English Diplomatic History, 1509–1783, Calendared in the Reports of the Historical Manuscripts Commission*, 1917. C. H. Firth and S. C. Lomas, *Notes on the Diplomatic Relations of England and France, 1603–88. Lists of Ambassadors from England to France and from France to England*, 1906, has references to all printed dispatches.

CONSTITUTIONAL AND LEGAL

For parliamentary proceedings the primary sources are *Journals of the House of Lords*, vols. ii–x, and *Journals of the House of Commons*, vols. i–viii. The former, in addition to recording the formal business before the house, supply copies of bills, letters, and other documents that are often of great value, especially for the civil war. 'The Manuscripts of the House of Lords' were calendared by the Historical Manuscripts Commission in its Third to Seventh *Reports*. They include papers addressed to the speaker of the lords or obtained for parliamentary inquiry, as well as minute books, drafts of bills, and other material supplementing the *Journals*. The *Journals of the House of Commons* have brief notes on the debates for the parliaments of the reign of James I and for the early part of the reign of Charles I. For the composition of the house of commons the blue book 69, *Members of Parliament*, often called 'Official Returns of Members of Parliament', vol. i (1878), includes the seventeenth century. There are also: D. Brunton and D. H. Pennington, *Members of the Long Parliament* (London, 1954); and Mary F. Keeler, *The Long Parliament, 1640–1641, a Biographical Study* (1954). *The Statutes of the Realm*, vol. iv, part 2, and vol. v, print the laws that received the royal assent, 1603–41. During 1642–60 parliament issued ordinances on its own authority. Most of these are reprinted in C. H. Firth and R. S. Rait, *Acts and Ordinances of the Interregnum, 1642–1660*. There are two collections of debates: *Parliamentary or Constitutional History of England*, 24 vols., 1751–62 (commonly known as the *Old Parliamentary History*), in which are many useful extracts from pamphlets published during 1642–60; and *The Parliamentary History of England*, ed. William Cobbett, 36 vols., 1806–20 (vols. i–iii cover the early Stuarts). Professors Wallace Notestein and Frances Relf, together with other American scholars, have been studying the parliamentary debates of this period, and, in addition to editing a number of diaries, have discussed the whole question of the sources for the commons' debates, in an excellent introduction to *The Commons' Debates for 1629*, 1921. Fine examples of well edited books are David Harris Willson, *The Parliamentary Diary of Robert Bowyer, 1606–1607*, 1931; *Commons' Debates, 1621*, ed. Wallace Notestein, Frances Helen Relf, and Hartley Simpson (7 vols., New Haven, 1935); *The Journal of Sir Simonds D'Ewes*, ed. Wallace Notestein for Nov. 1640 to March 1641, and by Willson Havelock Coates for Oct. 1641 to Jan. 1642 (New Haven, 1923 and 1942). A monograph on a special subject is Millicent B. Rex, *University Representation in England, 1604–90* (1954).

For legal history Sir William Holdsworth, *Sources and Literature of English Law*, 1925, and P. H. Winfield, *The Chief Sources of English Legal History*, 1925, supply excellent guides. Sir William Holdsworth, *A History of English Law*, 6th ed., 12 vols. (including Index), is the standard authority. It is broad and comprehensive in treatment, and contains much of value about the constitutional issues at stake under the early Stuarts. Its importance is the greater because the contest between prerogative and the common law was one of the chief areas of contention between king and parliament. It is unfortunate that, apart from Bacon, none of the many great lawyers of the period has an adequate biography. Sir James Stephen, *A History of the Criminal Law of England*, 3 vols., 1883, is useful for legal procedure, and Cobbett's *Complete Collection of State Trials*, 34 vols., 1809–28, for cases. However, the latter work is mainly a reprint of what had already been published, and is wholly uncritical in its selection. J. Bruce Williamson, *The History of the Temple, London*, 1924, is serviceable for legal training.

THE CENTRAL GOVERNMENT. Only one of the chief offices of state has been accorded an adequate history: Florence M. Grier Evans (Mrs. C. S. S. Higham), *The Principal Secretary of State*, 1923, which is based on thorough research. The privy council has attracted more attention. The late Edward Raymond Turner wrote two volumes on *The Privy Council of England, 1603–1784*, 1927, and two on *The Cabinet Council of England, 1622–1784*, 1930. Both works contain a great deal of valuable information, but it is difficult to see the wood for the trees. Naturally the primary source for conciliar history is the *Acts of the Privy Council*, which in 1957 reaches only the year 1628. Moreover the registers from 1602 to 1613 were burnt in the fire at Whitehall in January 1619. A helpful guide is E. R. Adair, *The Sources for the History of the Council*, 1924. *Tudor and Stuart Proclamations, 1485–1714, Vol. I, England and Wales*, calendared by Robert Steele, 1910, is extremely important.

LOCAL HISTORY. There are many guides to local history. Perhaps the most useful are A. L. Humphreys, *A Handbook to*

County Bibliography: Being a Bibliography of Bibliographies Relating to the Counties and Towns of Great Britain and Ireland, 1917, and Charles Gross, *A Bibliography of British Municipal History*, 1897. Many counties have found bibliographers. F. A. Hyett and William Bazeley, *The Bibliographer's Manual of Gloucestershire Literature*, 3 vols., 1895–1907, with a *Biographical Supplement* by F. A. Hyett and Roland Austin, 1915, is a model. The only general work that need be noted is the *Victoria History of the Counties of England*, ed. W. Page, H. A. Doubleday, and others, 1900– . This is still in progress. Its aim is to deal with the political, ecclesiastical, social, and economic history of each county and of London. A. H. A. Hamilton, *Quarter Sessions from Queen Elizabeth to Queen Anne*, 1878, is a good introduction to its subject. The quarter-sessions records for a number of counties have been published, sometimes as a calendar, sometimes as a series of extracts. Among the best of such sources for the early Stuarts are: *Hertfordshire County Records. Calendar to the Sessions Books, 1619 to 1657*, by William Le Hardy; *Middlesex County Records*, vols. ii–iii, by John Cordy Jeaffreson, c. 1887–8; *County of Middlesex. Calendar of the Sessions Records. New Series. Vol. I. 1612–1614*, by William Le Hardy, 1935; *Quarter Sessions Records of the County of Northampton*, by Joan Wake, 1924; *Nottingham County Records. Notes and Extracts from the Nottingham County Records of the 17th Century*, by H. Hampton Copnall, 1915; *Quarter Sessions Records for the County of Somerset*, by E. H. Bates Harbin, 3 vols., 1907–12; and *Worcestershire County Records. Calendar of the Quarter Sessions Papers. Vol. I. 1591–1643*, by J. W. Willis Bund, 1900. These records are invaluable, not only for their illustrations of local government, but also as throwing much light upon the daily habits of people who left virtually no literary remains.

ECCLESIASTICAL

There is no comprehensive ecclesiastical history for this period. In default of one, John Stoughton, *History of Religion in England*, 8 vols., 1881, may be used. Volumes v and vi in *A History of the English Church* deal with the period from the high-Anglican standpoint. The earlier volume, by W. H. Frere, 1904, is scholarly within rather narrow limits. The other, by W. H. Hutton, 1910, is marred by a failure to appreciate the moral strength of puritanism. W. K. Jordan, *The Development of Religious Toleration in England, 1603–1640* (1936) and its two sequels (1938–40), are based on extensive research especially in tracts. A valuable work is Roland G. Usher, *The Reconstruction of the English Church*, 2 vols., 1910, which is in the main an account of Bancroft's archiepiscopate. H. R. Trevor-Roper, *Archbishop Laud* (London, 1940), is detailed but unsympathetic. *Lectures on Archbishop Laud*, ed. by W. E. Collins, 1895, is useful. Recourse should be had to Peter Heylyn, *Cyprianus Anglicus*, 1668, and to *The Works of William Laud*, 7 vols., 1847–60. A life of Laud's rival, John Williams, called *Scrinia Reserata*, by John Hacket, 1693, is still worth reading in spite of its prolixity. For the later period W. A. Shaw, *A History of the English Church, 1640–1660*, 2 vols., 1900, is fully documented. The Society for Promoting Christian Knowledge has recently published a number of learned biographies of churchmen, including Godfrey Goodman, William Lloyd, and Jeremy Taylor. Robert S. Bosher, *The Making of the Restoration Settlement, 1649–1662* (Westminster, 1951), emphasizes the influence of the Laudians. *The Correspondence of Bishop Brian Duppa and Sir Justinian Isham, 1650–1660*, ed. Sir Gyles Isham (Northamptonshire Record Society, n.d., published in 1955), contains the letters of two devoted Anglicans in the days of their affliction.

The contemporary Thomas Fuller, *The Church History of Britain*, 1655, still has value, as has John Walker, *An Attempt towards Recovering an Account of the Numbers and Sufferings of the Clergy of the Church of England Who Were Sequester'd, Harass'd*, &c. *in the Late Times of the Grand Rebellion, 1714*. A modern study, G. B. Tatham, *Dr. John Walker and the Sufferings of the Clergy*, 1911, tends to vindicate Walker's accuracy. A. G. Matthews, *Walker Revised* (Oxford, 1948), has produced what is likely to remain the definitive edition. Henry Gee and William J. Hardy, editors of *Documents Illustrative of English Church History*, 1896, made a good selection. To supplement this the various collections edited by Edward Cardwell should be consulted. In the absence of a later work Felix Makower, *The Constitutional History of the Church of England*, 1895, may be used. A detailed study of facts and proposals regarding the livelihood of the clergy is C. Hill, *Economic Problems of the Church from Archbishop Whitgift to the Long Parliament* (1956).

On the whole nonconformists are better supplied with good

histories than are Anglicans. The earliest ecclesiastical English bibliography is John Whiting, *A Catalogue of Friends' Books*, 1708. More recent are the two works by Joseph Smith, *A Descriptive Catalogue of Friends' Books*, 2 vols., 1867, with a *Supplement*, 1893, and *Bibliotheca Anti-Quakeriana*, 1873. H. M. Dexter, *The Congregationalism of the Last Three Hundred Years as Seen in its Literature*, 1879, supplies over seven thousand titles. Even more complete is W. T. Whitley, *A Baptist Bibliography*, of which vol. i, 1916, covers 1526–1776. An excellent introduction to nonconformity in general is Rufus M. Jones, *Mysticism and Democracy in the English Commonwealth*, 1932. *Reliquiae Baxterianae* (1696) has much valuable autobiographical material with many controversial writings. F. J. Powicke has written Baxter's *Life*, of which vol. i (1924) goes down to 1661. Among modern treatments are: R. W. Dale, *History of English Congregationalism*, 1907; L. F. Brown, *The Political Activities of the Baptists and Fifth Monarchy Men in England during the Interregnum*, 1912; C. Burrage, *Early English Dissenters in the Light of Recent Research*, 2 vols., 1912; W. T. Whitley, *A History of British Baptists*, 1923; and, best of all, *The Beginnings of Quakerism*, by W. C. Braithwaite, 1912 (2nd ed. by H. J. Cadbury, 1955). William Haller's 2 vols., *The Rise of Puritanism* and *Liberty and Reformation in the Puritan Revolution* (New York, 1938 and 1955), are based on a thorough examination of sermons and tracts from 1570 to 1649. A great many sources of various kinds have been published. Among the most valuable are Benjamin Hanbury, *Historical Memorials Relating to the Independents*, 1839, and George Fox, *A Journal*, 1694—the most satisfactory modern editions are those of Norman Penney, 2 vols., 1911, and John L. Nickalls, 1952. Penney also edited *The Short Journal of George Fox*, 1925. The most elaborate life of a minister is *The Strenuous Puritan, Hugh Peter*, by Raymond Phineas Stearns (Urbana, 1954).

There are not many sources or later works for unitarianism, but the various writings of Alexander Gordon, including lives in the *Dictionary of National Biography*, always reach a high standard. *The Transactions of the Unitarian Historical Society*, 1917–, ed. W. H. Burgess, are indispensable. As for the Jews the following are very adequate: C. Roth, *Magna Bibliotheca Anglo-Judaica* (1937); the same author's *History of the Jews in England* (1941); Lucien Wolf, *Menasseh Ben Israel's Mission to Oliver Cromwell*, 1901; and H. S. Q. Henriques, *Return of the Jews to*

England, 1905. The *Transactions of the Jewish Historical Society,* 1894– , contain useful articles for this period.

David Mathew, *Catholicism in England, 1535–1935,* furnishes a good general sketch, but a detailed modern history of Roman catholicism in the seventeenth century is urgently needed. There is still nothing better than Charles Dodd (pseudonym of Hugh Tootel), *A Church History of England,* 3 vols., 1737–42 (a later edition, by M. A. Tierney, 5 vols., 1839–43, has serviceable additions and notes for 1603–25). Two valuable sources of information, however, are now available: Joseph Gillow, *A Literary and Biographical History or Bibliographical Dictionary of the English Catholics,* 5 vols., *c.* 1895–1902, which is fairly exhaustive from A to P; and Henry Foley, *Records of the English Province of the Society of Jesus,* 6 vols., 1875–80. A number of works on martyrology and persecution have been written, but none has superseded Richard Challoner, *Memoirs of Missionary Priests,* 2 vols., 1741–2. St. G. K. Hyland, *A Century of Persecution,* 1920, has some further information. Good accounts of the persecution to which a catholic gentleman was liable to be exposed at this time are contained in Margaret Blundell, *Cavalier,* 1933, and in two volumes edited by T. E. Gibson: *Crosby Records. A Cavalier's Note Book,* 1880, and *Crosby Records: A Chapter of Lancashire Recusancy,* 1887.

MILITARY

The *Journal of the Society for Army Historical Research,* 1921– , often has seventeenth-century material. M. J. D. Cockle, *A Bibliography of English Military Books up to 1642,* 1900, is a very satisfactory guide to writings on war. There is no military bibliography for the later years. Of modern books, Sir Charles Firth, *Cromwell's Army,* 1902 (3rd ed., 1921), is a profound study of the New Model army, and is invaluable for an understanding of the art of war as then practised, the raising of the army, its discipline, religion, and politics. The same author, in 'The Raising of the Ironsides' and 'The Later History of the Ironsides', *Transactions of the Royal Historical Society,* xiii and xv, 1899, 1901, traces the history of Cromwell's own regiment. For the campaigns, Gardiner is excellent. Sir Charles Firth assisted by Godfrey Davies traced the history of all regiments raised from 1645 onwards in *The Regimental History of Cromwell's Army*

(2 vols., Oxford, 1940). Godfrey Davies, *The Early History of the Coldstream Guards*, 1924, deals with a single regiment, Monck's, formed in 1650 from two existing regiments. A useful book for the earlier part of the century is Charles Dalton, *Life and Times of General Sir Edward Cecil, Viscount Wimbledon*, 2 vols., 1885.

Sources for the civil wars are numerous. John Vicars, *England's Parliamentarie Chronicle*, 3 vols., 1643–6, is of service to anyone who has not access to the pamphlets, &c., on which it is based. Joshua Sprigg, *Anglia Rediviva*, 1647, is a good relation of the first campaign of the New Model army; it, too, was largely written from published material. Sir Edward Walker, *Historical Discourses*, 1705, has narratives of the campaigns of Charles I in 1644 and 1645 and of Charles II in Scotland in 1650. C. E. H. Chadwyck-Healey edited *Bellum Civile*, 1902, which is a description of Hopton's campaigns, 1642–4. There are many works tracing the course of the civil wars in different localities. These sometimes take the form of a collection of tracts, sometimes of a history. An example of the former is *Bibliotheca Gloucestrensis*, ed. John Washbourne, 1825, and, of the latter, Mary Coate, *Cornwall in the Great Civil War*, 1933, an admirable contribution.

NAVAL

G. E. Manwaring, *Bibliography of British Naval History*, 1930, and W. G. Perrin, *Admiralty Library, Subject Catalogue of Printed Books*, 1912, are useful guides. There is no very satisfactory work covering the whole period, but within its field Martin Oppenheim, *A History of the Administration of the Royal Navy from 1509 to 1660*, 1896, is thoroughly sound. *The Royal Navy, a History*, by W. L. Clowes and others, vol. ii, 1897, is available. C. E. Penn, *The Navy under the Early Stuarts*, 1913, goes down to 1649 and is the best general treatment that has so far appeared. There are several very serviceable biographies: Granville Penn, *Memorials of Sir William Penn*, 2 vols., 1833; T. A. Spalding, *A Life of Richard Badiley*, 1899; J. B. Deane, *The Life of Richard Deane*, 1870; and F. R. Harris, *The Life of Edward Mountagu, first Earl of Sandwich* (2 vols., London, 1912). *The Journal of Mountagu*, ed. R. C. Anderson (Naval Records Soc., 1929), is valuable for the Restoration period. The most elaborate documentation is in the Navy Records Society, *Letters and Papers*

Relating to the First Dutch War, ed. S. R. Gardiner and C. T. Atkinson, 5 vols., 1898–1912. Some additional documents are printed in H. T. Colenbrander, *Bescheiden uit vreemde archieven omtrent de groote Nederlandsche Zeeoorlogen, 1652–1676*, 2 vols., 1919. Sir Julian Corbett, *England in the Mediterranean*, 2 vols., 1904, is the work of a recognized authority; but in relation to Algiers and North Africa in general corrections in it are made by Sir Godfrey Fisher, *Barbary Legend* (Oxford, 1957).

ECONOMIC

There is no comprehensive bibliography, but the *Economic History Review* (1927–) publishes bibliographies on different subjects from time to time. *The Dictionary of Political Economy*, ed. R. H. I. Palgrave, 3 vols., 1891-9 (later ed., 1925–6), has short bibliographies attached to the articles. An older work, J. R. McCulloch, *The Literature of Political Economy*, 1845, is useful. A large number of general economic histories is listed in Judith Blow Williams, *A Guide to the Printed Materials for English Social and Economic History, 1750–1850*, 1926. E. Lipson, *Economic History of England*, vols. ii and iii, 1931, is a good, if rather prosaic, summary of the age of mercantilism. It is invaluable as a storehouse of facts, but rather neglectful of major tendencies. W. Cunningham, *The Growth of English Industry and Commerce in Modern Times*, part i, 1919 (1st ed., 1882), was a great pioneer contribution. G. N. Clark, *The Wealth of England from 1496 to 1760* (Home University Library, 1946), is a very suggestive survey.

AGRICULTURE. Lord Ernle, *English Farming Past and Present*, 1927, is the best general guide. J. E. Thorold Rogers, *History of Agriculture and Prices in England*, 7 vols., 1866–1902 (vols. v and vi cover the seventeenth century), is still the only complete work on a most important subject. Its author was constitutionally inaccurate, and it has many defects, but, in default of anything better, is indispensable. Only the first volume has been published of the more ambitious work of Sir William (now Lord) Beveridge, *Prices and Wages in England*: this gives *Price-Tables: Mercantile Era* (1937). Reginald Lennard, *Rural Northamptonshire under the Commonwealth*, 1916, is an intensive study of a very interesting area. For inclosures the most thorough treatments are those by E. F. Gay: 'The Midland Revolt and the Inquisitions of Depopulation of 1607', in *Trans. Roy. Hist. Soc.*, new ser., xviii, 1904; and 'Inclosures in England in the Sixteenth Century', in *Quarterly Journal of Economics*, xvii. 576–97. Especially serviceable, too, is E. M. Leonard, 'The Inclosure of Common Fields in the Seventeenth Century', in *Trans. Roy. Hist. Soc.*, new ser., xix, 1905. A. H. Johnson, *The Disappearance of the Small Landowner*, 1909, is a good summary. E. C. K. Gonner, *Common Land and Inclosure*, 1912, is helpful, but should be used with caution. There are many contemporary pamphlets about inclosures. John Moore, *The Crying Sin of England*, 1653, and the answers it provoked, may be taken as specimens. For draining, no modern history exists, and recourse must be had to Sir William Dugdale, *The History of Imbanking*, 1652 or 1772. Much information is given in Sidney and Beatrice Webb, *English Local Government: Statutory Authorities for Special Purposes*, 1922.

INDUSTRY. George Unwin, *Industrial Organization in the Sixteenth and Seventeenth Centuries*, 1904, is valuable, although some of its conclusions can no longer be accepted. There are a number of works on separate industries: E. Lipson, *The History of the Woollen and Worsted Industries*, 1921; Herbert Heaton, *The Yorkshire Woollen and Worsted Industries*, 1920; Henry Hamilton, *The English Copper and Brass Industries*, 1926; A. P. Wadsworth and Julia de L. Mann, *Industrial Lancashire and the Cotton Industry*, 1931; and, best of all, J. U. Nef, *The Rise of the British Coal Industry*, 2 vols., 1932.

GILDS. Several books deal with them, but for this period Stella Kramer, *The English Craft Gilds*, 1927, is the most significant. A good article covering this field is T. H. Marshall, 'Capitalism and the Decline of the English Gilds', in *Cambridge Historical Journal*, iii.

TAXATION AND FINANCE. Stephen Dowell, *A History of Taxation and Taxes in England*, 4 vols., 1884, is the only comprehensive study at all modern, but badly needs revision. Frederick C. Dietz, *English Public Finance, 1558–1641*, 1932, is a recent treatment, whose defects are mainly due to an unavoidable cause, the disappearance of documents. M. P. Ashley, *Financial and Commercial Policies under the Cromwellian Protectorate*, 1934, is very useful though not exhaustive. To fill the gap left by these two monographs, there is W. O. Scroggs, 'English Finance under the Long Parliament', in *Quarterly Journal of Economics*, xxi. Only one tax of the period has received a special study:

M. D. Gordon, 'The Collection of Ship Money in the Reign of Charles I', in *Trans. Roy. Hist. Soc.*, 3rd ser., iv. W. Kennedy, *English Taxation, 1640–1799: An Essay on Policy and Opinion*, 1913, is not very satisfactory for this period. R. D. Richards, *The Early History of Banking in England*, 1929, sets forth the results of wide research in a field about which little has hitherto been known. E. M. Leonard, *The Early History of English Poor Relief*, 1900, embodies much research, although its main conclusions may be challenged. W. H. Price, *English Patents of Monopoly*, 1913, is a serviceable study of the legal aspects of a subject of great importance in this period.

TRADE. W. R. Scott, *The Constitution and Finance of English, Scottish, and Irish Joint-Stock Companies to 1720*, 3 vols., 1910–12, is an outstanding and indispensable work. W. A. S. Hewins, *English Trade and Finance*, 1892, is naturally out of date but is still worth reading. R. H. Tawney, *Religion and the Rise of Capitalism*, 1st ed., 1926, is profound if provocative.

WALES

No satisfactory history of Wales exists, but there is *A Bibliography of the History of Wales*, ed. R. T. Jenkins and William Rees, 1931. There is a useful sketch by Sir John Rhys and D. Brynmor-Jones, *The Welsh People*, 1900. J. C. Morrice, *Wales in the Seventeenth Century: Its Literature and Men of Letters and Action*, 1918, is mainly biographical and bibliographical. Valuable is A. H. Dodd, *Studies in Stuart Wales* (Cardiff, 1952). The puritan revolution is described in J. R. Phillips, *Memoirs of the Civil War in Wales and the Marches, 1642–1649*, 2 vols., 1874, useful for its documents, but sadly out of date; and T. Richards has written two serviceable books—*History of the Puritan Movement in Wales from 1639 to 1653*, 1920, and *Religious Developments in Wales, 1654–1662*, 1923. The late Miss Caroline A. J. Skeel made a careful study of *The Council in the Marches of Wales*, 1904. The Cymmrodorion Society's *Transactions* have many relevant papers.

SCOTLAND

It is curious that the best bibliography for Scottish history is George F. Black, *A List of Works Relating to Scotland*, 1916, which contains the titles of books owned by The New York Public

Library on 31 December 1914. Very useful in their respective ways are: C. S. Terry, *A Catalogue of the Publications of Scottish Historical and Kindred Clubs and Societies, 1780–1908*, 1909, with a continuation, 1928, by Cyril Matheson, for 1908–27; and C. S. Terry, *An Index to the Papers Relating to Scotland, Described or Calendared in the Historical MSS. Commission's Reports*, 1908.

Scotland is fortunate in possessing P. Hume Brown, *History of Scotland. Vol. II. From the Accession of Mary Stewart to the Revolution of 1689*, 1902, an excellent narrative.

There are not many monographs relating exclusively to this period. Two military studies are, however, important: C. S. Terry, *The Life and Campaigns of Alexander Leslie, First Earl of Leven*, 1899; and W. S. Douglas, *Cromwell's Scotch Campaigns, 1650–1651*, 1899. John Willcock, *The Great Marquess: Life and Times of Archibald, 8th Earl and 1st (and Only) Marquess of Argyll*, 1903, is a good biography of a leading Scotch covenanter. Another useful work is W. C. Mackenzie, *The Life and Times of John Maitland, Duke of Lauderdale*, 1923. The twenty-five or so family histories Sir William Fraser compiled during the second half of the nineteenth century, and his reports on Scottish private archives for the Historical Manuscripts Commission, have much information not available elsewhere.

The sources for Scottish history are very abundant. A number of the publications of the Scottish History Society are relevant: *Charles II and Scotland in 1650*, ed. S. R. Gardiner, 1894; *Scotland and the Commonwealth, 1651–1653*, 1895, and *Scotland and the Protectorate, 1654–1659*, 1899, both edited by C. H. Firth (these three volumes have valuable prefaces, which almost amount to a history of the times); *The Diplomatic Correspondence of Jean de Montereul and the Brothers De Bellièvre, French Ambassadors in England and Scotland, 1645–1648*, ed. J. G. Fotheringham, 2 vols., 1898–9; and *The Cromwellian Union*, 1902, and *Papers Relating to the Army of the Solemn League and Covenant, 1643–1647*, 2 vols., 1917—both works edited by C. S. Terry. *The Letters and Journals of Robert Baillie*, ed. David Laing, 3 vols., 1841–2, are of the utmost importance from the 1630's onwards.

J. Spottiswoode, *The History of the Church of Scotland*, 1655, is one of the chief sources for the reign of James VI. It is royalist and episcopal in sympathy. The presbyterian counterpart is D. Calderwood, *The True History of the Church of Scotland*, 1678. There is no similar work covering the rest of the period. J. K.

Hewison, *The Covenanters: A History of the Church in Scotland from the Reformation to the Revolution,* 2 vols., 1908, was written with strong covenanting sympathies, but, bias apart, is useful. New materials are used in G. Donaldson, *The Making of the Scottish Prayer Book of 1637* (1954), and D. Mathew, *Scotland under Charles I* (1955).

IRELAND

No bibliography, on an adequate scale, for Irish history has been published, but R. H. Murray, *Ireland, 1603–1714,* 1920, names the chief works. The best modern history is Richard Bagwell, *Ireland under the Stuarts,* 3 vols., 1909–16. E. A. Dalton, in his *History of Ireland,* vol. ii, 1547–1782 (1906), is more sympathetic to the native Irish than Bagwell. There is also G. B. O'Connor, *Stuart Ireland,* 1910. A number of monographs are pertinent: George Hill, *Historical Account of the Plantation in Ulster,* 1877; D. Murphy, *Cromwell in Ireland,* 1883; J. P. Mahaffy, *An Epoch in Irish History. Trinity College, Dublin, 1591–1660,* 1903; G. A. T. O'Brien, *Economic History of Ireland in the Seventeenth Century,* 1919; Lord Ernest William Hamilton, *The Irish Rebellion of 1641,* 1920; and St. J. D. Seymour, *The Puritans in Ireland, 1647–1661,* 1921.

Three personages have left much biographical material. *The Lismore Papers,* ed. A. B. Grosart, 10 vols., 1886–8, contains the diary of Richard Boyle, earl of Cork, and letters to and from him; Dorothea Townsend wrote *The Life and Letters of the Great Earl of Cork,* 1904, which to many will be a substitute for *The Lismore Papers.* William Knowler made a good selection in *The Earl of Strafforde's Letters and Dispatches,* 2 vols., 1740; and a modern study that deserves mention is W. H. A. O'Grady, *Strafford in Ireland,* 2 vols., 1923. T. Carte, *The Life of James, Duke of Ormond,* 2nd ed., 6 vols., 1851 (also 3 vols., 1735–6), is indispensable for its documents. A briefer and more attractive, but not wholly satisfactory, work is Lady Burghclere, *Life of James, Duke of Ormond,* 2 vols., 1912. Ormond's papers are preserved partly at Kilkenny Castle and partly at the Bodleian Library, Oxford. The former have been calendared by the Historical Manuscripts Commission, and those covering this period are in *Ormond Papers,* vols. i–ii, 1895–9, and new ser., vols. i–ii, 1902–3. For the Ormond papers in the Bodleian Library, there are reports by T. Duffus Hardy and J. S. Brewer,

1864, and by C. W. Russell and J. P. Prendergast, 1871. The documentary publications of Sir J. T. Gilbert are important for the period from 1641 onwards, especially because they give contemporary narratives of those opposed to the English rule in Ireland. From 1603 to 1670, the *Irish State Papers* were printed separately, 13 vols., 1872–1910, ed. C. W. Russell, J. P. Prendergast, and R. P. Mahaffy. For the commonwealth and protectorate, Robert Dunlop, *Ireland under the Commonwealth. Being a Selection of Documents Relating to the Government of Ireland from 1651 to 1659*, 2 vols., 1913, is fundamental.

THE COLONIES

For colonial history in general, there is a very handy little guide, C. S. S. Higham, *The Colonial Entry-Books. A Brief Guide to the Colonial Records in the Public Record Office before 1696*, 1921. *The Calendar of State Papers, Colonial Series*, covers this period so far as America and the West Indies (1860) are concerned, but stops short in 1634 for the East Indies, China, and Japan (1892). *The Acts of the Privy Council, Colonial Series*, ed. W. L. Grant and J. Munro, 6 vols., 1908–12, extracts from the privy-council registers the entries relating to colonies. The best brief history is J. A. Williamson, *Short History of British Expansion*, 1922; on a larger scale is the *Cambridge History of the British Empire*, vol. i, 1929. The work edited by C. P. Lucas, *Historical Geography of the British Colonies*, includes many sound volumes. D. W. Prowse, *A History of Newfoundland*, 1896, has not been superseded, although J. D. Rogers, *Newfoundland*, 1911, is excellent, if brief.

The writings on American history are very numerous. Edward Channing, A. B. Hart, and F. J. Turner, *Guide to the Study of American History*, 3rd ed., 1912, is now replaced by *Harvard Guide to American History*, ed. Oscar Handlin and others (Cambridge, Mass., 1954); since 1906 Grace G. Griffin, *Writings on American History*, has supplied an admirable bibliography of books and articles relating to United States and Canadian history during each year. A. P. C. Griffin edited a *Bibliography of American Historical Societies*, 2nd ed., 1907, which is invaluable. For the histories of colonies to 1660, C. M. Andrews, *The Colonial Period of American History. I. The Settlements*, 1934, is by an acknowledged authority. H. L. Osgood, *The American Colonies in the Seventeenth Century*, 3 vols., 1904–7, should be consulted for institutional and religious history. G. L. Beer, *The Origins of the British Colonial System, 1578–1660*, 1908, was a most influential publication.

For the West Indies there is a *Bibliography of the West Indies (Excluding Jamaica)*, 1909, compiled by Frank Cundall. The standard work, for a century at least, was Bryan Edwards, *The History, Civil and Commercial, of the British Colonies in the West Indies*, 3 vols., 1793, but it is of very little use for this period. Texts on *Colonising Expeditions to the West Indies, 1623–1667*, were edited by Vincent T. Harlow, 1925. Useful short books are by C. P. Lucas, *Historical Geography of the British Colonies, The West Indies*, 1890; and A. P. Newton, *The European Nations in the West Indies, 1493–1688* (1933). On the whole, this branch of colonial history is to be studied through separate accounts of the islands and a few monographs. J. A. Williamson is responsible for two careful publications, *English Colonies in Guiana and on the Amazon, 1604–1668*, 1923, and *The Caribee Islands under the Proprietary Patents*, 1926; N. D. Davis, *The Cavaliers and Roundheads of Barbados*, 1887, is still of service; Vincent T. Harlow, *The History of Barbados, 1625–1685*, 1926, is helpful. J. H. Lefroy, *Memorials of the Discovery and Early Settlement of the Bermudas or Somers Islands*, 2 vols., 1877–9, is exhaustive. E. Long, *The History of Jamaica*, 3 vols., 1774, has not been replaced. For the capture of Jamaica there is *The Narrative of General Venables*, edited, with a valuable introduction, by C. H. Firth, 1900. A popular subject is discussed in C. H. Haring, *The Buccaneers in the West Indies* (1910).

The history of the East Indies has attracted a great deal of attention, and there are a number of guides to records, the best being Shafaat Ahmad Khan, *Sources for the History of British India in the Seventeenth Century*, 1926. The standard history is W. W. Hunter, *The History of British India*, 2 vols., 1899–1900. A useful book is Shafaat Ahmad Khan, *The East India Trade in the Seventeenth Century*, 1923. The chief collections of documents are: *Letters Received by the East India Company*, ed. F. C. Danvers and W. Foster, 6 vols., 1896–1902; W. Foster, *The English Factories in India*, 1906–27, and the new series of the same edited by Sir Charles Fawcett (1936–   ), containing documents from the India Office, the British Museum, and the Public Record Office; and *Calendar of the Court Minutes of the East India Company, 1635–79*, ed. E. B. Sainsbury, 1907–38.

LITERATURE AND SCIENCE

Douglas Bush, *English Literature in the Earlier Seventeenth Century* (Oxford, 1946), is the standard work. It excludes the drama. Its bibliography is very full and well chosen. *The Cambridge History of English Literature*, ed. A. W. Ward and A. R. Waller, vol. vi, *The Drama to 1642*, 1919, and vol. vii, *Cavalier and Puritan*, 1920, furnish convenient summaries of the literature of the period. These volumes have little unity, but they contain several very good essays. *The Cambridge Bibliography of English Literature*, ed. F. W. Bateson, vol. i (1941), covers the years 600–1660. In *Studies in Philology*, there appears, annually, 'Recent Literature of the English Renaissance', which gives a list of the year's output beginning 1925. Annually too, since 1921, has been published a *Bibliography of English Language and Literature*. There is also a large number of bibliographies, among which Clark S. Northup, *Register of Bibliographies of the English Language and Literature*, 1925, and Arthur G. Kennedy, *Bibliography of Writings on the English Language*, 1927, should be mentioned. So far as it extends, the most interesting but not always accurate treatment is undoubtedly that by J. J. Jusserand, translated as *A Literary History of the English People*, 3 vols., 1906–9. No other work has so successfully connected literature with the history of the times in which it was written. For the drama Sir Edmund Chambers, *The Elizabethan Stage*, 4 vols., 1923, is a storehouse of facts. A continuation is by Gerald Eades Bentley, *The Jacobean and Caroline Stage* (5 vols., Oxford, 1941–56). Alfred Harbage, *Annals of English Drama, 975–1700*, supplies a record of all plays. Leslie Hotson, *The Commonwealth and Restoration Stage*, 1928, is valuable for the later years. For the masques, Allardyce Nicoll, *Stuart Masques and the Renaissance Stage* (London, 1938), can be used. W. W. Greg has published a monumental *Bibliography of the English Printed Drama to the Restoration* in three volumes, 1939–57. There is no point in enumerating the works of the different dramatists, but exceptions should be made in favour of C. H. Herford and Percy Simpson's edition of *Ben Jonson*, 11 vols., 1925–52, and A. Glover and A. R. Waller's edition of the plays of Beaumont and Fletcher, 10 vols., 1905–12.

POETRY. There is an excellent selection, with valuable introductions, in *The Poetry of the English Renaissance, 1509–1660*, ed. J. W. Hebel and H. H. Hudson, 1932. A general history is W. J.

Courthope, *History of English Poetry*, 6 vols., 1895–1910. Well edited are: *The Works of George Herbert*, ed. F. E. Hutchinson (Oxford, 1941); *The Poetical Works of Robert Herrick*, ed. F. W. Moorman (Oxford, 1921); *The Poems of John Donne*, ed. H. J. C. Grierson (2 vols., Oxford, 1912). The greatest poet of the age has received a full biography: David Masson, *The Life of John Milton*, 7 vols., 1859–1904. A very useful guide is J. H. Hanford, *A Milton Handbook* (4th ed., New York, 1946). There is a worthy edition of his many writings, *The Works of John Milton*, edited for the Columbia University Press, 1931–40. David H. Stevens, *Reference Guide to Milton*, 1930, is the most complete bibliography. No one has attempted to write a general account of the ballads of the period, but there are, fortunately, some very valuable collections printed. William Chappell and J. W. Ebsworth edited, for the Ballad Society, *The Roxburghe Ballads*, 9 vols., 1874–97; and Hyder E. Rollins edited *Old English Ballads, 1553–1625*, 1920, *A Pepysian Garland, 1625–1639*, 1922, *Cavalier and Puritan, 1640–1660*, 1923, and *The Pepys Ballads*, 8 vols., 1929–32. The use that may be made of this kind of ephemeral literature is well illustrated by Sir Charles Firth, 'Ballad History of the Reign of James I' and a similar article for Charles I, in *Trans. Roy. Hist. Soc.*, 3rd ser., v and vi.

NEWSPAPERS. Their history is to be found mainly in the various works of J. G. Muddiman (who used to write as J. B. Williams). His *History of English Journalism to the Foundation of the Gazette*, 1908, and *The King's Journalist*, 1923, reveal much knowledge of the newsbooks of the time, a remark that is also applicable to W. M. Clyde, *The Struggle for the Freedom of the Press from Caxton to Cromwell*, 1934. The best bibliographies are *Tercentenary Handlist of English & Welsh Magazines, Newspapers, & Reviews*, published by *The Times*, 1920, and compiled by J. G. Muddiman; *A Census of British Newspapers and Periodicals, 1620–1800*, by R. S. Crane and F. B. Kaye, 1925; and *A Catalogue of English Newspapers and Periodicals in the Bodleian Library, 1622–1800*, ed. R. T. Milford and D. M. Sutherland (Oxford Bibl. Soc. IV, part ii, 1936), a model compilation.

POLITICAL SCIENCE. The political theories of the time are dealt with in J. N. Figgis, *The Theory of the Divine Right of Kings*, 1896; G. P. Gooch, *The History of English Democratic Ideas in the Seventeenth Century*, 1898; W. A. Dunning, *A History of Political Theories from Luther to Montesquieu*, 1905; John William Allen,

English Political Thought, 1603–1660 (1938); J. W. Gough, *Fundamental Law in English Constitutional History* (1955); Lewis H. Berens, *The Digger Movement in the Days of the Commonwealth*, 1906, is largely superseded by *The Works of Gerrard Winstanley*, ed. George H. Sabine (Ithaca, N.Y., 1941); and Theodore Calvin Pease, *The Leveller Movement*, 1916. Selected writings have been edited by William Haller and Godfrey Davies, *The Leveller Tracts*, and by Don M. Wolfe, *Leveller Manifestoes* (both New York, 1944). There are other studies of the Levellers and of radical theories too numerous to mention. Two very good short monographs are George L. Mosse, *The Struggle for Sovereignty in England* (East Lansing, 1950), and Margaret Atwood Judson, *The Crisis of the Constitution* (New Brunswick, 1949). Among the original works, the most important are *The Political Works of James I*, with an introduction by Charles Howard McIlwain, 1918; Thomas Hobbes, *Leviathan, or the Matter, Forme, and Power of a Commonwealth Ecclesiastical and Civil*, 1651 (there are later editions, edited by A. R. Waller, 1904, and W. G. Pogson Smith, 1909); and James Harrington, *Commonwealth of Oceana*, 1656 (there are later editions, edited by H. Morley, 1883, and S. B. Liljegren, 1924, and a study by H. F. Russell Smith, *Harrington and His Oceana*, 1914). For the political theories in the army, as expressed in the debates in the army council in 1647, see *The Clarke Papers*, ed. C. H. Firth, vol. i, 1891. A. S. P. Woodhouse has re-edited these debates and added valuable documents in *Puritanism and Liberty* (London, 1938).

SCIENCE. W. C. D. Dampier-Whetham, *A History of Science*, 1929, is a good general guide. More ambitious is A. Wolf, *A History of Science, Technology, and Philosophy in the 16th & 17th Centuries*, 1935, with over 300 illustrations. It is not, however, by any means abreast of modern knowledge in some sections. Of an entirely different character is Basil Willey, *The Seventeenth Century Background*, 1934, which examines the thought of the time in relation to its poetry and religion. A book of modest dimensions could not deal with so large a subject definitively, but this work is extremely stimulating, even fascinating. More concentrated is Paul H. Kocher, *Science and Religion in Elizabethan England* (1953), with much of value for the early Stuarts. E. A. Burtt, *The Metaphysical Foundations of Modern Science*, 1925, may also be consulted. In addition to these general treatments, several studies of separate branches of science have appeared.

M. Cantor, *Vorlesungen über die Geschichte der Mathematik*, 4 vols., 1880–1908, is the standard publication. Much briefer are two books by W. W. Rouse Ball: *A Short Account of the History of Mathematics*, 1888; and *A History of the Study of Mathematics at Cambridge*, 1889. Francis R. Johnson, *Astronomical Thought in Renaissance England*, 1937, is a study of English scientific writings from 1500 to 1645 and contains a chronological list of astronomical books. His 'Gresham College' in the *Journal of the History of Ideas* (Oct. 1940) is a valuable essay. For medicine a number of summary accounts is available, such as Charles Singer, *Short History of Medicine*, 1928. For a time when the plague was so prevalent, C. Creighton, *A History of Epidemics in Britain*, 2 vols., 1891–4, is important, as is F. P. Wilson, *The Plague in Shakespeare's London*, 1927. D'Arcy Power wrote a life of *William Harvey*, 1897. Very helpful for biographical purposes is W. R. Munk, *The Roll of the Royal College of Physicians of London*, 2 vols., 1861, or 3 vols., 1878. J. von Sachs, *History of Botany*, translated by H. E. F. Garnsey, 1890, and C. Singer, *Short History of Biology*, 1931, are of service. Among the older works John Ward, *The Lives of the Professors of Gresham College*, 1740, and Thomas Sprat, *The History of the Royal Society of London*, 1667, have much useful information. The two later histories of the Royal Society, by T. Birch, 4 vols., 1756–7, and by C. R. Weld, 2 vols., 1848, still leave room for an up-to-date study. R. T. Gunther, *Early Science in Oxford*, 10 vols., 1923–35, has much of interest for this period.

THE ARTS AND MUSIC

PAINTING AND SCULPTURE. For a general survey, C. H. Collins Baker, *British Painting* (with a chapter on primitive painting, by Montague R. James), 1933, is best. It is profusely illustrated. More detailed are C. H. Collins Baker and W. G. Constable, *English Painting of the Sixteenth and Seventeenth Centuries*, 1930, and C. H. Collins Baker, *Lely and the Stuart Portrait Painters*, 2 vols., 1912. The source of much information about artists and paintings has long been Horace Walpole, *Anecdotes of Painting in England*, 4 vols., 1762–71, or 3 vols., 1849. The material George Vertue collected, which supplied the base for Walpole's work, has been printed by the Walpole Society, under the title, *Vertue Note Books*, 6 vols. This society has many publications of value for this period. There is a number of interesting articles in the

Burlington Magazine. B. S. Long, *British Miniaturists,* 1929, is first-rate. Margaret Whinney and O. Millar, *English Art, 1625–1714* (Oxford History of English Art, 1957), is an excellent textbook for its period and incorporates much new work.

Katharine A. Esdaile, *English Monumental Sculpture since the Renaissance,* 1927, is a very convenient guide.

ARCHITECTURE. There are many general histories, most of which are profusely illustrated. Among them are: *Architecture of the Renaissance in England,* by J. A. Gotch, assisted by W. T. Brown, 2 vols., 1894; G. H. Birch, *London Churches of the Seventeenth and Eighteenth Centuries,* 1896; Sir Reginald Blomfield, *A History of Renaissance Architecture in England,* 2 vols., 1897; and J. A. Gotch, *Early Renaissance Architecture in England,* 1901, and *The Growth of the English House,* 1909. H. M. Colvin, *Biographical Dictionary of English Architects* (1954), is a work of much learning.

TAPESTRY. W. G. Thomson, *A History of Tapestry,* 1906, is exhaustive on the Mortlake tapestries.

GARDENING. This is dealt with in such books as Sir Reginald Blomfield, *The Formal Garden in England,* 1892, and E. S. Rohde, *The Old English Gardening Books,* 1924.

FURNITURE. It is probable that most readers would find P. Macquoid and R. Edwards, *Dictionary of English Furniture,* 3 vols., 1924–7, amply sufficient, but for those who would like a more connected account, there is H. A. Tipping, *English Homes, 1066–1820,* 1920–6 (Period III, vol. ii, and Period IV, vol. i).

MUSIC. There is a very good book by Ernest Walker, *A History of Music in England,* 1907, and a more elaborate study in the *Oxford History of Music,* vol. iii: Sir Hubert Parry, *The Music of the Seventeenth Century,* 1902. For individual composers, recourse should be had to Sir George Grove's *Dictionary of Music and Musicians,* 5th ed., 9 vols., ed. Eric Blom, 1954.

SOCIAL

Shakespeare's England, 2 vols., 1916, is the most valuable work, both on account of its various essays, by acknowledged experts, on different aspects of social life, and for the bibliographical notes attached to each chapter. *Social England,* ed. H. D. Traill and J. S. Mann, vol. iv, 1895, has several good articles for this period. There is a number of general publications devoted to social life in the seventeenth century, all of which contribute something. Among these are: Mary Coate, *Social Life in Stuart England*, 1924; Rose M. Bradley, *The English Housewife in the Seventeenth and Eighteenth Centuries*, 1912; Elizabeth Godfrey (Jessie Bedford), *Social Life under the Stuarts*, 1904—she also wrote *Home Life under the Stuarts, 1603–1649*, 1925; Christian Hole, *English Sports and Pastimes* (1949), *The English Housewife in the Seventeenth Century* (1953), and other works. Henry Martyn Dexter and Morton Dexter, *The England and Holland of the Pilgrims*, 1906, devote Book I to social conditions.

In quite another category are Alice Clark, *Working Life of Women in the Seventeenth Century*, 1919, and Margaret James, *Social Problems and Policy during the Puritan Revolution, 1640–1660*, 1930, both of which are based on exhaustive research. The latter has a long list of sources. A useful book, dealing with still another kind of subject, is Chilton Latham Powell, *English Domestic Relations, 1487–1653*, 1917. *Englishmen at Rest and Play, 1558–1714*, ed. Reginald Lennard, 1931, has extremely interesting essays on watering-places, Sunday observance, country inns and ale-houses, and meals and meal-times. Wallace Notestein, *The History of Witchcraft in England*, 1911, and L. H. Berens, *The Digger Movement*, 1906, are concerned with special aspects of the social scene. Louis B. Wright, *Middle-class Culture in Elizabethan England*, 1935, is one of the most thorough studies of the cultural background of the period, and has a very comprehensive and accurate bibliography. Wallace Notestein, *The English People on the Eve of Colonization, 1603–1630* (New York, 1954), is the work of an acknowledged authority. It has an excellent bibliography. Although the emphasis of David Ogg, in *England in the Reign of Charles II*, 2 vols., 1934, is naturally on the years after 1660, he says much about social and economic life that is as applicable to the 1650's as to the 1660's. The edition of *The Diary of John Evelyn* by E. S. de Beer (6 vols., 1955) is a mine of accurate information on almost every aspect of social life.

Almost any kind of contemporary writing may be of value for social history, and all that can be done here is to indicate a few types. John Earle, *Microcosmography; or, A Piece of the World Discovered in Essays and Characters*, 1628 (ed. S. T. Irwin, 1897), is one of a number of similar books listed by Gwendolen Murphy, *A Bibliography of English Character-Books, 1608–1700*, 1925. Another valuable guide to the same kind of books is Chester Noyes Greenough, *A Bibliography of the Theophrastan*

Character, ed. J. Milton French (Cambridge, Mass., 1947). There are many guides to gentility, of which Richard Brathwait, *The English Gentleman; and the English Gentlewoman*, 3rd ed., 1641, and Henry Peacham, *The Compleat Gentleman*, 3rd ed., 1661, are the best-known. Francis Osborn, *Advice to a Son, or Directions for Your Better Conduct*, 6th ed., 1658, and the corresponding work of John Heydon, *Advice to a Daughter*, 1658, are equally interesting. The quarter-sessions records (listed under Local History) throw much light on contemporary habits, and George Roberts, in his *Social History of the People of the Southern Counties of England*, 1856, makes good use of local records. Memoirs and family correspondences are of even more value than conduct books, inasmuch as they relate actual behaviour and not merely rules for good behaviour. Practically all the quaker diaries, of which there are many for these years, contain excellent descriptions of the social life of the middle classes during the last decade of the period. It is almost unnecessary to say that they are particularly full on the prisons of England. The life of a nobleman is illustrated in *The Autobiography of Edward, Lord Herbert of Cherbury*, ed. Sidney Lee, *c.* 1906. *The Autobiography of Joseph Lister*, 1842, is a narrative of one who became a gentleman's servant in London. Of family correspondences, the best is *The Oxinden Letters, 1607–1642*, ed. Dorothy Gardiner, 1933. Lady Verney's *Memoirs of the Verney Family during the Civil War*, 2 vols., 1892, because it is so solidly founded on letters, contains the outstanding account of the fortunes of a county family during those troubled times. The observations of travellers are useful, because they often include comment on what the native may ignore because of its very familiarity. *England as seen by Foreigners in the Days of Elizabeth and James I*, ed. W. B. Rye, 1865; Edward Smith, *Foreign Visitors in England*, 1889; and *A Relation of a Short Survey of 26 Counties Observed, 1634, by a Captain, a Lieutenant, and an Ancient*, ed. L. G. Wickham Legg, 1904, are among the most valuable. *An English Garner. Social England Illustrated. A Collection of XVIIth Century Tracts*, ed. Andrew Lang, 1903, provides a good selection from the great number of tracts illustrating social history.

Amusements are dealt with in vol. ii of *Shakespeare's England*. One contemporary work, however, must be mentioned, as it is a classic—Izaak Walton, *The Compleat Angler*, 100th ed., 2 vols., 1888, ed. R. B. Marston.

EDUCATION. There is no general history of education, which has to be studied in various publications. Foster Watson, 'Scholars and Scholarship, 1600–1660', in *The Cambridge History of English Literature*, vol. vii, 1920, is very useful to begin with. Sir Charles Mallet, *History of the University of Oxford*, vol. ii, 1924, and J. B. Mullinger, *The University of Cambridge*, vols. ii–iii, 1873–84, deal with the two universities, the latter more thoroughly than the former. Montagu Burrows edited *The Register of the Visitors of the University of Oxford, 1647–1658*, 1881. Foster Watson, *The English Grammar Schools to 1660*, 1908, and *The Beginnings of the Teaching of Modern Subjects in England*, 1909, are based on exhaustive research but rather hard to read. In *The Cambridge History of English Literature*, vol. vii, J. B. Mullinger has a useful list of histories of schools. There are two excellent contemporary works that appeared conveniently near the beginning and end of the period, respectively: John Brinsley, *Ludus Literarius*, 1612, ed. E. T. Campagnac, 1917, and Charles Hoole, *A New Discovery of the Old Art of Teaching Schoole*, 1660, ed. E. T. Campagnac, 1913. No one seems to have made a study of the writing schools and the dames' schools, but Dorothy Gardiner, *English Girlhood at School*, 1929, describes female education. Sir John Sandys, *History of Classical Scholarship*, vol. ii, 1908, is a standard authority. Kathleen Lambley, in *The Teaching and Cultivation of the French Language during Tudor and Stuart Times*, 1920, has written a first-class monograph. There should be more of like quality to deal with other subjects.

LISTS OF THE HOLDERS OF CERTAIN OFFICES

In general these lists have not been continued beyond the outbreak of the civil war, after which there were often two sets of officials, one royal, one parliamentarian. Moreover parliament frequently appointed committees rather than individuals to carry on the work formerly done by the great officers of state.

Archbishops of Canterbury

1583 John Whitgift.
1604 Richard Bancroft.
1611 George Abbot.
1633 William Laud.
1645 See vacant until 1660.

Lord Chancellors and Keepers of the Great Seal

1596 Sir Thomas Egerton, Lord Ellesmere (1603), and Viscount Brackley (1616), keeper (chancellor, 1603).
1617 Sir Francis Bacon, Lord Verulam (1618), and Viscount St. Albans (1621), keeper (chancellor, 1618).
1621 John Williams, dean of Westminster, afterwards bishop of Lincoln, keeper.
1625 Sir Thomas Coventry, afterwards Lord Coventry, keeper.
1640 Sir John Finch, afterwards Lord Finch, keeper.
1641 Sir Edward Lyttelton, afterwards Lord Lyttelton, keeper.
       After the civil war began there were two seals, parliament making one and entrusting it to commissioners.

Lord High Treasurers and Lords Commissioners of the Treasury

1599 Thomas Sackville, Lord Buckhurst (1567), earl of Dorset (1604).
1608 Robert Cecil, Lord Cecil (1603), Viscount Cranborne (1604), earl of Salisbury (1605).
1612 Henry Howard, earl of Northampton (1604), and other commissioners.
1614 Thomas Howard, Lord Howard de Walden (1597), earl of Suffolk (1603).
1618 George Abbot, archbishop of Canterbury, and other commissioners.
1620 Henry Montagu, Baron Kimbolton and Viscount Mandeville (1620), earl of Manchester (1626).
1621 Lionel Cranfield, Lord Cranfield (1621), earl of Middlesex (1622).
1624 James Ley, Lord Ley (1624), earl of Marlborough (1626).

1628 Richard Weston, Lord Weston (1628), earl of Portland (1633).
1635 William Laud, archbishop of Canterbury, and other commissioners.
1636 William Juxon, bishop of London.
1641 Sir Edward Lyttelton, afterwards Lord Lyttelton, and other commissioners.
       With the outbreak of the civil war the old financial system fell into abeyance and was not revived until 1654.

Lords Privy Seal

1597 Robert Cecil, Lord Cecil, Viscount Cranborne, earl of Salisbury.
1608 Henry Howard, earl of Northampton.
1614 Robert Carr, Viscount Rochester (1611), earl of Somerset (1613), acting keeper.
1616 Edward Somerset, 9th earl of Worcester.
1628 Henry Montagu, earl of Manchester (d. 1642).

Lord High Admirals

1585 Charles Howard, Lord Howard of Effingham, earl of Nottingham (1596).
1619 George Villiers, earl of Buckingham (1617) and duke of Buckingham (1623).
1628 Richard Weston, Lord Weston, earl of Portland, and other commissioners.
1632 Richard Weston, Lord Weston, earl of Portland, and other commissioners.
1636 William Juxon, bishop of London, and other commissioners.
1637 Algernon Percy, earl of Northumberland, lord admiral (1638, lord high admiral acting for the duke of York), till 1642.
1643 Robert Rich, 2nd earl of Warwick (for the parliament).
1645 Algernon Percy, earl of Northumberland, and a parliamentary committee.
1648 Robert Rich, 2nd earl of Warwick, lord high admiral.
       An admiralty committee of the council of state took over many of the duties throughout the protectorate. For the actual administration there were commissioners.

Secretaries of State[1]

1596		Sir Robert Cecil, Baron Cecil, Viscount Cranborne, earl of Salisbury.
1600	John Herbert.	
1613		Robert Carr, Viscount Rochester, earl of Somerset, acting.
1614	Sir Ralph Winwood.	
1616		Sir Thomas Lake.

[1] *Public Record Office, Lists and Indexes*, no. xliii (1914).

1618	Sir Robert Naunton.	
1619		Sir George Calvert.
1623	Sir Edward Conway, Baron Conway (1625), and Viscount Conway (1627).	
1625		Sir Albertus Morton. Sir John Coke.
1628	Dudley Carleton, Baron Carlton (1626), Viscount Dorchester (1628).	
1632	Sir Francis Windebank.	
1640		Sir Henry Vane.
1641	Sir Edward Nicholas.	
1642		Lucius Cary, 2nd Viscount Falkland.
1643		George Digby, Lord Digby and 2nd earl of Bristol.

INDEX

1. ENGLAND AND WALES

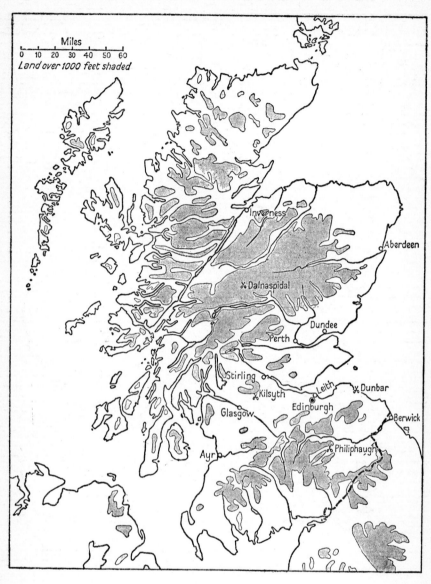

2. SCOTLAND

RESERVED FOR TRANSPLANTED IRISH

Londonderry

Belfast

Benburb

Drogheda

△ Dangan Hill

Rathmines ○ Dublin

Limerick

Kilkenny

Clonmel

Wexford

Waterford

Cork

Kinsale

▬▬▬ Boundaries of Provinces
.... " " Counties
▬▬▬ Area Reserved for Transplanted Irish
Land over 1000 feet shaded
Miles

0 10 20 30 40 50 60

3. IRELAND

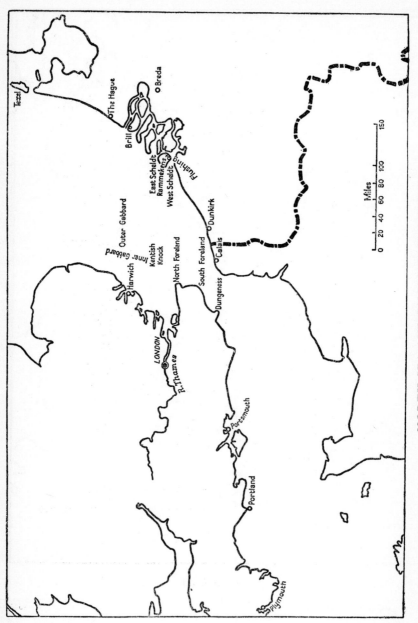

4. NORTH SEA AND ENGLISH CHANNEL

5. WESTERN EUROPE

6. INDIA AND EAST INDIES

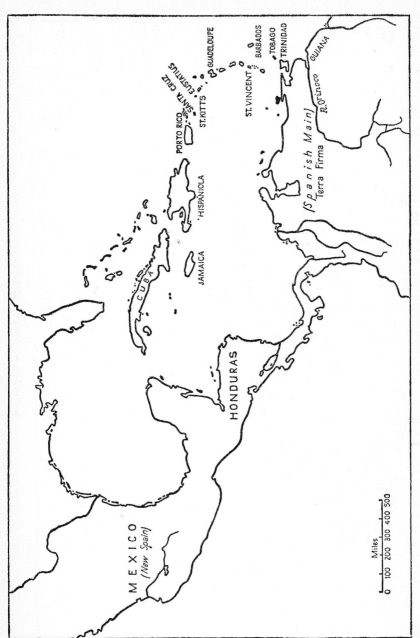

7. WEST INDIES

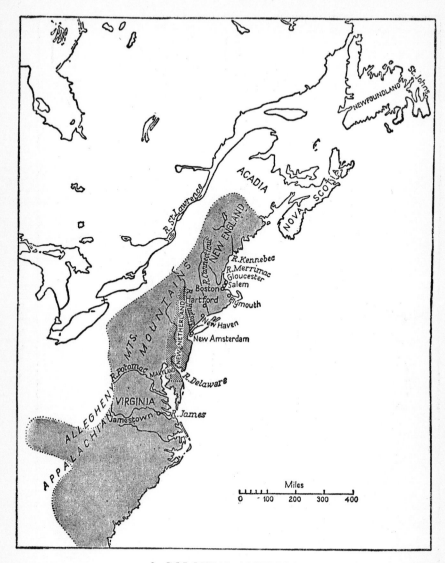

8. COLONIAL AMERICA

PRINTED IN GREAT BRITAIN
AT THE UNIVERSITY PRESS, OXFORD
BY VIVIAN RIDLER
PRINTER TO THE UNIVERSITY